T0299055

# Monetary Policy in Low-Inflation Economies

This volume collects the proceedings from a conference on monetary policy in low-inflation economies that was sponsored by the Federal Reserve Bank of Cleveland. The chapters make both theoretical and empirical contributions to that topic, and they fall under two broad themes. The first concerns the argument for low inflation. Several chapters reexamine the issue of inflation's costs and consequences. One advantage of the chapters collected here is that they approach the question from various theoretical perspectives. To motivate money demand, some chapters invoke standard distortions within a New Keynesian framework, one adopts an overlapping generations structure, and one a deep money perspective. The second set of chapters in this volume represents a collection of studies on diverse questions concerning the facts of operating in and transitioning to low-inflation economies. Broadly speaking, they investigate the complications (or the lack thereof) of implementing monetary policy at low rates of trend inflation; threshold effects on the costs of inflation; and the interaction of inflation, financial markets, and intermediation.

**David E. Altig**, senior vice president and director of research at the Federal Reserve Bank of Atlanta, was vice president and associate director of research at the Federal Reserve Bank of Cleveland when this book began to be compiled. He oversees the Atlanta Federal Reserve's blog, which is titled "Macroblog." His published research focuses on tax policy, business cycle issues, and monetary policy analysis. Dr. Altig has taught at a number of universities—The University of Chicago, Case Western Reserve University, Cleveland State University, John Carroll University, and Indiana University—and lectured in the Chinese Executive MBA Program, sponsored by the University of Minnesota and Lignan College of Sun Yat-Sen University. Dr. Altig earned his doctorate in economics from Brown University.

**Ed Nosal**, vice president and senior financial economist in the financial markets group at the Federal Reserve Bank of Chicago, was senior research advisor in the Research Department of the Federal Reserve Bank of Cleveland when this book began to be compiled. His research focuses on money and banking. Dr. Nosal has taught at the University of Chicago, University of Waterloo, University of British Columbia, University of New South Wales, and the National University of Singapore. Dr. Nosal earned his doctorate in economics from Queen's University in Canada.

# Monetary Policy in Low-Inflation Economies

Edited by

**DAVID E. ALTIG**
*Federal Reserve Bank of Atlanta*

**ED NOSAL**
*Federal Reserve Bank of Chicago*

CAMBRIDGE
UNIVERSITY PRESS

# CAMBRIDGE
## UNIVERSITY PRESS

32 Avenue of the Americas, New York NY 10013-2473, USA

Cambridge University Press is part of the University of Cambridge.

It furthers the University's mission by disseminating knowledge in the pursuit of education, learning and research at the highest international levels of excellence.

www.cambridge.org
Information on this title: www.cambridge.org/9781107514119

© Federal Reserve Bank of Cleveland 2009

First published 2009
First paperback edition 2015

A catalogue record for this publication is available from the British Library

Library of Congress Cataloguing in Publication data

Monetary policy in low-inflation economies / edited by David E. Altig, Ed Nosal.
    p.   cm.
Includes bibliographical references and index.
ISBN 978-0-521-84850-3 (hardback)
1. Monetary policy.   2. Inflation (Finance)   I. Altig, David, 1956–   II. Nosal, Ed.
III. Title.
HG230.3.M63755   2009
339.5′3–dc22          2009019724

ISBN 978-0-521-84850-3 Hardback
ISBN 978-1-107-51411-9 Paperback

# Contents

# Contents

# Contributors

**Costas Azariadis**
University of California–Los Angeles

**David K. Backus**
New York University

**Michael D. Bordo**
Rutgers University
National Bureau of Economic Research

**John Boyd**
University of Minnesota

**James Bullard**
Federal Reserve Bank of St. Louis

**Nicola Cetorelli**
University of California–Davis
Board of Governors of the Federal Reserve System

**Bruce Champ**
Federal Reserve Bank of Cleveland

**Wilbur John Coleman II**
Duke University

**Michael B. Devereux**
University of British Columbia

**Michael Dotsey**
Federal Reserve Bank of Philadelphia

## Contributors

**Eric O'N. Fisher**
The Ohio State University

**Scott Freeman**
(deceased)

**Marvin Goodfriend**
Federal Reserve Bank of Richmond

**Espen R. Henriksen**
University of Oslo

**Werner Hermann**
Swiss National Bank

**Boris Hofmann**
Center for European Integration Studies
University of Bonn

**Iikka Korhonen**
Bank of Finland

**Finn E. Kydland**
Carnegie Mellon University

**Raphael W. K. Lam**
University of California–Los Angeles

**John Landon-Lane**
Rutgers University

**Angela Redish**
University of British Columbia

**Guillaume Rocheteau**
Australian National University
Federal Reserve Bank of Cleveland

# Contributors

**Peter L. Rousseau**
Vanderbilt University

**Jack Selody**
Bank of Canada

**Shouyong Shi**
University of Toronto

**Pierre L. Siklos**
Wilfrid Laurier University

**François R. Velde**
Federal Reserve Bank of Chicago

**Jürgen von Hagen**
Center for European Integration Studies
University of Bonn
Indiana University
Centre for Economic Policy Research

**Paul Wachtel**
New York University

**Randall Wright**
University of Pennsylvania

**Tony Yates**
Bank of England

# Acknowledgments

This set of essays represents the collected contributions of those who participated in a conference sponsored by the Central Bank Institute of the Federal Reserve Bank of Cleveland in November 2003. The product is the result of much hard work by many industrious, committed, and, it must be admitted, patient people. We are deeply indebted above all to the contributors, who have waited an overly long time to see their excellent work published. We also extend our thanks to those who helped us arrange the conference. Special mention goes to Kathy Popovich, Mary Mackay, and especially Connie Jones for her patient and tireless administrative assistance. We thank Deborah Ring for editing the papers, Bonnye Albrecht and Ryan Hagler of Albrecht Design for their deft typesetting, Scott Parris for being our advocate at the Cambridge University Press, and Monica Crabtree-Reusser for overseeing the final pre-press production.

And, oh yes—the views expressed herein do not necessarily reflect those of the Federal Reserve Bank of Cleveland, the Board of Governors, or anyone else in the Federal Reserve System.

# Introduction

We live, we hope, in an era of low inflation. The global fiat-money standard in force today arguably began soon after World War II, notwithstanding the nominally gold-anchored Bretton Woods period. Using Alan Meltzer's (2005) proposed dating scheme, we might roughly divide history after the war into three subperiods: the post-Accord, the Great Inflation, and the Great Moderation episodes, covering, respectively, 1952–1964, 1965–1984, and 1984 onward. The annual rates of inflation in each of these subperiods, measured by the GDP deflator, averaged 1.8 percent in the first episode, 5.8 percent in the second, and 2.5 percent in the third.[1]

If we exclude from the latter episode the 1985–1991 period—which in retrospect has the appearance of a transition phase—the episode's annual rate of inflation falls to 2.2 percent. Perhaps more importantly, the volatility of inflation fell dramatically relative to the Great Inflation period, to a level even lower than that realized over the post-Accord episode.[2]

This inflation profile is, as most know, not unique to the United States. Summarizing research presented at a 2005 autumn meeting of central bank economists sponsored by the Bank of International Settlements, Will Melick and Gabriele Galati (2006) note that during the Great Moderation "the mean rate of inflation has often been judged to have fallen by the order of 10 percentage points" in industrialized countries, "while declines have been of the order of 20 to 30 percentage points for developing countries." The observation about disinflation in developing countries is also the theme of Paul Wachtel and Iikka Korhonen's contribution to this volume.

---

[1] We choose to make the comparison in terms of the chain-weighted GDP deflator rather than a measure of consumer prices because the GDP deflator is methodologically consistent over time (unlike the Consumer Price Index) and is available for the entire post-WWII period (unlike the chain-weighted Personal Consumption Expenditure index).

[2] The standard deviations of annual inflation were 0.86 from 1952–1964, 2.3 from 1965–1984, and 0.75 from 1985–2007 (or 0.58 from 1992–2007).

Though the rates of inflation are similar in the periods before and after the Great Inflation, there are several reasons that the attainment of relatively low and stable inflation has been scrutinized more closely now than in the earlier era. First, in the "don't know what you got 'till it's gone" category, the experience of the Great Inflation made abundantly clear the fact that price stability cannot be taken for granted. Second, the emergence and subsequent conquest of accelerating inflation highlighted the fact that, despite the undeniable influence of factors outside the control of monetary authorities, the long-run pace of price-level growth is, in the end, a policy *choice*. Third, the combination of advances in theory and empirical methodology with a great (if unhappy) natural experiment has provided the opportunity to productively revisit long-standing questions about inflation's costs and consequences.

This volume contains both theoretical and empirical contributions to that discussion, and the individual articles are divided along those lines. The theoretical papers of the first four chapters are largely (though not wholly) devoted to the question of optimal inflation. Ultimately, monetary economics is about the study of economies with frictions, and we suggest that the reader think about our collection of theory papers as a study in the types of frictions that motivate a monetary economy and the welfare implications that emerge as different types of frictions are introduced. In fact, we have chosen to order the papers in what we think of as a somewhat natural theoretical progression, from the traditional cash-in-advance, money-in-the-utility-function setups of Freeman, Henriksen, and Kydland and Devereux (albeit with interesting and nontrivial choices over transactions and pricing technologies), to the overlapping generations framework of Azariadis and Lam (in which uninsurable risks are paramount), to the modern search-theoretic paradigm developed by Rocheteau and Wright. Not surprisingly, conclusions about optimal policy turn out to be quite model dependent, in our opinion raising the stakes on establishing a consensus about which frictions really matter.

The four empirical chapters are somewhat more eclectic, taking up a variety of issues associated with monetary policy in—and in the transition to—a low-inflation environment. For purposes of this discussion, we organize the papers around three major themes: Evidence on the complications (or the lack thereof) of implementing monetary policy when rates of trend inflation are low; threshold effects on the costs of inflation; and the interaction of inflation, financial markets, and intermediation.

## THE THEORY CHAPTERS

The welfare economics of monetary policy starts with the Friedman rule, the simple proposition that the money supply should be deflated at the rate equal to the rate of time preference. The intuition behind the rule is straight-forward: Because the social cost of producing fiat money is essentially zero, individuals will hold the optimal amount of real balances only in the event that the private opportunity cost of holding money is also zero. In an abstract world with a single reference interest rate, this requires that the nominal interest rate reside at its zero lower bound. If the rate of preference is positive, implying that the real interest rate is positive, the central implication of the Friedman rule is that the optimal inflation rate is negative.

Despite the compelling intuition, the Friedman rule seems to clash with reality. Not only do policymakers avoid pursuing a Friedman rule–type policy, they become quite concerned even when inflation rates are at very low, but still positive, levels. The most common explanation for this aversion starts with the so-called New Keynesian framework, which is rapidly taking its place as the workhorse structural framework adopted by (at least the research departments of) most major central banks. The canonical version of this model is most completely explicated in Michael Woodford's (2003) enormously influential *Interest and Prices*. Due to the work of Woodford and many others, it is now well-known that the sticky-price element in this framework implies pursuing a policy that engineers very-near-absolute price stability.

Here, too, the intuition is straightforward: In the face of rigidities in the adjustment of goods prices, deviations in the aggregate price level away from zero generate inefficient changes in underlying firm-specific relative prices. Abstracting from other distortions, such as those emphasized by the Friedman rule or deadweight losses arising from the embedded assumption of imperfect competition in intermediate-goods-producing markets, zero infla-tion is the right way to go.[3]

That still leaves the question of why most central banks prefer to bound the inflation rate well above zero.[4] Here, too, an answer is often provided within the context of the standard New Keynesian framework. Policy in most variations of this model is implemented by manipulating a short-term inter-est rate (a characteristic that obviously describes monetary policy in most

---

[3] Another obvious friction would emanate from inflexible nominal wages. Christiano, Eichenbaum, and Evans (2005) demonstrate that this type of friction is important (among other things) for generating empirically plausible dynamics in New Keynesian models. Erceg, Henderson, and Levin (2000) show that the welfare implications of these models change when nominal wage rigidity is introduced.

[4] See, for example, the charts in Altig (2003).

central banks today). The fact that nominal interest rates cannot fall below zero places a potential constraint on monetary policy operations. The lower the rate of inflation, the more likely it is that an economy will periodically run up against this constraint.

It is not so clear how significant this problem really is. Ben Bernanke, Vincent Reinhart, and Brian Sack (2004), for example, note that targeted asset purchases that change the size and composition of the central bank's balance sheet can be effective even if short-term interest rates are at their zero bound, especially when combined with communications aimed at shaping expectations about the course of future interest rates. Roughly speaking, implementing a stimulative monetary policy simply requires printing plenty of money and convincing the public that you intend to keep at it. This is precisely the route taken by the Bank of Japan when it introduced the so-called quantitative easing policy in 2001. Though not uncontroversial, evidence presented by Bernanke, Reinhart, and Sack and in Mark Spiegel's 2006 review suggests that the approach was successful, at least in the sense of affecting longer-term interest rates.

Beyond providing a frame of reference for the welfare results collected in this volume, there are other obvious points to be made by the foregoing discussion. First, there is a nontrivial policy discussion to be had because the context of monetary policy begins with the belief that the relevant environment is not described by a friction-free Arrow-Debreu economy. Second, the nature of the best policy *potentially* depends on the details of how that environment deviates from the Arrow-Debreu benchmark. Depending on the nature of the distortion, a deviation from the Friedman rule may or may not be optimal.

It is in this light that the theoretical papers in this volume are best viewed. The first three papers in our theory section invoke "standard-type" monetary (and nonmonetary) distortions. Freeman, Henriksen, and Kydland (FHK) and Devereux introduce money via transactions-costs technologies, both contributing to the literature on familiar monetary environments by endogenizing key elements in their models. FHK enrich this environment by adding an endogenous cash/credit decision, but do not otherwise stray far from the money demand model pioneered by Robert Lucas and Nancy Stokey (1987). In a similar vein, Devereux extends an otherwise standard New Keynesian model by giving firms access to a costly flexible-price technology.

While FHK and Devereux operate in the general universe of transactions-based money demand, Azariadis and Lam motivate money demand through an overlapping generations structure. This alternative approach provides an opportunity to examine the robustness of results on the determinacy of monetary equilibrium under Taylor-rule operating procedures, an issue well-traveled within the more standard New Keynesian framework. Nonetheless, while the motivation for holding money is quite different from New Keynesian models—and from FHK and Devereux—the Azariadis and Lam analysis still invokes a fairly traditional monetary environment (albeit with the welfare question complicated by adding incomplete intragenerational risk-sharing and strategic interactions between monetary and fiscal authorities to the usual inefficiencies created by nonzero nominal rates).

As the theoretical structures of these three papers represent variations on traditional money-demand themes, it does turn out that the policy implications are fairly familiar as well. In FHK, agents would rather use inside money because it bears interest, but the existence of a transactions cost to doing so means that outside money (cash) is used in equilibrium. We know from past research—Cooley and Hansen (1991) being a prominent example—that deviations from the Friedman rule have somewhat limited welfare effects in models in which the inflation tax is the primary source of distortions. As John Coleman points out in his comments, given this result, it would be surprising if the FHK model actually generated large welfare costs of inflation: Households can simply use cash, so giving them the option to transact in alternative assets seems unlikely to make the welfare problems worse than in similar models in which the choice sets are more limited.

Both Coleman and Tony Yates make note of the fact that the quantitative results in FHK imply that the welfare cost of 400% inflation is about the same as 10% inflation. This, of course, is driven by the endogeneity of the trans-actions technology, which allows consumers to pay a fixed cost to adopt the credit technology, and thus avoid the inflation tax. This rather striking implication actually conforms to at least some other evidence on the cross-regime costs of inflation, a point we will return to below in our discussion of the Boyd-Champ and Wachtel-Korhonen contributions.

Just as the FHK model generates normative results that are similar to its no-price-friction predecessors, the Devereux sticky-price model generates normative results that are similar to those of the New Keynesian tradition. As Devereux proceeds from the vantage of a small open economy, there are really two issues in play. First, what is the nature of the optimal policy rule given the type of pricing friction studied? Second, what is the optimal exchange rate regime with sticky prices?

To the first question, given the availability of a price-flexibility technology, firms will choose greater price flexibility as the variability of demand shocks increases. As is often the case in New Keynesian models, there is a strategic complementarity in individual firms' choices because the demand for a firm that does not change its price is more volatile the more other firms change their prices. It is fairly easy, then, to see how the addition of an endogenous price-flexibility decision contributes to the possibility of multiple equilibria. This characteristic of the price-flexibility technology reinforcing the properties of standard exogenous-price-stickiness models carries over to the optimal policy results. Adopting price-flexibility is costly, so the optimal monetary policy is one that minimizes price flexibility. Once prices are inflexible, it is best to minimize the volatility in relative prices associated with the fact that some prices can adjust and others can't. Thus, in Devereux's model, price stability is optimal, as in standard sticky-price models.

To the second question, Devereux finds that when exchange rates are fixed, firms will choose fixed-price policy and, hence, will avoid the cost of adopting flexibility. The prescription is thus for fixed prices generally, and the policy regimes that support those choices.

Like FHK and Devereux, Azariadis and Lam uncover the power of old results in a familiar setting. Where FHK embark from a price-flexible neoclassical platform and Devereux from the New Keynesian, Azariadis and Lam appropriate the overlapping-generations structure in the tradition of Sargent and Wallace (1981). In fact, the starting point of Azariadis and Lam's analysis is Sargent and Wallace's indeterminacy result, famously known as the "unpleasant monetarist arithmetic." As is well-known, this kind of economic structure has both high-interest-rate and low-interest-rate equilibria, the former being efficient and the latter inefficient. It is precisely a low-inflation environment that is consistent with low nominal interest rates and hence efficient outcomes.

What is novel in Azariadis and Lam's analysis is the closing of the over-lapping-generations model with the monetary policy characterized by the Taylor rule. The familiar result from standard New Keynesian models that policymakers ought to respond to lagged inflation with a coefficient of greater than one[5] emerges here with the added consequence that the rule also steers the economy to the efficient low-interest-rate equilibrium.

How low is the "low" of the low-inflation environment in Azariadis and Lam's model? Once again, the answer is that it depends. Concerns about the zero nominal-interest-rate bound and risk-sharing considerations move the answer away from the Friedman rule. (In Azariadis and Lam, the inflation tax is the only tax mechanism available to finance transfers from high-income to low-income households.) That does not, however, justify the conclusion that real-world central banks are optimally bounding inflation at strictly positive levels. Azariadis and Lam raise the stakes by introducing strategic

---

[5] See, for example, Carlstrom and Fuerst (2001).

interactions between fiscal and monetary authorities, showing that even a benevolent and independent central bank may choose inflation rates that are too high if it is forced to deal with less-than-benevolent (essentially meaning impatient) fiscal policymakers.

Each of the three papers we have discussed represents useful and interesting variations on some familiar themes in models with particular types of frictions—fixed costs of credit in FHK, sticky prices in Devereux, impediments to intergenerational trade in Azariadis and Lam. The essence of the analysis by Guillaume Rocheteau and Randy Wright is that the optimal policy discussion should start in an environment in which the key frictions are those that give rise to the existence of money as a unique asset that is willingly held in positive quantities in equilibrium. In the tradition of the new "deep money" literature,[6] Rocheteau and Wright assume that periods exist in which trade is characterized by anonymity and the lack of a double coincidence of wants, which implies that some sort of asset is needed to facilitate trade during these periods.

In such an environment it is reasonable to suspect that the nature of trading technologies will loom large in the determination of what monetary policy ought to be. And this is exactly where Rocheteau and Wright go, focusing on trading frictions and three alternative pricing mechanisms: bargaining (standard search equilibrium), competitive price-taking, and price posting or directed search, called competitive search equilibrium by Rocheteau and Wright. The basic model has search externalities—that is, the property that the probability of matches is an increasing function of aggregate search intensity. This property makes the frequency of trade endogenous.

On the welfare question, the pricing structure matters. If prices are determined by bargaining or by competitive price-taking, social welfare may be increased by deviating from the Friedman rule. The rationale for this will be familiar to those schooled in this literature: Although inflation always distorts the level of production away from what is optimal, inflation may improve the frequency of trades, and, as a result, increase social welfare. Less well-known from previous research is the result that if prices are determined by a competitive search mechanism, the Friedman rule is, in fact, optimal.

With these theoretical observations as a foundation, Rocheteau and Wright proceed with a quantitative exercise to gauge the magnitude of inflation costs when policy deviates from its best steady-state setting. In the competitive search equilibrium, the welfare costs of, say, going from 0 to 10% inflation are

---

[6] Any list of seminal works in this literature would include Kiyotaki and Wright (1989, 1993), Trejos and Wright (1995), Shi (1997), and Lagos and Wright (2005).

not very big. They are, in fact, very close to Robert Lucas's (2000) well-known calculations derived from approximating the area under a quantified money demand curve.

When the economy is characterized by either bargaining or competitive price-taking—that is, when deviations from the Friedman rule are optimal—the costs to (high) inflation can be much higher. This is especially true of bargaining. The costs in the competitive price-taking environment are lower, but still higher than the Lucas benchmark. Apparently, the distortions that drive the optimal policy away from the Friedman rule are substantial enough that additional distortions created by inflation are not second-order.

A point made in the commentary by Jim Bullard is worth emphasizing. In all cases, Rocheteau and Wright calibrate their models to a standard-looking money demand curve. Despite the similarity of the reduced forms, welfare costs are very strongly related to the nature of the underlying structures that generate those reduced forms. This is an old lesson, but it is exactly why examining the frictions that generate monetary nonneutrality is so important. And why research like that represented in the first four papers of this volume drive the discussion forward.

## THE EMPIRICAL CHAPTERS

The distinction between the theory papers and the empirical papers in this volume is a bit artificial. With the exception of the Azariadis and Lam article, each of the other contributions we have labeled "theory" have quantitative analysis at their center. But where the contributions to the foregoing section share a thematic core in theoretical propositions about the welfare effects of inflation, the papers we have grouped into the empirical section of the volume represent a collection of studies on diverse questions concerning the facts of operating in and transitioning to low-inflation economies.

That does not mean that there are no common threads among the group we are calling the "empirical papers." We want to highlight three major themes: Evidence on the complications (or the lack thereof) of implementing monetary policy at low rates of trend inflation; threshold effects on the costs of inflation; and the interaction of inflation, financial markets, and intermediation.

### Implementing Monetary Policy in Low-Inflation Environments

Both the Bordo-Lane-Redish and von Hagen-Hofmann papers deal with the complicating factors facing policymakers when trend inflation is low. As noted in the discussion of the Azariadis-Lam paper, the dangers of the zero-nominal-interest-rate bound is a common theme in discussions of optimal monetary policy within the framework of the standard New Keynesian macroeconomic model. This theme, as noted, carries over into Azariadis and Lam's analysis, despite the fact that aspects of their overlapping-generations framework is, in many ways, quite different from the standard model.

But are theoretical complications alone sufficient to consistently drive the actions of central bankers? In particular, are problems that might arise in theory the main source of most modern central bankers' strong predilection to bound the average rate of inflation away from zero? We would claim that the answer is no. The tipping point apparently derives from the much-analyzed, and much-feared, example of Japan, whose troubles through a good part of the 1990s are often attributed to restrictions on monetary policy responses resulting from low nominal rates, themselves attributed in part to the belief that the Bank of Japan would not tolerate rates of inflation much above zero.[7]

Enter Bordo, Lane, and Redish, who warn that focusing on examples like Japan obscures the fact that deflation is not uniformly associated with bad times. Their primary reference is to the period from 1880 to 1914, when many countries were experiencing modest deflation coupled with strong productivity growth and economic expansion. Essentially, the evidence from this period confirms that productivity-driven deflation is not a bad thing. The key insight of Bordo, Lane, and Redish was summarized this way in the 2001 Annual Report of the Federal Reserve Bank of Cleveland:

> The key is the real interest rate: In good times, the productivity of capital is rising and the demand for funds to finance consumption and investment is high. In bad times, the opposite is true. Accordingly, real interest rates tend to rise during good times and fall during bad times. To the extent that zero nominal interest rates... represent the real dangers of deflation, the problems are most likely to occur in times of economic distress.
>
> Deflation alone—even anticipated deflation—does not necessarily imply zero nominal interest rates...provided the real interest rate is sufficiently positive (the normal state of affairs).

Thus, concerns that center on the zero-nominal-interest-rate bound are really concerns about episodic complications. Jürgen von Hagen and Boris Hofmann, on the other hand, suggest a more persistent and general problem with low-inflation environments: The possibility that the quality of inflation indicators may deteriorate as economies settle into low and, importantly, stable inflation regimes.

---

[7] See, for example, McCallum (2001).

Von Hagen and Hofmann articulate a sort of corollary to "Goodhart's law." Goodhart's law, familiar to most, is the notion that policy instruments lose their informational content exactly when policy is successful. If a central bank succeeds in adjusting the monetary thermostat to control the inflation temperature, it will appear that changes in policy have no impact on prices, even if it is the only thing influencing actual inflationary outcomes. The von Hagen-Hofmann corollary is that, as short-run noise in monetary policy declines, short-run fluctuations in the price level will be increasingly dominated by transitory nonmonetary influences on the price level. Though trend growth in the money supply remains the only determinant of trend inflation, the higher variance of transitory noise will make it increasingly difficult to detect the money-inflation connection in high-frequency data.

Von Hagen and Hofmann usefully put their argument in contemporaneous terms by making use of the equivalence between changes in money growth and changes in short-term interest rates characteristic of the New Keynesian framework. Although there has been a near-complete rhetorical replacement of monetary indicators with Taylor rule concepts such as the output gap, the von Hagen-Hofmann corollary applies with equal force to the latter.[8]

But there is an important distinction between the two types of indicators: Whereas money growth and output gaps are equivalent indicators at high frequencies in the simplest types of New Keynesian models, that equivalence does not hold at low frequencies: In the long run, the output gap is zero. Von Hagen and Hofmann conclude that, in the absence of reliable high-frequency-indicator variables for inflation, a central bank should shift its focus to reliable indicators of the long-term trend in inflation.

The happy news is that the data suggest the long-term relationship between money and inflation is a durable one. Von Hagen and Hofmann show a simple version of this relationship for the period from 1960 to 1990 in their figure 1. As an exercise, you can extend their cross-country plot of M2 growth and inflation to the period after 1990 and you will find that even though the positive relationship has weakened somewhat, it is still there.

### Threshold Effects on the Costs of Inflation

One of the intriguing results in the paper by Freeman, Henriksen, and Kydland is the discovery of significant "threshold effects." As noted above, their exper-

---

[8] In many quantitatively successful formulations of the New Keynesian model—the work of Frank Smets and Raf Wouters (2002) is a prime example—these transitory influences are often "mark-up shocks," essentially residuals in pricing equations outside of the output-gap features of the model.

iments indicate that the welfare costs of 10% inflation are not significantly different than the costs associated with 400% inflation. In other words, by the time an economy gets to the low double digits, most of inflation's damage has been done.

The interplay of inflation and its costs in FHK derives from certain properties of the banking system, the technology for accessing credit in particular. Though the credit market mechanism in FHK is specific and relatively simple, the threshold effects it generates are reflective of a broader set of empirical observations that connect inflation and financial-market phenomena more generally. John Boyd and Bruce Champ revisit this evidence, quoting from prior work by Boyd, Ross Levine, and Bruce Smith (2001):

> [T]here appears to be some evidence of a threshold in the empirical relationship between inflation and financial activity. At moderate inflation rates, there is a strong negative association between inflation and financial development. For countries whose inflation is above some critical level, the estimated intercept of the bank development relation is much lower than it is for countries below the threshold. Moreover, in economies with rates of inflation exceeding this threshold, the partial correlation between inflation and financial activity essentially disappears. (237)

The estimated threshold in Boyd, Levine, and Smith is a surprisingly low 15%. In his comments on the paper, Peter Rousseau suggests that the threshold may be even lower, in the range of about 7% to 14%.

These threshold effects may shed light on one of the observations made by Paul Wachtel and Iikka Korhonen in their study of disinflations in transition countries:

> ...stabilization programs usually take hold very quickly. [...] after an initial burst, the pace of disinflation slows down. A stabilization program brings inflation below 60% in about a year (the median for successful stabilizations is 13 months). The median time for inflation to fall from 60% to 30% is about four months. However, further progress in inflation reduction takes more time. The median time for inflation to fall from 30% to 15% is eight months, and from 15% to 7.5%, one year. The initial disinflation experiences are almost all rapid. Stabilization programs always bring inflation below 60% in about two years or less. Further progress is sometimes delayed.

Typically, the discussion on a threshold effect is framed in terms of the low incremental welfare losses once some critical level of the inflation rate is breached. As we discussed earlier, in FHK this appears to be occurring because high inflation induces agents to simply pay the fixed costs that allow them to skirt the resulting welfare losses. To the econometrician not privy to the structural model, this would look exactly like the adoption of an institutional structure (in the form of more active credit markets) that serves to keep the marginal cost of inflation low. But the argument is symmetric. If there is a range over which the marginal cost of higher inflation is low, it stands to reason that the marginal cost of lower inflation may well be lower over that range as well. Once certain thresholds are hit, however, regimes truly change in the sense that the necessary institutional arrangements and transaction practices fundamentally change. Progress near these "tipping points" will almost certainly be more painful and protracted. It may not be surprising, then, to see cases where early progress on reducing inflation is rapid to a point but "delayed" beyond that point.

### The Interaction of Inflation, Financial Markets, and Intermediation

The Boyd and Champ paper itself is all about how inflation interacts with the form and functioning of financial intermediation, which they view as a critical component of the engine of growth. The storyline is straightforward: Inflation reduces the vibrancy and depth of financial markets. Financial intermediaries, banks especially, can at best imperfectly adjust to the impediments that inflation presents. As a consequence, the returns to real capital are reduced (contra Goodfriend's comments on Azariadis and Lam). And to top it all off, the bad stuff kicks in at relatively low rates of inflation (per the aforementioned threshold effects).

Boyd and Champ's review of and contribution to the evidence suggest that these are in fact powerful ill effects. On an encouraging note, Werner Hermann points to the power of competitive pressures in financial markets to also set things right. Commenting on Wachtel and Korhonen, Hermann suggests:

> One additional reason why inflationary policies became less attractive in transition countries, which Wachtel and Korhonen do not mention, might have to do with the increasing threat of currency substitution. In the Commonwealth of Independent States, financing government expenditures by expanding the money supply was attractive during the first stage of transition because there were no inflation expectations, no established tax collection mechanism, no tradition of paying explicit taxes, and thus tax collection was extremely costly. An excess supply of money, of course, led to inflation. People adapted quickly and began to monitor the exchange rate of the domestic currency carefully.

*Soon the U.S. dollar became not only a stable store of value and tacit unit of account, but indeed the only commonly accepted means of payment for larger transactions, such as the sale of second-hand cars, even among residents. As more and more people tried to substitute dollars for domestic currency, inflationary policies became less attractive.* [emphasis added]

This focus on competitive pressure is of a piece with the theme that runs through this volume. The study of inflation and its effects can scarcely proceed without a serious accounting of the institutional settings that shape the technologies available for transacting and intermediating funds (including, Rocheteau and Wright emphasize, the market structures in which these activities take place). This may well be the next frontier in the quest to really understand the economic consequences of inflation, high and low.

## REFERENCES

Altig, D. 2003. Comment on Taking Intermediation Seriously. *Journal of Money, Credit and Banking* 35: 1367–77.

Bernanke, B., V. Reinhart, and B. Sack. 2004. Monetary Policy Alternatives at the Zero Bound: An Empirical Assessment. FEDS Working Paper No. 2004–48, Washington, D.C..

Boyd, J., R. Levine, and B. Smith. 2001. The Impact of Inflation on Financial Market Performance, *Journal of Monetary Economics* 47: 221–48.

Carlstrom, C., and T. Fuerst. 2001. Timing and Real Indeterminacy in Monetary Models. *Journal of Monetary Economics* 47: 285–98.

Christiano, L., M. Eichenbaum, and C. Evans. 2005. Nominal Rigidities and the Dynamic Effects of Monetary Policy. *Journal of Political Economy* 113: 1–45.

Cooley, T., and G. Hansen. 1991. The Welfare Costs of Moderate Inflation. *Journal of Money, Credit, and Banking* 23: 483–503.

Erceg, C., D. Henderson, and A. Levin. 2000. Optimal Monetary Policy with Staggered Wage and Price Contracts. *Journal of Monetary Economics* 46(2): 281–313.

Federal Reserve Bank of Cleveland. 2001. Deflation. *Annual Report.*

Kiyotaki, N., and R. Wright. 1989. On Money as a Medium of Exchange. *Journal of Political Economy* 97: 927–54.

Kiyotaki, N., and R. Wright. 1993. A Search-Theoretic Approach to Monetary Economics. *American Economic Review* 83: 63–77.

Lagos, R., and R. Wright. 2005. A Unified Framework for Monetary Theory and Policy Analysis. *Journal of Political Economy* 113: 463–84.

Lucas, R., and N. Stokey. 1987. Money and Interest in a Cash-in-Advance-Economy. *Econometrica* 55: 491–514.

Lucas, R., 2000. Inflation and Welfare. *Econometrica* 68: 247–74.

McCallum, B. 2001. Japanese Monetary Policy. Report to the Shadow Open Market Committee, April 30, http://wpweb2.tepper.cmu.edu/faculty/mccallum/JapanMonPol2.pdf.

Melick, W., and G. Galati. 2006. The Evolving Inflation Process: An Overview, Working Paper No. 196, Bank of International Settlements.

Meltzer, A. H. 2005. Origins of the Great Inflation. *Federal Reserve Bank of St. Louis Review* 87: 145–75.

Sargent, T., and N. Wallace.1981. Some Unpleasant Monetarist Arithmetic. *Federal Reserve Bank of Minneapolis Quarterly Review* 5:1–17.

Shi, S. 1997. A Divisible Search Model of Fiat Money. *Econometrica* 65: 75–102.

Smets, F., and R. Wouters. 2002. An Estimated Stochastic Dynamic General Equilibrium Model of the Euro Area, Working Paper No. 171, European Central Bank.

Speigel, M., 2006. Did Quantitative Easing by the Bank of Japan "Work"? *Federal Reserve Bank of San Francisco Economic Letter* 2006–18.

Trejos, A., and R. Wright. 1995. Search, Bargaining, Money, and Prices. *Journal of Political Economy* 103: 118–41.

Woodford, M. 2003. *Interest and Prices: Foundations of a Theory of Monetary Policy,* New Jersey: Princeton University Press.

# 1

## The Welfare Cost of Inflation

## in the Presence of Inside Money

*Scott Freeman, Espen R. Henriksen, and Finn E. Kydland*

In this paper, we ask what role an endogenous money multiplier plays in the estimated welfare cost of inflation. The model is a variant of that used by Freeman and Kydland (2000) with inside and outside money in the spirit of Freeman and Huffman (1991). Unlike models in which the money–output link comes from either sticky prices or fixed money holdings, here prices and output are assumed to be fully flexible. Consumption goods are purchased using either currency or bank deposits. Two transaction costs affect these decisions: One is the cost of acquiring money balances, which is necessary to determine the demand for money and to make the velocity of money endogenous. The other is a fixed cost associated with using deposits. This cost is instrumental in determining the division of money balances into currency and interest-bearing deposits. Faced with these two costs and factors that may vary over time in equilibrium (such as over the business cycle), households make decisions that, in the aggregate, determine the velocity of money and the money multiplier.

The model is consistent with several features of U.S. data: (1) M1 is positively correlated with real output; (2) the money multiplier and deposit-to-currency ratio are positively correlated with output; (3) the price level is negatively correlated with output in spite of conditions (1) and (2); (4) the correlation of M1 with contemporaneous prices is substantially weaker than the correlation of M1 with real output; (5) correlations among real variables are essentially unchanged under different monetary policy regimes; and (6) real money balances are smoother than money-demand equations would predict.

A key feature of the model is that households purchase a continuum of types of goods indexed by their size. It comes from assuming a Leontief-type utility function over these types. One could argue that the distinction between nondurable and (usually larger) durable consumption goods should also be taken into account. We shall not take that step here. Instead, compared with Freeman and Kydland (2000), we consider a more flexible utility function than before, which, in equilibrium, permits the implication that households wish to consume large goods in relatively greater quantities.

1

With the model economy calibrated to the usual long-run relations in the data—including the selection of values for the two transaction-cost parameters so as to make the model consistent with the empirical average deposit-to-currency ratio and the fraction of capital that is intermediated—the estimated welfare cost of inflation turns out to be rather small. An interesting finding is that the welfare cost as a function of the steady-state inflation rate is very steep for low inflation rates (well under 10%) but quite flat for higher inflation rates. Moreover, we find that the welfare cost is sensitive to the values of the transaction-cost parameters.

Beginning with Bailey (1956) and Friedman (1969), a long line of research addresses the question of the cost of inflation. Among recent contributions, the estimated gain from reducing inflation from 10% to 0% range from a consumption equivalent of 0.38% by Cooley and Hansen (1989), who address the question within a cash-in-advance model, to a consumption equivalent of around 1% by Lucas (2000), who analyzes a representative agent model with shopping time.[1]

## 1. MODEL ECONOMY

### 1.1 The Household's Problem

There is a continuum of good types of measure $c_t^*$, ordered by size and indexed by $j$ over $[0,1]$. The representative household has a Leontief-type instantaneous utility function over the continuum of good types,

$$\min \left[ \frac{c_t(j)}{(1-\omega)j^{-\omega}} \right],$$

which gives us the parameterized distribution function for $c_t(j)$ over $[0,1]$

(1)  $c_t(j) = (1-\omega)j^{-\omega}c_t^*.$

The representative household has time-separable preferences over total consumption $(c_t^*)$ and leisure $(d_t)$,

(2)  $\max E \sum_{t=0}^{\infty} \beta^t u(c_t^*, d_t),$

---

[1] Other recent contributions include Bullard and Russell (2000), Dotsey and Ireland (1996), Gomme (1993), Imrohoroglu and Prescott (1991), Jones and Manuelli (1995), and Lacker and Schreft (1996).

where the instantaneous utility is given by

$$(3) \quad u\left(c_t^*, d_t\right) = \frac{1}{1-v}\left[(c_t^*)^\zeta (d_t)^{1-\zeta}\right]^{1-v}.$$

There are three vehicles of savings available to the household: noninter-mediated capital $(a_t)$, nominal bank deposits $(h_t)$, and currency $(m_t)$. Both bank deposits $(h_t)$ and currency $(m_t)$ can be used to purchase consumption goods, but the use of deposits incurs an extra fixed cost, denoted by $\gamma$. Because of this fixed cost of using deposits for purchases, the deposit rate of the return net of transaction costs goes to negative infinity as purchase size $(j)$ goes to zero. Therefore, some $j^*$ exists below which currency is a preferred means of payment and above which deposits are preferred.

The household's good budget constraint is given by

$$(4) \quad c_t^* + a_t + \frac{h_t}{p_t} + \frac{m_t}{p_t} + \gamma\left(1 - j_t^*\right) = w_t\, l_t + r_t\, a_{t-1} + \tilde{r}_t\, \frac{h_{t-1}}{p_{t-1}} + \frac{m_{t-1}}{p_t} + \frac{x_t}{p_t},$$

where $p_t$ is the nominal price level, $w_t$ is the wage rate, $r_t$ is the real rate of return on capital, $\tilde{r}_t$ is the real rate of return on deposits, and $x_t$ is government lump-sum transfers.

Available time for the households is normalized to 1, and the time available is spent on leisure $(d_t)$, labor $(l_t)$, and the number of times that money balances have to be replenished each period $(n_t)$ multiplied by the time each replenishment takes $(\varphi)$. The time constraint is

$$(5) \quad 1 = d_t + l_t + n_t\, \varphi.$$

## 1.2 Production

Output is given by a constant-returns-to-scale production function with two inputs, capital $(k_t)$ and labor $(l_t)$:

$$y_t = z_t f(k_t, l_t).$$

The law of motion for the technology level $z_t$ is given by

$$z_t = p z_{t-1} + \varepsilon_t, \qquad z_t \sim N(\mu, \sigma^2), \ \mu > 0.$$

The depreciation rate is denoted by $\delta$, so the law of motion for the capital stock is

$$k_{t+1} = (1 - \delta)\, k_t + i_t,$$

where $i_t$ is gross investment.

### 1.3 Government

The government controls the supply of intrinsically worthless fiat money. The law of motion for the money stock is

$$M_t = \xi M_{t-1}.$$

Net revenues from printing money are transferred to the household in a lump-sum fashion,

$$x_t = (\xi - 1)\, M_{t-1}.$$

### 1.4 Financial Intermediation

Banks accept deposits, hold the required-reserves fraction ($\theta$) as cash, and invest the proceeds in capital. Free entry ensures zero profit, and the rate of return on deposits ($\tilde{r}$), therefore, is a linear combination of the real return on capital ($r_{t+1}$) and the return on holding currency ($p_t/p_{t+1}$):

$$\tilde{r}_{t+1} = (1-\theta)\, r_{t+1} + \theta\, \frac{p_t}{p_{t+1}}.$$

By definition, the total stock of fiat money (the monetary base) is equal to the combined stocks of currency and reserves,

$$M_t = m_t + \theta h_t,$$

whereas the total money stock (M1) is the sum of nominal deposits and currency, which can be rewritten as the product of the monetary base and the money multiplier:

$$\mathrm{M1}_t = m_t + h_t = M_t \left[ 1 + \frac{h_t(1-\theta)}{m_t + \theta h_t} \right].$$

For the representative household, the per-period holdings of real deposits ($h_t/p_t$) are

$$(6)\quad n_t \frac{h_t}{p_t} = \int_{j*}^{1} c_t(j)\, \mathrm{d}j = \int_{j*}^{1} (1-\omega) j^{-\omega} c_t^*\, \mathrm{d}j = [\, j^{1-\omega} c_t^* \,]_{j*}^{1} = \left( 1 - (j^*)^{1-\omega} \right) c_t^*,$$

and holdings of real fiat-money balances ($m_t/p_t$) are

$$(7)\quad n_t \frac{m_t}{p_t} = \int_{0}^{j*} c_t(j)\, \mathrm{d}j = \int_{0}^{j*} (1-\omega) j^{-\omega} c_t^*\, \mathrm{d}j = [\, j^{1-\omega} c_t^* \,]_{0}^{j*} = (j^*)^{1-\omega} c_t^*.$$

## 2. CALIBRATION

In the steady state, investment is one-quarter of output and the annual capital–output ratio, 2.5. The depreciation rate is then calibrated to 0.025. The parameter $\alpha$ in the production function is calibrated such that the labor share of national income is 0.64. The autocorrelation coefficient $\rho$ in the technology process is equal to 0.95, with a standard deviation of 0.0076.

Setting the average allocation of households' time (excluding sleep and personal care) to market activity equal to 0.30 restricts the value of the utility parameter $\zeta$. The risk-aversion parameter, $\upsilon$, is equal to 2, and the reserve-requirement ratio, $\theta$, is 0.10.

### 2.1 Utility Function

As an illustration, let the continuum of good types $c_t(j)$ be of measure $c_t^*=1$. Equation (1) can then be simplified as

$$c_t(j) = (1-\omega)j^{-\omega}.$$

In figure 1, $c_t(j)$ is plotted for three different values of $\omega$. As is apparent from the expression and visualized in the figure, for $\omega>-1$, the amount of a good that is consumed is a concave function of the size of the good, whereas for $\omega<-1$, the amount of a good that is consumed is a convex function of the size of the good.

**Figure 1: $c(j)$ for $0 \leq j \leq 1, c^* = 1$**

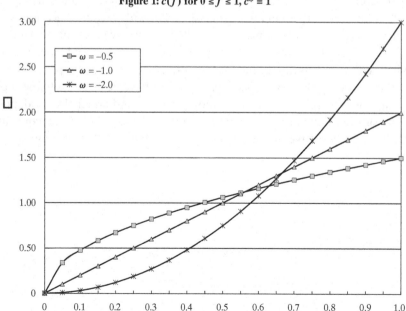

Combining equations (6) and (7) gives us the cutoff size for purchase, above which deposits are preferred over currency:

$$(8) \quad j^* = \left(1 + \frac{h_t}{m_t}\right)^{\frac{1}{\omega - 1}}.$$

The derivative of $j^*$ is negative, implying that, loosely speaking, the more convex $c_t(j)$, the higher $j^*$, or, conversely, the more concave $c_t(j)$, the lower $j^*$. Note that equations (6) and (7) combined with (8) imply

$$\int_{j^*}^{1} c_t(j)\,dj = \left(1 + \frac{m_t}{h_t}\right)^{-1} c_t^*$$

and

$$\int_{0}^{j^*} c_t(j)\,dj = \left(1 + \frac{h_t}{m_t}\right)^{-1} c_t^*.$$

In other words, the cutoff size of purchases for which deposits are preferred over currency is a function of $\omega$, whereas the share of total consumption $(c_t^*)$ for which deposits are preferred over currency (and vice versa) depends only on the deposit-to-currency ratio.

## 2.2 Business Cycle Properties

To get a sense of the reasonable values of $\omega$, we start by reexamining the business cycle findings of Freeman and Kydland (2000) with this modification of the utility function. As in Freeman and Kydland (2000), we examine the model's behavior under three different policy regimes (see figure 2): Under the first, policy A, the growth rate of fiat money is fixed at 3% in every period. Under the second, policy B, serially uncorrelated shocks have been added to the supply of fiat money, with a standard deviation of 0.5%. And under the third, policy C, the shocks to the growth rate of the monetary base are serially correlated with an autoregressive parameter of 0.7 and a standard deviation of 0.2.

**Figure 2: Cross-Correlations: Output and Price Level**

Policy A

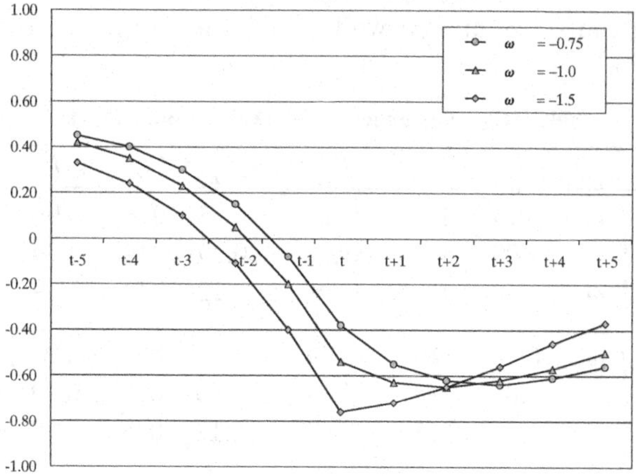

Policy B

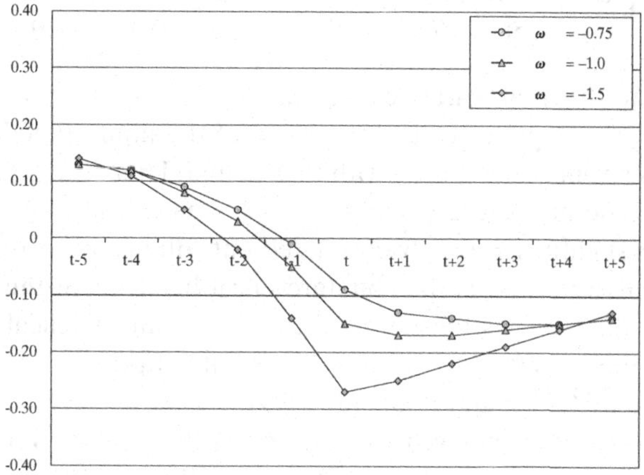

Policy C

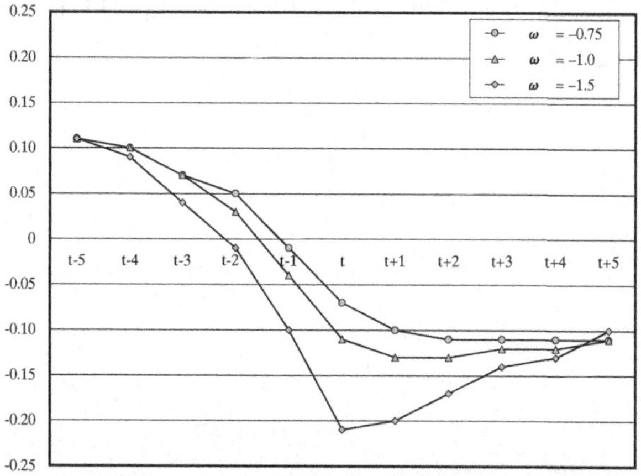

For these three policies, we examine the business cycle properties for $\omega = \{-0.75, -1.0, -1.5\}$. Table 1 presents the contemporaneous correlations with output, which can be compared with actual data presented by Gavin and Kydland (1999).

**Table 1: Contemporaneous Correlations with Output**

|  |  | M1 | P | $R_{nom}$ | C | I | L |
|---|---|---|---|---|---|---|---|
| Policy A: | $\omega = -0.75$ | 1 | –0.38 | –0.73 | 0.96 | 0.99 | 0.99 |
|  | $\omega = -1.00$ | 1 | –0.54 | –0.29 | 0.96 | 0.99 | 0.99 |
|  | $\omega = -1.50$ | 1 | –0.76 | 0.12 | 0.96 | 0.99 | 0.99 |
| Policy B: | $\omega = -0.75$ | 0.89 | –0.09 | –0.73 | 0.96 | 0.99 | 0.99 |
|  | $\omega = -1.00$ | 0.85 | –0.15 | –0.29 | 0.96 | 0.99 | 0.99 |
|  | $\omega = -1.50$ | 0.78 | –0.27 | 0.12 | 0.96 | 0.99 | 0.99 |
| Policy C: | $\omega = -0.75$ | 0.82 | –0.07 | –0.36 | 0.96 | 0.99 | 0.99 |
|  | $\omega = -1.00$ | 0.78 | –0.11 | –0.09 | 0.96 | 0.99 | 0.99 |
|  | $\omega = -1.50$ | 0.72 | –0.21 | 0.02 | 0.96 | 0.99 | 0.99 |

Notice that the real variables—*C, I,* and *L*—are hardly affected by changes in monetary policy or the curvature of the utility function. We also see that M1 is strongly correlated with real output. Under policy A, in which there is no randomness, the correlation is 1. Under the two other policy regimes, M1 is slightly less tightly correlated but still highly correlated.

An interesting pattern is the countercyclical behavior of the price level. We see that, for all policies, the price level is more countercyclical for $\omega = -1.5$ than for the other two values, which is consistent with the business cycle statistics reported by Gavin and Kydland (1999).

We also notice that the cyclical behavior of the nominal interest rate is closer to what is observed in the data for $\omega = -1.5$ (figure 3). For the other two values of $\omega$, the nominal rate of return ($R_{nom}$) is countercyclical, whereas for $\omega = -1.5$, the nominal interest rate is weakly procyclical. This is consistent with reported business cycle statistics.

**Figure 3: Cross-Correlations: Output and Nominal *R***

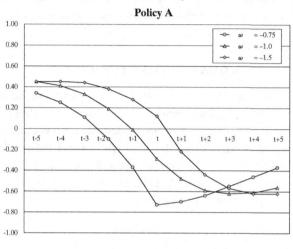

**Policy A**

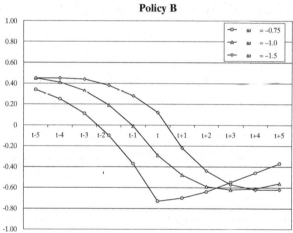

**Policy B**

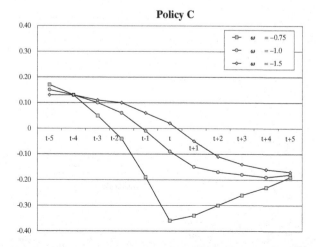

**Policy C**

Until we have data from which we can map more directly to $\omega$, we choose $\omega = -1.5$ as our benchmark value because this value gives business cycle statistics closest to those observed.

## 3. QUANTITATIVE FINDINGS

We will begin by describing the steady-state properties of our economy under different inflation regimes. The economy is calibrated such that for an annual inflation rate equal to 0.03, the currency-to-deposit ratio is equal to 9 and the nonreserve portion of M1 divided by the capital stock is 0.05. This gives us calibrated values for $\gamma = 0.00529$ and $\varphi = 0.00060$, which implies that at this inflation rate, the fixed cost, $\gamma(1-j^*)$, is 0.36% of gross domestic product and $\varphi$ corresponds to approximately 55 minutes per quarter.

### 3.1 Steady State

Figures 4 and 5 (figure 4 is just a subset of figure 5) plot the benchmark welfare cost function $\lambda$, defined such that

$$u[\lambda c(\pi), d(\pi)] = u[c(\tilde{\pi}), d(\tilde{\pi})],$$

where $\tilde{\pi}$ equals the average inflation rate over the last 15 years, about 3%.

**Figure 4: Welfare Cost of Inflation Relative to Net Annual Inflation of 0.03**

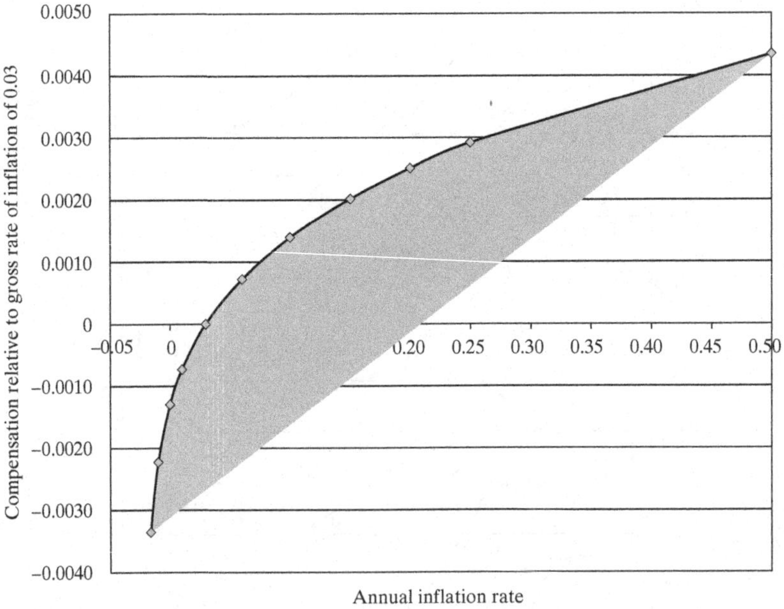

**Figure 5: Welfare Cost of Inflation Relative to Net Annual Inflation of 0.03**

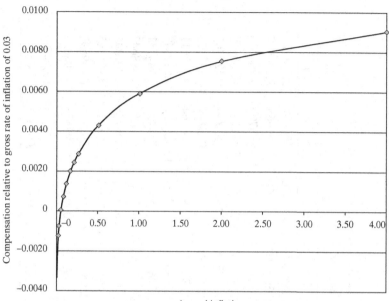

Annual inflation rate

We see from figures 4 and 5 that as steady-state inflation approaches an annual rate of 50%, the welfare cost is slightly less than 0.4% of consumption compared with the steady state associated with 3% inflation. As the steady-state inflation rate increases further, the associated welfare flattens out. At an annual inflation rate of 400%, the cost of inflation in terms of consumption compensation is still less than 0.8%.

The most striking feature of the graph is the predicted welfare gain from reducing inflation to below 3% annually. As we see from the graph, the effect of reducing inflation to its lower bound of −0.01644% gives a welfare improvement of almost the same magnitude as the welfare cost of increasing inflation from 3% to 50%.[2]

The main variables underlying these results are presented in table 2. As inflation increases, individuals become less and less willing to hold non-interest-bearing assets such as currency. The cutoff value of $j^*$, below which currency is preferred over deposits, is decreasing and eventually converges to zero as inflation increases towards infinity. Hence, the deposit-to-currency ratio

---

[2] In this model, there is a uniquely defined lower bound of inflation that is weakly greater than the inverse of the real rate of return on capital. At this lower bound, no one will hold deposits and the total money stock is equal to the monetary base (M1 = $M$).

**Table 2: Steady-State Welfare Costs, Benchmark Calibration**

Annual Inflation Rate

| | −0.0164 | 0.00 | 0.01 | 0.03 | 0.06 | 0.10 | 0.25 | 0.50 |
|---|---|---|---|---|---|---|---|---|
| $n$ | 1.320681 | 1.192505 | 1.171063 | 1.209201 | 1.309609 | 1.446476 | 1.600991 | 2.311321 |
| $l$ | 0.299345 | 0.299722 | 0.299879 | 0.300000 | 0.300038 | 0.300018 | 0.299965 | 0.299597 |
| $a$ | 9.713202 | 9.566608 | 9.516885 | 9.500000 | 9.521467 | 9.557323 | 9.593700 | 9.700938 |
| $h$ | 0.000000 | 2.331871 | 3.358631 | 4.736842 | 5.927637 | 6.810877 | 7.441156 | 8.736977 |
| $m$ | 1.000000 | 0.766813 | 0.664137 | 0.526316 | 0.407236 | 0.318912 | 0.255884 | 0.126302 |
| $h/m$ | 0.000000 | 3.040992 | 5.057136 | 9.000000 | 14.555766 | 21.356580 | 29.080149 | 69.175101 |
| $j^*$ | 1.000000 | 0.572012 | 0.486511 | 0.398107 | 0.333613 | 0.288561 | 0.256264 | 0.182611 |
| $p$ | 3.327290 | 4.948311 | 6.309454 | 8.526316 | 11.118960 | 13.827927 | 16.529927 | 27.529942 |
| $c$ | 0.746847 | 0.746759 | 0.746644 | 0.746420 | 0.746132 | 0.745815 | 0.745490 | 0.744131 |
| $d$ | 0.699650 | 0.699370 | 0.699229 | 0.699079 | 0.698965 | 0.698880 | 0.698816 | 0.698643 |
| $u$ | −1.398807 | −1.399235 | −1.399496 | −1.399835 | −1.400167 | −1.400477 | −1.400765 | −1.401841 |
| $k$ | 9.978158 | 9.990729 | 9.995970 | 10.000000 | 10.001267 | 10.000614 | 9.998846 | 9.986565 |
| $l$ | 0.299345 | 0.299722 | 0.299879 | 0.300000 | 0.300038 | 0.300018 | 0.299965 | 0.299597 |
| $y$ | 0.997816 | 0.999073 | 0.999597 | 1.000000 | 1.000127 | 1.000061 | 0.999885 | 0.998656 |
| $\lambda_{0.03}$ | −0.0022 | −0.0013 | −0.0007 | 0.0000 | 0.0007 | 0.0014 | 0.0020 | 0.0043 |
| $\lambda_{0.00}$ | −0.0009 | 0.0000 | 0.0006 | 0.0013 | 0.0020 | 0.0027 | 0.0033 | 0.0057 |

increases and more resources in the economy are spent on facilitating transactions, both through the fixed cost for purchasing goods with deposits, $\lambda(1-j^*)$, and the time spent to withdraw currency $(n^*\varphi)$.

Steady states with lower inflation rates display the mirror image of the high-inflation regimes: Because the alternative value of holding deposits over holding currency diminishes, the cutoff value $j^*$ increases and the deposit-to-currency ratio decreases. Henceforth, the welfare costs associated with individual liquidity management decrease.

### 3.2 Sensitivity/Alternative Calibration

The qualitative results presented in the previous section turn out to be insensitive to the calibration of the model economy. The quantitative results, however, depend strongly on the way the data are mapped to the model and, in particular, on the calibration of the transaction parameters, $\gamma$ and $\varphi$.

Both the deposit-to-currency ratio and the nonreserve portion of M1 divided by the capital stock are hard to measure. Our empirical deposit-to-currency ratio, which excludes an estimate of the ratio of currency held abroad, ranges from 12 early in the sample to 7 late in the sample. We have encountered estimates of the nonreserve portion of M1 divided by the capital stock as low as 0.03 and as high as 0.20.

Table 3 shows how the values $\gamma$ and $\varphi$ vary as we change the deposit-to-currency ratio and the nonreserve portion of M1 divided by the capital stock. The last column of table 3 shows the welfare gain from reducing inflation from 0.03% to 0.00% annually. The values for $\varphi$ and $\gamma$ reported in the last row correspond to 19.7 hours per quarter and 1.58% of output, respectively.

As we see from the last row of this table and from figure 6, the steady-state welfare gains increase by a factor of about five with this alternative calibration. The welfare gain from reducing inflation from 3% annually to the lower bound is about 1.5%, whereas the cost of increasing inflation from 3% to 50% is about 2%.

**Table 3: Alternative Calibrations of $\varphi$ and $\gamma$**

|  | $\dfrac{h}{m}$ | $\dfrac{M1-\theta h}{k}$ | $\varphi$ | $\gamma$ | $\gamma_{0.03 \to 0.00}$ |
|---|---|---|---|---|---|
| Benchmark | 9 | 0.05 | 0.0007614 | 0.005948 | 0.0013 |
| Alt. 1 | 7 | 0.05 | 0.0009014 | 0.006993 | 0.0017 |
| Alt. 2 | 9 | 0.20 | 0.01236 | 0.02379 | 0.0052 |
| Alt. 3 | 7 | 0.20 | 0.01466 | 0.02798 | 0.0067 |

**Figure 6: Welfare Costs, Alternative Calibration**

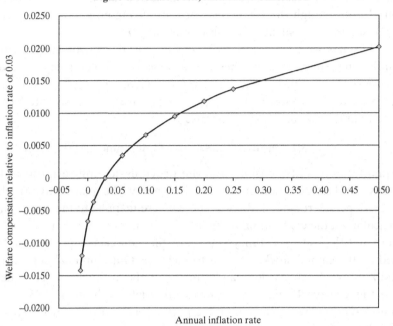

Annual inflation rate

### 3.3 Transition

Restricting the comparison to steady states ignores some important aspects that are relevant to answering our question. Therefore, we conduct a series of policy experiments in which we reduce inflation from moderate levels (0.03%, 0.06%, 0.10%, and 0.25%) to zero. When conducting these policy experiments, we calibrate the economy to the benchmark case for $\gamma$ and $\varphi$.

Table 4 and figure 7 present the results of these experiments. The welfare gains from reducing inflation are smaller than when comparing the steady states and range from 0.07% for an initial inflation rate of 3% to 0.35% for an initial inflation rate of 25%.

Comparing steady states, the welfare gains come solely from the reduction in resources spent on facilitating transactions. In addition, we have the effect of changes in expectations of monetary policy. If the rate of money growth ($\xi$) is decreased, anticipated inflation decreases, demand for real money balances increases, and the price level must decrease in equilibrium. This is known as the *Friedman surge effect*.

**Table 4: Transition between Steady States**

|  | 0.03→0.00 | 0.06→0.00 | 0.10→0.00 | 0.15→0.00 | 0.25→0.00 |
|---|---|---|---|---|---|
| *h/m* initial | 9.0000 | 14.5558 | 21.3566 | 29.0801 | 42.6042 |
| *h/m* new st. st. | 3.0419 | 3.0419 | 3.0419 | 3.0419 | 3.0419 |
| *j** initial | 0.3981 | 0.3336 | 0.2886 | 0.2563 | 0.2209 |
| *j** new st. st. | 0.5720 | 0.5720 | 0.5720 | 0.5720 | 0.5720 |
| *c* initial st. st. | 0.7464 | 0.7461 | 0.7458 | 0.7455 | 0.7450 |
| *c* new st. st. | 0.7468 | 0.7468 | 0.7468 | 0.7468 | 0.7468 |
| *c* change (net) | 0.0005 | 0.0008 | 0.0013 | 0.0017 | 0.0024 |
| *d* initial st. st. | 0.6991 | 0.6990 | 0.6989 | 0.6988 | 0.6987 |
| *d* new st. st. | 0.6994 | 0.6994 | 0.6994 | 0.6994 | 0.6994 |
| *d* change (net) | 0.0004 | 0.0006 | 0.0007 | 0.0008 | 0.0009 |
| *k* initial st. st. | 10.0000 | 10.0013 | 10.0006 | 9.9988 | 9.9969 |
| *k* new st. st. | 9.9906 | 9.9906 | 9.9906 | 9.9906 | 9.9906 |
| *k* change (net) | −0.0009 | −0.0011 | −0.0010 | −0.0008 | −0.0006 |
| output initial st.st. | 1.0000 | 1.0001 | 1.0001 | 0.9999 | 0.9997 |
| output new st. st. | 0.9991 | 0.9991 | 0.9991 | 0.9991 | 0.9991 |
| output change (net) | −0.0009 | −0.0011 | −0.0010 | −0.0008 | −0.0006 |
| welfare gain | 0.0007 | 0.0014 | 0.0022 | 0.0029 | 0.0035 |

**Figure 7: Welfare Comparisons**

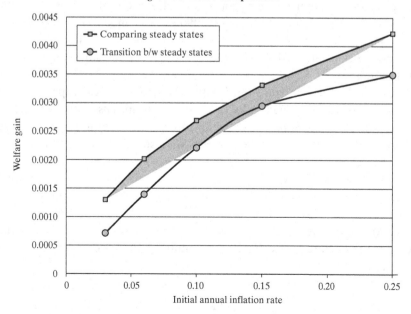

## 4. CONCLUDING REMARKS

Compared to the existing literature on the welfare cost of inflation, the model in this paper contains some novel features. For one, people make purchases using both inside and outside money. The proportions of purchases made by either are determined by economic decisions in which the liquid assets' relative returns play an important role. The model allows for two transactions costs, one associated with using deposits (checks) when making purchases, and one incurred when liquid balances are replenished during the period. In equilibrium, people make small purchases with currency and large purchases with deposits. The transaction-cost parameters are calibrated to the average currency–deposit ratio and to the fraction of the economy's total capital that is intermediated. The extent to which these costs kick in for various inflation rates plays a major role in our quantitative estimates. Moreover, because banks invest individuals' deposits in capital, another interesting feature is an effect of steady-state inflation on the total capital stock, which in our model may go in the reverse direction of what is commonly called the *Tobin effect*.

Our welfare-cost estimates are somewhat lower than those that Cooley and Hansen (1989) and Lucas (2000) report. An interesting finding is that the welfare-cost curve is quite concave, meaning that the cost goes up steeply with steady-state inflation for low inflation rates (especially around 5% and lower) before flattening out considerably.

We have not taken into account fiscal considerations, such as replacing lost seigniorage revenue using proportional taxes on labor and/or capital income rather than lump-sum taxes; we believe our model has little new to say in that regard. It would probably replicate Lucas's (2000) finding that fiscal considerations affect the welfare-cost estimates noticeably only for very low inflation rates.

We consider the estimate's sensitivity to several features. In particular, it is quite sensitive to the magnitudes of the two quantities used to calibrate the transaction-cost parameters. This is an interesting finding because these quantities have changed over the decades. We also study the transition paths from one steady-state inflation rate to another. These converge very quickly and make little difference to the welfare costs. Initially, they do contain a sizable amount of the so-called Friedman surge effect, which a central bank might wish to avoid for some reason or another that is not included in this model. An interesting but not trivial extension, then, could be to evaluate the effect on the welfare-cost estimate of combining the current model with a price-smoothing rule.

## ACKNOWLEDGMENTS

Dr. Henriksen gratefully acknowledges the financial support of the SEB Group and the William Larimer Mellon Fund.

## REFERENCES

Bailey, M. 1956. The Welfare Cost of Inflationary Finance. *Journal of Political Economy* 64: 93–110.

Bullard, J., and S. Russell. 2000. How Costly Is Sustained Low Inflation for the U.S. Economy? Unpublished working paper.

Coleman, J. 1996. Money and Output: A Test of Reverse Causation. *American Economic Review* 86(1): 90–111.

Cooley, T. F., and G. D. Hansen. 1989. The Inflation Tax in a Real Business Cycle Model. *American Economic Review* 79(4): 733–48.

Cooley, T. F., and G. D. Hansen. 1991. The Welfare Costs of Moderate Inflations. *Journal of Money, Credit, and Banking* 23(3): 483–503.

Dotsey, M., and P. Ireland. 1996. On the Welfare Costs of Inflation in General Equilibrium. *Journal of Monetary Economics* 37(1): 29–47.

Freeman, S., and G. W. Huffman. 1991. Inside Money, Output, and Causality. *International Economic Review* 32(3): 645–67.

Freeman, S., and F. E. Kydland. 2000. Monetary Aggregates and Output. *American Economic Review* 90(5): 1125–35.

Friedman, M. 1969. *The Optimum Quantity of Money and Other Essays.* Chicago: Aldine.

Gavin, W. T., and F. E. Kydland. 1999. Endogenous Money Supply and the Business Cycle. *Review of Economic Dynamics* 2: 347–69.

Gomme, P. 1993. Money and Growth Revisited: Measuring the Costs of Inflation in an Endogenous Growth Model. *Journal of Monetary Economics* 32(1): 51–77.

Imrohoroglu, A., and E. C. Prescott. 1991. Seigniorage as a Tax: A Quantitative Evaluation. *Journal of Money, Credit, and Banking* 23(3): 462–75.

Jones, L., and R. Manuelli. 1995. Growth and the Effects of Inflation. *Journal of Economic Dynamics and Control* 19: 1405–28.

Lacker, J., and S. Schreft. 1996. Money and Credit as a Means of Payment. *Journal of Monetary Economics* 38: 3–23.

Lucas, R. E. 2000. Inflation and Welfare. *Econometrica* 68(2): 247–74.

# Commentary

*Wilbur John Coleman II*

Estimating the welfare cost of inflation has had a long presence in the literature, extending as far back as Bailey (1956) and Friedman (1969). In many ways, the evolution of answers to this question reflects the advances in technology that we use to address all sorts of questions in economics. The research of Bailey and Friedman was conducted in the spirit of treating money as an object of choice, which led them to examine the area under its demand curve to conduct welfare analysis. Later, as tools for examining economic dynamics began to be developed and research focused more on how money is used, Cooley and Hansen (1989) and Lucas (2000) studied the issue of the welfare cost of inflation using variants of cash-in-advance models of an economy with fully dynamic optimizing households and firms. At roughly the same time, more effort was being put into developing richer models of how money is used in an economy so that models could meaningfully distinguish currency, reserves, checkable deposits, and credit. Papers along these lines include King and Plosser (1984), Lucas and Stokey (1987), Coleman (1996), and Freeman and Kydland (2000). The current paper by Freeman, Henriksen, and Kydland uses and extends this recent line of research to examine the welfare cost of inflation in a model with multiple means of payment.

Let me first step back and ask whether Freeman, Henriksen, and Kydland offer a useful framework for generating new insights into the issue of estimating the welfare cost of inflation. One way to interpret some of the earlier welfare-cost literature is that even if people are forced to hold cash, as they are in a cash-in-advance model, estimates of the welfare cost of inflation are small. Models with multiple means of payment allow households (and possibly firms, depending on how money is modeled) to avoid holding cash and instead to hold other interest-bearing assets for transactions purposes. It is difficult to imagine, then, that in such a model you would estimate the welfare cost to be larger than in a model without these alternative means of payment. In Freeman, Henriksen, and Kydland, households can choose to transact only in cash, which would effectively transform this model into a cash-in-advance economy.[1] Of course, a different model changes the calibration of the model's parameters, so it is possible that the welfare estimates may change as well. Nonetheless, overall Freeman, Henriksen, and Kydland do not find large welfare costs, and I suspect it is due to this feature of a model with multiple means of payment.

---

[1] They would just set $j^* = 1$.

18

Lucas (2000) found that a significant portion of the welfare gain from reducing inflation comes as a result of reducing inflation from a value that is slightly higher than the lower bound of the negative of the real interest rate. Freeman, Henriksen, and Kydland replicate this finding and thereby show that this result is not sensitive to the particular models Lucas had used to establish this result. This is an important issue because it seems that an objective of modern economies is to maintain inflation at low levels (with inflation, say, anywhere from 1% to 3%). If Lucas and Freeman, Henriksen, and Kydland are right, then roughly as much welfare gain can be achieved by reducing inflation from low levels to its lower bound than from high to low levels. This strikes me as an important contribution.

It is an interesting question to ask why central bankers seem to prefer low inflation rates over slightly negative inflation rates. Surely, one response is that they perceive short-term interest rates to be an important tool of monetary policy and that maintaining, on average, slightly positive nominal interest rates gives them the option to reduce them when needed. In this light, perhaps Japan during the 1990s offers an important lesson on the difficulty of pursuing an expansionary monetary policy when nominal interest rates are close to zero. Maintaining an option value of monetary policy may be an important counterbalance to the results of Lucas and Freeman, Henriksen, and Kydland—that much of the welfare gain from reducing inflation comes from reducing inflation at very low levels.

Examining the welfare cost of inflation surely extends beyond just looking at average inflation rates. Even in developed countries such as the United States, considerable resources are devoted to managing the volatility of the value of financial assets that stems from variation in, say, nominal interest rates. This cost extends to the time wasted refinancing mortgages, the time wasted by financial institutions speculating on future interest rates, or even the time wasted by so-called Fed watchers. If short-term nominal interest rates were set to 1% forever with perfect certainty, then all interest rates would have to be 1%. The resources saved by eliminating nominal interest rate uncertainty are surely substantial. It strikes me that these are interesting issues for future research on the welfare costs of inflation.

In terms of the various features of the model presented by Freeman, Henriksen, and Kydland, there seem to be many other potential uses of the model that highlight the strengths of such an approach. The model seems particularly well suited to examining the welfare consequences of paying interest on reserves, examining the implications of technological change in managing monetary assets (such as ATMs), or considering how to best accommodate shocks to things such as the currency–deposit ratio. Freeman, Henriksen, and Kydland have developed a tractable model that should be useful for studying a wide variety of issues in monetary economics.

REFERENCES

Bailey, M. 1956. The Welfare Cost of Inflationary Finance. *Journal of Political Economy* 64: 93–110.

Friedman, M. 1969. *The Optimum Quantity of Money and Other Essays.* Chicago: Aldine.

Coleman, W. J. 1996. Money and Output: A Test of Reverse Causation. *American Economic Review* 86(1): 90–111.

Cooley, T. F., and G. D. Hansen. 1989. The Inflation Tax in a Real Business Cycle Model. *American Economic Review* 79(4): 733–48.

Freeman, S., and F. E. Kydland. 2000. Monetary Aggregates and Output. *American Economic Review* 90(5): 1125–35.

King, R. G., and C. I. Plosser. 1984. Money, Credit, and Prices in a Real Business Cycle Model. *American Economic Review* 74(3): 363–80

Lucas, R. E. 2000. Inflation and Welfare. *Econometrica* 68(2): 247–74.

Lucas, R. E., and Nancy L. Stokey. 1987. Money and Interest in a Cash-in-Advance Economy. *Econometrica* 55(3): 491–513.

# Commentary

*Tony Yates*

## 1. INTRODUCTION

The story in Freeman and Kydland (2000) is this: A modern version of the Friedman and Schwartz (1963) idea is that because the business cycle component of money is positively correlated with the business cycle component of output, we have evidence that money shocks cause business cycles. But if you build a model that captures the reality that consumers can choose between two means of payment, money and deposits, you can get that output and (the sum of) money (and deposits) both rise following a positive productivity shock. When productivity rises, agents want to consume more large-ticket goods; for that reason, it becomes more economical to buy things with deposits rather than money (because larger purchases reduce the per-unit costs of using deposits), and banks respond to that demand by creating more deposits. A model with no frictions and no monetary shocks can generate the supposed evidence that money shocks cause output fluctuations.

Freeman, Henriksen, and Kydland present a paper that uses a model of this kind to study the welfare costs of inflation. In this model, as inflation rises, agents shift more of their portfolios into interest-bearing forms to avoid the inflation tax, but they have to pay the additional fixed cost of using interest-bearing deposits in transactions. The authors find that the costs of inflation are small. For example, in their baseline calibration, the gains from reducing inflation from 10% to 3% are about 0.13% (of steady-state consumption). This value is "small" in the sense that they estimate the welfare cost of 400% inflation to be about the same as Lucas's (2000) estimates for 10% inflation— a little under 0.8% of consumption. If the fixed costs of using deposits to transact are increased by a factor of five, then the welfare costs of inflation are multiplied by roughly the same factor. The authors observe that the marginal costs of inflation fall as inflation rises.

## 2. COMMENTS

### 2.1 Small Welfare Costs

One factor making the welfare costs small is that consumers can pay for all goods with either cash or deposits. Relative to a model in which there are cash-only and deposits-only goods, this reduces the welfare costs of inflation. One factor pushing the opposite way is that consumers cannot substitute between goods. If they could, then as inflation rose, they could move toward consuming larger goods and make the inflation-avoiding choice of paying for them with deposits, which would be more economical. So in a sense, within the confines of this model, whether we believe that the welfare costs of inflation are genuinely small depends on how seriously we take these particular modeling choices. We need good independent evidence to underpin the costs of inflation.

### 2.2 Isolating the Effect of the Deposit–Cash Choice

In my view, the fact that this model has no nominal or informational frictions is grounds for not taking the estimates of the costs of inflation it produces literally. More interesting is to compare the costs of inflation in this model with others without sticky prices. Flexible prices were a necessary part of Freeman, Henriksen, and Kydland's dialogue with economists who were prepared to argue that the positive correlation of money and output was sufficient evidence for sticky prices. But that debate has moved on. Economists who believed in sticky prices were forced to find microevidence that prices did not change frequently and demonstrate that models with these frictions matched the moments of the data better than those without them. I would contend that they found such microevidence and that models with these frictions do match the data better, although the task of embedding these within rigorously microfounded models is hardly finished. The case for there being something out there that causes prices to move slowly seems overwhelming. And we know that models of this type will give higher costs of inflation than other models.

The main contribution of this paper is to isolate the effect of the introduction of the deposit-cash choice on the costs of inflation relative to a flexible-price model without it. I would suggest that there is a premium on finding a way of nesting this model in a model without the choice. For example, if the fixed cost of making all transactions with deposits were set to infinity for all goods, then no one would hold deposits. If the fixed costs of using cash to pay for large goods were set to infinity and the fixed costs of paying for small goods with deposits were set to infinity, then you would have a model that is like the cash-credit goods model.

### 2.3 Are Large Ticket Items More Likely to Be Bought with Cash?

What is the best parable to tell about the constraints facing consumers? The Freeman–Henriksen–Kydland parable? A parable in which there are cash-only and credit-only (or more properly, deposit-only) goods? Or something in between (you can buy cash goods with credit, but at a premium, and you can buy credit goods with cash, but at a premium)?

**Figure 1: Cash Intensity of Retail Transactions by Type of Store, United Kingdom, 2001**

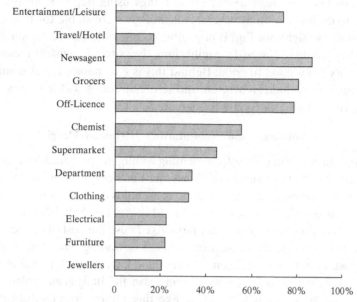

Source: APACS.

In the United Kingdom, we can get information on the cash intensity of spending on purchases of different goods and on purchases made at different categories of retail outlets. These things give some very basic support to the basic conjecture in Freeman, Henriksen, and Kydland's model and those that precede it: that large items are more likely to be paid for by deposits than small ones. So, for example, suppose that 20% of sales at furniture shops and jewelers are paid for by cash, whereas 80% of off-license (or, in American, liquor store) purchases are made with cash.

English (1999) reports evidence from the 1995 Survey of Currency and Transactions Account Usage that corroborates the U.K. evidence. The mean size of payments is $76 for household checks, $59 for credit cards, $20 for debit cards, and $11 for cash.

I conjecture that for many small or illegal transactions, even if you have a bank account, it is almost impossible to use deposits. For many large transactions, it is very costly to use cash. For all the rest, there is no difference in the cost of doing either at the point of sale. So the costs of using a particular payment technology, fixed or not, vary from good to good. They don't in Freeman, Henriksen, and Kydland's model. Whether the gap between the real world and the Freeman–Henriksen–Kydland parable is a sign of elegant abstraction—or something more worrying—is hard to say. It depends on how literally the authors want us to take their story. A defense of the parable might be this: If it were uneconomical to buy small things using deposits, no one would choose to do it if the inflation-costs technology were stable for long enough. And retailers might not find it profitable to offer the choice for small goods when they would for large. In equilibrium, the costs of payment technologies would vary from good to good: Behind this is a technology that is similar to that used by Freeman, Henriksen, and Kydland. But it is at least a possibility that there is an alternative, better parable.

### 2.4 Mulligan and Sala-i-Martin's "Extensive Margin"

Another observation comes from reading Mulligan and Sala-i-Martin (2000). According to the 1989 Survey of Consumer Finances, 59% of households had no interest-bearing assets, and 19% of households did not even have a checking account. So what? Well, the point of Mulligan and Sala-i-Martin (2000) is to argue that there is another very large fixed cost: the cost of participating in the banking system. That could be the cost of finding out about it or some other cost. Freeman, Henriksen, and Kydland have that all households make choices at the margin between deposits and cash. In Mulligan and Sala-i-Martin's world, some households will behave like this: Others won't substitute at all because they don't have enough assets to warrant paying the cost of being able to do the substitution. The effect of this is to overstate the costs of inflation at very low interest rates.

### 2.5 How Good an Approximation to Leave Out Firms' Holdings of Money?

One question is: Freeman, Henriksen, and Kydland don't model the fact that firms have to buy things with money or something else. Is this a good approximation? In the United Kingdom, we have data on the portions of different types of money held by different sectors. For example, in the United Kingdom, we think that about 90% of M0 is held by households. For M4, which includes notes and coin, interest and non-interest-bearing deposits, firms hold more: During the same period, households held only £657 billion out of £942 billion.

How important is it that Freeman, Henriksen, and Kydland—and most other papers—abstract from firms' money holdings? The veil that lies between consumers and producers in a general equilibrium model can generate some differences in the effects of inflation. When we have just households holding money, inflation reduces real incomes but increases the value of leisure. If we had firms (even firms wholly owned by those same households) using money in a production function, inflation would cause firms to substitute into other non-money factors, capital and labor, presumably raising real wages. This would have the effect of reducing the value of leisure. This extra distorting effect of inflation would presumably increase the welfare costs.

### 2.6 Falling Marginal Costs of Inflation

Freeman, Henriksen, and Kydland find that the marginal costs of inflation are falling in inflation. This is a property their results have in common with other studies of the costs of inflation. What should we make of that? Does it say something about the costs of inflation or about those models? The prejudice I start out with is that, at some point, the marginal costs of inflation start to increase again. Ferguson offers a colorful quote from the memoirs of a resident of Frankfurt who described life in 1923 in a way that suggests that the marginal costs of inflation don't flatten out:

> It was more than a disorder that smashed over people, it was something like daily explosions....The smallest, most private, the most personal events always had one and the same cause: the raging plunge of money....I [had] regarded money as something boring, monotonous...But now I suddenly saw it from a different, an eerie side—a demon with a gigantic whip, lashing at everything. (2001, 154)

English (1999) reports an anecdote in which the number of employees in the "D" banks in Germany doubled between 1920 and the end of the 1923 hyperinflation. Some of this could be due to the "benefit" of surprise inflation, but the rest could be a reflection of the rising marginal costs of inflation. He also finds that inflation is related to financial-sector size for medium- and high-inflation countries but unrelated for low-inflation countries. That could either be evidence of a rising marginal cost of inflation or the effect of other factors on financial-sector size dominating the effect of inflation in low-inflation countries.

The point is that, at some point, the marginal costs of inflation rise again. They might cause agents to coordinate on a new money or force them to barter and generate huge economic costs in the process. Something similar but less dramatic is happening in Mulligan and Sala-i-Martin (2000). At a certain point, once inflation is high enough, poor agents have to pay the fixed cost of learning about the banking system, and at that point, the marginal cost of inflation rises and then falls back again.

### 2.7 Falling Marginal Costs of Inflation Again: Inflation and the Returns to Investing in Deposit-Transactions Technology

In Freeman, Henriksen, and Kydland, the fixed costs of transactions in money and deposits are invariant to the steady-state rate of inflation. Imagine a world such as the following: The fixed costs of using deposits depend on the resources devoted to deposit-transactions technology. The resources devoted to deposit-transactions technology depend on the returns. The returns get higher as inflation gets higher. By way of an anecdote, I was once told that a disproportionate number of the patents in check-clearing technology are registered with Latin American countries. Those countries invested in making the costs of using deposits to pay for things less. If this comment has bite, then it says that perhaps we can't rely on these computations as steady-state welfare calculations, or at least we must take them as an upper bound. At some point, resources will be spent (itself obviously costly), allowing consumers to economize on the costs of holding cash.

### 2.8 Freeman, Henriksen, and Kydland and Wallace's Dictum

My next comment on Freeman, Henriksen, and Kydland is neither mine nor a comment directed at the authors in particular.

Wallace (1998) set out a dictum for monetary theory. The dictum is that "monetary theories should not contain an undefined object labeled *money*." Theories that don't satisfy the dictum include "models which assume that real balances are arguments of utility or production functions and models which assume cash-in-advance constraints." Theories that don't satisfy the dictum "cannot address questions about which objects constitute money." The reason was stated by Hahn (1965):[1]

> [A]n adequate foundation for a monetary theory...requires a precise statement of the methods of transactions open to an individual with their attendant costs...[and]...must specify rather precisely the conditions in which futures markets for various commodities would arise. For if there were futures markets in all goods and services....as in Debreu's world... there would be no problem of the non-coincidence of payments and receipts.

Models that assume that cash (or cash and deposits) are required in advance don't contain the imperfections that would lead to cash being required in advance or being useful. Hahn said, "We are told that there exist claims to debt....Why should transactions not be carried out by means of these claims to debt?" Applied to Freeman, Henriksen, and Kydland, the comment would be, why can't transactions be carried out with claims to nonintermediated capital? Neither Hahn nor Wallace are discussing this paper, but I would be interested to know how Freeman, Henriksen, and Kydland would respond to them if they were.

One defense might be this: We are not asking questions about which objects constitute money. We are asking what the welfare costs of policy are, conditional on certain objects having been chosen as money. But although

---

[1] I am grateful to Gertjan Vlieghe for pointing out that Hahn made this argument first.

Wallace himself concedes that it "it takes a model (that addresses the issue at hand) to beat a model (that addresses the issue at hand)." He also notes that "some [models] that satisfy the dictum do not imply the [Friedman] rule."[2]

The model of Lagos and Wright (2003) obeys the Friedman rule. But it shows that the conclusion that the welfare costs of deviations from the Friedman rule are small is not robust. Lagos and Wright's estimates of the cost of moving from 10% to 0% inflation are 2.3% of consumption, compared to Freeman, Henriksen, and Kydland's estimate of a 0.4% gain form reducing inflation from 50% to 0%. These models also have the property that, at some point, the marginal cost of inflation rises because money will not be chosen as a medium of exchange if inflation is high enough, and a barter equilibrium will result instead.

## ACKNOWLEDGMENTS

I benefited greatly from many conversations with Luca Benati, Matthew Hancock, Roman Sustek, and Gertjan Vlieghe.

## REFERENCES

English, W. 1999. Inflation and Financial Sector Size. *Journal of Monetary Economics* 44: 379–400.

Ferguson, N. 2001. *The Cash Nexus: Money and Power in the Modern World, 1700–2000.* New York: Basic Books.

Freeman, S., and F. Kydland. 2000. Monetary Aggregates and Output. *American Economic Review* 90(5): 1125–35.

Friedman, M., and A. Schwartz. 1963. *A Monetary History of the United States, 1867–1960.* Princeton, NJ: Princeton University Press.

Hahn, F. H. 1965. On Some Problems of Proving the Existence of an Equilibrium in a Monetary Economy. In *The Theory of Interest Rates*, ed. F. H. Hahn and F. P. R. Brechling. London: Macmillan.

Lagos, R., and R. Wright. 2003. A Unified Framework for Monetary Theory and Policy Analysis. Unpublished manuscript, Princeton University.

Lucas, R. 1984. Money in a Theory of Finance. *Carnegie–Rochester Conference Series on Public Policy* 21: 9–45.

---

[2] Sentiments such as these can be found in Plosser's (1984) comments on Lucas (1984). For example, Plosser states, "[H]ow financial and monetary institutions will change in the face of variations in the economic environment can never be done satisfactorily in models where the institutions arise from exogenously imposed constraints" (52).

Lucas, R. 2000. Inflation and Welfare. *Econometrica* 68(2): 247–74.

Mulligan, C., and X. Sala-i-Martin. 2000. Extensive Margins and the Demand for Money. *Journal of Political Economy* 108(5): 961–91.

Plosser, C. 1984. Money in a Theory of Finance: Some Observations on the Lucas Paper. *Carnegie–Rochester Conference Series on Public Policy* 21: 47–52.

Wallace, N. 1998. A Dictum for Monetary Theory. *Federal Reserve Bank of Minneapolis Quarterly Review* 22(1): 20–26.

# 2

# An Open-Economy Model of Endogenous Price Flexibility

*Michael B. Devereux*

## 1. INTRODUCTION

Theoretical studies incorporating nominal rigidities into dynamic general equilibrium models have been developed to an increasing degree of sophistication in recent years (e.g., Woodford 2003). These models have been very influential in making the case for price stability as an optimal monetary policy, both in closed-economy settings as well as in the open economy (e.g., Benigno and Benigno 2003). But in most of these models, the rules used by firms to adjust prices are assumed to be an exogenous part of the environment. Recently, some authors (e.g., Dotsey, King, and Wolman 1999) have pursued a line of research in state-dependent pricing models. In these models, a firm always has an option to adjust its price at any time period, subject to incurring a fixed cost of price change. The firm continually trades off the benefits of adjusting the price against the costs of price change.

This paper develops an intermediate framework between models of fixed prices and models of state-dependent pricing. In this model, firms can choose in advance whether to have flexible prices. By incurring a fixed cost, a firm can invest in flexibility. If the firm incurs this fixed cost, then it can adjust prices ex post in the face of shocks to its demand or marginal cost. If it chooses not to incur this cost, it must set its price in advance. By assuming that firms face differential fixed costs of price flexibility, we can integrate this framework into a general equilibrium model of a small open economy and investigate the determinants of equilibrium price flexibility. In particular, we focus on the relationship between price flexibility and exchange rate policy.

A classic argument for flexible exchange rates is that they enhance the ability of the economy to respond to shocks in the presence of nominal rigidities (Friedman 1953). By allowing the exchange rate to do the adjusting, a flexible exchange rate policy reduces the need for adjustment in the real economy. But the standard argument takes the degree of nominal price stickiness as given. In our framework of endogenous price flexibility, we show that the exchange rate regime choice may be a critical determinant of price flexibility, so much so that the standard trade-off between exchange rate stability and output volatility may be reversed.

In the model, the incentive for ex post price flexibility for any firm is higher as the variance of nominal demand that it faces for its good becomes greater. A fixed exchange rate may increase or reduce the variance of nominal aggregate demand depending on the source of shocks. If shocks come from the domestic economy in the form of movements in the velocity of money, then a fixed exchange rate reduces the variance of nominal demand (offsetting velocity shocks) and reduces price flexibility. But if exchange rate volatility is mostly determined by world demand shocks, then a fixed exchange rate will increase the variance of nominal demand and increase price flexibility. The variance of nominal demand facing any one firm will also depend on the degree of price flexibility itself. This introduces a strategic interaction between the pricing decisions of firms. If most firms adjust prices, then the variability in demand for any one firm is very high, and it has a greater incentive to adjust prices itself. Therefore, there is a key strategic complementarity in the choice of flexibility. This may give rise to multiple equilibria in the degree of price flexibility.

How does the presence of endogenous price flexibility affect optimal monetary policy rules? I show that the optimal exchange rate policy in the model acts to minimize the degree of price flexibility. Hence, as in the conventional sticky price models of Woodford (2003) and others, price stability remains an objective of monetary policy. In this framework, because firms incur fixed costs of flexibility, it is optimal for monetary policy to minimize these costs. Simultaneously, an optimal monetary policy rule minimizes the variance of gross domestic product (GDP).

As discussed previously, the paper is related to the literature on state-dependent pricing and menu costs of price change (Ball and Romer 1991; Dotsey, King, and Wolman 1999). The model is most closely related to Ball and Romer (1991). They show the possibility of multiple equilibria in an environment in which price setters can choose ex post whether to adjust prices, given a common menu cost of price change, within a one-country environment. The present analysis differs because it allows a distribution of firm-specific menu costs and assumes that price setters choose in advance whether to have the ex post flexibility to adjust prices. This is more in line with the view that a large change in monetary policy regime (e.g., fixing the exchange rate) may lead to structural changes in the flexibility of contracts within a monetary economy. Finally of course, I use an open-economy model.

The next section sets out the basic technology of endogenous price flexibility for a given firm. Section 3 incorporates this into an open-economy model. Section 4 examines the link between price flexibility and the exchange rate regime. Section 5 investigates the predictions of the model for optimal exchange rate policy under endogenous price flexibility. Some conclusions follow.

## 2. THE FIRM AND THE CHOICE OF PRICE FLEXIBILITY

In models of state-dependent pricing, the firm chooses whether to adjust its price ex post, given realizations of demand and costs. The firm's choice is based on trading off the benefits of price adjustment relative to the direct (e.g., menu) costs of price change. By contrast, in our model, a firm invests ex ante in flexibility. That is, a firm must choose ex ante whether to have the flexibility to adjust its price ex post after observing the realized state of the world. It incurs a fixed cost in order to have this flexibility. We might think of this as describing the way changes in monetary policy or other structural features of the economy would affect the institutional characteristics of nominal price or wage setting. In this section, we focus on the decision made by a single firm.

Firm $i$ has the production function

(2.1) $\quad Y_i = (H_i - D_i \, \Phi_i)^\alpha$,

where $Y_i$ is the firm's output, $H_i$ is total employment, and $\Phi_i$ is a firm-specific fixed cost of flexibility. The firm knows $\Phi_i$. Let $D_i$ be an indicator variable. $D_i = 1$ ($D_i = 0$) if the firm chooses to (not to) incur the cost of ex post price flexibility. Assuming that $0 < \alpha < 1$, (2.1) indicates the presence of a firm-specific factor of production, which is combined with labor to produce output for sale.

The firm faces market demand

(2.2) $\quad X_i = (\dfrac{P_i}{P})^{-\lambda} X$,

where $P_i$ is the firm's price, $P$ is the (possibly stochastic) industry price, $\lambda > 1$ is the elasticity of demand, and $X$ is a demand shock. Assume the firm faces a stochastic wage $W$. From the production technology (2.1), the firm's total operating cost is

(2.3) $\quad W(Y_i)^{\frac{1}{\alpha}} + W D_i \, \Phi_i$.

The firm evaluates expected profits using a stochastic discount factor $\Gamma$![1] Then discounted expected profits may be written as

(2.4) $\quad E\Gamma \left\{ P_i \left(\dfrac{P_i}{P}\right)^{-\lambda} X - W \left[ \dfrac{P_i^{-\lambda}}{P} X \right]^{\frac{1}{\alpha}} - W D_i \, \Phi_i \right\}$.

---

[1] In the next section, we determine from the preferences of the firm's household shareholders.

The firm chooses $P_i$ to maximize (2.4). If $D_i = 1$, then the firm can choose its price after observing $P$, $X$, and $W$, and it sets the following price:

$$(2.5) \quad \tilde{P}_i = \delta[W^\alpha (\hat{X})^{1-\alpha}]^\omega$$

where

$$\delta = \left(\frac{\lambda}{\alpha(\lambda-1)}\right)^{\alpha\omega}, \quad \omega = \frac{1}{\alpha + \lambda(1-\alpha)}$$

and $\hat{X} = P^\lambda X$. When $\alpha = 1$, the firm's price is a constant markup over the wage. But when $\alpha < 1$, the optimal price will depend on a geometric average of the wage and market demand.

When $D_i = 0$, the firm must set its price in advance. The optimal preset price is given by

$$(2.6) \quad \bar{P}_i = \delta \frac{E[\Gamma W (\hat{X})^{\frac{1}{\alpha}}]^{\alpha\omega}}{E(\Gamma\hat{X})^{\alpha\omega}}.$$

When the wage and market demand are known ex ante, (2.5) and (2.6) give the same answer. But in general, the two prices will differ.

Now, substituting (2.5) and (2.6), respectively, into the expected profit function (2.4), we can evaluate the firm's expected profits (excluding fixed costs) under $D_i = 1$ and $D_i = 0$. Let $\Theta = \{\Gamma, W, \hat{X}\}$, then

$$(2.7) \quad \tilde{V}(\Theta) = \Psi E\Gamma (W^{\alpha(1-\lambda)}\hat{X})^\omega$$

$$(2.8) \quad \bar{V}(\Theta) = \Psi(E\Gamma W\hat{X}^{\frac{1}{\alpha}})^{(1-\lambda)\alpha\omega} (E\Gamma\hat{X})^{\lambda\omega},$$

where $\Psi = \delta^{1-\lambda} - \delta^{-\frac{\lambda}{\alpha}}$. The firm will choose $D_i = 1$ whenever the gain in discounted expected profits exceeds the discounted expected fixed costs. That is, $D_i = 1$ whenever

$$\tilde{V}(\Theta) - \bar{V}(\Theta) \geq E\Gamma W \, \Phi_i.$$

Because $\Phi_i$ is known to the firm ex ante, $E\Gamma W \, \Phi_i = \Phi_i E\Gamma W$. We can therefore rewrite this condition as

$$(2.9) \quad \Delta(\Theta) \equiv \frac{[\tilde{V}(\Theta) - \bar{V}(\Theta)]}{E\Gamma W} \geq \Phi_i,$$

where $\Delta(\Theta)$ represents the gain to price flexibility.

## 2.1 Approximation of Equation (2.9)

We evaluate the gains to price flexibility by taking a second-order logarithmic approximation to $\Delta(\Theta)$ around the mean value $E \ln (\Theta)$. In the appendix, it is shown that

$$(2.10) \quad \Delta(\Theta) \approx \frac{\Omega \alpha}{2} \left\{ \sigma_w^2 + \left[ \frac{(1-\alpha)}{\alpha} \right]^2 \sigma_x^2 + 2 \frac{(1-\alpha)}{\alpha} \sigma_{wx} \right\} > 0$$

where

$$\Omega = \frac{V[\exp (E \ln \Theta)]}{\exp [E(1\mathrm{n}\, \Gamma + \ln W)]} \; \lambda(\lambda-1)\omega^2 > 0, \; V[\exp(E \ln \Theta)]$$

represent profits evaluated at the mean $E \ln(\Theta)$ and $\sigma_w^2$, $\sigma_x^2$, $\sigma_{wx}$ represent the variance of the wage, market demand, and their covariance.

Up to a second order, the incentive for a firm to incur the costs of price flexibility depends on the variance of the wage, the variance of market demand, and their covariance. If $\alpha = 1$ and marginal cost is independent of output, then uncertainty in market demand has no impact on the incentive to change prices. Then the gains from flexibility depend only on uncertainty in wages. Intuitively, if $\alpha = 1$, then optimal expected profits are linear in market demand. Furthermore, if the wage is known, then the firm's price is the same whether it is set before or after $\Theta$ is observed. In this case, there is no gain to price flexibility. More generally, however, optimal profits are convex in $W$ when prices are flexible but linear in $W$ under a fixed price. Hence, wage volatility raises expected profits when prices are flexible relative to expected profits with preset prices. When $\alpha < 1$, optimal profits are concave in market demand $\hat{X}$, either when prices are flexible or fixed. But intuitively, the optimized profit function is more concave in demand when prices are fixed than when they are flexible. Hence, uncertainty in market demand increases the benefits to price flexibility because $\alpha < 1$.

Finally, (2.10) does not depend on the properties of the stochastic discount factor. Up to a second-order approximation, the discount factor affects profits under fixed and flexible prices in the same way.

## 2.2 Determination of Price Flexibility in the Aggregate

The left-hand side of (2.9) is common to all firms. Hence, firms will differ in their choice of price flexibility only because of differences in their specific fixed costs of flexibility. Without loss of generality, we let each firm $i$ draw from a distribution of fixed costs, $\Phi(i)$, described by $\Phi(0) = 0$, $\Phi'(i) > 0$. That is, firms are ranked according their fixed cost of flexibility. Then, we may describe the determination of price flexibility in the aggregate as the measure

$z$ of firms, $0 \le z \le 1$, who choose to incur the fixed cost of price flexibility. The following condition determines $z$:

(2.11) $\quad \Delta(\Theta) = \Phi(z), \quad 0 \le z \le 1$

(2.12) $\quad \Delta(\Theta) > \Phi(1) \quad z = 1.$

This condition gives a link between the underlying uncertainty facing firms and the aggregate degree of flexibility in the economy.

## 3. A MODEL OF A SMALL OPEN ECONOMY

We now take a model of a small open economy in which the aggregate variables impinging on the firm's choice of price flexibility are determined endogenously. In the economy, there is a continuum of households along the unit interval, consuming goods produced at home and goods imported from the rest of the world, and obtaining income from wages and the ownership of firms. The firms produce and choose their degree of price flexibility as described in the previous section.

### 3.1 Households

Household $i, i \in 2 (0,1)$, has preferences given by

(3.1) $\quad \ln C(i) + \chi \ln \dfrac{M(i)}{P} - \eta H(i),$

where $C(i)$ is a composite of the consumption of home and foreign goods, given by

(3.2) $\quad C(i) = \left( \dfrac{C_h(i)}{\gamma} \right)^{\gamma} \left( \dfrac{C_f(i)}{1-\gamma} \right)^{1-\gamma}.$

Here, $P$ is a price index given by $P = (P_h)^{\gamma} (SP_f^*)^{1-\gamma}$ where $P_f^*$ is the exogenous foreign currency price of foreign goods, $S$ is the exchange rate, $\gamma$ represents the relative preference for home goods, and $M(i)$ is the quantity of domestic money held. We assume $\chi$ is a random variable that will capture shocks to the consumption velocity of money.

Consumption of home goods are differentiated, so that for household $i$, the home good consumption and price indices are

(3.3) $\quad C_h(i) = \left[ \displaystyle\int_0^1 C_h(i,j)^{1-\frac{1}{\lambda}} dj \right]^{\frac{1}{1-\frac{1}{\lambda}}}, \quad P_h = \left[ \displaystyle\int_0^1 P_h(j)^{1-\lambda} dj \right]^{\frac{1}{1-\lambda}}$

where $\lambda > 1$.

The home household $i$ faces the budget constraint

$$(3.4) \quad PC(i) + M(i) = W(i)H(i) + M_0(i) + T(i) + \Pi,$$

where $M_0(i)$ represents initial money holdings, $T(i)$ is a transfer from the monetary authority, and $\Pi$ is total profits of home firms.

Households choose money balances, labor supply, and consumption of each good to maximize utility, subject to their budget constraint. We get the demand for each good, $C_h(i)$, demand for the foreign good, demand for money balances, and implicit labor supply as

$$(3.5) \quad C_h(i,j) = \left[\frac{P_h(j)}{P_h}\right]^{-\lambda} C_h(i), \quad C_h(i) = \frac{\gamma PC(i)}{P_h}, \quad C_f(i) = \frac{(1-\gamma)\, PC(i)}{P_f}$$

$$(3.6) \quad M(i) = \chi PC(i), \quad W = \eta H^{\Psi} PC(i).$$

### 3.2 The Foreign Sector

We assume that foreign demand for the home good $i$ may be described as

$$(3.7) \quad D_h^*(i) = \left[\frac{P_h(i)}{P_h}\right]^{-\lambda} \frac{S}{P_h} D^*,$$

where $D^*$ is a stochastic foreign demand disturbance term. Thus, in the aggregate, foreign demand for the composite home good has a relative price elasticity of unity. Here, we have normalized so that the foreign price index is 1.

### 3.3 Firms

Firms set prices based on the technologies described in the previous section, given demand coming from the home and foreign sectors. For instance, a measure $z$ of firms sets prices $\tilde{P}_h(j)$ after the state of the world is realized, and $(1 - z)$ sets prices $\bar{P}_h(j)$ in advance. The condition given by (2.11) (or 2.12) determines the size of the flexible price sector. Total profits of all firms are written as

$$(3.8) \quad \int_0^z \tilde{P}_h(j)\tilde{Y}(j)\,dj + \int_z^1 \bar{P}_h(j)\bar{Y}(j)\,dj - \int_0^1 WH(i)\,di.$$

### 3.4 Equilibrium

We focus on symmetric equilibria where all households are alike. Equilibrium is defined in the usual way. Given money market clearing, $M = M_0 + T$, households' ex post budget constraints are given by

$$(3.9) \quad PC = z\tilde{P}_h\tilde{Y}_h + (1-z)\bar{P}_h\bar{Y}_h.$$

The goods market for each category of firm implies that

$$(3.10) \quad \tilde{Y}_h = \left(\frac{\tilde{P}_h}{P_h}\right)^{-\lambda} \gamma\left[\frac{PC}{P_h} + \frac{SD^*}{P_h}\right]$$

$$(3.11) \quad \bar{Y}_h = \left(\frac{\bar{P}_h}{P_h}\right)^{-\lambda} \gamma\left[\frac{PC}{P_h} + \frac{SD^*}{P_h}\right].$$

Analogous conditions hold for the foreign economy.

We may define aggregate real GDP by aggregating over fixed and flexible price firms. Thus,

$$Y = \frac{z\tilde{P}_h\tilde{Y} + (1-z)\bar{P}_h\bar{Y}}{P_h}.$$

In what follows, we will assume that the two shocks $\chi$ and $D^*$ are log-normally distributed, so that $\ln \chi \ N(0, \sigma_\chi^2)$, $\ln D^* \ N(0, \sigma_{d^*}^2)$.

### 3.5 Solving the Model for Given Price Flexibility

Given $z$ and $z^*$, the equilibrium can be easily characterized. From the definition of aggregate GDP and the household budget constraint, we have $PC = P_h Y$. Hence, we may write the money market equilibrium condition as

$$(3.12) \quad M = \chi P_h Y.$$

Using this in combination with the goods market equilibrium, (3.10) and (3.11), and aggregating, we get solutions for both the exchange rate and GDP:

$$S = \frac{1-\gamma}{\gamma}\frac{M}{D^*\chi}, \qquad Y = \frac{M}{P_h\chi}.$$

A monetary expansion causes an exchange rate depreciation, whereas a velocity shock causes an appreciation. An increase in world demand $D^*$ toward home goods also causes an appreciation. Real GDP is determined by the value of real money balances, in terms of home goods, relative to the velocity shock.

Demand for the individual firm may be defined from (3.10) and (3.11). The nominal wage is given from (3.6). Then we may use (2.5) and (3.12) to define the flexible-price firm's price as

$$(3.14) \quad \tilde{P}_h = \delta \left[ \eta P_h^{(\lambda-1)} (1-\alpha) \frac{M}{\chi} \right]^\omega.$$

The discount factor for firms is given by the household's marginal utility of a dollar of home currency, which is $\Gamma = (PC)^{-1}$. Then we can write the fixed-price firm's price as

$$(3.15) \quad \bar{P}_h = \delta \frac{E[\eta (P_h^{\lambda-1} \frac{M}{\chi})^{\frac{1}{\alpha}}]^{\alpha\omega}}{E[P_h^{\lambda-1}]^{\alpha\omega}}.$$

The domestic good price index is then defined as

$$(3.16) \quad P_h = \left[ z \tilde{P}_h^{1-\lambda} + (1-z) \bar{P}_h^{1-\lambda} \right]^{\frac{1}{1-\lambda}}$$

### 3.6 The Determination of Optimal Price Flexibility

To determine equilibrium price flexibility, we use condition (2.11) (or 2.12) from the previous section in combination with the values of $\Gamma$, $W$, and $\hat{X}$ implied by the general equilibrium model. From the model equilibrium, market demand and wages are written as

$$(3.17) \quad \hat{X} = P_h^{\lambda-1} \frac{M}{\chi}, \quad W = \eta \frac{M}{\chi}.$$

This, in combination with equations (3.14)–(3.16) and (2.11), determines the equilibrium values of $W$, $\hat{X}$, $\tilde{P}_h$, $\bar{P}_h$, $P_h$, and $z$ for the home economy.

For $z = 0$, the model has a simple analytical solution given by (3.13) and (3.15). But there is no analytical solution when $0 < z < 1$. However, we may describe an approximate solution using the second-order approximation used in (2.10). In order to determine the gains to price flexibility using (2.10), we must obtain the variance of $\ln(W)$ and $\ln(\hat{X})$. We can write

$$(3.18) \quad \ln(W) = \ln(M) - \ln(\chi)$$

$$(3.19) \quad \ln(\hat{X}) = (\lambda-1) \ln(P_h) + \ln(M) - \ln(\chi).$$

For given $z$, the model is log linear, except for the price index equation (3.16). In the appendix, it is shown that $P_h$ may be approximated around the mean value $E \ln P_h$ (we use lowercase letters to denote deviations from means, i.e., $p_h = \ln(P_h) - E \ln(P_h)$) as

$$(3.20) \quad p_h = \frac{\varphi(z)\omega(m-\hat{\chi})}{1-(1-\alpha)\omega(\lambda-1)\varphi(z)}$$

Here, $\hat{\chi}$ represents the log deviation of the velocity shock from its mean value, and $\varphi(z)$ is an increasing function of $z$, which satisfies $\varphi(0) = 0$, $\varphi'(z) > 0$, $\varphi''(z) > 0$, and $\varphi(1) = 1$. Note that, by the definition of $\omega$, we have $(1-\alpha)\omega(\lambda-1) < 1$.

Substituting (3.20) into (3.19) and (3.18) and then substituting into (2.10), we obtain the conditions

$$(3.21) \quad \frac{\Omega}{2\alpha}\left[\frac{1}{1-(1-\alpha)(\lambda-1)\,\omega\varphi(z)}\right]^2 (\sigma_m^2 + \sigma_{\hat{\chi}}^2 + 2\sigma_{m\hat{\chi}}) = \Phi(z), \quad 0 \leq z \leq 1$$

$$(3.22) \quad \frac{\Omega}{2\alpha}\left[\frac{1}{1-(1-\alpha)(\lambda-1)\,\omega}\right]^2 (\sigma_m^2 + \sigma_{\hat{\chi}}^2 + 2\sigma_{m\hat{\chi}}) = \Phi(1), \quad z=1.$$

Figure 1a illustrates the determination of $z$. The VV locus illustrates the left-hand side of condition (3.21). This represents the benefit of price flexibility to the marginal price setter, as measured along the horizontal axis. This is higher as the variance of nominal aggregate demand $m - \hat{\chi}$ becomes higher. The CC locus represents the fixed flexibility cost facing the marginal price setter. The CC locus is upward sloping because marginal firms (by assumption) have higher costs of price flexibility. The VV locus is also upward sloping (and convex). This is explained by the link between the decisions made by all other firms and the incentive of any one firm to have flexible prices. When more firms choose to have flexible prices because $\lambda > 1$, this makes any one firm's *desired* ex post price $\tilde{P}_h$ more volatile. But the benefit to the firm of having flexible prices is greater as there is more volatility in its desired ex post price.

This introduces a strategic complementarity into the pricing decisions of firms: The greater the measure of other firms adjusting to shock, the greater the incentive of any one firm to adjust its own price.

Although figure 1A describes the case of a unique equilibrium, figure 1B characterizes a situation in which the VV curve intersects twice with the CC curve. Hence, there may be multiple equilibria in price-flexibility decisions. In the figure, there are three equilibria corresponding to low $z$, $z = 1$, and an intermediate value of $z$ (unstable based on the usual reasoning). In the low $z$ equilibrium, a small fraction of firms choose price flexibility, weakening the incentives of other firms to have flexible prices. But when $z = 1$, the volatility of demand is so great that all firms willingly pay the costs for flexibility because all others do. Therefore, multiple equilibria are generated by strategic complementarity in price setting. This strategic complementarity, as well as the possibility of multiple equilibrium, is greater as $\alpha$ becomes lower and $\lambda$ becomes higher.

**Figure 1A**

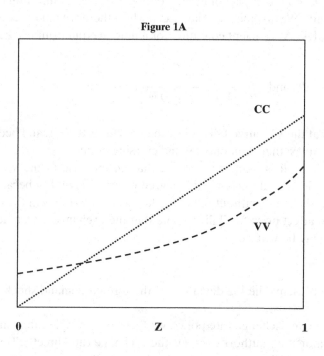

**Figure 1B**

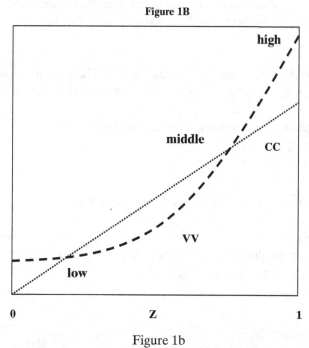

Figure 1b

## 4. PRICE FLEXIBILITY AND THE EXCHANGE RATE REGIME

We now focus on the impact of monetary policy on the equilibrium degree of price flexibility. We first focus on the case in which there is a unique equilibrium, as in figure 1A. A sufficient condition for a unique equilibrium is that $\Phi(i)$ is uniform;

$$\Phi(i) = \overline{\Phi}_i, \text{ and } \frac{\Omega}{2\alpha} \left[ \frac{1}{1-(1-\alpha)(\lambda-1)\,\omega} \right]^2 (\sigma_m^2 + \sigma_\chi^2 + 2\sigma_{m\hat{\chi}}) < \overline{\Phi}.$$

This says that the VV curve falls below the CC curve at $z = 1$, and because VV is strictly convex, there can only be one crossing point.

From (3.21), it is immediate to see that an increase in the volatility of money or velocity will increase the degree of price flexibility because it will shift up the VV curve without affecting the CC curve. How will the exchange rate regime affect price flexibility? Note that the exchange rate, in log deviation form, may be written as

(4.1)   $s = m - \hat{\chi} - d^*$,

where $d^*$ represents the log deviation of the foreign demand shock, $D^*$, from its mean.

To define an exchange rate policy, we focus on a simple monetary rule in which the monetary authority targets the exchange rate directly. This has the advantage that it allows us to vary the importance that exchange rate stability plays in policy. The monetary authority, therefore, follows the rule

(4.2)   $m = -\mu s$,

where $\mu$ is the degree of exchange rate intervention. The value $\mu = 0$ corresponds to a freely floating exchange rate, and $\mu \to \infty$ corresponds to a fixed (or pegged) exchange rate.

Under this rule, the exchange rate can be described as

$$s = \frac{-(\hat{\chi} + d^*)}{1 + \mu},$$

Using this and (3.21), we may establish proposition 1.

### PROPOSITION 1

The degree of price flexibility, $z$, is higher under a fixed exchange rate (flexible exchange rate) when $\sigma_{d*}^2 > \sigma_\chi^2 \,(\sigma_{d*}^2 < \sigma_\chi^2)$.

**Proof:** Under the assumptions made, $z$ is determined by

$$(4.3) \quad \frac{\Omega}{2\alpha}\left(\frac{1}{(1+\mu)^2}\sigma_\chi^2 + \frac{\mu^2}{(1+\mu)^2}\sigma_{d*}^2\right) = \Psi(z)$$

where $\Psi(z) = \bar{\Phi}z(1-(\lambda-1)(1-\alpha)\varphi(z)\omega)^2$.

The left-hand side is higher when $\mu \to \infty$ (fixed exchange rate) than under $\mu = 0$ (floating exchange rate) if and only if $\sigma_{d*}^2 > \sigma^2$. Then, as long as the equilibrium is unique, the right-hand side must be increasing in $z$. If $\sigma_{d*}^2 < \sigma^2\chi$, the logic holds in reverse.

Thus, the proposition says that a pegged exchange rate will increase equilibrium price flexibility whenever the volatility of the world demand shock exceeds that of the domestic velocity shock.

To see the result more intuitively, note that equilibrium price flexibility will be higher whenever the variance of $m - \hat{\chi}$ is higher. In order to keep the exchange rate from changing in the face of world demand shocks, the variance of $m$ must rise. Thus, in the face of $d^*$ shocks, an exchange rate peg tends to increase $z$. On the other hand, in the absence of world demand shocks, a pegged exchange rate stabilizes the variance of $m - \hat{\chi}$ and tends to reduce $z$.

How are these results related to the discussion of the introduction? Is there a trade-off between exchange rate flexibility and output volatility in this model? In the model, output is given by

$$Y = \frac{M}{P_h\chi}.$$

Taking a linear approximation, using the approximation for the home price index given by (3.20), we can write

$$(4.4) \quad y = \frac{(m-\hat{\chi})[1-\varphi(z)]}{1-(1-\alpha)\omega(\lambda-1)\varphi(z)}.$$

From this expression, we may establish proposition 2.

## PROPOSITION 2

If an exchange rate rule increases the volatility of output, holding the degree of price flexibility constant, then it will also increase the degree of price flexibility.

**Proof:** Expression (4.4) makes clear that output volatility will rise for a given $z$ whenever the volatility of $m - \hat{\chi}$ rises. But this is exactly the same condition for an increase in price flexibility under proposition 1.

Proposition 2 makes clear the impact that endogenous price flexibility will have on the trade-off between exchange rate volatility and output volatility.

Output volatility, for a given $z$, is determined by the volatility of nominal aggregate demand $m - \hat{\chi}$. But from proposition 1, this is exactly the same factor that governs the degree of price flexibility. If an exchange rate policy reduces exchange rate volatility at the expense of a higher volatility of output, for a given degree of price flexibility, then it will also increase the incentive for firms to invest in greater price flexibility. But from (4.4), output volatility is declining in $z$. Hence, allowing for endogenous price flexibility acts as an indirect compensating force, which reduces the direct effect of exchange rate policy on the volatility of output.

Figure 2 provides a quantitative illustration of this result. We focus on a case in which the only shocks faced by the economy are to world demand.[2] We set the elasticity of substitution between categories of goods at 6, corresponding to a 20% monopolistic markup. We assume that the distribution $\Phi(i)$ is uniform. In the calibration, we choose the cost function so that if all firms were choosing ex post price flexibility, the total cost of this would be only 3% of GDP. This corresponds to the quantification of the costs of price change measured by Zbaracki et al. (2000) and the calibration used in Dotsey, King, and Wolman (1999). Finally, we set $\alpha = 0.75$.

**Figure 2**

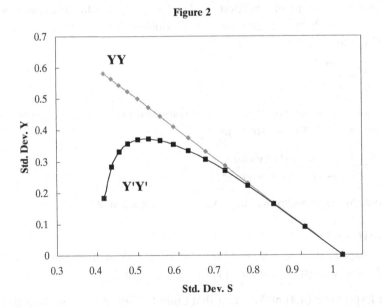

---

[2] Alternatively, we can think of this as a case in which the monetary rule offsets velocity shocks directly rather than indirectly through exchange rate intervention.

Figure 2 illustrates the relationship between the standard deviation of the exchange rate and the standard deviation of output for different values of the exchange rate intervention coefficient $\mu$. First, take the case in which price flexibility is exogenous and $z = 0$, so that all firms set prices in advance.[3] Then $\mu = 0$ (a pure floating exchange rate) ensures that output volatility is zero. But in this case, the volatility of the exchange rate is $\sigma_s = \sigma_{d*}$ (see 4.1). Increasing the degree of exchange rate intervention will reduce $\sigma_s$ but will also increase output volatility, $\sigma_y$. This is illustrated by the locus YY in figure 2. Clearly, in this case, there is a negatively sloped relationship between $\sigma_s$ and $\sigma_y$. A policy of stabilizing the nominal exchange rate must simultaneously destabilize GDP.

Now, focus on the case of endogenous price flexibility, in which $z$ is determined by the condition (3.21). This is illustrated by the locus Y'Y'. Beginning at $\mu = 0$, an increase in the degree of exchange rate intervention will reduce $\sigma_s$ and increase $\sigma_y$. Thus, at low levels of exchange rate intervention, there is a still a negative relationship between exchange rate volatility and output volatility. But as $\mu$ rises, increasing the variance of nominal aggregate demand, $\sigma_{m-\hat{x}}$, more and more firms choose to invest in ex post price flexibility, so that in the aggregate, $z$ increases. Thus, the trade-off between exchange rate volatility and output volatility becomes less negative as the direct effect of higher aggregate demand volatility on output is offset by the greater degree of aggregate price flexibility. Moreover, as $\mu$ continues to increase, the trade-off *changes sign*; the increase in price flexibility is so great that overall output volatility falls, even though the volatility of nominal aggregate demand is increasing. Thus, the trade-off between output volatility and exchange rate volatility may be reversed in the presence of endogenous price flexibility.

## 5. OPTIMAL EXCHANGE RATE RULES

In this section, we investigate the optimal exchange rate rule. Assume the monetary authority chooses a value of $\mu$ to maximize expected utility, taking into account the way prices are set. This represents the optimal monetary rule under policy commitment. We proceed in two steps: We first describe the optimal rule when all prices are sticky, or equivalently, when the cost of ex post flexibility is prohibitive for any one firm. We show that the optimal rule for the small economy is one that minimizes the variance of output. We then extend the environment to one in which firms can choose ex post price flexibility in the manner described in section 2. Moreover, we assume that the monetary authority, in choosing an optimal exchange rate rule, takes into account the

---

[3] This is achieved by setting $\Phi$ at a very high value in (3.21).

way prices are set. Our results indicate that endogenous price flexibility has no affect on the optimal monetary rule.

Following most of the literature (e.g., Obstfeld and Rogoff 2002), assume that the optimal monetary rules maximize expected utility net of the utility of real balances. Thus, optimal policy focuses only on the distortion generated by sticky prices, ignoring the implicit distortion associated with deviations from the Friedman rule.

If all prices are sticky, then the home country price may be written as

$$(5.1) \quad P_h = \eta^\alpha \delta_{\bar{\omega}}^{\frac{1}{\omega}} \left[ E\left(\frac{M}{\chi}\right)^{\frac{1}{\alpha}} \right]^\alpha.$$

It is straightforward to show that equilibrium consumption and employment in the home country are given by

$$(5.2) \quad C = \frac{M}{\chi P_h^\gamma (S)^{1-\gamma}} = \gamma \left[\frac{M}{\chi P_h \gamma}\right]^\gamma \left[\frac{D^*}{(1-\gamma)}\right]^{1-\gamma}$$

$$(5.3) \quad H = \left[\frac{M}{\chi P_h}\right]^{\frac{1}{\alpha}}.$$

From (5.3) and (5.1), we can show that

$$\eta E H = \eta \frac{E\left(\frac{M}{\chi}\right)^{\frac{1}{\alpha}}}{P_h^{\frac{1}{\alpha}}} = \Omega_1 \frac{E\left(\frac{M}{\chi}\right)^{\frac{1}{\alpha}}}{E\left(\frac{M}{\chi}\right)^{\frac{1}{\alpha}}},$$

which is a constant ($\Omega_1$ is a constant function of parameters). Hence, for monetary policy evaluation, the expected utility depends only on the expected value of log composite consumption.

We may then write out the expected utility objective function for the home country's monetary authority (ignoring constants):

$$(5.4) \quad E \ln C = E\gamma \left(\ln \frac{M}{\chi} - \ln P_h\right) + E(1-\gamma)\ln D^*.$$

Using (5.4), we may establish proposition 3.

## PROPOSITION 3

When all prices are preset, the optimal degree of exchange rate intervention is (a)

$$(5.5) \quad \mu = \frac{\sigma_\chi^2}{\sigma_{d*}^2}$$

and (b) the optimal intervention rule minimizes the variance of GDP.

**Proof:** From (5.4), because $E \ln (M)$ is independent of $\mu$, the optimal intervention rule is derived by minimizing the expression

$$E \ln (E (\exp (\ln(M) - \ln (\chi))))$$

$$(5.6) \quad = E \ln \left[ \exp \left( \Omega_2 + \frac{\mu}{1+\mu} Ed^* - \frac{1}{1+\mu} E\hat{\chi} + \frac{1}{2} \left( \frac{\mu^2}{(1+\mu)^2} \sigma_{d*}^2 + \frac{1}{(1+\mu)^2} \sigma_{\hat{\chi}}^2 \right) \right) \right]$$

where $\Omega_2$ is a constant.

The equality follows because the shocks $D^*$ and $\chi$ are log-normal, with $Ed^* = E\hat{\chi} = 0$. Hence, the optimal intervention rule is obtained by minimizing

$$\frac{\mu^2}{(1+\mu)^2} \sigma_{d*}^2 + \frac{1}{(1+\mu)^2} \sigma_{\hat{\chi}}^2$$

The solution to this problem is

$$\frac{\sigma_{\hat{\chi}}^2}{\sigma_{d*}^2}.$$

Part (b) of the proposition holds because it may be readily seen that minimizing the foregoing expression, given the assumed monetary rule, is equivalent to minimizing the variance of output from (4.4).

Proposition 3 establishes that when all prices are preset, if there are only external demand shocks, then the optimal exchange rate policy is to completely stabilize output and allow the exchange rate to adjust to the shocks, with an intervention coefficient of zero. Thus, in terms of figure 1, we should be at point 1 on the locus YY. On the other hand, if shocks are solely the result of domestic velocity disturbances, then the optimal policy is a fixed exchange rate where $\mu \to \infty$.

Optimal exchange rate policy under preset prices is based on precisely the same factors that determine whether an exchange rate peg stimulates price flexibility. If real external shocks tend to dominate, then the optimal policy leans toward greater exchange rate flexibility. But in this case, an exchange rate peg would stimulate greater flexibility in prices when $z$ is endogenous. On the other hand, if shocks to the velocity of money dominate, then the exchange rate should be stabilized. But in this case, a flexible exchange rate would tend to generate more price flexibility under endogenous $z$.

How do these results change when we allow for endogenous price flexibility? In this case, there is no closed-form analytical solution for the model. But the model may be solved numerically for a given assumption on the distribution of shocks processes. Using this procedure, we find that the optimal exchange rate intervention rule is unchanged from proposition 3. That is, the optimal rule in the numerical solution accords exactly with (5.5). Intuitively, this is easy to understand given the structure of the model. As the appendix shows, the distribution of consumption and employment, through the solution for prices and $z$, depend only on the nominal aggregate demand term $\frac{M}{\chi}$. Thus, the rule (5.5), which minimizes the variance of nominal aggregate demand, conditional on the assumed form of the exchange rate intervention rule, continues to be an optimal policy in the environment with endogenous price flexibility.

Hence, we conclude that the presence of endogenous price flexibility does not alter the standard prescriptions for optimal monetary policy in a small open economy. More generally, this implies that an optimal exchange rate rule in an environment of endogenous price flexibility acts to minimize the degree of price flexibility. Because price flexibility is costly, the monetary authority designs an intervention rule to minimize the resources that firms invest in flexibility. From another perspective, the results imply that the basic prescription toward price stability that arises in models of sticky prices extends to models with endogenous price flexibility.

## 6. CONCLUSIONS

Theoretical studies of the benefits of exchange rate flexibility almost always take the structure of price determination to be independent of the exchange rate regime choice. But in policy circles, it is often emphasized that exchange rate commitments may help to affect private-sector expectations and alter the institutional structure of wage contracting and price setting. Many Latin American countries pursued exchange-rate-based stabilizations in the 1990s on the hope that the fixed exchange rate would feed directly into private-sector actions. Countries that adopt a currency board or fully dollarize emphasize that a prerequisite for success is the flexibility of internal prices (e.g., Latter 2002).

This paper has developed a theoretical model of the link between exchange rate regime choice and nominal price flexibility. We built up from the basic microeconomics of a firm's decision to invest in price flexibility and then integrated this into a small open-economy model in which there are monetary and real shocks.

The paper is illustrative rather than realistic. But in principle, there is no difficulty in extending the basic choice of flexibility outlined in section 2 into more realistic dynamic general equilibrium environments. It may be that this type of extension could alter many of the predictions of the impact of monetary policy in sticky price environments.

APPENDIX

### A.1 Obtaining the Approximation (2.10)

We first describe how the approximation given in (2.10) is obtained. Note that

$$(A.1) \quad \Delta(\Theta) = \frac{\Psi}{E\Gamma W} [E\Gamma (W^{\alpha(1-\lambda)}\hat{X})^\omega - (E\Gamma W\hat{X}^{\frac{1}{\alpha}})^{(1-\lambda)\alpha\omega} (E\Gamma\hat{X})^{\lambda\omega}]$$

This may be written in the form

$$(A.2) \quad \Delta(\Theta) = \frac{\Psi}{E\exp(\ln\Gamma + \ln W)} [E\exp(\ln\Gamma + \omega(\alpha(1-\lambda)\ln(W) + \ln X))$$
$$- (E\exp(\ln\Gamma + \ln W + \frac{1}{\alpha}\ln\hat{X}))^{(1-\lambda)\alpha\omega} (E\exp(\ln\Gamma + \ln\hat{X}))^{\lambda\omega}]$$

Now, take a second-order logarithmic approximation of $\Delta(\Theta)$ around the mean $E\ln\Theta$. This gives

$$(A.3) \quad \Delta(\Theta) \approx \Delta(\exp(E\ln\Theta))$$

$$+ \Xi E(g + \omega(\alpha(1-\lambda)w + x)$$

$$- \Xi E(((1-\lambda)\alpha + \lambda)\omega g + (1-\lambda)\alpha\omega w + ((1-\lambda)\omega + \lambda\omega)x)$$

$$+ \Delta(\exp(E\ln\Theta))E(g + w)$$

$$+ \frac{1}{2}\Xi E(g^2 + (\omega(\alpha(1-\lambda)))^2 w^2 + \omega^2 x^2 + 2\omega\alpha(1-\lambda)gw + 2\omega gx + 2\omega^2\alpha\ (1-\lambda)wx)$$

$$- \frac{1}{2}\Xi[(1-\lambda)\alpha\omega E\ (g^2 + w^2 + \alpha^{-2}x^2 + 2gw + 2\alpha^{-1}gx + 2\alpha^{-1}wx) +$$
$$\lambda\omega E\ (g^2 + x^2 + 2gx)]$$

$$- \frac{1}{2}\Xi(1 - ((1-\lambda)\alpha + \lambda)\omega)Eg(g + w)$$

$$- \frac{1}{2}\Xi(\omega\alpha\ (1-\lambda) - (1-\lambda)\alpha\omega)Ew(g + w)$$

$$- \frac{1}{2}\Xi(1 - ((1-\lambda)\alpha + \lambda)\omega)Ex(g + w)$$

where small-case letters denote logarithmic deviations from their mean levels: $g = \ln\Gamma - E\ln\Gamma, w = \ln W - E\ln W, x = \ln\hat{X} - E\ln\hat{X}$, and

$$\Xi \equiv \frac{V(\exp(E\ln\Theta))}{\exp(E\ln\Gamma + E\ln W)}.$$

Using the definition of $\Delta(\Theta)$ in (2.9), it must be that $\Delta(\exp E\ln\Theta) = 0$ because profits for fixed or flexible price firms are equal, evaluated at the constant value of $E\ln\Theta$. Hence, the first term on the right-hand side of (A.3) must be zero.

The second, third, and fourth terms represent first order effects, evaluated around $E\ln\Theta$. The second and third terms are also zero by definition because

$Eg = Ew = Ex = 0$. The fourth term, capturing the first-order effects of the terms in the denominator of (A.2), is zero for the same reason. The fifth and sixth terms capture the second-order effects coming from the numerator of (7.2), and the seventh, eighth, and ninth terms capture the second-order effects coming from the denominator of (A.2). These last three terms are zero, given the defi nition $\omega = \dfrac{1}{\alpha + \lambda(1-\alpha)}$ . Intuitively, the second-order effects coming from the denominator of (A.2) are zero because they interact with expected profits in the flexible and fixed price case in ways that exactly cancel out.

Then, defining $Ew^2$ as $\sigma_w^2$, etc, the fourth and fifth terms in expression (7.3) may be rearranged after canceling out terms in $\sigma_g^2$, $\sigma_{gx}$, and $\sigma_{gw}$ as

$$(A.4) \quad \frac{\Omega\alpha}{2} \left[ \sigma_w^2 + \frac{(1-\alpha)^2}{\alpha^2} \sigma_x^2 + 2\frac{(1-\alpha)}{\alpha} \sigma_{wx} \right],$$

which is just expression (2.10) in section 2 of the text.

### A.2 Approximating $P_h$

We first approximate $P_h$ around the mean $E \ln P_h$. Because $\bar{P}_h$ is predetermined, we have

$$(A.5) \quad p_h = \varphi(z) \, \tilde{p}_h$$

where

$$\varphi(z) \equiv \frac{z \exp\left[E \ln \tilde{P}_h (1-\lambda)\right]}{z \exp\left[E \ln \tilde{P}_h (1-\lambda)\right] + (1-z) \exp\left[E \ln \bar{P}_h (1-\lambda)\right]}$$

is an increasing function of $z$ and satisfies the properties $\varphi(0) = 0$, $\varphi(1) = 1$, as well as $\varphi''(z) > 0$[4]. This approximation allows for the fact that the mean values $E \ln \tilde{P}_h$ and $E \ln \bar{P}_h$ will not, in general, be the same.

From (3.14) in the paper, we may write

$$(A.6) \quad \tilde{p}_h = \omega\alpha\psi h + \omega(\lambda-1)(1-\alpha)p_h + \omega(m-\hat{\chi}).$$

### A.3 Optimal Policy with Endogenous Price Flexibility

With endogenous price flexibility, the property that the expected utility of employment is independent of the distribution of money no longer holds. But

---

[4] This latter property holds because the preset prices are higher in the mean than the mean of the flexible prices.

the expected utility of log consumption (5.4) is written in the same way. Thus, the objective function for the monetary authority may be described as

(A.7)   $E\gamma(\ln \dfrac{M}{\chi} - \ln P_h) + E(1-\gamma)\,(\ln D^*\chi^* - \eta EH.$

The monetary authorities choose an intervention rule $\mu$ to maximize (A.7) subject to the conditions on prices, employment, and the determination of $z$ from the text. These are:

(A.8)   $\tilde{P}_h = \delta\left[\eta P_h^{(\lambda-1)(1-\alpha)}\,\dfrac{M}{\chi}\right]^{\omega}$

(A.9)   $\bar{P}_h = \delta\,\dfrac{E[\eta(P_h^{\lambda-1}\frac{M}{\chi})^{\frac{1}{\alpha}}]^{\alpha\omega}}{E[P_h^{\lambda-1}]^{\alpha\omega}}$

(A.10)   $P_h = \left[z\tilde{P}_h^{1-\lambda} + (1-z)\bar{P}_h^{1-\lambda}\right]^{\frac{1}{1-\lambda}}$

(A.11)   $H = \left[z\left(\dfrac{\tilde{P}_h}{P_h}\right)^{-\frac{\lambda}{\alpha}} + (1-z)\left(\dfrac{\bar{P}_h}{P_h}\right)^{-\frac{\lambda}{\alpha}}\right]\left(\dfrac{M}{\chi P_h}\right)^{\frac{1}{\alpha}} + \displaystyle\int_0^z \Phi(z)\,dz$

(A.12)   $\Delta(\Theta(z)) = \Phi(z)$

From an inspection of these equations, we see that the only stochastic elements enter in the form $\dfrac{M(\epsilon)}{\chi}$, which, given the intervention rule, is equal to (in logs, ignoring constants) $\dfrac{mu}{1+\mu}\,d^* + \dfrac{1}{1+\mu}\,\hat{\chi}$. Thus, the optimal monetary rule remains the same as that with all prices preset.

### ACKNOWLEDGMENTS

I thank the participants of the 2003 Federal Reserve Bank of Cleveland Central Banking Conference, especially Michael Dotsey, for very helpful comments on this paper. I thank the Social Sciences and Humanities Research Council, the Royal Bank of Canada, and the Bank of Canada for financial assistance.

## References

Ball, L., and D. Romer. 1991. Sticky Prices as Coordination Failure. *American Economic Review* 81: 539–52.

Basu, S., and J. Fernald. 1997. Returns to Scale in U.S. Production: Estimates and Implications. *Journal of Political Economy* 105: 249–83.

Baxter, M., and A. Stockman. 1989. Business Cycles and the Exchange Rate Regime: Some International Evidence. *Journal of Monetary Economics* 23: 377–400.

Benigno, G., and P. Benigno. 2003. Price Stability in Open Economies. *Review of Economic Studies* 70: 743–64.

Chari, V. V., P. J. Kehoe, and E. McGrattan. 2002. Can Sticky-Price Models Generate Volatile and Persistent Real Exchange Rates? *Review of Economic Studies* 69: 533–63.

Cooper, R., and A. John. 1988. Coordinating Coordination Failures in Keynesian Models. *Quarterly Journal of Economics* 103: 441–63.

Corsetti, G., and P. Pesenti. 2001. Welfare and Macroeconomic Interdependence. *Quarterly Journal of Economics* 116: 421–45.

Dotsey, M., R. G. King, and A. Wolman. 1999. State-Dependent Pricing and the Equilibrium Dynamics of Money and Output. *Quarterly Journal of Economics* 114: 656–89.

Frankel, J., and A. Rose. 1998. The Endogeneity of the Optimal Currency Area Criteria. *Economic Journal* 108: 1009–45.

Friedman, M. 1953. The Case for Flexible Exchange Rates. In *Essays in Positive Economics*, by M. Friedman, 157–203. Chicago: University of Chicago Press.

Helpman, E. 1981. An Exploration in the Theory of Exchange Rate Regimes. *Journal of Political Economy* 89: 865–90.

King, R., and A. Wolman. 1999. What Should the Monetary Authority Do When Prices Are Sticky? In *Monetary Policy Rules*, ed. J. Taylor, 349–98. Chicago: Chicago University Press.

Kollmann, R. 2000. The Exchange Rate in a Dynamic Optimizing Business Cycle Model: A Quantitative Investigation. *Journal of International Economics* 55: 243–62.

Latter, T. 2002. Hong Kong's Currency Board Today: The Unexpected Challenge of Deflation. *Hong Kong Monetary Authority Quarterly Bulletin*, August, 48–53.

Mussa, M. 1986. Nominal Exchange Rate Regimes and the Behavior of Real Exchange Rates: Evidence and Implications. *Carnegie–Rochester Conference Series on Public Policy* 25: 117–213.

Obstfeld, M., and K. Rogoff. 1995. Exchange Rate Dynamics Redux. *Journal of Political Economy* 103: 624–60.

Obstfeld, M., and K. Rogoff. 2002. Global Implications of Self-Oriented National Monetary Rules. *Quarterly Journal of Economics* 117: 503–35.

Woodford, M. 2003. *Interest and Prices: Foundations of a Theory of Monetary Policy*. Princeton, NJ: Princeton University Press.

Zbaracki, M., M. Ritson, D. Levy, S. Dutta, and M. Bergen. 2000. The Managerial and Customer Dimensions of the Cost of Price Adjustment: Direct Evidence from Industrial Markets. Unpublished manuscript.

# Commentary

*David K. Backus*

I'm delighted to be here, but I have both good news and bad news to report. The good news is that I have the opportunity to comment on a terrific paper. Michael Devereux has done his usual superb job of characterizing an important issue in a transparent and elegant way. The bad news is that his paper involves monetary economics and exchange rates, two topics I've successfully avoided for most of my life. The papers at this conference remind us that monetary economics involves not only practical questions of policy but also deep philosophical questions about the value of colored pieces of paper and why anyone would exchange something of value for paper, or even the promise of future paper or a bank liability exchangeable for paper. Devereux's model has two kinds of paper and revolves around the price at which one is exchanged for the other. I'm lost already, and maybe you are, too.

The question that Devereux addresses is how the exchange rate (the relative price of two kinds paper) affects the allocation of resources. Is the allocation better if the exchange rate is fixed or if we allow it to vary in response to various shocks that hit the economy? It's a classic question, but we are a long way from a definitive answer. It's relatively easy to write down models in which the exchange rate is irrelevant. If we layer the quantity theory on top of a frictionless real model—which is more or less what the early cash-in-advance models did—then the equilibrium of the real model is generally efficient on its own, and the addition of money and exchange rates doesn't change that. That's my starting point, but there's a sense in which it is unfair to the question. If there were no frictions, there would be little reason to have money—or exchange rates—in the first place. But what frictions? The most common one in this line of work is rigid or sticky nominal prices. Devereux cites Friedman as arguing that a flexible exchange rate can be superior if it moderates the adverse impact of such nominal rigidities. Another friction is incomplete financial markets. The modern study of exchange rate regimes begins, in my view, with Helpman and Razin (1982), with a nod to Helpman's earlier work. Those authors, as well as Neumeyer (1998), suggest that flexible exchange rates might again moderate the impact of a friction—in this case, by expanding the set of assets available to manage risk. In both cases, exchange rate flexibility can be useful in overcoming a friction or rigidity elsewhere in the economy.

These examples illustrate the potential benefits of exchange rate flexibility in economies with frictions, but Devereux's paper does something more difficult: He develops a model in which, despite frictions, a fixed exchange rate is superior to a flexible exchange rate. This counterintuitive result apparently depends on a number of features of his model. As I understand it, there are two major frictions:

- Nominal rigidity: Firms (producers of differentiated products) can either set prices one period in advance or pay a fixed cost for the option of changing prices after markets have opened. This is a little different from most models of menu costs because firms must pay the cost prior to knowing the value of changing prices.

- Incomplete financial markets: Devereux studies a small open economy, so there are effectively incomplete markets in the sense that agents absorb all the risk of shocks to their economy rather than share some of it with the rest of the world.

The former gets most of the attention. Because price flexibility is endogenous, it depends on the exchange rate regime, among other things. In this model, a flexible exchange rate tends to make price flexibility valuable to firms, and because price flexibility is costly, optimal policy calls for less exchange rate flexibility.

The bottom line is that a fixed exchange rate system can lead to a superior allocation of resources. It is a neat result, not only for its exchange rate implications. It makes the general point that frictions may interact in complex ways with policy choices.

Where do we go from here? I continue to be reasonably happy ignoring money most of the time, but I suppose I should stay quiet about that with this audience. To me, one of the insights gained from this line of work is the value of fixed costs as a device for modeling frictions. They have the great virtue of allowing flexibility when it is most needed, allowing some adaptation of behavior to changes in the environment. Alvarez, Atkeson, and Kehoe (2002) provide another good example of how this device can be used to account for the behavior of prices and exchange rates, and I'm sure we can look forward to more in the future.

### REFERENCES

Alvarez, F., A. Atkeson, and P. J. Kehoe. 2002. Money, Interest Rates, and Exchange Rates with Endogenously Segmented Markets. *Journal of Political Economy* 110: 73–112.

Helpman, E., and A. Razin. 1982. A Comparison of Exchange Rate Regimes in the Presence of Imperfect Capital Markets. *International Economic Review* 23: 365–88.

Neumeyer, P. A. 1998. Currencies and the Allocation of Risk: The Welfare Effects of a Monetary Union. *American Economic Review* 88: 246–59.

# Commentary

*Michael Dotsey*

In "An Open-Economy Model of Endogenous Price Flexibility," Michael Devereux has developed an interesting idea, namely, that when firms have the ability to choose when to set prices, that choice is generally influenced by the form of the monetary policy rule. In particular, he analyzes how varying degrees of exchange rate flexibility interact with firms' decisions to adjust prices. In turn, the fraction of firms that adjust prices affects the relative variability of output and the exchange rate. Thus, the trade-off between exchange rate volatility and output volatility is influenced by the degree of endogenous price flexibility. Furthermore, endogenous price flexibility implies that the trade-off between output and exchange rate volatility can vary in surprising ways when firms are able to choose their price-setting behavior. This result is very interesting in and of itself. It also opens up the possibility that endogenous price flexibility would have serious implications for optimal exchange rate stabilization. Unfortunately, for the simple open-economy model employed in the paper, that is not the case. The optimal policy is independent of the degree of endogenous price flexibility, and it is the same as the case in which all firms have preset prices. However, in terms of optimal policies, this may not be a general result, and the framework developed in the paper can serve as a springboard for analyzing richer sets of policies and models. My comments will focus on one such example.

Before investigating some simple alternatives to the model, I will briefly restate the features of the model that are important for the welfare results. The analysis of the economic effects of state-dependent price setting is a central contribution of the paper. The model is essentially static, and firms must make a decision before the state of nature is realized. They draw a fixed cost indicating how costly it will be to adjust their price upon seeing the state, but they must decide whether to pay the cost prior to learning the state. If they don't invest in the price-setting technology, they must set their price in advance.

Firms that pay the fixed cost of buying a price-adjusting technology can reset their price after observing current disturbances. Those firms set a price, $\tilde{p}_h$, according to

(1) $\quad \tilde{p}_h = \delta^{1/\omega}\, \eta^\alpha [M/(\chi a)],$

where $M$ represents nominal money balances; $\delta$ is an expression involving both the price elasticity of demand, $\lambda$, and the production elasticity, $\alpha$; $\eta$ governs the disutility of work effort; and $\chi$ and $a$ are stochastic disturbances to money demand and technology, respectively. I have added a technology disturbance to the production structure of the model because it highlights some of the features of optimal policy that I wish to address. Both shocks are log-normally distributed. According to equation (1), the realization of the shocks to money demand and technology directly influences the prices that are set by flexible price setters, as will any disturbance that affects the level of the money stock.

A firm that chooses to operate with a preset price sets that price, denoted $\bar{p}_h$, as follows,

$$(2) \quad \bar{p}_h = \delta \left[ \frac{E(\eta p_h^{((\lambda-1)/\alpha)} (M/(\chi\alpha))^{1/\alpha}}{E p_h^{\lambda-1}} \right]^{\alpha\omega}$$

where $p_h$ is the aggregate price index of home-produced goods given by

$$(3) \quad p_h = [z\tilde{p}_h^{1-\lambda} + (1-z)\bar{p}_h^{1-\lambda}]^{1/(1-\lambda)}.$$

In equation (3), $z$ is the fraction of firms that endogenously choose to have flexible prices. The log-normality of the shocks implies that their volatility will influence the preset price. Furthermore, the more volatile the shocks, the greater the chance that the preset and flexible prices will differ substantially and that the profits of the price setters will be significantly greater than those of firms with preset prices. Thus, volatility will influence the fraction of firms that decide to change their prices, and, in turn, that fraction will influence the behavior of the economy. Devereux shows that the interaction of a policy that tries to stabilize the exchange rate to varying degrees both influences the fraction of firms that choose price flexibility and, in turn, influences output–exchange rate volatility in a very nonlinear way. Given the interesting and complex interaction between price setting and monetary policy, it is somewhat surprising that the optimal degree of exchange rate stabilization is not influenced by the fraction of firms that choose to adjust prices.

To understand this result, consider a case in which all firms set their prices in advance. In this environment, equation (3) collapses to

$$(4) \quad \bar{p}_h = \delta^{1/\omega} \eta^\alpha \{ E[M/(\chi\alpha)]^{1/\alpha} \}^\alpha.$$

Next, there are some features of the specification on the household side of the model that contribute importantly to the welfare results. Because the model is static, there is no borrowing and lending between countries. Given the utility function

$$U(C, M/P, H) = \ln(C) + \chi \ln(M/P) - \eta H,$$

where $C$ is a Cobb-Douglas aggregate of the consumption of home- and foreign-produced goods, $M$ represents nominal money balances, $P$ is the aggregate price level, and $H$ is hours worked, the Cobb-Douglas consumption aggregate implies that the aggregate price-level index is given by $P=(p_h)^\gamma(Sp_f^*)^{1-\gamma}$, where $S$ is the nominal exchange rate and $p_f^*$ is the exogenous price of the foreign good, which is normalized to 1. The condition that the value of imports equals the value of exports, along with the structure of the demand aggregators, implies that $(1-\gamma)PC = \gamma SD^*$, where $D^*$ represents a stochastic foreign demand shock, which is also log-normally distributed. Because the demand for money in the model is $M = PC$, the exchange rate is determined by the following equation:

$$(5) \quad S = \frac{1-\gamma}{\gamma} \frac{M}{\chi D^*}.$$

Importantly, the exchange rate is influenced only by demand-side disturbances, irrespective of the pricing decisions of firms. Thus, as we will see, exchange rate stabilization cannot offset the effects of technology shocks in this model.[1] In an intertemporal model with incomplete markets, that would not be the case, and technology shocks would influence the nominal exchange rate.

Taking the log of equation (5.2) in Devereux's paper, the log of aggregate consumption is shown to behave according to

$$\ln(C) = \gamma \ln(M) - \gamma \ln(\chi) - \gamma \ln(p_h) + (1-\gamma)\ln D^* - (1-\gamma)\ln\frac{1-\gamma}{\gamma}.$$

The important observation from this equation is that the only avenue through which the variability of shocks can influence the expected value of log consumption—and hence expected utility—is through $p_h$, which involves expectations of log-normally distributed disturbances. It is through this term that the variability of technology and money demand shocks enter.

We now have reproduced the essential features of the model that allow us to investigate the welfare implications of exchange rate stabilization. Let the money supply be governed by $(M/\bar{M}) = (S/\bar{S})^{-\mu}$, so that the money supply is contracted when the exchange rate depreciates. With this policy,

---

[1] This is also a feature of a model with complete asset markets. In this case, optimal ex ante risk sharing implies that the exchange rate is given by $S = [P(s)/P^*(s)]\,[C(s)/D^*(s)]$, where $s$ indexes the state of the economy and the foreign price level is normalized to 1. Thus, the exchange rate is proportional to nominal money balances in the complete market setting.

$$S_t = \frac{1-\gamma}{\gamma}\left(\frac{1}{\chi D^*}\right)^{1/(1+\mu)}$$

and the money stock behaves as $M = (\chi D^*)^{\mu/(1+\mu)}$.

Rearranging, one observes that

(6)     $M/\chi = \chi^{-1/(1+\mu)} D^{*\mu/(1+\mu)}$

Looking at the case in which all prices are preset, $EH$ is a constant, and ignoring constants,

(7)     $E \ln C = -\gamma E \ln \bar{p}_h = -\gamma E \ln\{E[M/(\chi\alpha)]^{1/\alpha}\}^\alpha$
          $= -\alpha\gamma[(1/(1+\mu))^2 (\sigma_x^2/2) + (\mu/(1+\mu))^2 (\sigma_{D*}^2/2) + (\sigma_\alpha^2/2)].$

The parameter $\mu$, which governs the degree of exchange rate stabilization, does not interact with the technology shock. Thus, under a policy of exchange rate stabilization, the more volatile the productivity shock, the worse off the representative agent will be. Under exchange rate stabilization, the best the monetary authority can do is set $\mu = \sigma_x^2/\sigma_{D*}^2$, which is the optimal policy derived in the paper. Furthermore, the shocks to money demand and goods demand enter the endogenous pricing decision in exactly the same way they enter the welfare criterion. Thus, endogenous pricing scales welfare, but it does not influence the trade-off between money demand volatility and the volatility of foreign demand.

Working out the optimal policy with the addition of a technology shock would require solving the model computationally, which goes beyond the scope of my comments. But intuitively, it appears that with the inclusion of technology shocks, there is additional scope for a trade-off. Increased flexibility should serve to ameliorate the effects of technology volatility on consumption and labor effort because more flexibility means that a greater proportion of the shock falls on prices and less on real activity. As prices become more flexible, the economy comes closer to achieving an optimal response to the technology shocks. The monetary authority may, therefore, find it optimal to set $\mu$ in such a way that price flexibility is enhanced more than if it set $\mu$ as a ratio of the two demand shock variances. In this situation, it appears that endogenous price flexibility would influence the optimal policy problem.

In the presence of technology shocks, employing a monetary policy of stabilizing the exchange rate does not seem like the optimal policy because the exchange rate is unaffected by technology shocks, and it is not a good instrument for countering the effects of their volatility. Suppose instead that the monetary authority sought to stabilize the price of the home-produced good. Can that policy do better? The answer is yes. Replace the money supply rule with $(M/\bar{M}) = (p_h/\hat{p}_h)^{-\mu}$, where $\hat{p}_h$ is the nonstochastic price level of the economy and equal to $\delta^{1/\omega}\eta^{\alpha}$. To see how this rule operates to achieve a better welfare result, first consider a case in which all prices are preset. Substituting this alternative money supply rule into equation (4) implies that

$$\bar{p}_h = \delta^{1/\omega}\eta^{\alpha}\{E[1/(\chi\alpha)]^{1/\alpha}\}^{\alpha/(1+\mu)},$$

and that

$$E\bar{p}_h = \frac{1}{2\alpha(1+\mu)}(\sigma_x^2 + \sigma_a^2),$$

where constants have again been omitted. To maximize the utility from consumption, one minimizes the preceding expression, which requires setting $\mu = \infty$, or pegging the price of home-produced goods. In the case in which some firms choose to preset their prices, stabilizing the price of home-produced goods is still optimal because the flexible prices set by firms is $\tilde{p}_h = \delta^{1/\omega}\eta^{\alpha}\{1/(\chi\alpha)]^{1/(1+\mu)}$, which under a price-level peg implies that $\tilde{p}_h = \delta^{1/\omega}\eta^{\alpha} = \hat{p}_h$. Under this rule, price adjusters and firms that preset their prices choose the same price, implying that no firm will optimally choose to pay the adjustment cost. Furthermore, expected labor effort is a constant in this setting, just as it was under exchange rate stabilization. By pegging the price that home firms charge, the monetary authority gets rid of the relative price distortions that occur when some firms adjust and some do not. Because $p_h$ is a constant, there is no avenue for the volatility of the various shocks to affect welfare. Thus, in this simple setting, stabilization of prices dominates exchange rate stabilization. The resulting optimal volatility of the exchange rate is derived from equation (5) and depends directly on the volatility of both demand disturbances.

There are, of course, many other ways to enrich the model and many other economic questions that can be addressed using the model. My comments here are mainly intended to explore one such modification and to examine alternative monetary policies. There are certainly a number of other interesting extensions. For example, putting the framework in a dynamic context would allow for borrowing and lending across countries. Doing so would make the exchange rate a more interesting object because it would be influenced by shocks other than those to demand, which, in turn, would make it an instrument that could be used to deal with the welfare effects of these shocks. One could also investigate how various asset market structures affect pricing behavior and how endogenous price flexibility influences economic behavior in these richer settings.

Because his paper introduces a methodology that can be widely applied in richer environments—and shows that pricing behavior substantially influences the way an economy behaves—Devereux has made a valuable contribution. I hope that my discussion in some way adds to researchers' desire to more fully explore the implications of endogenous price flexibility in new open-economy macro models.

### ACKNOWLEDGMENTS

The views expressed herein are the author's and do not represent the views of the Federal Reserve Bank of Philadelphia or the Federal Reserve System.

# 3

# Efficient Inflation Targets
# for Distorted Dynamic Economies

*Costas Azariadis and Raphael W. K. Lam*

## 1. THE TASKS OF MONETARY POLICY

Most central banks in OECD countries intervene in credit markets to achieve a target level of the short-term nominal interest rate and the long-term inflation rate (Bernanke and Mishkin 1992). The influential paper by Taylor (1993) suggests that Federal Reserve policy is well characterized by a simple rule in which the central bank sets the short-term nominal interest rate as a linear function of the lagged inflation rate and of lagged output deviations from their target values. Taylor argues that an active policy rule, with the coefficient on inflation greater than one, ensures macroeconomic stability. If the nominal interest rate has a more than one-for-one response to any change in inflation, then the central bank is able to influence the real interest rate and deter inflationary pressures.[1]

Benhabib, Schmitt-Grohe, and Uribe (2001a), on the other hand, observe that active policy rules may have unintended consequences if one considers the zero bound on the nominal interest rate. The steady-state equilibrium for an active policy rule may be locally unique, but at the same time, multiple trajectories may exist around the steady state that eventually converge to a deflationary liquidity trap with a zero nominal interest rate. This *global* indeterminacy is robust to wide variations of parametric values (e.g., slope of Taylor rule, the long-run inflation target, consumption velocity of money, etc.) and holds for a fairly general class of monetary models with both flexible and sticky prices.

The possibility of indeterminacy under an active policy rule is followed up in a number of studies (Benhabib, Schmitt-Grohe, and Uribe 2001b; Bernanke and Woodford 1997; Carlstrom and Fuerst 2000, 2001) that cast doubt on the stability of active policy rules. These studies generally stress the drawbacks of active policy rules when the interest rate responds to forecasts of future inflation.

---

[1] Active policy rules were shown to be stabilizing in a number of earlier papers in the context of nonoptimizing models (Levin, Wieland, and William 1999), in optimizing models with flexible prices (Leeper 1991), or with nominal rigidities (Rotemberg and Woodford 1997, 1999).

When the inflation trigger for the interest rate instrument consists of an inflation forecast, the Taylor rule may lead to equilibria that respond to arbitrary
changes in agent expectations. To solve this problem, the central bank needs
to focus on lagged interest rates rather than lagged inflation rates.[2]

Selecting instruments and targets has become the key challenge for monetary
authorities operating in distorted real-world economies. In these economies,
simple laissez-faire rules of zero nominal interest rates or zero inflation,
suggested respectively by Friedman (1969) for representative household
environments and Freeman (1993) for lifecycle ones, are not sufficient to deliver
macroeconomic stability.[3] This paper studies efficient monetary policy
responses to three types of distortions that afflict simple dynamic economies.

Paralleling the literature on Taylor rules, we first examine indeterminacy
in economies with lifecycle consumers in which monetary policy is nonneutral
because it redistributes resources between generations.[4] A Laffer curve
describes seigniorage from inflation in these economies: Any small, fixed
government deficit may be financed at either a relatively high or a relatively
low inflation rate. In fact, we know from Sargent and Wallace (1981) that certain
types of passive monetary and fiscal policies (constant nominal yield, constant
fiscal deficits) generate a continuum of Pareto-ranked perfect foresight
equilibria bounded by the two steady states. One steady state is stable, dynamically inefficient with high inflation; a permanent increase in the nominal interest
rate has the "unpleasant monetarist arithmetic" property of raising the
steady-state inflation rate by more than the interest rate hike. The other steady
state has exactly the reverse properties. Between those states lies a continuum
of dynamic equilibria that converge monotonically to the inefficient state. We
show that both indeterminacy and the "unpleasant monetarist arithmetic"
property are cured by a backward-looking Taylor rule that sets a low inflation

---

[2] Benhabib, Schmitt-Grohe, and Uribe (2003) propose an inflation trigger that looks backward
and consists of lagged terms as smoothing factors. In this case, an instrument rule with
sufficiently backward-looking elements can help central banks neutralize self-fulfilling
fluctuations. This is easier to achieve when the nominal interest rate depends not only on
measures of inflation and the output gap, but also on lagged nominal interest rates that do
not appear in the original Taylor rule but are included here as smoothing variables.
Theoretical work by Giannoni and Woodford (2002a, 2002b) and Rotemberg and Woodford
(1999) justifies the inclusion of lagged nominal interest rates in policy rules. This body of
work shows that, if the sum of coefficients on smoothing variables exceeds one, a locally
unique equilibrium emerges; otherwise indeterminacy and equilibrium cycles remain.

[3] Bewley (1983) examines the optimality of the Friedman rule in an economy with uninsurable
income risks and infinitely lived agents; Paal and Smith (2001) and Edmond (2002) redo that
exercise in lifecycle economies.

[4] Azariadis and Kaas (2002) study an endowment economy in which the planning horizon of
infinitely lived households is finite due to recurring and endogenous debt constraints.

target, a relatively high nominal interest target, and pursues those targets by aggressively boosting nominal yields when inflation heats up.

Uninsurable idiosyncratic income risks are the second distortion we examine, and one that compels any benevolent central bank to aid in the provision of social insurance when private insurance is unavailable. Social insurance in our context means exactly the same thing as in Edmond's (2002): lump-sum payments to older individuals, financed by printing currency (or monetizing fiscal deficits), and imposing an inflation tax on the young generation. The monetary authority is called upon to balance the distortion from missing markets against the distortion from inflation. It does so by selecting a higher inflation target than it would in an economy with complete markets for contingent claims.

A similar inflationary bias shows up when the independent monetary authority interacts strategically with an equally independent, and less patient, fiscal authority. The noncooperative nature of this interaction distorts policy choice for reasons similar to those discovered by Dixit and Lambertini (2003) in a static Keynesian framework: The fiscal authority and the monetary authority want different things. The two authorities have different inflation and output targets in Dixit and Lambertini (2003). In this paper, the authorities trade off consumption in youth and old age differently: Being less patient, the fiscal authority places a lower weight on old-age consumption, and by extension on robust asset returns, than the average household or the benevolent central bank. Conflicts about lifecycle consumption profiles and real rates of interest lend to a *strategic complementarity* under which the best response of each authority depends positively on the play of the other.

For example, the response of the monetary authority to higher fiscal spending is to raise the nominal interest rate in order to protect old-age consumption. Higher fiscal spending is also the best fiscal response to higher nominal interest rates. The outcome is higher inflation and higher nominal rates than either authority desires. Long-run inflation is then the likely result of noncooperative policymaking by government agencies with different objectives, just as it is in the static Keynesian world of Dixit and Lambertini.

The rest of this paper is organized as follows: Section 2 lays out the economic environment. Section 3 describes equilibria for exogenous policies and calculates the payoffs from these policies for a benevolent central bank and a slightly less benevolent Treasury. Section 4 designs targets and instruments to defeat indeterminacy and "unpleasant monetarist arithmetic." Section 5 analyzes the inflationary bias from the provision of social insurance in incomplete markets. Section 6 examines noncooperative games with commitment between monetary and fiscal authorities, and section 7 summarizes conclusions and discusses extensions.

## 2. THE ENVIRONMENT

We study an exchange economy that consists of an infinitely lived monetary authority (MA), an infinitely lived fiscal authority (FA), and a countable infinity of two-period-lived overlapping cohorts, indexed by $v = 0,1,\ldots$ . Time extends from one to infinity. The monetary authority is benevolent; it seeks to maximize the expected lifecycle utility of the average household in the steady state by manipulating the sequence of $\{R_t^N\}_{t=0}^{\infty}$ of nominal yields on public and private debt. The fiscal authority is slightly less benevolent; it has the same objective as the FA but discounts old-age consumption more than the MA. The fiscal authority issues public debt to pay for a sequence of transfers $\{\tau_t\}_{t=1}^{\infty}$ to old-age households or for a sequence of $\{z_t\}_{t=1}^{\infty}$ of public goods purchases. For reasons we discuss below, no taxes are levied on households.

### 2.1 The Public Sector

Value is stored in the form of two assets: safe debt and currency. Debt is issued at each period $t$ by the fiscal authority and purchased by the households and the monetary authority. It pays a real yield $R_t = R_t^N/i_t$, where the inflation factor $i_t = P_{t+1}/P_t$ measures the change in the price level $P_t$. Currency is issued by the central bank and purchased by young households for "transaction services."

We denote $B_t$ as the real stock of public debt issued at $t$ with maturity at $t + 1$, by $D_t$ the monetary authority demand for real debt, and by $g_t$ the real fiscal deficit. The budget constraint for the fiscal authority is

(1)  $g_t + R_{t-1} B_{t-1} = B_t.$

A similar constraint for the monetary authority reads,

(2)  $D_t - R_{t-1} D_{t-1} = m_t - m_{t-1}/ i_t,$

where $m_t = M_t /P_t$ describes the real value of currency. Both of these budget constraints equate the flow of expenditure to the flow of revenue at each period $t$.

### 2.2 The Private Sector

Cohorts are made up of a unit mass of households, indexed by their youthful endowment $\theta \in [\underline{\theta},\overline{\theta}]$. Youthful endowment describes the birth state of each household that is a random draw from a fixed distribution $G$ on $[\underline{\theta},\overline{\theta}]$ such that $G(\underline{\theta}) = 0, G(\overline{\theta}) = 1$, and $\int \theta \, dG = 1$. The endowment vector of household $\theta$ in cohort is

(3a)  $\omega_t(\theta) = (\theta, \tau_{t+1})$ if $t \geq 1$

   $\quad\quad\quad = \tau_o \quad\quad\quad t = 0.$

This endowment contains an idiosyncratic uninsurable risk $\theta$, and a deterministic lump-sum transfer from the fiscal authority. We assume that the fiscal authority *does not have the power to levy income taxes.* If it did, income risks would be perfectly shared by taxing away all youthful income and distributing the proceeds as lump-sum transfers without harm to private incentives.

Households with any birth state $\theta$ share a common lifecycle utility function of the form

$$(3b) \quad u_t(\theta,\beta) = \log\left\{\min[c_t\,(\theta), m_t^d\,(\theta)/v]\right\} + \beta \log x_{t+1}\,(\theta)$$

$$+ \gamma\,[\log z_t + \beta \log z_{t+1}],$$

which depends on youthful consumption $c_t(\theta)$, old-age consumption $x_{t+1}\,(\theta)$, youthful money demand $m_t^d\,(\theta)$, and a vector of $(z_t, z_{t+1})$ of public goods consumption. Here we assume that $\beta \in (0,1)$, $v \geq 0$ is the reciprocal of the consumption velocity of money, and $\gamma > 0$ is a parameter that controls the marginal rate of substitution between private goods consumption and public goods consumption.

Household $\theta$ has period-by-period budget constraints,

$$(4a) \quad c_t\,(\theta) + m_t^d\,(\theta) + b_t^d\,(\theta) = \theta$$

$$(4b) \quad x_{t+1}\,(\theta) = \tau_{t+1} + m_t^d\,(\theta)\,/i_t + R_t\,b_t^d,\,(\theta),$$

in which $b_t^d$ is the demand for debt. These constraints are summed up in the lifecycle constraint

$$(5) \quad c_t\,(\theta) + \frac{r_t^N}{R_t^N}\,m_t^d(\theta) + \frac{x_{t+1}\,(\theta)}{R_t} = y_t\,(\theta) = \theta + \frac{\tau_{t+1}}{R_t}\,,$$

where $r_t^N = R_t^N - 1$ is the nominal interest rate and $y_t(\theta)$ is the value of lifecycle income.

An optimal consumption plan requires that $m_t^d(\theta) = vc_t\,(\theta)$ whenever $R_t^N > 1$. In that case, we rewrite (5) in the following form:

$$(5') \quad c_t(\theta)\,/\,\Psi_t + x_{t+1}(\theta)/R_t = y_t(\theta),$$

where

$$(6) \quad 1/\Psi_t = 1 + v\,(r_t^N/R_t^N)$$

is a variable controlled by the central bank.

Maximizing the utility function (3b) subject to constraint (5′) generates the following household demand schedules:

(7a) $\quad c\,(\theta) = \dfrac{\Psi_t\, y_t\,(\theta)}{1+\beta}\,,$

(7b) $\quad x_{t+1}(\theta) = \dfrac{\beta}{1+\beta}\, R_t\, y_t(\theta),$

(7c) $\quad m_t^d\,(\theta) = vc\,(\theta) \qquad$ if $R_t^N > 1$

$\qquad\qquad\quad\; = +\infty \qquad\qquad$ if $R_t^N = 1,$

(7d) $\quad b_t^d(\theta) = \theta - c_t(\theta) - m_t^d\,(\theta)\,.$

Integrating over households, we derive economy-wide demand schedules that depend on the instrument vector $(\tau_t, \Psi_t)$:

(8a) $\quad c_t = \int c_t\,(\theta)\, dG\,(\theta) = \dfrac{\Psi_t\,(1 + \tau_{t+1}/R_t)}{1+\beta}\,,$

(8b) $\quad x_t = \int x_t\,(\theta)\, dG\,(\theta) = \left(\dfrac{\beta}{1+\beta}\right)(R_{t-1} + \tau_t),$

(9a) $\quad m_t^d = \int m_t^d\,(\theta)\, dG\,(\theta) = vc_t\;$ if $R_t^N > 1$

(9b) $\qquad\qquad\qquad\qquad\qquad\quad = +\infty$ if $R_t^N = 1$

(9c) $\quad b_t^d = \int b_t^d\,(\theta)\, dG\,(\theta) \quad = 1 - c_t - m_t^d.$

### 3. EQUILIBRIUM FOR EXOGENOUS POLICIES

Policies are vectors $(\tau_t, z_t, R_t^N)$ that describe real transfers to the old, purchases of public goods, and settings of the nominal yield instrument. For each $t \geq 1$, these vectors satisfy the inequalities

(10) $\quad z_t \geq 0,\; R_t^N \geq 1,\; \tau_t + z_t \leq 1,$

which constrain the provision of public goods and the nominal interest rate from being negative, and prevent the fiscal authority from spending more than the entire national income.

Any policy is feasible if it is consistent with clearing in the goods, bonds, and money market for each $t \geq 1$, that is, if

(11a) $\quad c_t + x_t + z_t = 1,$

(11b) $\quad D_t + b_t^d = B_t,$

(11c) $\quad m_t^d = m_t.$

The first of these equates total spending on consumption and public goods to aggregate income; the second equates the demand for public debt by the central bank and by households to the debt supplied by the Treasury; and the third balances the demand for real currency with the corresponding supply.

Given the budget constraints (1) and (2) for the monetary and fiscal authorities, all three markets will clear if the goods market does. Substituting (8a) and (8b) into (11a), we obtain a nonautonomous first-order difference equation in the real yield $R_t$, that is,

(12) $\beta R_{t-1} + \tau_{t+1} \dfrac{\Psi_t}{R_t} = (1+\beta)(1-z_t) - \beta \tau_t - \Psi_t.$

This equation ties equilibrium outcomes to the choice of the fiscal instruments $(\tau_t, z_t)$ and the monetary instrument $(\Psi_t)$. In particular, *passive policies* of the form $\pi_t = (\tau_t, z_t, \Psi_t) = (\tau, z, \Psi) \equiv \pi$, for all $t$ lead to the indeterminacy originally pointed out by Sargent and Wallace (1981). Solving (12) for $R_t$, we obtain

(13a) $R_t = \dfrac{\tau \Psi}{A(\pi) - \beta R_{t-1}},$

where

(13b) $A(\pi) \equiv (1+\beta)(1-z) - \beta \tau - \Psi$ is decreasing in $\pi = (\tau, z, \Psi),$

(13c) $\Psi \equiv \left(1 + \dfrac{vr^N}{R^N}\right)^{-1}$ is decreasing in $R^N.$

From equation (13a), we identify steady states as positive solutions to the equation

(14) $f(R) \equiv \beta R^2 - A(\pi) R + \tau \Psi = 0.$

Therefore, any policy $\pi \equiv (\tau, z, \Psi)$ that satisfies

(15) $A(\pi) > 2\sqrt{\beta \tau \Psi}$

is consistent with two steady states, $0 < R_1^*(\pi) < R_2^*(\pi)$ (shown in figure 1), as intersections of the solid line with the diagonal. Given $R^N$, the state $R_1^*$ has higher inflation than the state $R_2^*$. The inequality (15) requires that the fiscal deficit, $\tau + z$, be "not too large," and the nominal yield $R^N$ "not too small." Otherwise, the supply of loanable funds to the fiscal authority will be unable to offset the corresponding demand.

The challenge for a monetary authority in this environment is to *keep the economy away from the high-inflation state $R_1^*(\pi)$*, which is afflicted with

**Figure 1: Dynamic Equilibria and Indeterminacy**

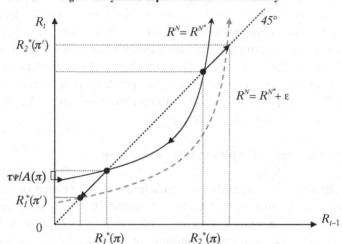

the triple problem of indeterminacy, dynamic inefficiency, and what Sargent and Wallace called "unpleasant monetarist arithmetic."[5]

Indeterminacy is a serious problem because the high-inflation state attracts any equilibrium path whose initial real yield is in the interval $(R_1^*, R_2^*)$. Dynamic inefficiency arises because the polynomial $f(R)$ in equation (14) cannot have two roots above +1, which means that the interest rate $R_1^*$ is *necessarily* below the growth rate. Finally, "unpleasant monetarist arithmetic" is the counterintuitive property of inflation being caused by tight monetary policies (high $R^N$) and by lax fiscal policies (high $z$ or $\pi$). For example, a permanent rise in nominal yield $R^N$ will displace the equilibrium frontier in figure 1 from the solid line to the dotted line, thereby lowering the steady-state real yield from $R_1^*(\pi)$ to another real yield $R_1^*(\pi')$ even though the nominal yield has gone up. This requires the steady-state inflation rate to move up *by more than* the nominal yield.

The low-inflation state $R_2^*(\pi)$ is free of two of these problems and, for some policy choices, of all three. Specifically, if the fiscal deficits $(\tau, z)$ are sufficiently low and $R^N$ is sufficiently high, then $A(\pi) > (\tau + \Psi)$. In that case, equation (14) says that

(16) $R_1^*(\pi) < 1 < R_2^*(\pi)$.

---

[5] Recent literature on unpleasant monetarist arithmetic includes Espinosa and Russell (1993) and Bhattacharya, Guzman, and Smith (1998).

For these policies, the low-inflation state is dynamically efficient (in the restricted sense of supporting desirable intertemporal allocations of aggregate private consumption between two coexisting cohorts) if we ignore static inefficiencies that are caused by missing markets for income risks and by the possible misallocation of resources between private and public consumption.

To steer the economy away from the high-inflation state, the monetary authority can exploit the fact that dynamic economic behavior, as described by equation (12), responds to the choice of the monetary instruments ($\Psi_t$).

## 4. CONTROLLING INDETERMINACY

Can the monetary authority manipulate the interest rate instrument $R_t^N$ to nudge the economy toward the low-inflation steady state? Taylor (1993) suggests that the Federal Reserve system has done so in the past through rules of the form

(17) $R_t^N = T(i_{t-1})$,

where the function $T : \Re_+ \rightarrow [1, \infty)$ has the property of *overreaction* near the inflation target $i^*$, that is,

(18) $T'(i^*) > 1$.

We examine next the impact of these instrument rules on the dynamic properties of equilibrium in the neighborhood of a dynamically efficient steady state $R_2^*(\pi) > 1$, which we assume to be supported by some policy for which $R_N^*$ is an appropriate nominal interest target, and $i^* = R_N^* / R_2^*(\pi)$ is the inflation target. By construction, these targets eliminate the high-inflation state as a possible equilibrium.

Substituting the Taylor rule (17) into the market-clearing condition (12) produces a dynamical system in $(R_t^N, i_t)$, namely,

(19a) $i_t = H(R_{t-1}^N, i_{t-1})$,

(19b) $R_t^N = T(i_{t-1})$,

where

(20) $H(R, i) \equiv \dfrac{1}{\tau}\left[(1+\beta)(1-z) - \beta\left(\tau + \dfrac{R}{i}\right)\right][(1+v)T(i) - v] - \dfrac{T(i)}{\tau}.$

A unique steady state $(R_N^*, i^*)$ has been built into this system. Dynamic behavior in the neighborhood of that state is controlled by two real eigenvalues $T'(i^*)$ and $H_R(R_N^*, i^*)$, where $H_R$ is the partial derivative of the function $H$ with respect to $R$, evaluated at the steady state. It is easy to check that

$$(21) \quad H_R = \frac{(1+v)R_N^* - v}{\tau i^*} < -1,$$

if $R_I^* < 1$, that is, if the high-inflation state is dynamically inefficient.

The other eigenvalue equals to the slope of the Taylor rule. If that rule overreacts to past inflation as in inequality (18), then the steady state ($R_N^*, i^*$) is locally unique; otherwise it is indeterminate. We conclude that, in simple lifecycle economies, Taylor rules defeat indeterminacy, reverse the "unpleasant monetarist arithmetic" property, and steer the economy toward dynamically efficient outcomes.

## 5. THE INFLATIONARY BIAS FROM INCOMPLETE MARKETS

Achieving determinate, dynamically efficient aggregate outcomes is not equivalent to optimality in environments of incomplete markets, especially ones in which asset markets are too weak to provide insurance against income risks. Edmond (2002) and Paal and Smith (2001) study economies in which low-inflation policies are suboptimal. To understand why, let us ignore public goods and think instead of the policy $(\tau_t, R_t^N) = (0,1) > \forall t$, which pays no old-age subsidy, delivers the golden rule outcome with zero inflation, and provides maximal liquidity for consumers.

What is wrong with this policy is that *it does nothing to insure individuals against uninsurable income risks.* Unlucky households with very low realized income will do very poorly; lucky ones with high income will do splendidly. A modest amount of inflation is helpful in this setting. A small inflation tax generates seigniorage that will finance lump-sum payments to all households. The outcome is to make after-tax income less sensitive to the luck of the draw $\theta$ without unduly distorting intertemporal consumption decisions. In a setting similar to ours, Edmond (2002) shows that it is optimal to raise the inflation target above zero.

To illustrate, suppose that currency yields no utility services ($v = 0$), and that there is no independent fiscal authority. The government monetizes all fiscal deficits; it expands money supply at the gross rate $\mu \geq 1$ to finance an old-age transfer $\tau_t$ at time $t$, that is,

$$(22) \quad M_t = \mu M_{t-1}.$$

This implies a consolidated government budget constraint,

$$P_t \tau_t = M_t - M_{t-1} = (1-1/\mu)M_t.$$

Equivalently, we have

$$(23) \quad \tau_t = \left(1 - \frac{1}{\mu}\right)m_t,$$

where $m_t = M_t/P_t$ is the supply of real currency balances.

We skip issues connected with indeterminacy, which can be cured by Taylor rules, focusing instead on stationary monetary equilibria. The stationary form of equation (23) is

(23′) $\tau = \left(1 - \dfrac{1}{\mu}\right) m.$

Assume that the pretax endowment profile is $(\theta, 0)$, and the after-tax profile is $(\theta, \tau)$ for a household of type $\theta$ in any cohort $t = 1, 2, \ldots$. Since money is the only store of value with steady-state yield $R = 1/\mu$, saving by a household with income profile $(\theta, \tau)$ at that yield is

(24)  $s(\theta) = \dfrac{1}{1+\beta}\left(\beta\theta - \dfrac{\tau}{R}\right) = \dfrac{1}{1+\beta}(\beta\theta - \tau\mu).$

Aggregate saving equals the stock of real currency balances in equilibrium because private debts cancel out. Thus,

(25)  $m = \int s(\theta)\, dG.$

Combining (23′), (24), and (25), we obtain

(26)  $\tau = \dfrac{(1 - 1/\mu)\beta}{\beta + \mu},$

$m = \dfrac{\beta}{\beta + \mu}.$

Equilibrium consumption profiles for agents of type $\theta$ are $[c(\theta), x(\theta)]$, where

(27a)  $x(\theta) = \dfrac{\beta}{\mu}\, c(\theta),$

(27b)  $c(\theta) = \left(\dfrac{1}{1+\beta}\right)\left(\dfrac{\theta + \beta(\mu - 1)}{\beta + \mu}\right).$

These expressions say that high steady-state inflation benefits unlucky individuals. In fact, $c(\theta)$ is increasing in $\mu$ for all $\theta$ because low rates of return tilt consumption toward youth. It is also easy to check that $x(\theta)$ is increasing in $\mu$ for "sufficiently small" $\theta$ and $\mu$, that is, for $\theta < \beta(2\mu - \mu^2 + \beta)/(\beta + \mu)^2$. Old-age consumption for unlucky agents benefits from inflation because the income effect from a bigger old-age pension overwhelms the adverse substitution effect of a lower yield on saving.

Lucky agents are the only ones hurt by inflation. To balance conflicting household attitudes toward inflation, we assume that the central bank chooses $\mu \geq 1$ to maximize expected (or average) utility in the steady state, that is,

$$V(\mu) = E_\theta\{\log[c(\theta)] + \beta\log[x(\theta)]\}.$$

Substituting (27a) and (27b) into this expression and ignoring constants, we obtain the concave payoff function

$$(28) \quad V(\mu) = -\beta\log\mu + (1+\beta)\log\left[\theta + \frac{(\mu-1)\beta}{\beta+\mu}\right],$$

defined for every $\mu \geq 1$.

It is straightforward to see from the first-order condition for a maximum that the optimal inflation rate is $\mu^* > 1$. In fact,

$$(29) \quad \frac{1}{\beta}V'(\mu) = -\frac{1}{\mu} + \left(\frac{1+\beta}{\mu+\beta}\right)^2 E_\theta\left[\frac{1}{(1+\beta)\,c\,(\theta)}\right],$$

which implies

$$\frac{1}{\beta}V'(1) = -1 + E_\theta\left[\frac{1}{(1+\beta)c\,(\theta)}\right]$$

$$> -1 + \left[\frac{1}{(1+\beta)E_\theta c(\theta)}\right] \qquad \text{by Jensen's inequality}$$

$$> -1 + \frac{1}{E\theta} \qquad\qquad \text{by equation (27b)}$$

$$= 0 \qquad\qquad\qquad \text{by assumption}$$

Therefore, the solution to $V'(\mu) = 0$ requires positive inflation. If we expand $1/c\,(\theta)$ around $E(\theta) = 1$ and ignore terms of order higher than two, the equation $V'(\mu) = 0$ reduces to

$$(30) \quad \sigma_\theta^2 = J(\mu) \equiv \frac{(1+\beta)\,(\mu-1)\mu^2}{(\mu+\beta)^2},$$

where $\sigma_\theta^2$ is the variance of the youthful income. Since $J(.)$ is an increasing function that attains the values $J(1) = 0$ and $J(\mu) \to \infty$ as $\mu \to \infty$, equation (30) has a unique optimum $\mu^* > 1$ for each value of $\sigma_\theta^2 > 0$ and of the discount rate $\beta > 1$. This optimum is an increasing function of both income variance and the discount rate; a high value of $\beta$ weighs the social insurance benefit from old-age transfers more heavily than the inflation distortion.

Two examples will give a sense of how large the optimum inflation rate may be. For the parameter values $(\sigma_\theta^2, \beta) = (1,1)$, that is, no discount and unitary coefficient of variation for income, we obtain from (30) a $\mu^*$ slightly above 2 that corresponds to an annual inflation rate of about 2.5% compounded over a 30-year span. At the other end of plausible parameter values, the choice $(\sigma_\theta, \beta) = (0.5, 0.5)$ reduces the optimum annual inflation rate to nearly 1%.

## 6. STRATEGIC MOTIVES FOR MONETARY POLICIES

### 6.1 The Issues

Independent central banking has become the norm for advanced societies because citizens do not altogether trust the Treasury to coordinate both monetary and fiscal policy. One particular fear is that the electoral cycle makes the Treasury too willing to tolerate inflation and fiscal deficits as it pursues short-term gains in output or transfers resources to key voting blocks. The citizens seem willing to give up the obvious advantage of policy coordination in the hope of entrusting some of the levers of economic policy to institutions with more congenial or benevolent motives. Less tolerance for inflation may be one of these motives, advocated by Rogoff (1985) and documented in Eijffinger and de Haan (1996) and other studies.

This section analyzes policy outcomes in a society with two independent policymakers: a benevolent monetary authority (MA) that evaluates outcomes exactly the same way as the average household and a fiscal authority (FA) that is inherently less patient than the household or the central bank. Ideal social outcomes in this setting correspond to the bliss point of the average household or the MA: Policy delivers an ideal division of resources between public and private consumption, between current and future consumption, but not necessarily among households facing uninsurable income risks.

On the other hand, if the Treasury coordinates all policies, then it will deliver the bliss point of the FA. Consumption will favor public goods over private ones, the young over the old, and deficit spending. To finance the resulting public debt, the FA needs higher nominal yields and needs to be willing to tolerate higher inflation than the central bank would.

To understand these outcomes, we study a simplified version of the model economy from section 2 with zero transfer payments throughout. The endowment vector is $(\theta,0)$, the utility function is exactly as in equation (3b), and policies are constant vectors $\pi = (z, R^N)$ such that $z \in [0,1]$ and $R^N \geq 1$. The FA controls the first element of the policy vector, the MA controls the second. Each authority commits to a fixed choice that maximizes its own payoff function. The central bank maximizes the expected steady-state value of household utility shown in equation (3b). The Treasury maximizes an identical function with uniformly more impatience, that is, with $\delta \in (0,\beta)$ replacing $\beta$ in equation (3b).

Ignoring old-age transfers, and also setting old-age endowment at zero, brings to our analysis two considerable simplifying advantages: indeterminacy is no longer a problem and social insurance is no longer a motive for policy. Inspecting equations (5'), (7a), (7b), and (12), we see that the lifecycle income vector $[c(\theta), x(\theta)]$ is exactly proportional to $\theta$. Also, the term $R_t$ vanishes from the law of motion for real yields that now becomes

(31)  $\beta R = (1+\beta)(1+z) - \Psi$

in the steady state.

These two observations mean that our special model does *not* allow policy to manipulate the present value of lifecycle income or to influence the number of equilibria. *Equilibrium is unique and social insurance is infeasible in this section.*

### 6.2 Ideal Policies

For any constant policy $(z, R^N)$, or equivalently $(z, \Psi)$, stationary equilibrium obeys equations (7a), (7b), and (31), that is,

(31)   $\beta R = (1+\beta)(1-z) - \Psi,$

(32a)  $(1+\beta)c(\theta) = \theta\Psi,$

(32b)  $(1+\beta)x(\theta) = \theta[(1+\beta)(1-z) - \Psi],$

where

(32c)  $\Psi = \dfrac{1}{1+v - v/R^N}.$

From (31), it is clear that a unique stationary equilibrium exists for any *feasible policy* such that

(33)   $(1+\beta)(1-z) - \Psi > 0.$

Suppressing constants, we substitute equations (31) and (32) into (3) to compute the payoff functions for the monetary and fiscal authorities. These are

(34a)  $W^M(z, \Psi) = \log\Psi + \beta\log[(1+\beta)(1-z) - \Psi] + \gamma(1+\beta)\log z$

for the monetary authority and

(34b)  $W^F(z, \Psi) = \log\Psi + \delta\log[(1+\beta)(1-z) - \Psi] + \gamma(1+\delta)\log z$

for the fiscal authority.

The ideal policy for the MA is the joint solution $(z_M^*, \Psi_M^*)$ to the first-order conditions

$$W_z^M \equiv \frac{\partial W^M}{\partial z} = 0 \qquad W_\Psi^M \equiv \frac{\partial W^M}{\partial \Psi} = 0.$$

Equivalently, we have

(35a) $\quad \Psi = 1 - z, \quad \Psi = (1 + \beta)\left[1 - \left(1 + \frac{\beta/\gamma}{1+\beta}\right)z\right].$

Proceeding similarly, we obtain the ideal policy $(z_F^*, \Psi_F^*)$ for the FA from

$$W_z^F \equiv \frac{\partial W^F}{\partial z} = 0 \quad W_\Psi^F \equiv \frac{\partial W^F}{\partial \Psi} = 0,$$

which leads to

(35b) $\quad \Psi = \left(\frac{1+\beta}{1+\delta}\right)(1-z), \quad \Psi = (1+\beta)\left[1 - \left(1 + \frac{\delta/\gamma}{1+\beta}\right)z\right].$

From equations (35a) and (35b), it is clear that the MA desires a higher interest rate for each given $z$ than does the FA, and also a lower flow of the public good for each given interest rate. The MA prefers a high value of $R^N$, or low $\Psi$, at each given $z$ because, by equation (30), higher nominal yields lead to higher real yields, which, in turn, tilt private consumption toward old age. The same mechanism explains why the FA likes public goods more than the MA at each given $\Psi$: Higher values of $z$ lower real yields and redistribute private consumption towards the young generation.

Bliss points in the policy space $(z, \Psi)$ are surrounded by ellipsoidal indifference contours for each policymaker. Figure 2 displays indifference contours for the MA with continuous lines, and for the FA with broken lines. Differences in contours are due to the fact that the line $W_z^F = 0$ lies above the line $W_z^M = 0$ and the line $W_\Psi^F = 0$ lies above the line $W_\Psi^M = 0$.

The optimal policy for the household is, by assumption, the MA bliss point. However, equilibrium outcomes are sensitive to the institutional setting within which the two authorities interact. If policy is coordinated by the Treasury, the outcome is the bliss point of the FA with more public spending, a lower interest rate, and higher inflation than the household wants. All of these are obvious from figure 1, except for the inflation differential. To see that the FA desires higher spending and higher inflation than the MA, we solve equations (35a) and (35b) separately to obtain ideal policies $\pi_M^*$ and $\pi_F^*$ for the monetary and fiscal authorities. These policies are, respectively,

**Figure : Ideal and Actual Policies**

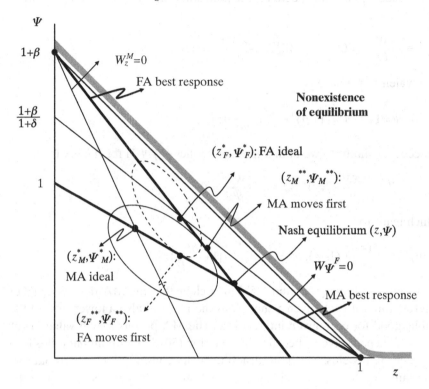

(36a) $\quad \pi_M^* \equiv (z_M^*, \Psi_M^*) = \left( \dfrac{\gamma}{1+\gamma}, \dfrac{1}{1+\gamma} \right)$,

(36b) $\quad \pi_F^* \equiv (z_F^*, \Psi_F^*) = \left( \dfrac{\gamma}{\dfrac{1+\delta}{1+\beta}+\gamma}, \dfrac{1}{1+\gamma \dfrac{1+\beta}{1+\delta}} \right)$

If the fiscal authority is less patient than the central bank, then $\delta < \beta$, which leads to $z_F^* > z_M^*$, and $\Psi_F^* < \Psi_M^*$.

Each policy $\pi = (z, \Psi)$ implies a unique inflation target that we can extract easily from equation (31). Using the definition of $\Psi$ in equation (32c), we rewrite equation (31) in the form

(37) $\quad i = \dfrac{\beta v}{[(1+\beta)(1-z)-\Psi][1+v-1/\Psi]}$ .

Inflation targets for the two authorities' bliss points are computed from equations (36a), (36b), and (37), that is,

(38a) $i_M^* = \dfrac{v}{1-z_M^*}$.

(38b) $i_F^* = \left(\dfrac{\beta(1+\delta)}{\delta(1+\beta)}\right) \dfrac{v}{1-z_F^*}$.

Clearly, for any $\beta > \delta > 0$, the fiscal authority's inflation target exceeds the monetary authority's inflation target.

### 6.3 Equilibrium Policies

Suppose now that policymaking is a one-shot strategic game with commitment, played by the two authorities: The MA selects $\Psi \in [1/(1+v),1]$ and the FA selects $z \in [0,1]$. As we know already, no equilibrium exists if $(1+\beta)(1-z) < \Psi$. Should we expect the outcome of the game to lie between the two bliss points $(z_F^*,\Psi_F^*)$ and $(z_M^*,\Psi_M^*)$ in the space of policies? Is the equilibrium a compromise between competing ideals?

Dixit and Lambertini (2003) show that expectation is generally incorrect in a static Keynesian model: Equilibrium is typically *outside* the interval defined by ideal policies. Both fiscal spending and the nominal interest rate turn out to be higher than either policymaker's targets because of strategic complementarities. To see why, note from figure 2 that the best response function for each player, $R^N(z)$ and $z(R^N)$, is an increasing function of the other player's action.

For example, the equilibrium of a simultaneous move game lies on the intersection of the two best-response functions: the MA best response is $W_\Psi^M = 0$. and the FA best response is $W_z^F = 0$. From (35a) and (35b), we have the Nash equilibrium

(39) $\overline{\pi} = (\overline{z}, \overline{\Psi}) = \left(\dfrac{\gamma}{\gamma + \gamma/\beta}, \dfrac{\delta/\beta}{\gamma + \delta/\beta}\right)$.

Comparing (36a), (36b), and (37), we verify that the Dixit and Lambertini (2003) intuition extends to dynamic non-Keynesian economies, that is,

(40) $\overline{z} > z_F^* > z_M^*, \qquad \overline{\Psi} < \Psi_F^* < \Psi_M^*$.

Nash equilibrium specifies more fiscal spending, a higher nominal yield, and (as easily shown) more inflation than *either* player ideally desires. This is also clear from figure 2.

Outcomes may come closer to a player's bliss point if that player moves first. For example, if the MA is the Stackelberg leader, then the equilibrium will be a tangency between the monetary authority's indifference contours and the fiscal authority's best response line, as shown in figure 2. It is easy to show that equilibrium policy in that case is

$$(41) \quad \pi_M^{**} = (z_M^{**}, \Psi_M^{**}) = \left( \frac{\gamma}{1+\gamma}, \frac{\beta+(1+\beta)\gamma}{\delta+(1+\beta)\gamma}, \frac{1}{1+\gamma} \right).$$

A comparison of (36a,b) with (41) reveals that

$$(42) \quad \Psi_M^{**} = \Psi_M^*, \qquad z_M^{**} > z_F^* > z_M^* .$$

If the central bank moves first, we conclude that the Stackelberg equilibrium achieves the ideal interest rate for households and the MA, but fiscal spending is *still higher* than the ideal for either player. The lack of policy coordination in noncooperative games causes difficulties not just for simultaneous moves but for *any* sequence of moves.

## 7. CONCLUSIONS AND EXTENSIONS

This paper has sequentially examined three challenges for monetary policy: controlling indeterminacy by Taylor rules, providing social insurance under incomplete markets, and attempting to exert strategic influence over the direction of fiscal policy. Our main findings are in line with earlier work by Taylor (1993), Edmond (2002), and Dixit and Lambertini (2003). In a simple lifecycle model of dynamic general equilibrium, we find that Taylor rules do a good job, at least near efficient steady states, of defeating indeterminacy if a sufficiently low inflation target is selected.

This reassuring conclusion is tempered by two other findings: The inflation target cannot be very low if the fiscal authority wishes to provide social insurance for privately uninsurable, idiosyncratic income risks, and also because strategic complementarities between the monetary authority and the fiscal authority will raise the equilibrium rate of inflation above the level desired by either authority. We do not know yet if Taylor rules are globally stable in lifecycle economies, or exactly how to strike the right balance of cooperation and competition between monetary and fiscal instruments.

Extensions of this work should look at policymaking that *simultaneously* confronts all of the three challenges described previously. The conclusions we can draw from an exercise of that type will carry more conviction if the fiscal authority is allowed to tax incomes, rather than just issue debt; if strategic play is repeated without commitment in an environment with uncertainty, rather than being one-shot with commitment under certainty; and if individuals trade more frequently than the simplest two-period lifecycle framework permits.

## ACKNOWLEDGMENTS

Support from the Program for Dynamic Economics at the University of California, Los Angeles, is gratefully acknowledged, as are comments by Eric Fisher and Marvin Goodfriend.

## REFERENCES

Azariadis, C., and L. Kaas. 2002. Asset Price Fluctuations without Aggregate Shocks. Unpublished manuscript, University of California, Los Angeles.

Benhabib, J., S. Schmitt-Grohe, and M. Uribe. 2001a. The Perils of Taylor Rules. *Journal of Economic Theory* 96(1): 40–69.

Benhabib, J., S. Schmitt-Grohe, and M. Uribe. 2001b. Monetary Policy and Multiple Equilbria. *American Economic Review* 91(1): 167–86

Benhabib, J., S. Schmitt-Grohe, and M. Uribe. 2003. Backward-Looking Interest-Rate Rules, Interest-Rate Smoothing, and Macroeconomic Instability. Working Paper No. 9558, National Bureau of Economic Research.

Bernanke, B., and F. Mishkin. 1992. Central Bank Behavior and the Strategy of Monetary Policy: Observations from Six Industrialized Countries. In *NBER Macroeconomics Annual,* vol. 7, edited by Olivier Jean Blanchard and Stanley Fischer, 183–228. Cambridge, MA: MIT Press.

Bernanke, B., and M. Woodford. 1997. Inflation Forecasts and Monetary Policy. Working Paper No. 6157, National Bureau of Economic Research.

Bewley, T. 1983. A Difficulty with the Optimum Quantity of Money. *Econometrica* 51: 1485–1504.

Bhattacharya, J., M. Guzman, and B. Smith. 1998. Some Even More Unpleasant Monetarist Arithmetic. *Canadian Journal of Economics* 31: 596–623.

Carlstrom, C., and T. Fuerst. 2000. Forward-Looking versus Backward-Looking Taylor Rules. Working Paper No. 0099, Federal Reserve Bank of Cleveland.

Carlstrom, C., and T. Fuerst. 2001. Timing and Real Indeterminacy in Monetary Models. *Journal of Monetary Economics* 47: 285–98.

Dixit, A., and L. Lambertini. 2003. Interactions of Commitment and Discretion in Monetary and Fiscal Policies. *American Economic Review* 93: 1522–42.

Edmond, C. 2002. Self-Insurance, Social Insurance, and the Optimum Quantity of Money. *American Economic Review* 92: 141–47.

Eijffinger, S., and J. de Haan. 1996. The Political Economy of Central Bank Independence. Princeton Special Papers in International Economics No. 19, Princeton University.

Espinosa, M., and S. Russell. 1993. Monetary Policy, Interest Rates, and Inflation: Budget Arithmetic Revisited. Working Paper No. 9312, Federal Reserve Bank of Atlanta.

Freeman, S. 1993. Resolving Differences over the Optimal Quantity of Money. *Journal of Money, Credit, and Banking* 25: 801–11.

Friedman, M. 1969. The Optimum Quantity of Money. In *The Optimum Quantity of Money, and Other Essays,* by Milton Friedman. Chicago: Aldine.

Giannoni, M., and M. Woodford. 2002a. Optimal Interest Rate Rules: I. General Theory. Unpublished manuscript, Princeton University.

Giannoni, M., and M. Woodford. 2002b. Optimal Interest Rate Rules: II. Applications. Unpublished manuscript, Princeton University.

Leeper, E. 1991. Equilibria under "Active" and "Passive" Monetary and Fiscal Policies. *Journal of Monetary Economics* 27: 129–47.

Levin, A., V. Wieland, and J. William. 1999. Robustness of Simple Monetary Policy Rules under Model Uncertainty. In *Monetary Policy Rules*, edited by J. Taylor. Chicago: University of Chicago Press.

Paal, B., and B. Smith. 2001. The Sub-Optimality of the Friedman Rule and the Optimum Quantity of Money. Unpublished manuscript, University of Texas at Austin.

Rogoff, K. 1985. The Optimal Commitment to an Intermediate Monetary Target. *Quarterly Journal of Economics* 100: 1169–89.

Rotemberg, J., and M. Woodford. 1997. An Optimization-Based Econometric Framework for the Evaluation of Monetary Policy. In *NBER Macroeconomics Annual,* vol. 12, edited by Ben S. Bernanke and Julio Rotemberg, 297–346. Cambridge, MA: MIT Press.

Rotemberg, J., and M. Woodford. 1999. Interest-Rate Rules in an Estimated Sticky Price Model. In *Monetary Policy Rules,* edited by J. Taylor. Chicago: University of Chicago Press.

Sargent, T., and N. Wallace. 1981. Some Unpleasant Monetarist Arithmetic. *Federal Reserve Bank Minneapolis Quarterly Review* 5: 1–17.

Taylor, J. 1993. Discretion versus Rules in Practice. *Carnegie–Rochester Series on Public Policy* 39: 195–214.

# Commentary

*Eric O'N. Fisher*

Keynes (1936) was right to emphasize that the investors' expectations have a paramount effect on the evolution of the national economy. Indeed, an important part of the role of the financial services sector in a modern economy is to try to forecast how the central bank will react to macroeconomic shocks, and any Wall Street economist worth his or her salt has a rule of thumb—a model drawn perhaps from some collective economic unconscious—that predicts how the Federal Open Market Committee will react to a bad inflation number or to a high unemployment figure. The high priest of the caste of economic forecasters—the Carl Jung of Wall Street economists—is John Taylor, whose elegant description (1993) of the Fed's putative policy rule has become a workhorse for modern macroeconomic analysis.

The essence of a simple version of Taylor's rule is that the Fed should raise nominal interest rates sharply if there is bad inflation news. This is the crux of how the Fed builds "credibility" in financial markets. Whenever there is a bad inflation number, the market is faced with a quandary: Is this a sign that the Fed is loosening monetary policy, or is it a signal that the Fed will tighten future interest rates to cool down a national economy that is perhaps over-heated? Once investors have assimilated Taylor's "activist" policy rule, the market will react to an inflation shock assuming (correctly) that the Federal Open Market Committee is serious about maintaining low inflation.

An important added benefit is that the Fed itself will know how the market will react to rising nominal interest rates, and this knowledge cuts through the Gordian knot of higher-order expectations that Keynes first described in his famous passage on financial markets as beauty contests in chapter 12 of *The General Theory*. The Fed no longer needs to guess how investors will act in response to their own forecasts of the Fed's prediction of how private markets will divine the latest news about how a member of the Federal Open Market Committee might react to her staff's using the newest (public) inflation number to make a forecast of the national economy in the next quarter! The right kind of Taylor rule makes it easier for the central bank to maintain *both* low inflation and full employment because there is a built-in stability in market expectations.[1]

This observation is the essence of the first of the three themes that Azariadis and Lam explore. In a wide class of macroeconomic models, there

---

[1] The reader should not think that this line of reasoning about the role of endogenous expectations is just a theoretical curiosum; Duffy and Fisher (2005) show that these ideas have real empirical bite.

is a fundamental indeterminacy in the set of perfect foresight equilibria. The nominal values of monetary variables are not tied down, and this fact can have unpleasant consequences for monetary and fiscal policy. In fact, there are typically many different inefficient equilibria, and it would be an improvement in the sense of Pareto if somehow all of these suboptimal equilibria were eliminated. Azariadis and Lam emphasize that a simple Taylor rule based upon past inflation suffices to insure that the unique perfect foresight equilibrium is the best one possible.

Azariadis and Lam's second theme has to do with the distributional effects of inflation. They actually study a model in which some agents are born poor and others are born rich. Since there is no bequest motive, each unborn soul faces idiosyncratic risk about where she will fall in the grand scheme of all things economic.[2] Think of a Rawlsian All Souls' Convention where every agent who will ever be born meets outside of time and behind a veil of ignorance. Since everyone is in a symmetric situation, not knowing whether he or she will be born poor or rich, there is a unique steady-state inflation rate—and concomitant uniform lump-sum transfer of seignorage —that maximizes the expected well-being of every ignorant soul. This policy of moderate inflation has the strong philosophical benefit that it would be adopted unanimously against any other inflation rate in a vote of pair-wise policies at the All Souls' Convention.

Azariadis and Lam's third theme builds on recent work by Dixit and Lambertini (2003). There is an important earlier literature that assumes a passive fiscal policy and then explores the effects of monetary policy using applied game theory, but Dixit and Lambertini make the important observation that the existence of independent fiscal and monetary authorities makes it necessary to model the strategic interaction between the two. Having worked at both the Federal Reserve Board and the Treasury, I know that Dixit and Lambertini's basic insight captures an important aspect of the reality of macroeconomic policy in the United States.

Azariadis and Lam explore this idea within their model. Using a simplified version of their basic model, the authors assume a benevolent monetary authority whose policy preferences actually coincide with those of the representative household. They also assume that the fiscal authority is less patient that the monetary authority; this assumption captures an important aspect of representative democracies in which elected officials typically serve

---

[2] Azariadis and Lam plausibly rule out the first-best policy of a 100% income tax that is redistributed in lump-sum equally among all agents, rich and poor. The political implications of such a policy in our world surely outweigh its theoretical benefits in this model's stylized universe.

shorter terms than an appointed governor of the central bank. The upshot of this assumption is that the Nash equilibrium of the game played by the fiscal and monetary authorities has too much inflation *and* too much government spending. Thus, Azariadis and Lam extend Dixit and Lambertini's ideas from a static Keynesian framework to a dynamic general equilibrium model.

In sum, Azariadis and Lam have given the reader a macroeconomic symphony in three movements. The theme of the first movement is that a simple backward-looking policy rule for nominal interest rates removes the generic indeterminacy that plagues many models of monetary economies. The second movement is an allegro divertimento describing why moderate rates of inflation may help in a world with incomplete markets and idiosyncratic risks to individual incomes. The theme of the third movement is that the interplay between the independent monetary and fiscal authorities—so much a part of the political economy of any modern industrialized country—gives rise to an inflation rate that is too high and also to too much public spending. The power of a symphony is to make harmony from otherwise discordant voices, and it is a pleasure to see how these authors blend these three themes in a dynamic macroeconomic model.

REFERENCES

Dixit, A., and L. Lambertini. 2003. Interactions of Commitment and Discretion in Monetary and Fiscal Policies. *American Economic Review* 93: 1522–42.

Duffy, J., and E. O'N. Fisher. 2005. Sunspots in the Laboratory. *American Economic Review* 95: 510–29.

Keynes, J. M. 1936. *The General Theory of Employment, Interest, and Money.* London: Macmillan.

Taylor, J. 1993. Discretion versus Rules in Practice. *Carnegie–Rochester Series on Public Policy* 39: 192–214.

# Commentary

*Marvin Goodfriend*

This paper studies some consequences of monetary policy for three sorts of fiscal policies: a passive fiscal policy, fiscal social insurance, and a regime where the fiscal authority is less patient than a monetary authority.

The passive fiscal policy regime is similar to one studied by Sargent and Wallace (1981) in their "unpleasant monetarist arithmetic" article. In this regime, the fiscal authority must raise a given real revenue that must be financed by an inflation tax. There are two steady-state equilibrium points on a Laffer curve that raise the required revenue—one equilibrium with a high inflation tax rate and the other with a low tax rate. There is no income tax or other source of revenue, so the inflation tax on real money balances is the only source of revenue for the government. The authors show that the low inflation tax equilibrium is locally saddle point stable when the monetary authority can commit to a Taylor rule in which the real interest rate reacts to the lagged inflation rate.

In the fiscal social insurance regime, markets are assumed to be incomplete so that households are subject to uninsurable idiosyncratic income risks at birth. The authors show that a small inflation tax is welfare improving because it generates revenue that can be redistributed to households to make after-(inflation) tax income less sensitive to the idiosyncratic income risk.

The third fiscal regime analyzes outcomes when the monetary authority is independent of the fiscal authority. In this case, both the monetary and the fiscal authorities are assumed to maximize household utility, but the fiscal authority is assumed to be less patient than the monetary authority. The policy instruments are public goods purchases, controlled by the fiscal authority, and the real interest rate, controlled by the monetary authority.

The authors consider three institutional frameworks. They show that the household optimum is achieved when the monetary authority dominates the fiscal authority. Not surprisingly, when the fiscal authority is assumed to be dominant, there is more public spending, a lower real interest rate, and higher inflation than households would like.

Finally, the authors consider a noncooperative game between the monetary authority and the fiscal authority. In this case, the authors find that the outcome is higher fiscal spending than *either* the monetary authority or the fiscal authority would like. This suboptimal outcome occurs even if the monetary authority "plays first." Apparently this is so because the fiscal authority is too impatient and does not fully internalize the cost of the inflation tax on its choice of public spending.

This paper is an interesting exercise in thinking through some issues of monetary and fiscal policy coordination; however, I find the models unsuitable for use in thinking seriously about real-world institutions, at least in developed economies such as the United States. First, there is no other source of revenue for the government besides the inflation tax in these models, which emphasizes the fiscal constraints on monetary policy much more than is deserved. I doubt that the issues focused on in the paper would matter much quantitatively for monetary policy in a model with more sources of revenue.

Second, the analysis leans heavily on a feature of the overlapping-generations model employed in the paper that gives the monetary authority permanent leverage over the real interest rate. I am uncomfortable with a model with much leeway for monetary policy to influence the real interest rate in the long run. In the standard growth model with infinitely lived agents, or dynastic families, productivity growth governs consumption growth in the steady state. And the real interest rate that is consistent with balanced growth is determined recursively by the intertemporal elasticity of consumption. There is little or no leeway for monetary policy to have a permanent effect on the real interest rate in such models. More importantly, I interpret "cheap money" experiments run by the world's central banks in the past as proof that easy-money policies geared to maintaining low real interest rates are unsustainable.

Even though I believe that the *analysis* in the paper is more of academic than practical interest, I very much agree with the *spirit of* the paper. Fiscal issues do potentially have first-order effects on monetary policy even when there is little pressure to raise revenue with the inflation tax as in the United States. today. Here are three ways in which monetary policy should take account of fiscal issues.

First, a few years ago, government budget surpluses threatened to reduce the outstanding stock of Treasury securities, and the Fed was forced to reconsider its asset acquisition policy. In fact, in October 2001, this Cleveland Fed conference held a panel discussion on the implications of declining Treasury debt.[1] The issue is less pressing today than it was, but it is important to think through how the Fed should operate under all possible circumstances in the future.

In an article with Al Broaddus that I summarized in that panel discussion, we made the following points (Broaddus and Goodfriend 2001): The Fed's asset acquisition policies should adhere to two closely related principles to support monetary policy by strengthening the Fed's independence—asset

---

[1] See Goodfriend, Kohn, and McCauley (2002).

acquisition should respect the integrity of fiscal policy and should minimize the risk of political entanglements involving Fed credit allocation. We proposed that the Fed and the Treasury cooperate, under the auspices of Congress if need be, to enable the Fed to continue to rely on Treasury securities even as the publicly held debt is paid down.

Second, in light of the potential for interest rate policy to be constrained by the zero bound, there is another more pressing reason to think about greater cooperation between the central bank and the fiscal authorities. Short-term government securities are perfect substitutes for the monetary base at the zero bound, so the Fed would have to buy longer-term government securities or private assets for quantitative easing to be effective there.

This means that the central bank may need more fiscal support for quantitative policy at the zero bound than is usually granted by the fiscal authorities. For one thing, there may not be enough outstanding long-term government bonds to purchase, or government budget deficits to monetize, to make quantitative policy effective. On the other hand, buying private domestic assets or foreign assets, or lending to banks on a large scale, involves problems that Al Broaddus and I emphasized in the article mentioned above. Finally, the central bank would be exposed to capital losses that might leave it with insufficient assets to reverse a potentially inflationary monetary overhang after quantitative policy has succeeded. Cooperative arrangements between the central bank and the fiscal authorities could make quantitative policy fully effective and credible at the zero bound (Broaddus and Goodfriend 2004; Goodfriend 2000).

Third, recently Congress has been considering legislation that would empower the Fed to pay explicit interest on bank reserves. Elsewhere, I pointed out that this fiscal innovation would have important advantages over current practice stemming from the fact that it would enable the central bank to implement interest rate policy by paying and varying interest on reserves *without maintaining an interest opportunity cost of reserves* (Goodfriend 2002). For instance, the interest-on-reserve regime would perfectly preserve the central bank's leverage over interest rates against technological innovations that threaten to reduce the use of the monetary base in making payments. The interest-on-reserves regime would also entirely eliminate the distortions in financial markets due to the tax on reserves. In particular, an abundance of costless, safe reserves would substitute for the costly and risky extension of private and central bank credit in the process of making payments. Additionally, the interest-on-reserves regime might very well be self-financing. The central bank would have to pay the federal funds rate on reserve deposits currently held by banks. However, eliminating the tax on reserves would cause the demand for reserves to increase substantially, enabling the central bank to increase its holdings of Treasury bills and other assets whose returns exceed the federal funds rate on average.

## REFERENCES

Broaddus, J. A., and M. Goodfriend. 2001. What Assets Should the Federal Reserve Buy? *Federal Reserve Bank of Richmond Economic Quarterly* 87: 7–22.

Broaddus, J. A., and M. Goodfriend. 2004. Sustaining Price Stability. *Federal Reserve Bank of Richmond Economic Quarterly* 30: 3–20.

Goodfriend, M. 2000. Overcoming the Zero Bound on Interest Rate Policy. *Journal of Money, Credit, and Banking* 32: 1007–35.

Goodfriend, M. 2002. Interest on Reserves and Monetary Policy. *Federal Reserve Bank of New York Economic Policy Review* 8: 77–83.

Goodfriend, M., D. Kohn, and R. McCauley. 2002. Panel Discussion: Implications of Declining Treasury Debt. *Journal of Money, Credit, and Banking* 34: 941–66.

Sargent, T., and N. Wallace. 1981. Some Unpleasant Monetarist Arithmetic. *Federal Reserve Bank of Minneapolis Quarterly Review* 5: 1–17.

4

# Inflation and Welfare in Models

# with Trading Frictions

*Guillaume Rocheteau and Randall Wright*

## 1. INTRODUCTION

We study the effects of inflation in models with various trading frictions. Our economic environment is based on recent search-theoretic models of monetary exchange following Lagos and Wright (2005), in that trade takes place periodically in both centralized and decentralized markets. However, following Rocheteau and Wright (2005), we extend previous analyses of that framework in two ways. First, by endogenizing the composition of agents in the market, we analyze the extensive margin (the frequency of trade) and the intensive margin (the quantity exchanged per trade). Second, we study several alternative trading or pricing mechanisms, including bargaining (as in previous studies), but also competitive price taking and price posting. The main contribution here is as follows: In Lagos and Wright (2005), the welfare costs of inflation are found to be considerably higher than in previous estimates. But in Rocheteau and Wright (2005), we show qualitatively that this conclusion can depend critically on the assumed mechanism. Here we ask, *how much?* That is, we study the quantitative effects of inflation under the different mechanisms.

To do this, we present a version of the framework that is simple enough to take to the data, yet general enough to capture some of the key ideas discussed in the relevant literature. One such idea is that the frequency of trade should be endogenous. We use something like the standard matching function from equilibrium search theory to capture the time-consuming nature of trade and how it depends on the endogenous composition of agents in the market.[1] Modeling the extensive margin explicitly is important because inflation may affect it differently than the way it affects output along the intensive margin. As we will see, endogenizing the frequency of trade not only affects the magnitude of the cost of inflation, it also can change its sign—depending

---

[1] In this sense, our framework is similar to much of the search-based labor literature, which relies heavily on composition effects (so-called market tightness and an aggregate matching function). See Pissarides (2000) for a textbook treatment. Some related work in monetary theory is discussed later.

on parameters and the assumed trading mechanism, inflation may actually increase output or welfare, at least over some range.

The three trading and pricing mechanisms we consider have been used before in various contexts. Bilateral bargaining is the assumption most often used in the microfoundations of money in the search tradition since Shi (1995) and Trejos and Wright (1995); we refer to equilibrium in the model with bargaining as *search equilibrium*. Price taking is the standard Walrasian assumption used in monetary theory in, say, the overlapping-generations models of Wallace (1980) and the turnpike models of Townsend (1980); we refer to it as *competitive equilibrium*. By the final mechanism, we mean more than simply price posting, which has been used in monetary models by several authors; we mean the combination of posting and directed search. This combination had not been studied in monetary theory before Rocheteau and Wright (2005), although it has been used in search models of the labor market since Shimer (1996) and Moen (1997). Following that literature, we refer to this model as *competitive search equilibrium*.[2]

We calibrate the model to match standard real and monetary observations and ask how the welfare cost of inflation differs across mechanisms. Our findings are as follows: In competitive search equilibrium with price posting, our estimated welfare cost is similar to previous estimates (Lucas 2000; Cooley and Hansen 1989, 1991); going from 10% to 0% inflation is worth between 0.67% and 1.1% of consumption, depending on the calibration. In search equilibrium with bargaining, the estimated cost can be between 3% and 5%—considerably bigger than what is found in most of the literature, although it is consistent with Lagos and Wright (2005). Further, we find something here that cannot happen in Lagos and Wright (2005) or in the extensions in Rocheteau and Wright (2005): In those models, with bargaining the Friedman rule is always the optimal policy, while this is not necessarily the case here. In competitive equilibrium, the cost of inflation is sensitive to parameter values, but for a benchmark case it tends to be between the estimates of the posting and bargaining models. Also, with price taking, the optimal inflation rate may again exceed the Friedman rule. The result that some inflation with either bargaining or competitive pricing may improve welfare is sensitive to the calibration, but nevertheless interesting. For example, for

---

[2] The essential feature of competitive search equilibrium is that agents get to direct their search to locations posting attractive prices, which induces competition among price setters. Price setting with undirected (purely random) search is a very different equilibrium concept. See Curtis and Wright (2004) for a discussion and citations.

some (perfectly anticipated, long-run) parameters, inflation can have a positive effect on output.[3]

The intuition for our results is as follows. To trade in the decentralized market, buyers must invest by acquiring cash. If the terms of trade are bargained ex post, buyers do not get the full return on their investment—a standard *holdup problem*.[4] This holdup problem reduces the value of money, and this makes trade inefficient along the intensive margin in search equilibrium. By contrast, in competitive equilibrium or competitive search equilibrium, there is no holdup problem, and inflation is less costly on the intensive margin. Along the extensive margin search equilibrium is also inefficient. In principle, inflation can amplify or mitigate this problem, but for our calibration it usually amplifies it. In competitive equilibrium the Friedman rule achieves the efficient outcome along the intensive but not the extensive margin. For some parameters inflation makes things better on the extensive margin and worse on the intensive margin, but the latter effect is second order near the Friedman rule, and the net effect is positive. In competitive search equilibrium, the Friedman rule is efficient on both margins, so inflation is always bad but the effect is second order near the Friedman rule.

It is interesting to compare these results with Shi (1997). In his model a household is composed of a large number of members, and it chooses the fractions to be buyers and sellers each period.[5] Buyers and sellers from different households meet and bargain. In equilibrium the number of sellers may be too high, in which case a deviation from the Friedman rule improves welfare by reducing the seller–buyer ratio. It is not true here that when the number of sellers is too high, a deviation from the Friedman rule necessarily improves welfare. However, we show by example that inflation may improve welfare when the number of sellers is inefficiently low. A difference in the models is that Shi imposes a bargaining procedure that avoids the holdup

---

[3] There is some evidence this may be true, at least for moderate inflation rates (Bullard and Keating 1995).

[4] It is well known in some applications of search theory that the holdup problem vanishes if bargaining power is just right—that is, if the Hosios (1990) condition holds. However, in our model this condition requires buyers to have all of the bargaining power, and this means there will be no sellers in equilibrium, so the market shuts down. Thus, it is *not* possible in general to achieve efficiency on both the intensive and extensive margins here.

[5] The large household assumption allows family members to share money at the end of each trading round, which means that in equilibrium all buyers hold the same amount of money at the start of the next period. One does not need this assumption in the Lagos–Wright framework because individuals have periodic access to centralized markets where they can adjust their cash balances, so we get all buyers to hold the same amount of money in equilibrium without invoking large families.

problem, meaning that the intensive margin is efficient close to the Friedman rule.[6] In fact, our results are closer to those of Shi when we impose competitive price taking. Nevertheless, for some parameters inflation may actually increase output or welfare.

The rest of the paper is organized as follows: Section 2 describes the basic environment. Section 3 presents the different trading and pricing mechanisms. Section 4 analyzes the welfare cost of inflation through a series of calibration experiments. Section 5 concludes.

## 2. THE ENVIRONMENT

Time is discrete and continues forever. Each period is divided into two subperiods, called *day* and *night*. During the day there will be a centralized and frictionless market, while at night trade occurs in more or less decentralized markets, subject to frictions that will be described in detail.[7] In the centralized day market, all agents can produce consumption goods from labor using a linear technology. At night, each agent can do one of two things: He can produce intermediate goods, or he can use these intermediate goods to produce a consumption good at home after the night market has closed. This generates a simple double-coincidence problem in the decentralized market: Some agents can make intermediate goods at night, but they do not have the home technology to use them, while others do have the home technology but cannot produce intermediate goods or anything else to trade for them in the night market.[8]

Assuming a $[0, 1]$ continuum of agents, let $n$ measure those who have the technology for intermediate goods production but not home production, and $1-n$ measure those who have the technology for home production but not intermediate goods production. Because of the way they interact in the decentralized market, we call the former *sellers* and the latter *buyers*. By letting

---

[6] For a comparison of the bargaining solutions in these models and the implications for the optimality of the Friedman rule, see Berentsen and Rocheteau (2003).

[7] The day–night story introduced in Lagos and Wright (2005) is convenient but not at all necessary in this class of models. In Williamson (2006), for example, there are both centralized and decentralized markets running simultaneously each period, with agents subject to random location shocks; that setup is basically the same for most purposes.

[8] The only reason for invoking home production—as opposed to generating a double-coincidence problem by having one type with a direct preference for the goods produced by another type, for instance—is that we want to allow agents to choose their type, and some people seem to find the choice of preference less palatable than the choice of technology. Calling it "home production" matters for little else, except maybe the way we do national income accounting when we calibrate the model.

an agent choose whether to be a seller or a buyer, we endogenize the composition of the decentralized market—that is, the buyer–seller ratio—and therefore the number of trades.[9] We assume that goods are nonstorable. We also assume that buyers in the decentralized market are anonymous; hence, they cannot get credit in the night market because they can default without fear of punishment, and this makes money essential (Kocherlakota 1998; Wallace 2001). Let the quantity of money at $t$ be $M_t > 0$ and assume $M_{t+1} = \gamma M_t$ where $\gamma$ is constant and new money is injected by lump-sum transfers to all agents.

The utility function of an agent within a full day–night period is

(1) $\; \mathcal{U} = U(x) - C(y) + \beta[u(q) - c(l)]$,

where $x$ is consumption and $y$ is production (equal to the labor supply) of the day good, while $q$ is consumption of the home-produced good and $l$ is intermediate goods production (equal to the labor supply) at night. Agents discount between day and night, but not between night and the next day; this is without loss in generality because, as in Rocheteau and Wright (2005), all that matters is the total discount between one day–night period and the next. In any case, because buyers consume home-produced goods but do not produce intermediate goods—while the opposite is true for sellers—and because by a change of notation we can always make home output equal to the input, $q = l$, we may as well write buyers' and sellers' utility functions as follows:

(2) $\; \mathcal{U}^b = U(x) - C(y) + \beta u(q)$

(3) $\; \mathcal{U}^s = U(x) - C(y) + \beta c(q)$.

An assumption that is crucial in terms of tractability, although not crucial in principle if one adopts more sophisticated computational methods, is that utility is linear in day labor: $C(y) = y$. This assumption is what makes the Lagos–Wright framework easy to study analytically, because it implies that all agents of a given type (for example, all buyers) will choose to carry the same amount of money out of the centralized market, independent of their histories. That is, conditional on type, there will be a degenerate distribution of money holdings in the decentralized market. This assumption makes our model similar to some previous well-known inflation studies, such as Cooley and Hansen (1989), as well as many other macro models following Rogerson

---

[9] Again, this is similar to the model in Shi (1997), where households choose the fraction of members to be buyers and sellers. Other methods of introducing extensive margin effects include Li (1995, 1997), Berentsen, Rocheteau, and Shi (2006), and Lagos and Rocheteau (2005), who assume endogenous search intensities, and Rocheteau and Wright (2005), who allow entry on one side of the market. The method used here is slightly easier for calibration purposes.

(1998), which also assume that utility is linear in labor. In terms of the other functions, we assume $U'(x)>0$, $U''(x)<0$, $u'(q)>0$, $u''(q)<0$, $u(0)=c(0)=c'(0)=0$, $c'(q)>0$, $c''(q)>0$, and $c(\bar{q})=u(\bar{q})$ for some $\bar{q}>0$. Let $q^*$ denote the solution to $u'(q^*)=c'(q^*)$ and $x^*$ the solution to $U'(x^*)=C'(x^*)=1$; $q^* \in (0,\bar{q})$ exists by the previous assumptions, and we assume that such an $x^*>0$ also exists.

The final important element of the model is that we assume there are trading frictions in the decentralized market: At night, a buyer gets an opportunity to trade with probability $\alpha_b = \alpha(n)$, and a seller gets an opportunity with probability $\alpha_s = (1-n)\alpha(n)/n$. One can interpret the buyer trading probability $\alpha(n)$ as being derived from an underlying constant returns to scale matching technology, although other interpretations are possible, and $n\alpha_s = (1-n)\alpha_b$ so that one can think of trade as bilateral if so desired. We assume $\alpha'(n)>0$, $\alpha(n)>\alpha'(n)n(1-n)$, $\alpha(n) \leq \min\{1, n/(1-n)\}$, $\alpha(0)=0$, and $\alpha(1)=1$. Let

(4)  $\eta(n) = \dfrac{\alpha'(n)n(1-n)}{\alpha(n)}$

be the contribution of sellers to the trading process. For example, if $\alpha(n)=n$, as in models like Kiyotaki and Wright (1991, 1993), then $\eta(n)=1-n$.[10]

This completes the description of the physical environment, and we now begin to describe what happens. Let $V^b(m)$ and $W^b(m)$ be the value functions of a buyer with $m$ dollars in the night and day market, respectively. Similarly, let $V^s(m)$ and $W^s(m)$ be the value functions for sellers. We omit the time subscript $t$ and shorten $t+1$ to $+1$, etc., in what follows. As we said previously, agents choose to be buyers or sellers of intermediate goods at the beginning of each period (by stationarity, they effectively could choose this once and for all). Therefore, the payoff to an agent with $m$ at the start of the day is

(5)  $W(m) = \max[W^b(m), W^s(m)]$.

The Bellman equation for a buyer in the decentralized night market is

(6)  $V^b(m) = \alpha_b(n)\{u[q(m)]+W_{+1}[m-d(m)]\}+[1-\alpha_b(n)]W_{+1}(m)$,

---

[10] More generally, if $\alpha(n)$ is derived from an underlying matching technology, $\eta$ is the elasticity of this matching function with respect to the measure of sellers. To see this, write the matching function as

$M(b,s)=b\alpha\left(\dfrac{s}{b+s}\right)$,

where $b$ is the measure of buyers and $s$ the measure of sellers. Then $\eta = M_s(b,s)s/M(b,s)$.

where, in general, the quantity of intermediate goods he buys ($q$) and the dollars he spends ($d$) may depend on his money holdings. Given $V^b(m)$, the problem for a buyer in the centralized market is

(7)   $W^b(m) = \max\limits_{\hat{m},x,y}\{U(x)-y+\beta V^b(\hat{m})\}$

(8)   s.t. $x+\phi\hat{m}=y+\phi(m+T)$,

where $\phi$ is the price of money in terms of goods, $T$ is the lump-sum transfer, and $\hat{m}$ is the money taken into the night market. Substituting $y$ from equation (8) into equation (7), we obtain[11]

(9)   $W^b(m) = \max\limits_{\hat{m},x}\{U(x)-x-\phi(\hat{m}-T-m)+\beta V^b(\hat{m})\}$

Several things are clear from equation (9): The maximizing choice of $x$ is $x^*$, where $U'(x^*)=1$; the maximizing choice of $\hat{m}$ is independent of $m$; $W^b$ is linear in $m$ with $W^b_m = \phi$; and if the solution is interior, then $\hat{m}$ satisfies

(10)   $\phi=\beta V^b_m(\hat{m})$.

Condition (10) sets the marginal cost of taking money out of the centralized market equal to the marginal benefit, in terms of what it will do for you in the decentralized market. As long as $V^b$ is strictly concave, $\hat{m}$ is unique. For the alternative specifications of the model discussed later, strict concavity holds under fairly weak conditions, and hence all buyers will choose the same $\hat{m}$.[12] This result is due to the quasi-linearity assumption $C(y)=y$, which, heuristically speaking, eliminates wealth effects on money demand and implies that all agents of a given type will choose the same $\hat{m}$ regardless of the $m$ they bring into the centralized market.

Because sellers do not want to purchase anything in the decentralized night market, they all choose $\hat{m} = 0$ (Rocheteau and Wright 2005). Hence, we ignore the argument of $V^s$ in what follows. Also, given that sellers carry no money at night, each buyer carries $M^b = M/(1-n)$, and the Bellman equation for a seller in the decentralized market becomes

(11)   $V^s=\alpha_s(n)\{-c[q(M^b)]+W_{+1}[d(M^b)]\}+[1-\alpha_s(n)]W_{+1}(0)$,

---

[11] We do not impose nonnegativity on $y$, but after finding an equilibrium one can easily adopt conditions to guarantee $y\geq0$ (Lagos and Wright 2005).

[12] As we will see below, under price taking the strict concavity of $V^b$ is a direct consequence of $u''<0$. See Lagos and Wright (2005) for details under bargaining and Rocheteau and Wright (2005) under price posting.

where $d=d(M^b)$ and $q=q(M^b)$ are the equilibrium terms of trade. The seller's problem in the centralized market is similar to a buyer's problem, and after substituting the budget equation can be written,

$$(12) \quad W^s(m) = \max_x \{U(x) - x + \phi(m+T) + \beta V^s\}.$$

As in the buyer's problem, we again have $x = x^*$, and $W^s$ is again linear in $m$ with $W_m^s = \phi$.

Next, to discuss each agent's choice to be a buyer or a seller of intermediate goods, linearity implies $W^b(m) = \phi m + W^b(0)$ and $W^s(m) = \phi m + W^s(0)$. Therefore, from (5), $W(m) = \phi m + \max[W^b(0), W^s(0)]$. Consequently, the decision to be a buyer or a seller is independent of one's money holdings, and $n$ is determined simply by $W^b(0) = W^s(0)$. Substituting (6) into (9) and (12) into (11), this condition can be reduced to

$$(13) \quad -\phi_{+1} M^b \left( \frac{\phi}{\beta \phi_{+1}} - 1 \right) + \alpha_b(n)[u(q) - \phi_{+1}d] = \alpha_s(n)[\phi_{+1}d - c(q)].$$

This has a simple interpretation: The left side is the expected payoff of being a buyer, and the right side is the expected payoff of being a seller in the decentralized night market. The first term on the left is the cost for buyers of carrying $M^b$ dollars into this market.[13]

To close this section, we define welfare as the utility of a representative agent within a period composed of a night and the following day,

$$(14) \quad W = (1-n)\alpha(n)[u(q) - c(q)] + U(x) - x.$$

On the intensive margin, the first-best allocation requires $x = x^*$ and $q = q^*$, where $U'(x^*) = C'(x^*) = 1$ and $u'(q^*) = c'(q^*)$. On the extensive margin, it requires that we maximize the number of trades, $(1-n)\alpha(n)$, which means

$$(15) \quad (1-n)\alpha'(n) = \alpha(n).$$

If $\alpha(n) = n$, for example, (15) implies $n = 1/2$.[14] In any case, using the definition of $\eta(n)$ in (4), (15) can be expressed generally as

$$(16) \quad n = \eta(n).$$

---

[13] This is easiest to see if we use the fact that in steady state $\phi_{+1} = \phi/\gamma$ and the inflation rate is $\pi = \gamma - 1$. Then defining the nominal interest rate by $1+i = (1+r)(1+\pi)$, the first term is simply $-\phi_{+1}M^b i$, or the real cost of forgone nominal interest.

[14] This is reminiscent of a result in search-based monetary models such as Kiyotaki and Wright (1993), generalized in Rocheteau (2000) and Berentsen (2002), that says efficiency dictates equal numbers of buyers and sellers.

Hence, efficiency implies the fraction of sellers must equal their contribution in the matching process.

## 3. EQUILIBRIUM

Here we consider the following three mechanisms: bargaining, price taking, and price posting. The first we refer to as *search equilibrium*, the second *competitive equilibrium*, and the third *competitive search equilibrium*. We present each in turn.

### 3.1 Search Equilibrium (Bargaining)

We assume that in the decentralized market, as in most search models, agents are matched bilaterally and the terms of trade $(q, d)$ are determined by the generalized Nash bargaining solution

(17)  $\max_{(q,d)} [u(q) - \phi_{+1}d]^{\theta} [-c(q) + \phi_{+1}d]^{1-\theta}$ s.t. $d \leq M^b$,

where $\theta$ is the bargaining power of a buyer.[15] In any monetary equilibrium the constraint $d \leq M^b$ binds in this model; intuitively, it should be clear that you would not bring to the decentralized market money what you do not want to spend (but see Lagos and Wright [2005] for details). Hence, the seller receives $d = M^b$ and produces the quantity that solves the first-order condition for $q$, which we write as $\phi_{+1}M^b = g(q)$, where

(18)  $g(q) = \dfrac{\theta u'(q)c(q) + (1-\theta)c'(q)u(q)}{\theta u'(q) + (1-\theta)c'(q)}$ .

From this we have $q'(m) = \phi_{+1}/g'(q)$.

Now consider the centralized market price $\phi$. From (6), we have

$V_m^b(m) = \alpha_b(n)u'(q)q'(m) + [1 - \alpha_b(n)]\phi_{+1}$, and therefore[16]

(19)  $V_m^b(m) = \left[\alpha_b(n)\dfrac{u'(q)}{g'(q)} + 1 - \alpha_b(n)\right]\phi_{+1}$.

Inserting this into the first-order condition $\phi = \beta V_m^b(M)$ and using the fact that $\phi = \gamma\phi_{+1}$ in steady state, after minor simplification we get

---

[15] To derive this, observe that the surplus (payoff minus threat point) of a buyer is
$u(q) + W_{+1}(m-d) - W_{+1}(m) = u(q) - \phi_{+1}d$, using the linearity of $W$. The surplus of a seller is similar.

[16] For $V^b$ to be strictly concave, we need $u'(q)/g'(q)$ strictly decreasing in $q$. Lagos and Wright (2005) show this will be satisfied if $c(q)$ is linear and $u'(q)$ is log-concave, or if $\theta$ is close to 1.

(20)   $\dfrac{i}{\alpha_b(n)} + 1 = \dfrac{u'(q)}{g'(q)}$ ,

where $i = \dfrac{\gamma-\beta}{\beta}$ is the nominal interest rate defined by $1+i=(1+r)(1+\pi)$, with $r=\beta^{-1}-1$ and $\pi=\gamma-1$ (as is standard, if we open a market for bonds they will not trade in equilibrium, but we can still price them). For future reference, we use $\tilde{q}$ to denote the solution to (20) when $i=0$, and note that $\tilde{q}<q^*$ unless $\theta=1$.

Also, the condition (13) determining the composition of buyers and sellers can be simplified using $\phi_{+1} M^b = g(q)$ to

(21)   $-ig(q)+\alpha_b(n)[u(q)-g(q)]=\alpha_s(n)[g(q)-c(q)]$.

We can now define an equilibrium for this model: In what follows, when we say an "equilibrium," we mean a steady-state monetary equilibrium.

**DEFINITION 1.** A search equilibrium is a pair $(q, n)$ that satisfies (20) and (21).

The existence and uniqueness or multiplicity of equilibrium can be analyzed using methods similar to those used by Rocheteau and Wright (2005) in a different but closely related model. Instead, our goal here is to describe things quantitatively, which we will do in the next section. As a benchmark, however, consider equilibrium at the Friedman rule, $i=0$.[17] From (20) and (21), this implies

(22)   $q_F=\tilde{q}$

(23)   $n_F = \dfrac{(1-\theta)c'(\tilde{q})}{(1-\theta)c'(\tilde{q})+\theta u'(\tilde{q})}$ .

Because (20) implies that $q<\tilde{q}$ for all $i>0$, the Friedman rule maximizes q. If $\theta<1$, we have $\tilde{q}<q^*$; *if* $\theta=1$, we have $n_F=0$. This reflects a tension between the intensive and extensive margins: $q=q^*$ requires giving all the bargaining power to buyers, but then no one chooses to become a seller and the night market shuts down.

Given $q=\tilde{q}$, comparing (16) and (23) we see that $n_F$ coincides with the efficient $n^*$ iff

---

[17] The condition $i=0$ is equivalent to $\gamma=\beta$; in this model there is no difference between nominal interest targeting, money-supply targeting, or inflation targeting. As is standard, it is impossible to set $i<0$ ($\gamma<\beta$) here because monetary equilibrium exists only if $\gamma\geq\beta$.

$$(24) \quad \eta(n_F) = \frac{(1-\theta)c'(\tilde{q})}{(1-\theta)c'(\tilde{q})+\theta u'(\tilde{q})} .$$

This is the familiar Hosios (1990) condition: The measures of buyers and sellers are efficient iff the seller's share of the surplus from matching equals their contribution to the trading process. Given that $\eta$ is independent of $\theta, u$, and $c$, this condition will not hold in general, and it is possible for $n$ to be either too high or too low in equilibrium. Therefore, in theory, having the composition of buyers and sellers endogenous may either exacerbate or mitigate the welfare cost of inflation, and it is even possible that some inflation could improve welfare.

### 3.2 Competitive Equilibrium (Price Taking)

Consider imposing a standard Walrasian mechanism at night: Agents in the intermediate goods market now trade in large groups taking the price as given, and the price adjusts to clear the market. In order to have trading frictions in this setting, we assume that agents need to spend a stochastic amount of time before being able to trade. This idea is clearly related to Lucas and Prescott's (1974) search model, where agents incur a cost to move from one competitive market to another. More precisely, in each period, a buyer gets into the competitive market with a probability of $\alpha_b(n)$, whereas a seller gets in with a probability of $\alpha_s(n)$. Therefore, in each period, only a measure $(1-n)\alpha(n)$ of buyers and sellers trade each night.[18] We still call the night market decentralized, even though it has competitive pricing. Also, as long as agents are anonymous in this market, money will still be essential.

A buyer who gets into the market at night maximizes $u(q^b)-\phi_{+1} pq^b$ subject to $q^b \le \frac{M^b}{p}$, where $p$ is the nominal price of the intermediate good. A seller who gets in maximizes $-c(q^s)+\phi_{+1} pq^s$. The price clears the market, which with equal numbers on each side requires $q^s = q^b = q$. Therefore,

$$(25) \quad c'(q)=p\,\phi_{+1}$$

$$(26) \quad q= \frac{M^b}{p},$$

---

[18] We assume that equal measures of buyers and sellers get into the night market, but of course this does not mean $n=1/2$; $n$ is the total measure of sellers, not all of whom get in. In any case, the assumption that the measures of buyers and sellers who get in are equal is used to make the different trading mechanisms more comparable because, if so desired, one can still think of trade as bilateral even if pricing is Walrasian. As Rocheteau and Wright (2005) show, this can easily be relaxed to allow a different measure of buyers and sellers to get in, although of course trade cannot in general be bilateral.

where we have used the fact that $q^b \leq \frac{M^b}{p}$ is binding in equilibrium (Rocheteau and Wright 2005). In this model,[19]

(27)  $V_m^b (M^b) = \alpha_b (n) u' \left( \frac{M^b}{P} \right) \frac{1}{P} + [1 - \alpha_b (n)] \phi_{+1}.$

Inserting this into $\phi = \beta V_m^b (M^b)$, using (25) and rearranging, we get

(28)  $\dfrac{i}{\alpha_b (n)} + 1 = \dfrac{u'(q)}{c'(q)}.$

Also, (25) and (26) imply that $\phi_{+1} M^b = c'(q)q$, and so (13) reduces to

(29)  $-iqc'(q) + \alpha_b (n) [u(q) - qc'(q)] = \alpha_s (n) [qc'(q) - c(q)].$

**Definition 2.** A competitive equilibrium is a pair $(q, n)$ that satisfies (28) and (29).

The equilibrium conditions are generally different from those in the search equilibrium. Now the Friedman rule implies

(30)  $q_F = q^*$

(31)  $n_F = \dfrac{q^* c'(q^*) - c(q^*)}{u(q^*) - c(q^*)}.$

From (30), $q$ is always efficient at the Friedman rule in competitive equilibrium. This is because when agents are price takers, there is no holdup problem in money demand. From (31), $n_F = 0$ if $c(q)$ is linear because profit is zero, so no one would want to be a seller. Hence, we need $c$ to be nonlinear for this model to be interesting.

Finally, (16) and (31) coincide and $n = n^*$ iff

(32)  $\eta(n_F) = \dfrac{q^* c'(q^*) - c(q^*)}{u(q^*) - c(q^*)}.$

This is again a Hosios condition, but different from the one in search equilibrium. It is again not likely to hold, as it relates the properties of $\eta$ with those of $u$ and $c$. Because the Friedman rule gives $q = q^*$, it is possible that inflation in excess of the Friedman rule could generate a welfare improvement if it moves $n$ in the right direction—which is possible because $n$ could be too big or too small. It is true that inflation also reduces $q$, which is bad along the intensive margin, but the effect on welfare of a change in $q$ is second order near $i = 0$. Hence, it is again possible that some inflation could improve welfare.

---

[19] The strict concavity of $V^b$ requires only $u'' < 0$ here.

### 3.3 Competitive-Search Equilibrium (Posting)

We now consider a price-posting mechanism where the terms of trade are publicly announced and agents can direct their search. There are still trading frictions because agents may or may not get to trade at that price. This corresponds to the notion of competitive-search equilibrium in Moen (1997) and Shimer (1996). Several interpretations of the mechanism have been proposed, and here we adopt the one used by Moen (1997) and Mortensen and Wright (2002). This story is that there are competing *market makers* who can open *submarkets,* where a given submarket is characterized by the terms $(q, d)$ at which agents commit to trade and by the fraction of sellers $(n)$. Obviously, this assumes a certain amount of commitment; this is the essence of posting and competitive search. One could argue whether this type of commitment is reasonable, but we emphasize that logically it does not make money inessential: Committing to the terms of decentralized trade within the period is not the same as committing to the repayment of credit.

The different submarkets are announced at the beginning of each period, and agents can choose to go to any open submarket at night. In each submarket, buyers and sellers are matched bilaterally and at random, and hence get to trade with probabilities $\alpha_b(n)$ and $\alpha_s(n)$, respectively. The sequence of events is as follows: At the beginning of every period, each agent chooses to be a buyer or a seller. Then market makers announce the terms of trade; we find it convenient to write these terms as $(q, z)$ here, where $z = \phi_{+1}d$. Market makers compete to attract buyers and sellers to their submarkets because they charge entry fees, although in equilibrium this fee is zero because there is free entry into market making.[20]

In designing submarkets, market makers effectively maximize the expected utility of buyers, subject to the constraint that they can attract some sellers to their submarket. Let $S$ be the set of active submarkets described by $(q, z, n)$, let $s$ denote an element of $S$, and let $V \equiv \max_{s \in S} \{\alpha_s(n) [-c(q)+z]\}$ be the expected utility of sellers in equilibrium. Then for any active submarket, the problem can be formulated as

$$(33) \quad \max_{(q, z, n)} \{\alpha_b(n)[u(q)-z]-iz\}$$

---

[20] We assume that market makers must charge the same fee of buyers and sellers, because they cannot identify types when they enter (see Faig and Huangfu [2006] for an analysis of the case when the fees can differ). In any case, market makers are not crucial for the competitive-search equilibrium concept; alternatively, one can let buyers or sellers post prices in order to attract potential trading partners (Acemoglu and Shimer 1999).

(34) s.t. $\alpha_s(n)[-c(q)+z]=V$.

Rocheteau and Wright (2005) show that, except for at most a countable number of values for $V$, the solution to this problem is unique, and so all sub-markets are the same in equilibrium.[21] Hence, assume there is only one active submarket.

Rocheteau and Wright (2005) also show that the correspondence $n(V)$ emerging from this program is nonempty and upper hemicontinuous, and any selection from $n(V)$ is decreasing in $V$. Furthermore, the maximum expected utility of the buyer defined by (33) is continuous and decreasing in $V$. This means there is a unique $V$ such that the expected utility of a buyer is equal to the expected utility of a seller, and this determines the equilibrium. Substituting $z$ from (34) into (33) and taking the first-order conditions for $q$ and $n$, we get

(35) $\dfrac{u'(q)}{c'(q)} = 1 + \dfrac{i}{\alpha(n)}.$

(36) $\eta(n)[u(q)-c(q)] = \left\{1 + \dfrac{i}{\alpha(n)}[1-\eta(n)]\right\} \dfrac{nV}{\alpha(n)\,(1-n)},$

where $\eta(n)$ is as defined above. Notice that (35), which determines $q$ for any given $n$, is the same as the equilibrium condition (28) from competitive equilibrium. To derive the equilibrium condition for $n$, substitute $V$ from (34) and $i/\alpha(n)$ from (35) into (36) to obtain

(37) $-c(q)+z = \dfrac{c'(q)\eta(n)}{c'(q)\eta(n)+u'(q)[1-\eta(n)]}\,[u(q)-c(q)].$

From this we see the terms of trade in competitive-search equilibrium coincide with those in search equilibrium when the seller's bargaining power is given by $1-\theta=\eta(n)$. Equivalently, the seller's effective bargaining power (that is, the trading surplus) adjusts to reflect his contribution to the matching process. Hence, $z$ satisfies a condition analogous to (18) where $\theta$ is replaced by $1-\eta$,

(38) $z = f(q,n) = \dfrac{[1-\eta(n)]\,u'(q)c(q)+\eta(n)c'(q)u(q)}{[1-\eta(n)]\,u'(q)+\eta(n)c'(q)}.$

---

[21] When the solution is not unique, buyers and sellers obtain the same expected payoff regardless of the solution chosen by the market maker.

Finally, (13) implies

(39) $-i \times f(q,n) + \alpha_b(n)[u(q)-f(q,n)] = \alpha_s(n)[f(q,n)-c(q)]$ .

**DEFINITION 3.** A competitive-search equilibrium is a pair $(q, n)$ that satisfies (35) and (39).

From (35), the intensive margin is efficient and $q = q^*$ in competitive-search equilibrium iff $i = 0$, as in competitive equilibrium, but generally not search equilibrium. Posting again eliminates the holdup problem in money demand. Furthermore, at $i = 0$ and $q = q^*$ (39) becomes

$$nu(q^*) + (1-n)\, c(q^*) = [1-\eta(n)]c(q^*) + \eta(n)u(q^*) ,$$

which reduces to $n = \eta(n)$. Hence, posting endogenously generates the Hosios condition, and therefore it is also efficient along the extensive margin when $i = 0$. To summarize, the Friedman rule in competitive-search equilibrium generates the first-best allocation, $q=q^*$ and $n=n^*$. A corollary is that any deviation from the Friedman rule must reduce welfare, although for a small deviation the effect is second order.

## 4. QUANTITATIVE ANALYSIS

We now move to the quantitative experiments. While the period length in this model can be anything, and while it may seem that a shorter period makes more sense in terms of the story, for now we set it to a year because we want to use the same methods and compare our results to Lucas (2000). The results are actually quite robust to period length, however, as we will discuss briefly. For now, we set $\beta^{-1} = 1.03$, as in Lucas. The utility function for goods traded in the centralized market is $U(x)-y$, and we use $U(x)=A \ln x$; except for notation, $A \ln x - y$ is exactly what Cooley and Hansen (1989) use. With $U(x)=A \ln x$, notice that $x^* = A$.

The utility function over home-produced goods is

$$u(q) = \frac{(q+b)^{1-a} - b^{1-a}}{1-a} ,$$

where $a > 0$ and $b \in (0,1)$. This generalizes the typical CRRA (constant relative risk aversion) utility function to guarantee that $u(0) = 0$ for any $a$, which is a maintained assumption in the model; for calibration, we actually set $b \approx 0$ so that $u(q)$ is close to the standard CRRA specification. Regarding the disutility of production for sellers of the intermediate input, we take $c(q)=q^\delta/\delta$ with $\delta \geq 1$. We set $\alpha(n) = n$, which is a common specification in search-theoretic models of money.

We now choose the vector of parameters $\Omega=(a, A, \delta, \theta)$. Regarding the bargaining power parameter $\theta$, which is only relevant in search equilibrium, we start with the symmetric case $\theta = 0.5$ and then check to see how varying $\theta$ affects the results. For the other parameters, we follow Lucas (2000) and choose $\Omega$ to match the money-demand data. Thus, we define $L = M/PY = L(i)$, where $P$ is the nominal price level and $Y$ is real output. One can think of this as money demand in the sense that desired real balances $M/P$ are proportional to real spending $Y$, with a factor of proportionality $L(i)$ that depends on the nominal interest rate. We measure $i$ by the short-term commercial paper rate, $Y$ by gross domestic product, $P$ by the GDP deflator, and $M$ by M1, as in Lucas; as he points out, the choice of M1 is somewhat arbitrary, but we use it here to make the analyses comparable. We consider the period 1900–2000, which is just slightly longer than Lucas's sample; for the sake of comparison, we will also consider the shorter period 1959–2000.

In the model, $L$ is constructed as follows: In the decentralized market we measure output by the production of intermediate goods (because home-produced goods are not traded). Nominal output in this market, therefore, is $(1-n)\alpha(n)M^b$. Nominal output in the centralized market is $x^*/\phi_{+1}$. Hence, $PY=(1-n)\alpha(n)M^b+x^*/\phi_{+1}$. Using the fact that $M=(1-n)M^b$, $z=\phi_{+1}M^b$ and $x^* = A$, we have

$$(40) \quad L = \frac{(1-n)z}{A+(1-n)\alpha(n)z}.$$

Because the endogenous variables $z$ and $n$ depend on the nominal interest rate through the equilibrium conditions of the model, (40) defines a relation $L=L(i)$ where $L(i)$ depends on the underlying parameter vector.

We first tried to choose $(a, A, \delta)$ to minimize the squared residuals between $L$ in the data and $L$ in the model. However, numerically we were not able to pin down the parameters precisely; roughly speaking, the routine picks $A$ to adjust the level of $L$ and $(a, \delta)$ to adjust the curvature, and there is more than one combination of $(a, \delta)$ that can generate basically the same curvature. Therefore, we let the data identify $(A, a)$ and set $\delta$ to an arbitrary value. We chose $\delta = 1.1$ so that $c(q)$ is close to linear, and therefore close to the specification for $C(y)$. We cannot take $\delta = 1$ because this implies that sellers earn zero profit, and hence there are no sellers in competitive equilibrium (this is not an issue in search equilibrium or competitive search equilibrium). We will discuss how the value of $\delta$ matters.

We measure the welfare cost of $\pi = \gamma - 1\%$ inflation by asking how much agents would be willing to give up in terms of total consumption to reduce $\gamma$ to 1. Expected utility for an agent given $\gamma$ is measured by $W_\gamma$, defined in

(14). Suppose we reduce $\gamma$ to 1 but also reduce consumption of all goods by a factor $\Delta$. Expected utility becomes

$$W_1(\Delta)=(1-n_1)\,\alpha\,(n_1)[u(q_1\Delta)-c\,(q_1)]+U\,(x^*\Delta)-x^*,$$

where $q_\gamma$ and $n_\gamma$ are the equilibrium values for $n$ and $q$ given $\gamma$. The welfare cost of inflation is the value of $\Delta_1$ that solves $W_1(\Delta)=W_\gamma$ (1). We also report how much consumption agents would be willing to give up to reduce $\gamma$ to $\beta$ (the Friedman rule). The measure $\Delta_F$ is interesting because the Friedman rule is the optimal monetary policy under some of the mechanisms we consider. In the following, we let $\bar{\Delta}_1$ = 100 $(1-\Delta_1)$ and $\bar{\Delta}_F$ =100 $(1-\Delta_F)$ and take as a benchmark $\gamma$ = 1.1; that is, $\bar{\Delta}_1$ is the percentage of total consumption that agents would give up to have 0% instead of 10% inflation, and $\bar{\Delta}_F$ is the percentage they would give up to have the Friedman rule instead of 10% inflation.

### 4.1 Competitive Search Equilibrium

We present our quantitative results in a different order from the way we presented the theory, beginning with competitive search equilibrium, because this mechanism delivers the first-best allocation at the Friedman rule, and hence offers a natural benchmark. When we fit the model to the data, we find that $(a, A)$ = (0.0976, 0.9562). As the upper panels of figure 1 show, this simple procedure generates a very good fit, where the left panel shows the whole sample (1900–2000) and the right panel shows the shorter sample (1959–2000). The lower diagrams show the equilibrium values of $q$ and $n$ as functions of $i$ implied by the fitted parameter values in each case.

At the Friedman rule, in competitive search equilibrium we have $q = 1$ and $n = 0.5$, corresponding to the first-best allocation. We find that a 10% inflation is worth just over 1% of consumption: $\bar{\Delta}_1$ = 1.11 and $\bar{\Delta}_F$ = 1.22. This is a little bigger than most previous estimates—for example, Cooley and Hansen (1989) or Lucas (2000)—but it is in the same ballpark (Lucas reports slightly less than 1%). The results are fairly robust to changes in $\delta$. For example, if we assume that $\delta$ = 1.2, we obtain $(a, A)$ = (0.0156, 0.8766), $\bar{\Delta}_1$ = 1.09, and $\bar{\Delta}_F$ = 1.20. An upper bound is obtained at $\delta$ = 1, which yields $(a, A)$ = 0.1797, 1.0519, $\bar{\Delta}_1$ = 1.13, and $\bar{\Delta}_F$ = 1.25. The cost shrinks when we consider more recent data: Going back to the case $\delta$ = 1.1, if we fit the model to the 1959–2000 data, we find that $(a, A)$ = (0.1946, 1.5987), $\bar{\Delta}_1$ = 0.67, and $\bar{\Delta}_F$ = 0.74.

106 *Guillaume Rocheteau and Randall Wright*

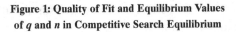

**Figure 1: Quality of Fit and Equilibrium Values**
**of $q$ and $n$ in Competitive Search Equilibrium**

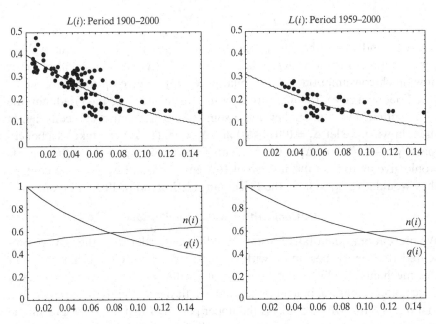

As figure 1 illustrates, the implied parameters from either sample indicate
that an increase in inflation reduces $q$ and increases $n$. To see how this works,
we represent the equilibrium conditions (35) and (39) by the curves $Q$ and $N$
in figure 2. As $i$ increases, $Q$ shifts to the left and $N$ shifts upward; the black
curves correspond to $i=0.03$ and the gray curves to $i=0.13$. In any case, to
summarize, we have seen that competitive search equilibrium generates a
welfare cost of inflation that is very much in line with estimates found in the
previous literature, including Lucas (2000). This is interesting, we believe,
because it shows that introducing frictions in the trading process does not
necessarily raise the cost of inflation if one is willing to adopt a particular
mechanism.

**Figure 2: Competitive Search Equilibriuim**

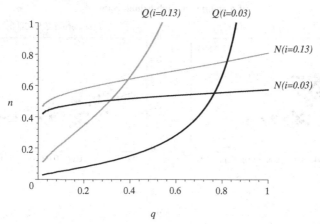

### 4.2 Search Equilibrium

We now move to search equilibrium. As a benchmark, consider symmetric bargaining, $\theta = \frac{1}{2}$. Now when we fit the model $(a, A) = (0.2450, 0.8942)$. For these parameters, a 10% inflation implies $\overline{\Delta}_1 = 3.10$, and $\overline{\Delta}_F = 3.77$. These measures are bigger than those in most of the literature and what we found under competitive search, but similar to what is reported in Lagos and Wright (2005) (which is also a bargaining model, but without extensive margin effects). If we recalibrate to the 1959–2000 data, the results do not change very much: We find that $(a, A) = (0.4064, 1.4671)$, $\Delta_1 = 3.02$ and $\Delta_F = 3.82$. In figure 3, we represent the fit and the equilibrium values of $q$ and $n$ as a function of $i$. Again, the left panel represents the whole sample, 1900–2000, and the right panel represents the shorter sample, 1959–2000.

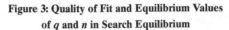

**Figure 3: Quality of Fit and Equilibrium Values
of *q* and *n* in Search Equilibrium**

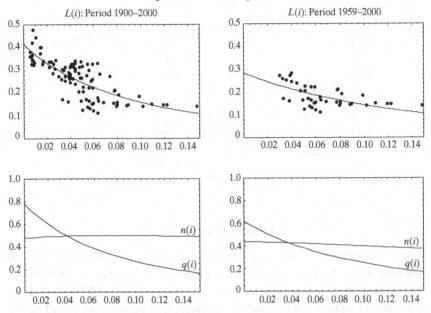

To explain the difference across models, first note that under bargaining there is a holdup problem in money demand. Second, when agents decide to become sellers, they do not internalize the effect of their decisions on the composition of the market and the frequency of trade. These two frictions raise the cost of inflation. Interestingly, $n$ is now nonmonotonic in $i$. This reflects the fact that inflation has two effects on agents' incentives to become sellers. First, it raises the opportunity cost of holding money, which hurts buyers. Second, it reduces $q$, which affects buyers' and sellers' shares of the match surplus. The buyer's share in equilibrium is

$$\frac{\theta u'(q)}{\theta u'(q)+(1-\theta)c'(q)},$$

which is decreasing in $q$. Therefore, as $i$ increases, $q$ decreases, and buyers extract a larger fraction of the gains from trade. This first effect dominates for low values of $i$, while the second dominates for larger values. To illustrate these two effects, we represent (20) and (21) by the curves $Q$ and $N$ in figure 4.

**Figure 4: Equilibrium under Bargaining**

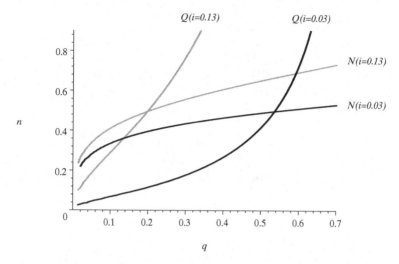

The cost of inflation depends on $\theta$, and a change in bargaining power can mitigate or exacerbate the effects. As $\theta$ gets bigger the holdup problem should be less severe, but the effect on the extensive margin is less obvious. To investigate this, we first vary $\theta$ while keeping $(a, A)$ constant. As table 1 reports, in this case $\overline{\Delta}_F$ decreases with $\theta$, whereas $\Delta_1$ is actually nonmonotonic and, in particular, smaller at $\theta = 0.2$ than $\theta = 0.5$. This is because at $\theta = 0.2$, inflation has a positive effect on the number of trades. However, this positive effect on the extensive margin is outweighed by the negative effect on the intensive margin, and so any inflation is still bad for welfare at $\theta = 0.2$. At $\theta = 0.8$, on the other hand, the positive effect on the extensive margin outweighs the effect on the intensive margin, and a small deviation from the Friedman rule is good for welfare (see figure 5). This happens because when $\theta$ is big, the holdup problem is not too severe. We think it is always interesting to see a model where inflation may be beneficial, simply because the Friedman rule is so robust in monetary economics.[22]

---

[22] As discussed in the introduction, some inflation may also be good in the model of Shi (1997), for different but not unrelated reasons. This contrasts sharply with the model in Rocheteau and Wright (2005), where the extensive margin is captured using free entry by sellers, and we can prove that the Friedman rule is optimal in search equilibrium for any bargaining power.

*Guillaume Rocheteau and Randall Wright*

**Table 1: Equilibrium and Welfare**

| $\theta$ | 0.2 | 0.4 | 0.5 | 0.6 | 0.8 |
|---|---|---|---|---|---|
| $\Delta_1$ | 2.78 | 3.21 | 3.10 | 2.95 | 2.83 |
| $\Delta_F$ | 4.14 | 4.11 | 3.77 | 3.40 | 2.95 |
| $q_{1.1}$ | 0.07 | 0.17 | 0.20 | 0.21 | 0.16 |
| $q_F$ | 0.63 | 0.74 | 0.78 | 0.83 | 0.92 |
| $n_{1.1}$ | 0.75 | 0.58 | 0.49 | 0.40 | 0.20 |
| $n_F$ | 0.77 | 0.57 | 0.48 | 0.38 | 0.19 |

**Figure 5. Welfare Cost of Inflation When $\theta = 0.8$**

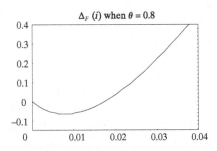

We repeat that in the above calculations, we vary $\theta$ but keep the same $(a, A)$. We can also do the exercise where we refit $(a, A)$ for each value of $\theta$. As table 2 reports, the cost of inflation is now a nonmonotonic function of $\theta$ and tends to be bigger when $\theta$ is further from $1/2$. In all cases shown in table 2, the Friedman rule is the optimal monetary policy. Also, we can show how the extensive margin matters by computing $\Delta_F$ when $n$ is exogenous and equal to its value at the Friedman rule, as shown in table 3. A comparison of tables 2 and 3 shows that having $n$ endogenous mitigates the cost of inflation when $\theta$ is small and exacerbates it when $\theta$ is high. The reasoning is that for low values of $\theta$, inflation has a positive effect on the extensive margin while for high values of $\theta$ it has a negative effect.

**Table 2: Equilibrium and Welfare**

| $\theta$ | 0.2 | 0.4 | 0.5 | 0.6 | 0.8 |
|---|---|---|---|---|---|
| $\Delta_1$ | 7.41 | 4.01 | 3.10 | 2.56 | 4.48 |
| $\Delta_F$ | 10.14 | 5.06 | 3.77 | 2.99 | 5.44 |
| $q_{1.1}$ | 0.08 | 0.17 | 0.20 | 0.22 | 0.16 |
| $q_F$ | 0.55 | 0.73 | 0.78 | 0.81 | 0.78 |
| $n_{1.1}$ | 0.71 | 0.58 | 0.49 | 0.39 | 0.10 |
| $n_F$ | 0.76 | 0.57 | 0.48 | 0.38 | 0.18 |

**Table 3: Welfare Cost of Inflation When $n$ Is Exogenous**

| $\theta$ | 0.2 | 0.4 | 0.5 | 0.6 | 0.8 |
|---|---|---|---|---|---|
| $\Delta_F$ | 10.97 | 5.03 | 3.78 | 3.03 | 3.36 |

Although symmetric bargaining may be a natural benchmark, another way to pick $\theta$ is to choose it to generate a markup, $\mu$ (price over marginal cost), that is consistent with the data. We target $\mu = 1.1$, which is standard following Basu and Fernald (1997). In the model, real marginal cost is $c'(q)$ and nominal marginal cost is $c'(q)/\phi_{+1}$. The price in the decentralized market is $M^b/q$. Therefore, the markup in the decentralized market is $\phi_{+1}M^b/[c'(q)q] = z(q)/[c'(q)q]$. The markup in the centralized market is 1. We aggregate markups using the shares of output produced in each sector. A markup of $\mu = 1.1$ implies $\theta = 0.3$, $(a, A)$, yielding $(0.2615, 0.4964)$, and this yields $\overline{\Delta}_1 = 5.36$ and $\overline{\Delta}_F = 7.03$. One has to interpret this somewhat cautiously, however. If there are other reasons for a positive markup, such as elements of monopolistic competition in the centralized market, one may not want to attribute $\mu = 1.1$ entirely to bargaining in the decentralized market.

To summarize, in the presence of bargaining, the welfare cost of inflation is bigger than what is usually found in studies adhering to the competitive paradigm. Although the exact numbers depend on some details, for the most reasonable calibrations $\overline{\Delta}_1$ is in a range of approximately 3% to 5%. The key feature of the model is the holdup problems, which are common in environments with bargaining. We find that extensive margin effects tend to mitigate the cost of inflation when the bargaining power of buyers is low and exacerbate the cost when it is high. Usually the Friedman rule is the optimal policy, although we find examples where it is not.

### 4.3 Competitive Equilibrium

In this model, the data yield $(a, A) = (0.0983, 1.1144)$.[23] A 10% inflation now implies $\bar{\Delta}_1 = 1.54$ and $\bar{\Delta}_F = 1.65$, which is smaller than the measure we obtained under bargaining but still a bit bigger than typical measures in the literature. In competitive equilibrium, the monetary holdup problem vanishes $(q_F=1)$, which reduces the cost of inflation as compared to search equilibrium. However, the market-clearing price does not internalize the effects on the extensive margin because $n_F = 0.45 < 0.5 = n^*$. This inefficiency explains the relatively higher cost of inflation.

In this case, if we refit the model to the period 1959–2000, the best fit is obtained for $a \approx 0$. When we restrict $a$ to be greater than 0.01, we get $(a, A) = (0.01, 0.2478)$ and $\bar{\Delta}_1 = 0.82$ Again, the estimated cost of inflation is lower in the more recent sample. For these parameter values, a deviation from the Friedman rule is optimal, and welfare is maximized for $i \approx 0.01$. To explain this result, note that for these parameters $n_F = 0.9$. An increase in $i$ above the Friedman rule reduces $n$ and, therefore, raises the number of trades and welfare. While this result is sensitive to the calibration, we think it is interesting that a case where the optimal policy is $i > 0$ can be derived for parameters that are not implausible.

**Figure 6: Quality of Fit and Equilibrium Values
of $q$ and $n$ in Competitive Equilibrium**

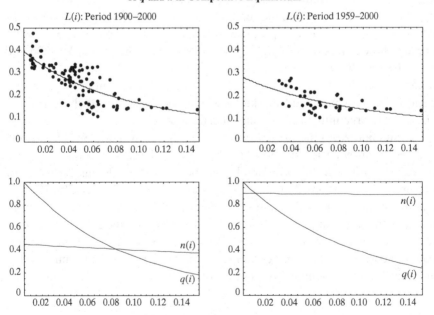

---

[23] This model was somewhat harder to fit to the money-demand data. It seems to work better when we omit one observation—the year 1981—which is a bit of an outlier.

Generally, the results for competitive equilibrium are sensitive to the choice of parameter values.[24] If we keep $(A, a)$ constant but increase $\delta$, we find that a deviation from the Friedman rule is welfare improving for all values of $\delta$ larger than 1.13. For these parameters, $n_F > 0.5$ and a deviation from the Friedman rule brings $n$ closer to $n^*$. Because $q = q^*$ at the Friedman rule, a small change in $q$ has only a second-order effect and the positive welfare effect on $n$ dominates. Furthermore, if $\delta$ is large enough (larger than 1.3), a deviation from the Friedman rule also has a positive effect on output. This is interesting because is some empirical evidence of a positive output effect of inflation for low inflation economies (Bullard and Keating 1995).

To summarize, in competitive equilibrium the welfare cost of inflation is sensitive to parameter values, but under our benchmark calibration it is bigger than usually found in the literature because of the endogenous composition of buyers and sellers. It is smaller than under bargaining, however, because there is no holdup problem on money demand. In some cases, a deviation from the Friedman rule can improve welfare if it happens to raise the number of trades, and it can also increase output for moderate inflation rates.[25]

## 5. CONCLUSION

In this paper we have analyzed inflation in some models with trading frictions. We did this under three alternative trading mechanisms: bargaining, price taking, and price posting. The quantity of output one gets in exchange for money as well as the frequency of trade are endogenous in the model, which allowed us to distinguish the effects of inflation on the intensive and extensive margins. We calibrated parameters to match some simple observations and calculated the welfare cost of inflation under various scenarios.

The main conclusions are as follows. First, the cost of inflation is big under bargaining: Assuming symmetry, eliminating a 10% inflation is worth about 3% of consumption. This is due to the holdup problem in money demand emphasized in Lagos and Wright (2005). That problem is absent under price

---

[24] For example, if $\delta = 1.2$, we get $(a, A) = (0.3915, 1.8643)$ and $\bar{\Delta}_F = 3.96$, and if $\delta = 1.5$, we get $(a, A) = (0.6496, 2.0866)$ and $\bar{\Delta}_F = 9.12$. The point is simply that results are very sensitive to parameter values with this mechanism.

[25] We checked the robustness of our results to the period length by taking the period to be a month. That is, we did not use monthly data, but transformed the data and model into monthly equivalents. Given this, we also fit a more general function $\alpha(n) = \mu n$ to capture the trading frictions because when the period is shorter, it makes more sense to allow $\alpha(n) < 1$ even at $n = 1$. In any case, the results did not change substantially. For example, the competitive search equilibrium model now implies $\bar{\Delta}_F = 1.23$, almost exactly the same as the yearly model, while the search equilibrium model with $\theta = 0.5$ now implies $\bar{\Delta}_F = 2.93$, only slightly smaller than the yearly model.

taking or posting. Under price taking, the cost of inflation can still be big, but for a different reason: The frequency of trade is generally inefficient, and inflation can make this worse. Depending on parameter values, inflation can also raise the frequency of trade, in which case a deviation from the Friedman rule may be optimal. Under price posting, the cost of inflation is close to previous estimates—around 1%.

Several extensions seem worth exploring. First, we endogenized the frequency of trades by allowing agents to choose to be either buyers or sellers. This modeling choice was mainly to make calibration easier. More work remains to be done to see how the results compare to models that capture the extensive margin in other ways, including endogenous search intensity. It would be interesting to introduce other distortions to see how they interact with the effects in our model. Certainly there is a lot more to be done in terms of fitting the model to the data; we followed the simple approach used by Lucas (2000) mainly to facilitate comparison, but this can be considered a preliminary step. Finally, we studied only economies where the distribution of money holdings across buyers is degenerate in equilibrium. It is known that the cost of inflation changes when one considers models that do not have this property, such as Molico (2006). Exploring these extensions is left to future work.

## ACKNOWLEDGMENTS

We thank seminar participants at MIT and the Universities of Chicago, Minnesota, Northwestern, and Pennsylvania. We also thank Boragan Aruoba, James Bullard, Paul Chen, Miguel Faig, Ricardo Lagos, and Shouyong Shi for their input. We are grateful to the Central Bank Institute at the Federal Reserve Bank of Cleveland for research support. Dr. Wright thanks the National Science Foundation and Dr. Rocheteau thanks the faculty of economics and commerce of the Australian National University for their support.

## REFERENCES

Acemoglu, D., and R. Shimer. 1999. Holdups and Efficiency with Search Frictions. *International Economic Review* 40: 827–49.

Basu, S., and J. Fernald. 1997. Returns to Scale in U.S. Production: Estimates and Implications. *Journal of Political Economy* 105: 249–83.

Berentsen, A. 2002. On the Distribution of Money Holdings in a Random-Matching Model. *International Economic Review* 43: 945–54.

Berentsen, A., and G. Rocheteau. 2003. On the Friedman Rule in Search Models with Divisible Money. *Contributions to Macroeconomics* 3. www.bepress.com/bejm/contributions/vol3/iss1/art11.

Berentsen, A., G. Rocheteau, and S. Shi. 2006. Friedman Meets Hosios: Efficiency in Search Models of Money. Forthcoming, *Economic Journal.*

Bullard, J., and J. Keating. 1995. The Long-Run Relationship between Inflation and Output in Postwar Economies. *Journal of Monetary Economics* 36: 477–96.

Cooley, T., and G. Hansen. 1989. The Inflation Tax in a Real Business Cycle Model. *American Economic Review* 79: 733–48.

Cooley, T., and G. Hansen. 1991. The Welfare Costs of Moderate Inflations. *Journal of Money, Credit, and Banking* 23: 483–503.

Curtis, E., and R. Wright. 2004. Price Setting and Price Dispersion in a Monetary Economy; Or, the Law of Two Prices. *Journal of Monetary Economics* 51(8): 1599–1621.

Faig, M., and X. Huangfu. 2006. Competitive Search Equilibrium in Monetary Economies. Forthcoming, *Journal of Economic Theory.*

Hosios, A. 1990. On the Efficiency of Matching and Related Models of Search and Unemployment. *Review of Economic Studies* 57: 279–98.

Kiyotaki, N., and R. Wright. 1991. A Contribution to the Pure Theory of Money. *Journal of Economic Theory* 53: 215–35.

Kiyotaki, N., and R. Wright. 1993. A Search-Theoretic Approach to Monetary Economics. *American Economic Review* 83: 63–77.

Kocherlakota, N. 1998. Money is Memory. *Journal of Economic Theory* 81: 232–51.

Lagos, R., and G. Rocheteau. 2005. Inflation, Output and Welfare. *International Economic Review* 46: 495–522.

Lagos, R., and R. Wright. 2005. A Unified Framework for Monetary Theory and Policy Analysis. *Journal of Political Economy* 113: 463–84.

Li, V. 1995. The Optimal Taxation of Fiat Money in Search Equilibrium. *International Economic Review* 36: 927–42.

Li, V. 1997. The Efficiency of Monetary Exchange in Search Equilibrium. *Journal of Money, Credit, and Banking* 29: 61–72.

Lucas, R. 2000. Inflation and Welfare. *Econometrica* 68: 247–74.

Lucas, R., and E. Prescott. 1974. Equilibrium Search and Unemployment. *Journal of Economic Theory* 7: 188–209.

Moen, E. 1997. Competitive Search Equilibrium. *Journal of Political Economy* 105: 385–411.

Molico, M. 2006. The Distribution of Money and Prices in Search Equilibrium. Forthcoming, *International Economic Review.*

Mortensen, D., and R. Wright. 2002. Competitive Pricing and Efficiency in Search Equilibrium. *International Economic Review* 43: 1–20.

Pissarides, C. 2000. *Equilibrium Unemployment Theory.* 2nd ed. Cambridge, MA: MIT Press:

Rocheteau, G. 2000. La quantité optimale de monnaie dans un modèle avec appariements aléatoires [Inventories, Money Holdings and the Optimal Quantity of Money in a Search Economy]. *Annales d'economie et statistique* 58: 101–42.

Rocheteau, G., and R. Wright. 2005. Money in Search Equilibrium, in Competitive Equilibrium, and in Competitive Search Equilibrium. *Econometrica* 73: 175–202.

Rogerson, R. 1998. Indivisible Labor, Lotteries and Equilibrium. *Journal of Monetary Economics* 21: 3–16.

Shi, S. 1995. Money and Prices: A Model of Search and Bargaining. *Journal of Economic Theory* 67: 467–96.

Shi, S. 1997. A Divisible Search Model of Fiat Money. *Econometrica* 65: 75–102.

Shimer, R. 1996. Contracts in Frictional Labor Market. Unpublished manuscript.

Townsend, R. 1980. Models of Money with Spatially Separated Agents. In *Models of Monetary Economies,* edited by John Kareken and Neil Wallace, 265–303. Minneapolis: Federal Reserve Bank of Minneapolis.

Trejos, A., and R. Wright. 1995. Search, Bargaining, Money, and Prices. *Journal of Political Economy* 103: 118–41.

Wallace, N. 1980. The Overlapping Generations Model of Fiat Money. In *Models of Monetary Economies,* edited by John Kareken and Neil Wallace, 49–82. Minneapolis: Federal Reserve Bank of Minneapolis.

Wallace, N. 2001. Whither Monetary Economics? *International Economic Review* 42: 847–69.

Williamson, Steve. 2006. Search, Limited Participation, and Monetary Policy. Forthcoming, *International Economic Review.*

# Commentary

*James Bullard*

## 1. THE CONVENTIONAL WISDOM OUTLINED BY LUCAS

This fascinating paper by Rocheteau and Wright makes a contribution to the welfare cost of inflation literature. The authors use a version of the search-theoretic approach to monetary economics that emphasizes periodically centralized and decentralized markets. The centralized markets do not require the use of money, but agents may wish to hold money in order to facilitate exchange in the decentralized markets. Models in this class are known for highly stylized abstraction and typically emphasize purely theoretical findings. However, in this paper, the authors attempt a quantitative-theoretic assessment of the welfare cost of inflation under alternative price formation mechanisms.[1] That they were able to do anything like this is what makes the paper fascinating.

The authors make progress by following the approach that Robert Lucas used in his 2000 *Econometrica* article "Inflation and Welfare." That model was also highly stylized, but Lucas was able to use available data over the past century to calibrate the model's implied money demand. He then computed the welfare cost of inflation armed with the calibrated values for key parameters. Rocheteau and Wright use the same procedure and, in fact, keep the analysis completely comparable to Lucas by using nearly the same data and the same definition of a time period, which is one year.

But there is an important difference between Lucas on one hand and Rocheteau and Wright on the other. The difference is that Lucas induces a demand for money by including money as an argument in the utility function,[2] whereas Rocheteau and Wright create a demand for money by introducing frictions into the trading environment in which agents operate. Lucas is perhaps the most prominent among a large group of economists who hold the belief that placing money in the utility function is a convenient fiction that does not cause too much damage when evaluating the merits of a relatively low steady-state rate of inflation against a relatively high steady-state rate of inflation. This group presumably includes many of the large number of economists who are now working on versions of Woodford's (2003) approach to monetary policy analysis. In that literature, money is in the utility function,

---

[1] Quantitative assessments of the welfare cost of inflation have been carried out in several closely related papers in this literature, such as Lagos and Wright (2005).

[2] See Lucas (2000, sec. 3).

if indeed money is in the model at all. Rocheteau and Wright would like to understand whether providing explicit microfoundations for money exposes a flaw in the convenient-fiction argument. They want to know whether a money-demand relation that seemingly looks the same when compared to data might, when tracing back through the equilibrium relationships of the model, have very different implications for household welfare.

A moment's reflection might suggest, a priori, that Rocheteau and Wright will be able to successfully locate a model with explicit microfoundations that has different policy implications when compared to Lucas. This is because, in specifying explicit microfoundations, Rocheteau and Wright have considerable leeway. The number of plausible models that could be written down is large, and it is likely that some will have important quantitative implications for the welfare cost of inflation. The authors have identified at least one such model in this paper; I do not think it was easy to find it. I also think the nature of the friction that causes the departure from Lucas is somewhat surprising, and therefore it provides an important addition to our knowledge in this area. Still, there are a lot of possible models out there. This literature will eventually have to provide microeconomic evidence concerning the frictions that are introduced in order to sort out which ones provide the most compelling theory of pricing and trade in actual decentralized markets. I will not dwell on this point, as I think it is widely understood that any frictions introduced need to be quantitatively appealing. The spirit of the analysis is more of the form: Are there any frictions at all, even ones that may not later pass a data-based test, that could shake the logic of the Lucas argument?

## 2. INTERPRETING THE MAIN FINDINGS

Because there is perhaps not much direct evidence on the nature of actual pricing and trade in decentralized markets—at least not that decisively settles the matter—the authors examine the consequences of several different mechanisms. The heart of the paper shows how the nature of these mechanisms can matter for a policy issue of major consequence. The mechanisms are culled from the recent search-theoretic literature in both monetary theory and labor economics. The first is what might be thought of as the standard, bilateral bargaining that yields what the authors term *search equilibrium*. The second is Walrasian price taking that yields what the authors call *competitive equilibrium*. The third is price posting with directed search, implying what the authors refer to as *competitive search equilibrium*. It turns out that competitive search equilibrium is more comparable to the Lucas analysis than what is here called *competitive equilibrium*. Therefore, for the purposes of simplifying this discussion, I will focus on just two of the three cases—namely, search equilibrium and competitive search equilibrium, which is to say, bargaining versus price posting with directed search.

The innovation in this paper is not just the variety of mechanisms. The authors also endogenize the composition of agents participating in markets so that inflation affects both the frequency of trade, the extensive margin, and the usual quantity exchanged per trade, the intensive margin. This means there are two ways that inflation may distort macroeconomic outcomes, and indeed, a simple way to understand the paper is to consider mechanism–margin pairs. In search equilibrium, trade is inefficient along both margins, and both of these inefficiencies are generally exacerbated by inflation. In competitive search equilibrium, low (Friedman-rule) inflation is efficient on both margins, and inefficiency arises only as inflation increases. This latter case sounds more like the Lucas analysis, and in fact, the authors find that for this mechanism, when comparing 10% versus zero inflation, the consumption-equivalent welfare cost is about 1%. The ratio of 10 percentage points of inflation to 1 percentage point of welfare cost is about what the literature has reported to date and is consistent with Lucas. The key contribution of the paper is actually this particular finding regarding competitive search. The finding that under bargaining, eliminating a 10% inflation has a much larger welfare benefit of about 4% of consumption, was known from Lagos and Wright (2005).

One conclusion might be that the Lucas (2000) money-in-the-utility function approximation is valid if the mechanism is posted pricing with directed search. The authors could be viewed as having identified a mechanism that rationalizes Lucas's convenient fiction in a microfounded model. Furthermore, this mechanism avoids the holdup problem that is at the heart of the large welfare cost associated with the search equilibrium and so might be viewed as more reasonable.

But a different and, in my opinion, better take on this paper is that the "pure money-demand" welfare cost of inflation may be much larger than the profession has thought to date. This take puts more emphasis on the findings associated with search equilibrium and on the authors' efforts to better understand this phenomenon. I was so impressed in looking at the upper left-hand panels of figures 1, 3, and 6 in this paper and comparing them to figures 2 and 3 in Lucas (2000, 251). The figures are not appreciably different in the two papers. Given Lucas's extensive discussion of the area under the demand curve as a reasonable approximation of the welfare cost of inflation—as worked out originally by Bailey (1956)—one cannot help but think that the Rocheteau and Wright model will deliver conclusions similar to Lucas. Yet it does not, at least in some cases. The area under the demand curve is not even remotely the right approximation in these cases.[3] This suggests to me that we have a great deal to learn from models that take the microfoundations of money seriously and that the conventional wisdom that has been handed down on this issue may be badly mistaken.

This is not the first paper to talk about relatively large welfare costs of inflation. What is interesting is that the large cost stems from the frictions that cause agents to value money in exchange. Other large welfare cost papers often bring in new issues. The rate of inflation might be a determinant of the long-run rate of output growth in an endogenous growth model, for instance, so that permanently higher inflation causes permanently lower rates of output growth and therefore has a very large welfare cost. Or tax systems, especially capital taxation, may be poorly indexed to inflation so that changes in inflation alter real tax rates and have substantial welfare costs.[4] These are completely valid, even critical concerns, but they are separate from the pure money–demand component of the welfare cost of inflation.

## References

Bailey, M. 1956. The Welfare Cost of Inflationary Finance. *Journal of Political Economy* 64: 93–110.

Bullard, J., and S. Russell. 2004. How Costly Is Sustained Low Inflation for the U.S. Economy? *Federal Reserve Bank of St. Louis Review* 86(3): 35–67.

Craig, B., and G. Rocheteau. 2005. State-Dependent Pricing, Inflation and Welfare in Search Economies. Working Paper No. 05–04, Federal Reserve Bank of Cleveland. www.clevelandfed.org/research/workpaper/2005/wp0504.pdf.

Lagos, R., and R. Wright. 2005. A Unified Framework for Monetary Theory and Policy Analysis. *Journal of Political Economy* 113(3): 463–84.

Lucas, R. 2000. Inflation and Welfare. *Econometrica* 68: 247–74.

Woodford, M. 2003. *Interest and Prices*. Princeton, NJ: Princeton University Press.

[3] Craig and Rocheteau (2005) provide a more detailed analysis of Bailey's (1956) approximation and its relationship to the findings in this and related papers.

[4] I think this is a major issue. See Bullard and Russell (2004).

# Commentary

*Shouyong Shi*

The welfare cost of inflation has long been a subject of academic research and public debate. Following a long tradition in monetary economics, Guillaume Rocheteau and Randall Wright model the behavior of money demand and reassess the cost of inflation. The general procedure closely follows the one used by Lucas (2000). First, they identify the parameters in the model by fitting the model's velocity into the U.S. data. Then they calculate the welfare cost of inflation as the percentage of steady-state consumption that agents are willing to give up to reduce inflation permanently. The critical difference between this paper and Lucas's is the use of a new class of models. Lucas used the cash-in-advance model and the model of money in the utility function; Rocheteau and Wright use the recently developed search models of money.

The basic structure of the model is as follows: There are two markets that are temporarily separated in each period. A centralized market operates in the day and a decentralized market at night. In the day market, the information about trading is centralized and there is no trading friction; money is not necessary there in principle. Nevertheless, some agents do sell goods for money because they anticipate they will need money in the night market. In the night market, the agents are anonymous, barter is difficult, and money plays an essential role in facilitating the exchange. Rocheteau and Wright investigate three different concepts of equilibrium—or rather, three market structures in the decentralized market. The first is the search structure, in which agents are randomly matched and bargain over the quantities of trade. The second is the competitive structure, in which agents take the price as given and the market clears. The third is the competitive search (directed) structure, where buyers create submarkets and announce the quantities of trade to compete for sellers.

Before summarizing and commenting on the main results of the paper, let me remark on the microfoundation for money in this paper. Why is such a microfoundation important for assessing the cost of inflation? The reason might simply be that it is difficult to understand what the numbers generated by a model mean if the model does not answer the question of why money performs an essential role in the first place.

Another possible contribution of this paper is that it may bring more attention to the quantitative properties of the search models. So far, research in the field has been largely theoretical. A few attempts to calibrate the models have not attracted much attention (Shi 1998; Wang and Shi 2001). For the field to expand, more quantitative works are necessary.

Now, let me turn to the main results of the paper. There are three main results:

1. Inflation above the Friedman rule can be welfare improving in the search structure and the competitive structure, but it can never be so in the competitive search structure.
2. The welfare cost of increasing inflation above zero is the highest in the search structure, lowest in the competitive search structure, and somewhat in between in the competitive structure.
3. The welfare cost of inflation in the search structure is much higher than in conventional monetary models. Agents are willing to give up about 3% of their consumption to reduce steady-state annual inflation from 10% to 0%. In comparison, the number in Lucas (2000) is about 1%.

Result (3) is very interesting. It illustrates that a serious monetary model can generate quite different quantitative results from ad hoc models. The relatively large welfare cost of inflation in result (3) arises from the holdup problem in trade. In particular, a buyer is invested in the past by producing goods to acquire money, but the seller in the current match will ignore the buyer's prior investment and try to exact too much surplus from the buyer. In the equilibrium, the value of money is low and the quantity of goods traded in a match is deficient. Inflation exacerbates the holdup problem by making the value of money deteriorate more quickly between periods.

In comparison, results (1) and (2) are much less surprising. It is well known by now that the Friedman rule can be suboptimal in the search structure because the search externalities are not internalized. It is also well known from the labor search literature that directed search (or competitive search) can internalize the search externalities by endogenously splitting the match surplus between the two sides of the market according to the so-called Hosios (1990) rule. As a result, the Friedman rule is optimal in a directed-search environment.

I have a few questions or suggestions.

First, there is an ambiguity in the measure of the cost of inflation. As Lucas (2000) did, Rocheteau and Wright measure the cost of inflation as the percentage of steady-state consumption that agents are willing to give up to reduce inflation. In Lucas's model, the goods are homogeneous. In the current paper, however, there are two types of goods—goods in the day market and goods in the night market. Rocheteau and Wright choose to measure the cost of inflation as a uniform reduction in consumption of the two goods. This uniform-compensation scheme is questionable because the two goods yield different marginal utilities. A certain amount of reduction in the consumption of one good is not the same as the other good.

To illustrate this point, consider the alternative scheme, which reduces agents' consumption of only one type of good in exchange for a reduction in inflation. Consider a reduction in inflation from an annual rate of 10% to 0% and set the parameters to the values used in the search equilibrium. If inflation is compensated through the consumption of the day goods alone, then agents are willing to give up 3.7% of consumption. This is similar to the 3% obtained under the uniform-compensation scheme. However, if inflation is compensated through the consumption of the night goods alone, then the compensation is 21.7% of consumption. This large number arises because the marginal utility of consuming the night goods is much lower than consuming the day goods. It is not clear which number should be taken as the welfare cost of inflation.

Second, the quantitative results may be sensitive to the matching frequency in the decentralized market. The authors set an agent's matching frequency in the night market to be at most once per period. This is unreasonably low, given that the length of a period is one year. Although one can reinterpret the length of a period to make this matching frequency reasonable, other parameters also need to be adjusted at the same time. Paradoxically, the authors claim the results are robust to the length of a period. This claim is counterintuitive. For what it is worth, the matching frequency embodies the search frictions. If agents could be matched infinitely quickly with each other, the search frictions would be negligible—and so would the holdup problem the authors emphasize for result (3).

To investigate how sensitive the results are to the matching frequency, let us conduct the following exercise. Let $k$ be the number of periods in a year, so that $1/k$ is the length of the period. Maintain the matching technology used in the paper and the assumption that an agent has at most one match per period. Let the discount factor between two adjacent periods be $\beta = 1.03^{1/k}$, so that the annual discount factor is equal to 1.03—the one used in the paper. Set annual velocity of money to 5, which is roughly what the data shows. Then, velocity during a period is $5/k$. Maintain the parameter values $a = 0.2450$, $\delta = 1.1$, and $\theta = 0.5$ that are used in the paper. For each chosen value of $k$, let us compute the model's prediction of velocity and match it to the value $5/k$ in the data. The model's prediction of velocity is

$$n(k) + \frac{A(k)}{z(k)\,[1-n(k)]}.$$

Here, $n(k)$ is the fraction of sellers in the market and $z(k)$ is the (shadow) value of money. Both are endogenous variables that depend on the chosen value of $k$. To perform the match, choose a nominal interest rate during a period, $i^*(k) = 1.042^{1/k} - 1$, which gives a realistic annual interest rate of 4.2%. At the interest rate $i^*(k)$, compute $n(k)$ and $z(k)$ from the model and equate this prediction on velocity to the number $5/k$. This procedure identifies the parameter $A$ as

$$A(k) = [1-n(k)]z(k)\left[\frac{5}{k} - n\ (k)\right].$$

This identification method approximates the one in the paper well. To see how close the two methods are to each other, set $k = 1$. This method yields $A(1) = 0.895$, while the methods in the paper yield $A = 0.8942$.

For each chosen value of $k$, we can identify $A(k)$ and then compute the equilibrium. Let $\Delta_1$ be the uniform reduction in consumption that agents are willing to give in exchange for a reduction of inflation from an annual rate of 10% to 0%—that is, from a rate of $(1.1)^{1/k} - 1$ per period to 0%. Let $\Delta_F$ be the similar compensation for reducing annual inflation from 10% to the Friedman rule. These welfare costs of inflation are listed below:

| $k$ | 1 | 3 | 6 |
|---|---|---|---|
| $\Delta_1$ (percent) | 3.2 | 0.7 | 0.3 |
| $\Delta_F$ (percent) | 3.9 | 0.8 | 0.3 |

When $k = 1$, the results are basically what Rocheteau and Wright have obtained. Now increase $k$ from 1 to 3. The welfare costs fall dramatically from above 3% to below 1%. When $k = 6$, the welfare costs are about 0.3%. This is 10 times less than the result obtained in the paper. I do not think it is unreasonable to think that an agent makes at least six matches in a year. In this regard, the authors have grossly overestimated the welfare cost of inflation.

Should we necessarily take this sensitivity as a bad result? Perhaps not. The sensitivity shows the welfare cost of inflation depends heavily on trading frictions. This is a result one would expect from an analysis that has an explicit microfoundation for money.

What have we learned from the analysis? The most important lesson may be that market structure is important for assessing the welfare cost of inflation. The same trading frictions may generate more pronounced inefficiencies in some market structures than in others. Another lesson may be that, at best, monetary policy alone is a limited solution to an inefficient market structure. To induce the creation of an efficient market structure, one should consider other types of policies. This brings us to the question of how the agents choose to adopt one market structure rather than another. More research is needed to answer this question.

## REFERENCES

Hosios, A. J. 1990. On the Efficiency of Matching and Related Models of Search and Unemployment. *Review of Economic Studies* 57(2): 279–98.

Lucas, R. E., Jr. 2000. Inflation and Welfare. *Econometrica* 68(2): 247–74.

Shi, S. 1998. Search for a Monetary Propagation Mechanism. *Journal of Economic Theory* 81(2): 314–52.

Wang, W., and S. Shi. 2001. The Variability of Velocity of Money in a Search Model. Forthcoming, *Journal of Monetary Economics.*

# 5

## Good versus Bad Deflation:

## Lessons from the Gold Standard Era

*Michael D. Bordo, John Landon-Lane, and Angela Redish*

### 1. INTRODUCTION

Concerns expressed by the Federal Open Market Committee at its meeting in May 2003 that the "balance of risks in the U.S. had shifted in favor of deflation"; similar concerns raised by an International Monetary Fund (IMF) report on deflation (2002) over the risk of deflation in Europe, especially Germany and Switzerland; and the experience of declining price levels in China and Japan have sparked new interest in the subject of deflation. In this paper, we examine the issue from a historical perspective. We focus on the experience of deflation in the late nineteenth century, when most of the countries of the world adhered to the classical gold standard. The period 1880–1914 was characterized by two decades of secular deflation followed by two decades of secular inflation.

The price level experience of the pre-1914 period has considerable resonance for recent concerns over the possibility of deflation's reemergence. Four elements of the earlier experience are relevant to today's environment: (1) Deflation was relatively low (1%–3% in most countries); (2) productivity advance was rapid; (3) the real economy was growing; and (4) the price level was anchored by a credible nominal anchor—adherence to gold convertibility.

Deflation has had a bad rap. Possibly as a consequence of the combination of deflation and depression in the 1930s, deflation is associated with (for some, it connotes) depression. In contrast, a basic tenet of monetary theory— the Friedman rule—suggests that deflation (albeit perfectly anticipated) is an outcome of optimal monetary policy. On the face of it, the evidence from the late nineteenth century was mixed: On one hand, the mild deflation during the period 1870–96 was accompanied by positive growth in many countries; however, growth accelerated during the period of inflation after 1896.

We distinguish between good and bad deflation. In the former case, falling prices may be caused by aggregate supply (possibly driven by technology advances) increasing more rapidly than aggregate demand. In the latter case, declines in aggregate demand outpace any expansion in aggregate supply.

For example, negative money shocks that are nonneutral over a significant period would generate a "bad" deflation. This was the experience in the Great Depression (1929–33) and the recession of 1919–21, and it may be the case in Japan today.[1] There is also a third possibility: the classical case in which deflation—for example, caused by negative money shocks—is neutral, as when monetary neutrality holds.[2]

We focus on the price level and growth experience of the United States, the United Kingdom, and Germany from 1880 to 1913. All three countries adhered to the international gold standard, under which the world price level was determined by the demand and supply of monetary gold, and each member followed the rule of maintaining the convertibility of its national currency into a fixed weight of gold. This meant that the domestic price level was largely determined by international (exogenous) forces.

We proceed by identifying separate supply shocks, money supply shocks, and nonmonetary demand shocks using a Blanchard-Quah methodology. We identify the shocks by imposing long-run restrictions on the impact of the shocks on output and prices and then do a historical decomposition to examine the impact of each shock on output and the price level.[3] We present three sets of empirical results: first, results for each country from estimating a panel over the period 1880–1913; results from estimating a panel over only the deflationary period, 1880–96; and finally, results from the entire period in a model in which gold supply shocks are included as an exogenous variable. Contrasting the first two series of results enables us to discuss the symmetry between the deflationary and inflationary period, whereas in the third set, we separate money supply shocks coming from gold shocks from those coming from intermediation shocks.

---

[1] The traditional explanation for this nonneutrality is nominal rigidities; more recently, balance-sheet effects have also been ascribed an important role (Bernanke 1983).

[2] Many people take issue with the term "good deflation" on the view that any departure from price stability is problematic. An alternative set of terms that we could use is "benign" versus "malignant" deflation or "the good, the bad, and the ugly," which is used by Borio and Filardo (2003). These terms connote productivity-driven deflation, as used by us; low deflation and stagnation, as has been the case in Japan; and the interwar experience.

[3] A similar methodology is followed in Bordo and Redish (2004). The results of the historical decompositions for the money stock, as well as the results from forecast error variance decompositions, are not presented in this paper for space reasons but are available from the authors on request. The results are consistent with those reported in this text.

The paper begins by briefly describing the data and historical environment. We then discuss the empirical methodology to be used. Our empirical analysis is presented in the next three sections, and the final section discusses the results and their implications and limitations.

Focusing on our interest in the deflationary episode, our results, in a nutshell, suggest that the deflation was generated by monetary factors, but these monetary factors do not explain much of the behavior of output. Output was determined by nonmonetary factors, and the deflation was essentially good or neutral.

## 2. THE CONTEXT

Figure 1 illustrates the behavior of the money stock, prices (gross domestic product [GDP] deflators) and real incomes in the three countries over the period 1880–1913. We use broad money (M2) as our measure of money stock, real GDP as our measure of real income, and the GDP deflator as our measure of prices.[4] Although there are differences in the patterns, there are a few common trends: Price levels declined—more so in the United States than elsewhere—over the period 1880 to the mid-1890s and subsequently rose. The money stock rose secularly, the most pronounced rise occurring in Germany, and in the United States, the growth rate increased after 1896. Income levels rose with a slight acceleration in the United States and United Kingdom after the 1890s, but German output growth decelerated (very slightly) from its very rapid post-1870s rate after the mid-1890s.

The period 1880–1913 encompassed a myriad of economic events. Technological changes occurred rapidly, and earlier changes were implemented at the production level. German and U.S. growth outpaced that of England. Early historians described the period before 1896 as a "great depression," but more recent historiography has recast the period as one of deflation without depression (Craig and Fisher 2000). Although there were very severe recessions, particularly in the early 1890s, secularly, incomes rose. Particularly noteworthy is the transmission of business cycles across economies, with all three of our economies experiencing common cycles.[5]

---

[4] Data are available from the authors on request. Sources: United States, Balke and Gordon (1986); United Kingdom, Mitchell (1998); Germany (prices), Sommariva and Tullio (1987); GDP, Mitchell (1998); money, Deutsche Bundesbank (1976). Real output is denominated in 1913 pounds sterling, whereas the nominal money supply is denominated in current pounds sterling. The GDP deflators are used as the price series, and these are based in 1913.

[5] See IMF (2002) and Bergman, Bordo, and Jonung (1998).

**Figure 1. Data for Core Countries**

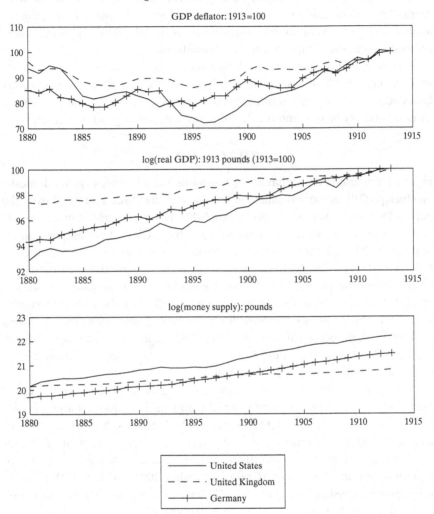

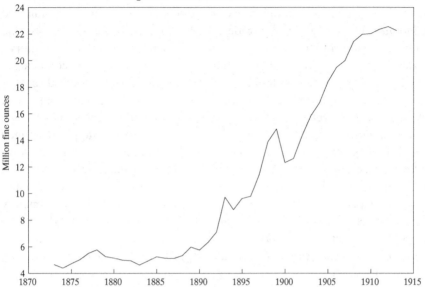

Figure 2. Gold Production, 1873–1913

At the monetary level, there were also secular trends and cyclical fluctuations. The gold standard tied the quantity of money to the stock of gold. Figure 2 shows that world gold production was constant and relatively low from 1870 to 1890, whereas after the early 1890s, it grew. The growth reflected gold discoveries in South Africa as well as in Australia and North America.

### 3. METHODOLOGY

Our empirical analysis is grounded in a model of money supply under the gold standard. The appropriate modeling strategy depends on the time horizon of interest: whether one is interested in the very long run, the long run, or business cycle frequency. We consider the "very long run" to be a period long enough for the quantity of gold mined to respond endogenously to macro-economic variables.[6] Given the short span of data available for our empirical analysis, we do not attempt to capture effects over this period and restrict ourselves to long-run and business cycle frequencies.

---

[6] For example, models in Bordo and Ellson (1985) and Dowd and Chappell (1997) allow the quantity of gold mined to respond endogenously to the price level through investment in refining technologies and exploration. See also Barro (1979) and Rockoff (1984). Rockoff argues that the increased gold production of the late nineteenth century was a response to the incentive of the high real price of gold (i.e., low price level).

The "long run" is defined here as a period over which purchasing power parity holds, and we model a world comprising several gold standard economies linked together by trade in gold, goods, and capital. We assume that in each economy, the quantity of money is a stable function of the country's stock of monetary gold, but the function is allowed to vary across countries to reflect, for example, the existence (or not) of a central bank, required reserve ratios, the degree of monetization, and the nature of the banking system. The world price level is determined by the world demand for money (which is determined by velocity and aggregate income) and the supply of money (which is determined by stocks of gold and the nature of intermediation). Individual economies take the world price level as exogenous. For each country, we identify three shocks that drive the joint behavior of prices, output, and the money stock: a money supply shock, a technology shock, and a nonmonetary demand shock, where the definition of each shock is implicit in the identifying assumptions described as follows.

We model output, prices, and money supply using the following trivariate VAR in differences:

$$(1) \quad \Delta y_t = D_t \alpha + \sum_{j=1}^{p} B_j \Delta y_{t-j} + \varepsilon_t,$$

where $y_t = (price_t, GDP_t, M_t)$ and $D_t$ is a matrix of deterministic variables that includes a constant and possibly a time trend. The data are tested for the presence of a unit root and are differenced to make them stationary.

Underlying the reduced-form specification, equation (1), is a set of structural innovations, $u_t$, that are orthogonal to each other and related to the reduced-form innovations in equation (1) by

$$(2) \quad \varepsilon_t = Cu_t.$$

Our aim is to identify orthogonal shocks, $u_t$, that can be interpreted as an aggregate supply shock, a nominal money supply shock, and a nonmonetary aggregate demand shock. To this end, we identify $C$ by imposing long-run restrictions on the structural impulse response functions implied by (1). These long-run restrictions are imposed using the method described in Blanchard and Quah (1989).

In order to exactly identify $C$ for each country, we need to impose at least three independent long-run restrictions on the impulse-response functions from (1). Our preferred identification is as follows: An aggregate demand shock is assumed to have zero long-run impact on output and prices. That is, the demand shock has no permanent impact on prices or output. We also assume that the aggregate supply shock, in the context of the gold standard, has no permanent impact on prices. That is, the long-run impact of an aggregate supply shock on prices is zero.

This identifying restriction follows from the fact that the countries in our sample were all strictly adhering to the gold standard during the sample period. An aggregate supply shock would initially be expected to lower the price level and increase real output. The decline in the price level would lead, in turn, to a gold inflow through the current account, raising the money supply and price level. Thus, gold flows have the effect of causing price levels, in the absence of further shocks, to return to their original levels.

These three long-run restrictions are enough to exactly identify $C$ and hence to identify the structural shocks, $u_t$. We impose no restrictions on the impact of the third shock. This is the only long-run influence on the price level and can be interpreted as a world price level shock or, in the context of our model, as a money supply shock. The aggregate demand shocks are presumably an aggregate of money demand shocks and temporary spending shocks, which cannot be disentangled. The effect of such an aggregate on prices and output in the short run would depend on its component mix, and we essentially treat this as a reduced-form construct.

A summary of our preferred identifying restrictions is as follows:
- An aggregate supply shock has no long-run impact on prices.
- An aggregate demand shock (combining the impact of velocity and spending shocks) has no long-run impact on either prices or output.
- The long-run (and short-run) impact of a nominal money supply shock on money, output, and prices is unrestricted.

The long-run impact of shocks to $u_t$, the structural innovation vector, is

(3)   $LR = [I - A(1)]^{-1} C$,

where $A(L) = I - A_1 L - \ldots - A_p L^p$ and $A(1) = I - \sum_{j=1}^{p} A_j$. Assuming that the structural innovation vector is ordered as $u_t = (money\ shock_t,\ supply\ shock_t,\ demand\ shock_t)'$ then the long-run impact matrix is

(4)   $LR = \begin{bmatrix} LR_{11} & 0 & 0 \\ LR_{21} & LR_{22} & 0 \\ LR_{31} & LR_{32} & LR_{33} \end{bmatrix}$.

In addition to our preferred identification, there are other possible long-run restrictions that could have been imposed. The most likely additional restriction is money neutrality, which would imply that the long-run impact of a money shock on output is zero. The addition of this long-run restriction leads to the long-run impact matrix

$$(5) \quad LR = \begin{bmatrix} LR_{11} & 0 & 0 \\ 0 & LR_{22} & 0 \\ LR_{31} & LR_{32} & LR_{33} \end{bmatrix}.$$

Clearly, this leads to an overidentified system. Following the method described in Amisano and Giannini (1997), the overidentifying restrictions imposed in equation (5) can be tested. If this extra long-run identification cannot be rejected, it will be imposed. However, we prefer not to impose money neutrality but to allow the data to tell us whether money neutrality holds during this sample. Only then do we impose this additional long-run restriction.

Another possible combination of the four long-run restrictions given in (4) and (5) would be

$$(6) \quad LR = \begin{bmatrix} LR_{11} & LR_{12} & 0 \\ 0 & LR_{22} & 0 \\ LR_{31} & LR_{32} & LR_{33} \end{bmatrix}.$$

In this specification, money neutrality would be imposed and the impact of the supply shock would be unconstrained. The set of constraints given in (6) exactly identifies the structural shocks. If equation (5) is rejected, we are left with a decision on whether to use (4) or (6); we opt for (4) on the basis of the historical context.

Given the small sample size inherent in the data, there are efficiency gains from pooling the data and estimating a panel VAR (PVAR) given by

$$(7) \quad \Delta y_{it} = D_t \, \alpha_i + \sum_{j=1}^{p} B_{ij} \, \Delta y_{it-j} + \varepsilon_{it} \quad \varepsilon_{it} \sim N(0, \Sigma_i).$$

The maintained assumption in this exercise is that the slope coefficient matrices, $B_{ij}$, are common across the countries in the panel. Different growth rates between countries and periods are allowed by permitting the constant terms in each VAR to be different. Also, the variance-covariance matrix of the innovations for each country-specific VAR, $\Sigma_i$, is allowed to differ across countries. This assumption allows for cross-sectional heteroscedasticity in the data. One implication of permitting cross-sectional heteroscedasticity is that individual countries are not constrained to have the same responses to structural shocks. All that is being assumed is that all countries have the same slope coefficient matrices in the reduced-form VAR. Also, the values of the slope coefficients do not change throughout the sample. These two assumptions are tested and the results are reported in tables 1 and 2.

The PVAR in (7) is estimated using the standard, seemingly unrelated regression estimator (SURE) with cross-equation restrictions imposed as defined previously. This allows us to exploit the panel structure and any contemporaneous correlation in shocks between countries to improve the efficiency of our estimates. After estimating our PVAR, we then estimate $C_i$ for each country using the scoring algorithm defined in Amisano and Giannini (1997) and use these estimates to calculate structural impulse response functions for each country. Once we have $C_i$, we are also able to construct the structural shocks implied by equation (2).

The structural impulse response functions isolate the impact of each of our identified shocks on each variable. Because we impose no restrictions on the impact effects of the shocks, we can use consistency between the theoretical predictions for the impact effects and the estimated impulse response functions to make the case that our economic interpretation of the estimated shock is valid. Having made that case, the historical decompositions allow us to do the counterfactual analysis that is inherent in our questions: How would output and prices have evolved if there had been no monetary shocks? What were the relative contributions of money and real shocks to the late-nineteenth-century deflation? These results are reported in the next sections.

## 4. RESULTS—FULL SAMPLE

Prior to estimation, we analyzed the time-series properties of the data and concluded that all the series were $I(1)$, and therefore we estimated the model in first differences. That is, we estimated (7). Information criteria tests suggested that a model with two lags fit the data well (that is, $p = 2$), and we included a trend break in all series in 1896. Given that the series are all nonstationary and that we estimated (7), the break in trend is handled by putting in a dummy variable that takes the value of 0 before 1897 and takes the value of 1 from 1897 until 1913. Clearly, using two lags in (7) would have severely affected the degrees of freedom of the estimator for the individual estimation. Table 1 reports the test of slope parameter equality across the countries in the sample. That is, table 1 reports Wald test results for the test given in (8):

(8)
$$H_0 : B_{ij} = B_{kj} \; \forall i, k \text{ for each } j$$
vs.
$$H_A : B_{ij} \neq B_{kj} \text{ for some } i, k, \text{ and for some } j.$$

This test was performed using data from the whole sample (1880–1913) and for the deflationary sample (1880–96). In both cases, the null hypothesis could not be rejected, so our assumption of similar short-run dynamics across

**Table 1. Test of Parameter Equality across Countries**

|  | Statistic | p value |
|---|---|---|
| Full sample (1880–1913) | 39.27 | .33 |
| Deflationary sample (1880–96) | 35.75 | .48 |
| Gold coefficients (gold) | 9.83 | .63 |

**Table 2. Chow Test of Slope Parameter Stability,**
**1880–96 and 1897–1913**

|  | Statistic | p value |
|---|---|---|
| United States | 21.18 | .270 |
| United Kingdom | 19.92 | .337 |
| Germany | 23.16 | .185 |
| Panel (full sample) | 15.23 | .646 |

**Table 3. Test of Overidentifying Restrictions**

|  | United States | | United Kingdom | | Germany | |
|---|---|---|---|---|---|---|
|  | Statistic | p value | Statistic | p value | Statistic | p value |
| Single equation | 9.19 | 0.003 | 3.53 | 0.061 | 5.18 | 0.025 |
| Panel (full sample) | 33.66 | 0.000 | 14.07 | 0.000 | 0.192 | 0.661 |
| Panel (deflation sample) | 26.28 | 0.000 | 2.97 | 0.085 | 0.057 | 0.811 |

the countries in our panel is not rejected by the data. Given that there appears to be a trend break in 1896, a test was performed to see whether there was also a structural break in the short-run dynamics of the VAR. That is, we tested to see whether the estimates of $B_{ij}$ were significantly different for the two different periods. Results from these tests are reported in table 2. For each country individually and for the panel estimate, there is no evidence of a structural break in the short-run dynamics of the system. Therefore, we account for the break in trend with intercept adjustments only.

Structural impulse response functions were estimated using identifications (4) and (5). The overidentifying restrictions in (5) were tested, and these results can be found in table 3. Estimating (1) using data from each country individually, we see that the overidentifying restrictions are rejected for each country. When we estimate (7) using the panel estimator, we see that neutrality is rejected for the United States and the United Kingdom but not for Germany. Therefore, we do not impose neutrality and use identification (4) to compute the structural impulse response functions.

Structural impulse response functions showing the impact of a 1% shock are reported in figures 3–5. Standard error bands show 90% approximate asymptotic confidence intervals calculated using the method described in Amisano and Giannini (1997).[7] We observe that for all countries, the money supply shock has a large, positive impact on output in the short run and a much smaller (zero for Germany) long-run positive impact. In the United States, prices and the money stock rise proportionately in response to the money shock, though in the other countries, the price effect is larger. In each case, the supply shock is observed to cause a significant temporary decline in prices (recall that the long-run impact is imposed to be zero). In the United States, the long-run income elasticity of money is roughly unitary (that is, the money stock increases proportionately with increases in income), whereas in Germany and the United Kingdom, it is somewhat less than unitary. Consistent with the interpretation as a demand shock, the direction of the impact of the third shock is the same for prices and output. In each case, the shock has a negative short-run impact on prices and output and a positive impact on money stocks, which is consistent with the interpretation that velocity shocks dominated the demand influences.

Historical decompositions for each shock are reported in figures 6–8. The three panels each contain plots of three series: the actual path of the variable; a baseline, which incorporates trends and shocks before the estimated period but none of the shocks during the estimated period; and a line showing the baseline plus the effect of one of the structural shocks. If the third line lies essentially on top of the baseline, then the isolated shock had no effect on the variable, whereas if the third line lies on top of the actual line, it shows that the isolated shock accounts for the behavior of the variable.

**Figure 3. Structural Impulse Response Functions, United States (Full Sample)**

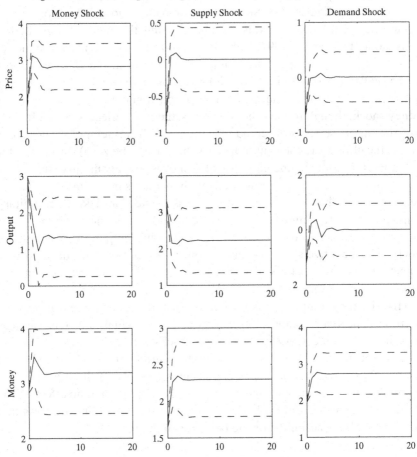

Note: The *y* axis for all impulse response functions is measured in percentage points.

**Figure 4. Structural Impulse Response Functions, United Kingdom (Full Sample)**

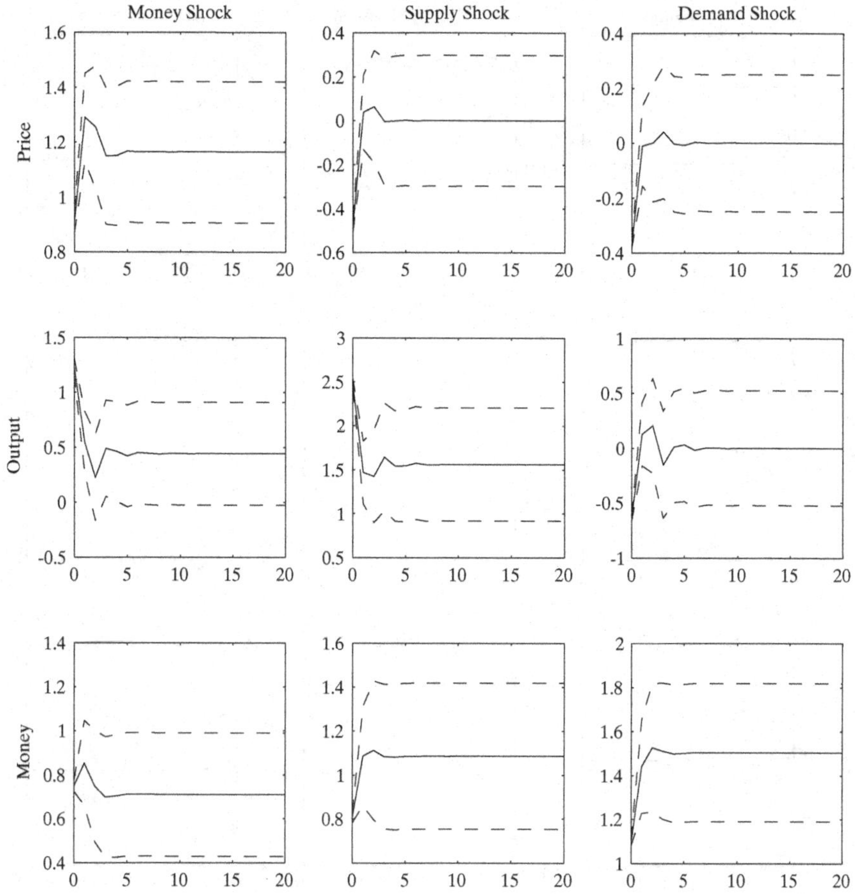

**Figure 5. Structural Impulse Response Functions, Germany (Full Sample)**

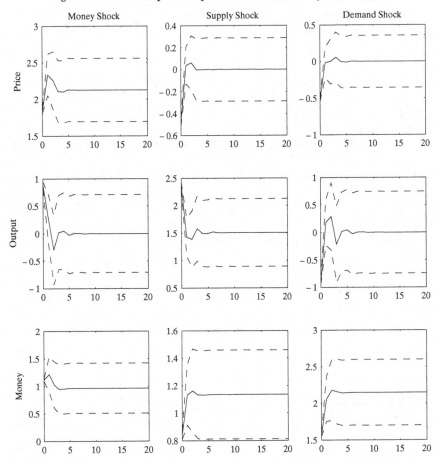

---

In fact, it is probably less than 90% given our small sample size.

**Figure 6A. Historical Decomposition of Prices, United States (Full Sample)**

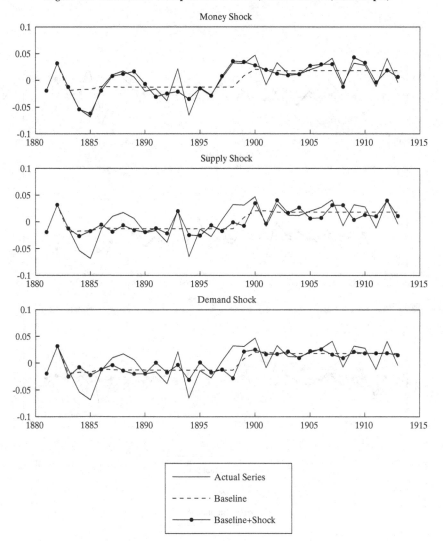

**Figure 6B. Historical Decomposition of Output, United States (Full Sample)**

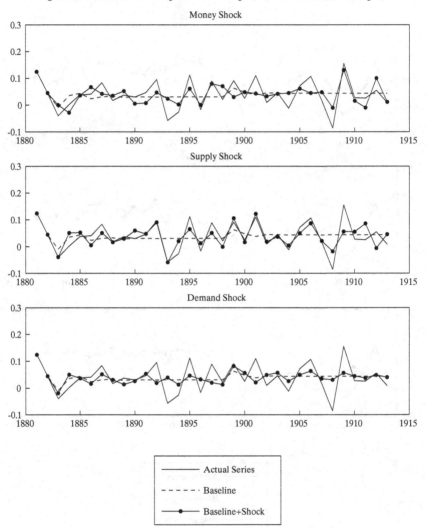

**Figure 7A.  Historical Decomposition of Prices, United Kingdom (Full Sample)**

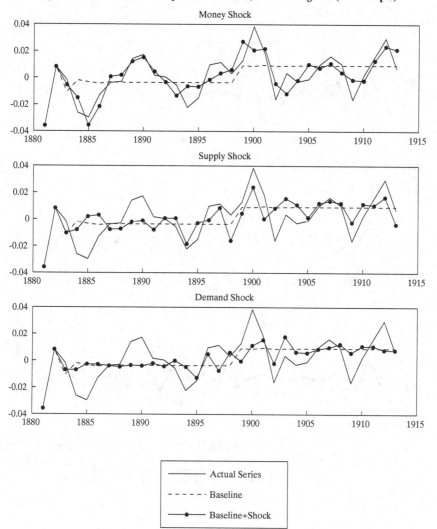

Money Shock

Supply Shock

Demand Shock

——— Actual Series

- - - - Baseline

—●— Baseline+Shock

**Figure 7B. Historical Decomposition of Output, United Kingdom (Full Sample)**

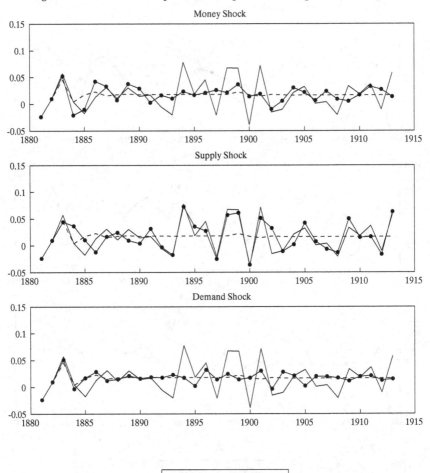

**Figure 8A.  Historical Decomposition of Prices, Germany (Full Sample)**

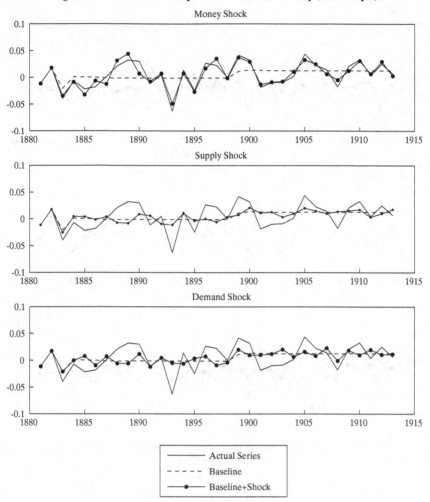

**Figure 8B. Historical Decomposition of Output, Germany (Full Sample)**

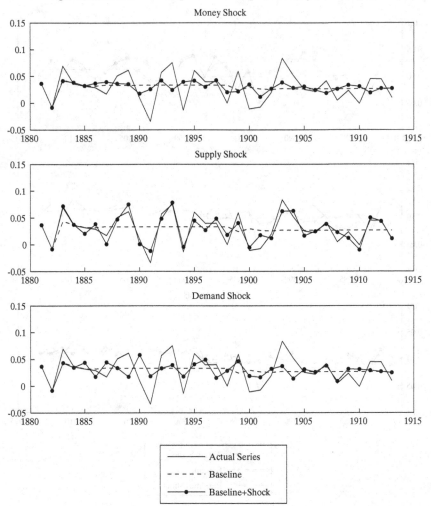

In all three countries, the behavior of the price level is driven by the money shock. That is, although the impulse response functions show that supply shocks have short-run price effects, the quantitative impact of those effects is negligible. More germane to our interests is the behavior of output. In the United Kingdom and Germany, supply shocks explain virtually all output fluctuations. In the United States, supply shocks are the dominant driving force; however, in a number of years, money supply shocks have a noticeable impact. This is consistent with the conventional wisdom that U.S. monetary institutions exacerbated output volatility in these periods. In all countries, the impact of the demand shocks was small.

The estimated structural shocks are shown in figure 9. Consistent with our interpretation of the history of the period, the money supply shocks are correlated across the three countries, as are the supply shocks. The demand shocks are uncorrelated, suggesting that there was a significant idiosyncratic component to the temporary shocks.

Two sensitivity analyses were carried out to check the robustness of our results. First, we replaced M2 with M0, the monetary base, as our measure of money stock. Second, we included dummy variables for 1907 and 1908, a period of financial crisis for the countries in our sample, in the VAR. In both cases, although the magnitudes of the impulse response functions were slightly different, the qualitative results described previously remain. This was the case for the benchmark VAR for the entire period and for the subsequent VAR, in which we added in the world gold stock as an exogenous variable.

## 5. DEFLATIONARY PERIOD RESULTS

Using the panel consisting of the three core countries, a PVAR is estimated using data from the period 1880–96. This period saw a substantial price deflation, as seen in figure 1. Taking into account the first three periods that are lost due to first differencing the data and the two lags used in the PVAR, there are 14 observations for each country. Clearly, this would not be enough data to estimate the VAR for each individual country in the sample. However, in the PVAR, data are pooled from the three countries in the panel so that we have a total of 42 observations at our disposal. The test statistic of the test of slope coefficient equality across countries is 35.75, with a $p$ value of .481 (see table 1). This means that there is no statistical evidence to suggest we cannot pool the data for the deflationary period.

We began by testing for the overidentifying restrictions in (5), and the results are reported in table 3. Similar to the full-sample case, we see that the test is rejected for the United States and is not rejected for Germany. However, for the United Kingdom, the $p$ value is now .08. Using the full sample

**Figure 9. Estimated Structural Shocks from the Panel (Full Sample)**

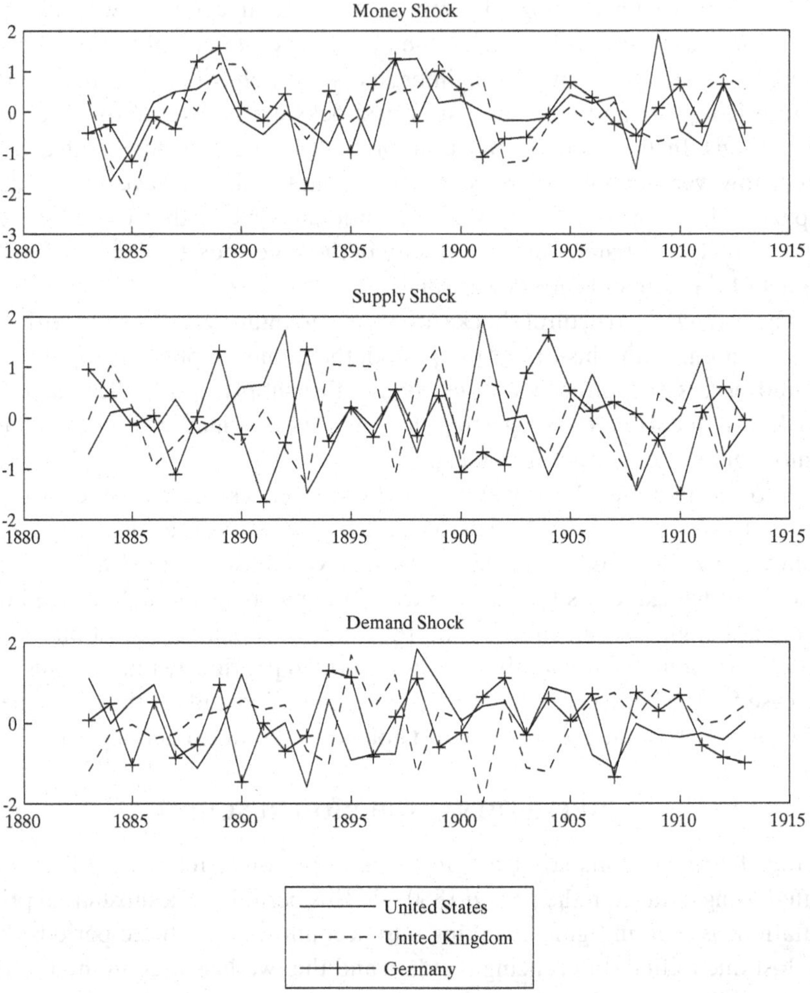

in the PVAR, the $p$ value for the United Kingdom is smaller than .001. Given that the point estimate of the long-run impact of money on output is similar, at about 0.5%, the change in the $p$ value is most likely the result of the smaller sample size, and hence larger standard errors, rather than any difference for the United Kingdom in the deflationary period. Therefore, we proceeded by estimating the model without monetary neutrality (that is, the model of equation [4]). Figures 10–12 report the structural impulse response functions for each country.

**Figure 10. Structural Impulse Response Function, United States (Deflationary Sample)**

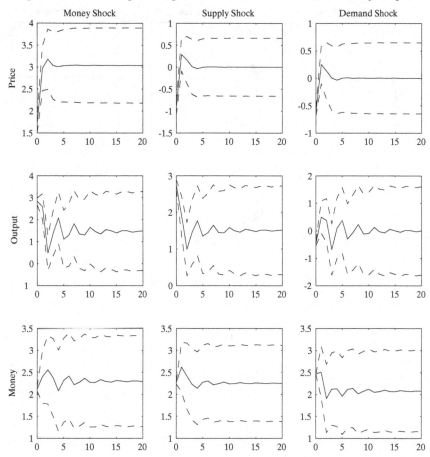

**Figure 11. Structural Impulse Response Function, United Kingdom (Deflationary Sample)**

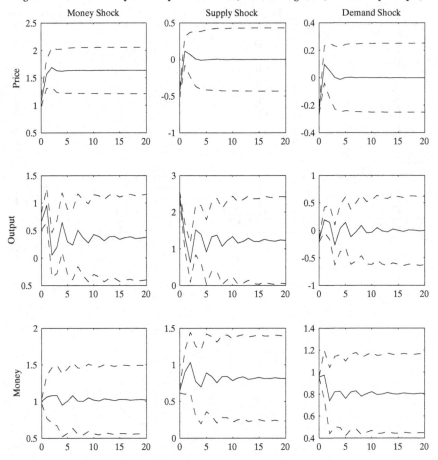

**Figure 12. Structural Impulse Response Function, Germany (Deflationary Sample)**

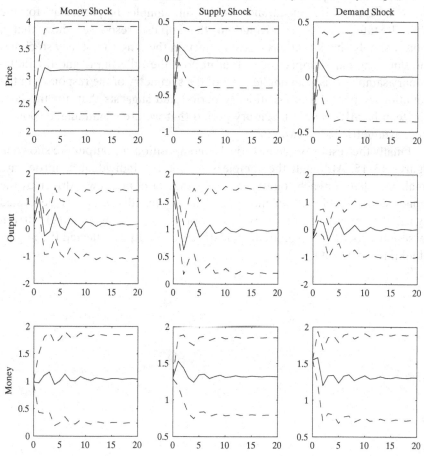

Overall, the impulse response functions for the deflationary period have the same qualitative appearance as the full sample. In particular, for the United States and United Kingdom, the impulse responses show that a money supply shock that has a given effect on the long-run money stock has the same estimated impact on output in both the full sample and the deflationary sample. This is an implicit test of the symmetry of the responses in the deflationary period and inflationary period and suggests that, for the late-nineteenth/early-twentieth-century period that we are examining, responses were symmetric in the two eras.

Finally the results of the historical decompositions of output are shown in figures 13–15. Although the sample sizes for the individual countries are small, it is clear for each country that the behavior of prices was driven by the money shock. That is, the deflation of the late nineteenth century was generated by negative monetary shocks. The behavior of output is again largely driven by supply shocks, although in the mid-1880s, U.S. output reflected the impact of all three types of shocks.

**Figure 13A. Historical Decomposition of Prices, United States (Deflationary Sample)**

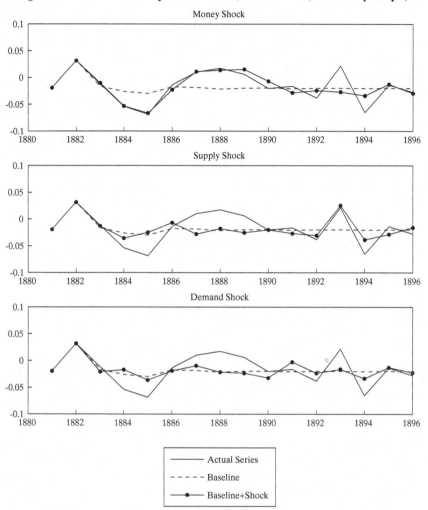

**Figure 13B. Historical Decomposition of Output, United States (Deflationary Sample)**

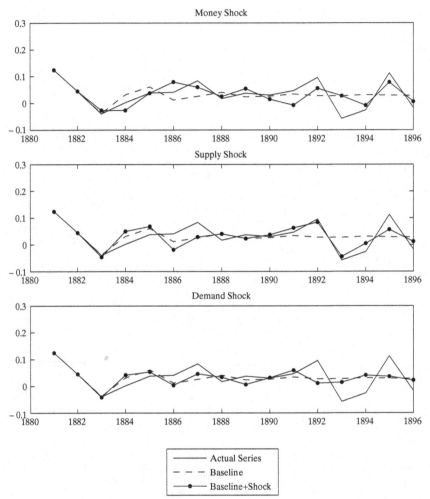

**Figure 14A. Historical Decomposition of Prices, United States (Deflationary Sample)**

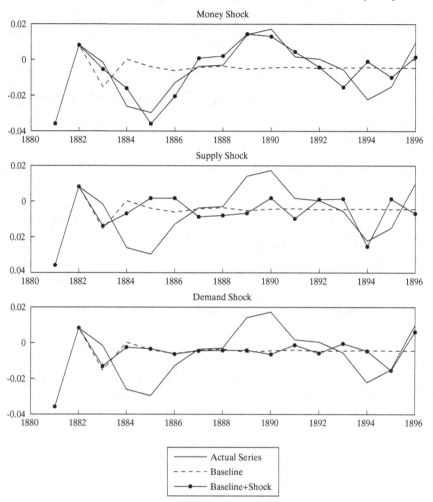

Actual Series
Baseline
Baseline+Shock

**Figure 14B. Historical Decomposition of Output, United Kingdom (Deflationary Sample)**

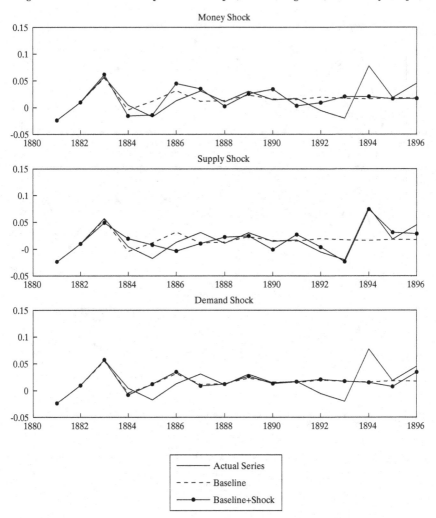

**Figure 15A. Historical Decomposition of Prices, Germany (Deflationary Sample)**

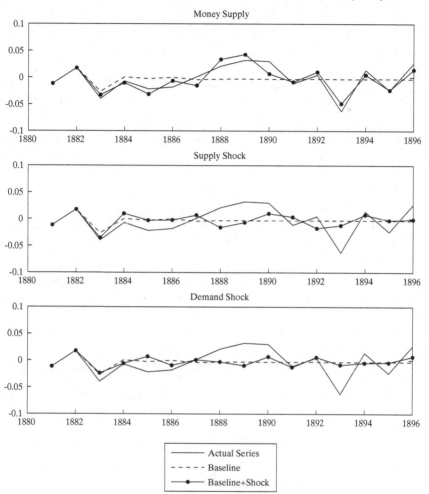

**Figure 15B.  Historical Decomposition of Output, Germany (Deflationary Sample)**

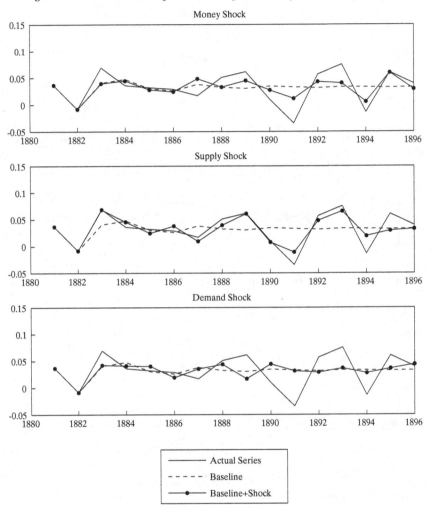

## 6. RESULTS FOR THE FULL PERIOD WITH EXOGENOUS GOLD SHOCKS

Our preferred identification, (5), is driven by the fact that during the period of our sample, the countries in our panel were all on the gold standard. We are therefore interested in knowing what role, if any, gold shocks played during this period. The model th at is estimated is

$$(9) \quad \Delta y_{it} = \alpha_{i0} + \alpha_{i1} D_{1896t} + \sum_{j=1}^{p} B_j \Delta y_{it-j} + \sum_{k=0}^{m} \gamma_k \Delta Gold_{t-k} + \varepsilon_{it},$$

where $Gold_t$ is the total world gold stock.[8] In this specification, gold is completely exogenous to the system. As we noted in section 3, at very long horizons, the world gold stock may be endogenous, but given the time span of our data, exogeneity is a reasonable assumption. Table 4 shows the results of a Hausman-type test for exogeneity. For all countries and all variables, we cannot reject the hypothesis that gold is exogenous to our variables.[9] A panel VAR is estimated using (9) with slope coefficients, $B_j$, and the impact coefficients of gold, $\gamma_j$, constrained to be equal across countries. Table 1 contains the results of the Wald test that gauges whether the coefficients on gold in (9) are common across the countries in the panel. The reported $p$ value for this test is .63, so the hypothesis that the gold coefficients are common across countries cannot be rejected.

**Table 4. Tests of Exogeneity of Gold**

| Dependent variable | United States Statistic | United States $p$ value | United Kingdom Statistic | United Kingdom $p$ value | Germany Statistic | Germany $p$ value |
|---|---|---|---|---|---|---|
| Price | 0.105 | 0.75 | 0.301 | 0.58 | 0.706 | 0.40 |
| Output | 0.108 | 0.74 | 0.018 | 0.89 | 0.483 | 0.49 |
| Money | 0.002 | 0.97 | 0.001 | 0.99 | 0.003 | 0.95 |

---

[8] Gold data are from the U.S. Gold Commission (1982), volume I, table SC-6.

[9] The Hausman test is really a test of whether ordinary least squares provide consistent estimates of (12). To conduct the Hausman test, we used $\Delta gold_{t-2}$ as the instrument for $\Delta gold_t$.

Figures 16–18 depict the structural impulse response functions calculated using the estimates of (9). These figures are qualitatively similar to the previous impulse response functions calculated when gold was not included into the VAR.[10] Figures 20–22 depict the historical decompositions. Again, we see that money contributes most to prices and the supply shock explains most of the observed variation in output. It is interesting to note that gold does not play an important role in the observed variation of prices and output.

We have also reestimated the model for the deflation sample alone (1880–96) but for space reasons do not include the figures here.[11] The historical decompositions for prices show that, as in the case without gold, supply shocks and the nonmonetary demand shock contribute little to the behavior of prices. But now, the price level is explained in part by gold shocks and in part by domestic money shocks. Gold shocks, however, explain little of the output fluctuations.

Figure 19 shows the impact of a 1% increase in gold supply on prices, output, and money supply. We see that the long-run impact of this gold shock is what we would expect under the gold standard. That is, the long-run impact of a 1% increase in gold supply is a 1% increase in prices, a 1% increase in the money supply, and no increase in output. This result suggests that our assumptions based on the gold standard are not unrealistic.

However, there is a puzzling result: The initial impact of the gold shock on prices is negative. One reason for this may be that the gold shocks that we are observing could be price led rather than being exogenous to the system. That is, lower prices lead to gold flows that appear in the data as positive gold supply shocks. This last observation would suggest that gold is not entirely exogenous and the possible endogeneity between price and gold should be modeled explicitly. How best to model this endogeneity is a difficult question, as gold supply probably has an endogenous component and an exogenous component. This problem is left for future research.

---

[10] The only qualitative difference is that the monetary shock has a small long-run negative impact on German output. When we estimate over only the deflationary sample, this result is overturned.

[11] Figures are available from the authors.

**Figure 16.  Structural Impulse Response Function, United States (Full Sample with Gold)**

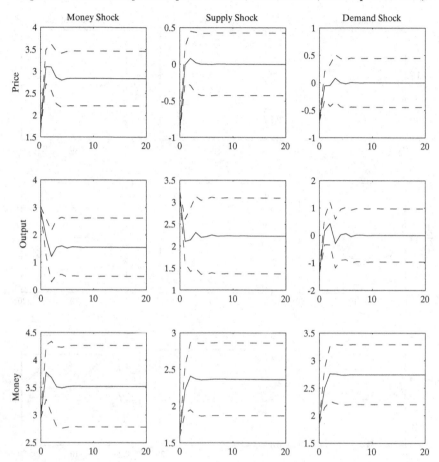

**Figure 17. Structural Impulse Response Function, United Kingdom (Full Sample with Gold)**

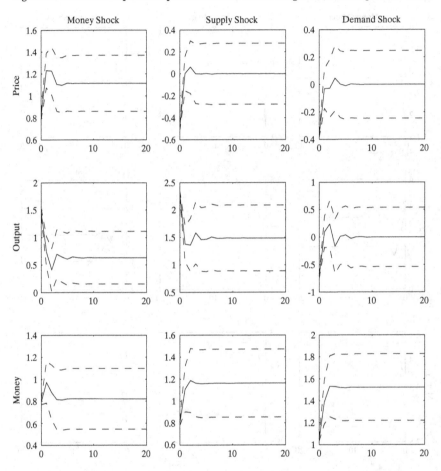

**Figure 18. Structural Impulse Response Function, Germany (Full Sample with Gold)**

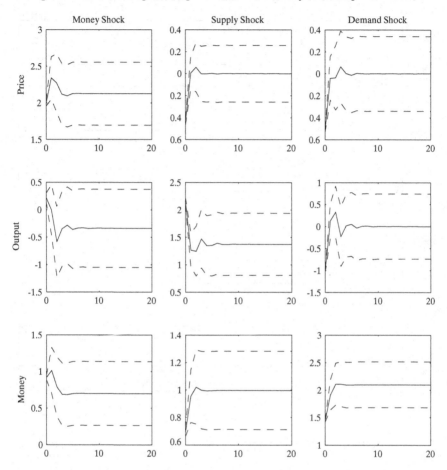

**Figure 19. Impulse Response to a 1% Increase in Gold**

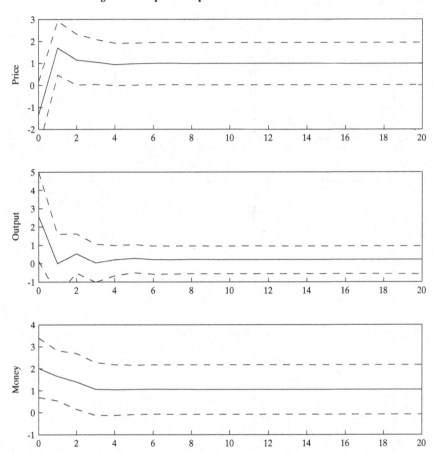

**Figure 20A.  Historical Decomposition of Price, United States (Full Sample with Gold)**

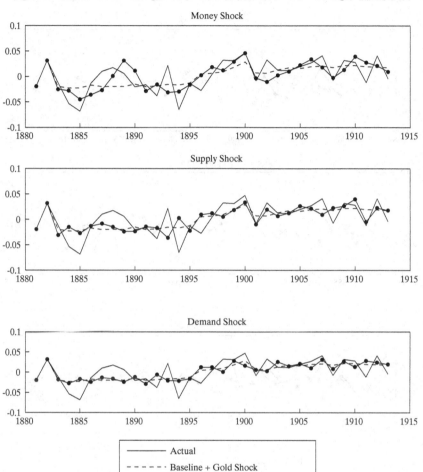

**Figure 20B.  Historical Decomposition of Output, United States (Full Sample with Gold)**

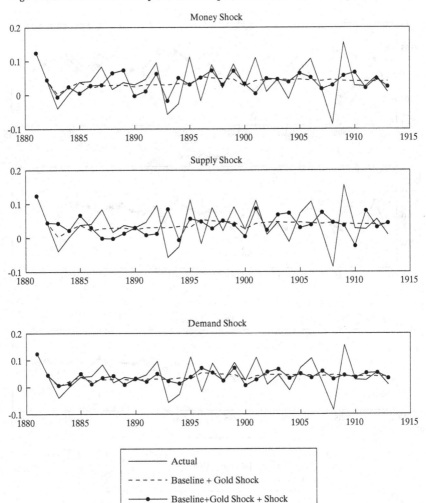

**Figure 21A. Historical Decomposition of Price, United Kingdom (Full Sample with Gold)**

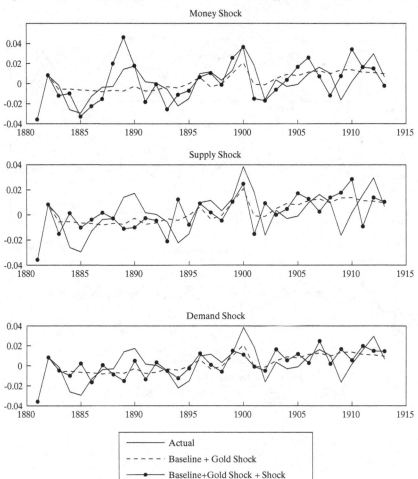

**Figure 21B. Historical Decomposition of Output, United Kingdom (Full Sample with Gold)**

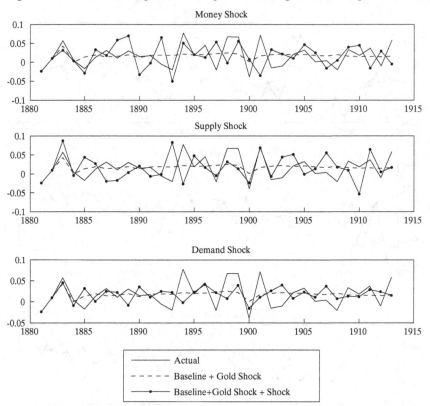

**Figure 22A. Historical Decomposition of Price, Germany (Full Sample with Gold)**

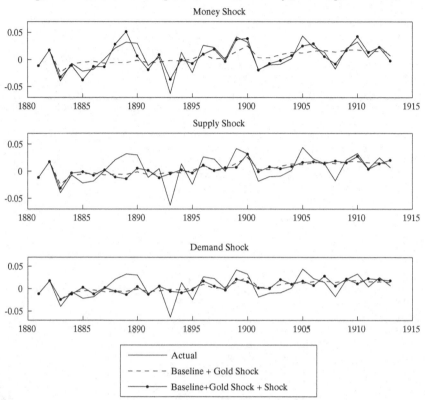

**Figure 22B. Historical Decomposition of Output, Germany (Full Sample with Gold)**

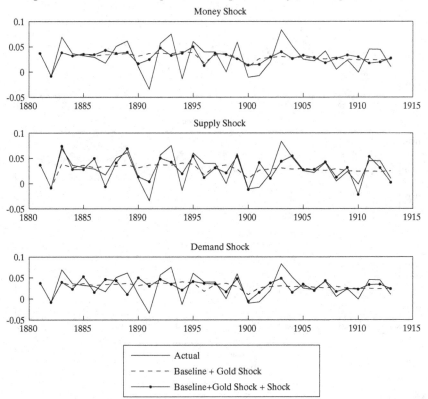

## 7. CONCLUSIONS

Inflation rates around the globe fell from historically high levels in the 1970s and 1980s to numbers close to zero as the twentieth century ended. Indeed, some countries have experienced actual deflation. Yet output growth rates remain positive. Not since the turn of the nineteenth century have economies experienced such low inflation associated with nonnegative growth, and it seems natural to turn to that period to learn about macro behavior in low inflation or possibly deflationary environments.

Deflation can reflect the impact of positive aggregate supply shocks (in the absence of offsetting positive demand shocks) or negative demand shocks. In the latter case, if the aggregate supply curve is nonvertical, the deflation will be "bad" in that it will be accompanied by negative output effects.

Our results show that the deflation of the late-nineteenth-century gold standard era in three key countries reflected both positive aggregate supply and negative money supply shocks. Yet the negative money shock had only a minor effect on output. This, we posit, is because the aggregate supply curve was very steep in the short run. Thus, our empirical evidence suggests that deflation in the late nineteenth century was primarily good.

Important issues for today's environment arise from our findings. We need to be clear about what is different between the late-nineteenth-century environment and that of the twentieth and twenty-first centuries. First, the historical era we analyze was the classical gold standard regime, under which all three countries were linked together by a common adherence to the gold standard convertibility rule, and all faced a common money shock—the vagaries of the gold standard.

Second, aggregate supply seems to have been an important source of the shocks that we identify. This is likely in contrast to the other major deflationary episodes of the twentieth century, including 1920–21, 1929–33, and Japan in the 1990s, which many observers posit reflected the consequences of severe monetary contraction.[12] Today's environment in the United States, Canada, and the European Union may indeed be closer to the pre-1914 era than the earlier twentieth-century episodes.

Third, the short-run aggregate supply seems to have been very steep before 1913. This means that negative demand shocks did not have much of a contractionary bite. This result is in sharp contrast to the experience of 1929–33. Many attribute the catastrophic declines of output in the face of monetary contraction then to the presence of nominal rigidities, in particular sticky wages (Bordo, Erceg, and Evans 2000).

---

[12] For a contrary view, see Kehoe and Prescott (2002).

Our analysis has not dealt with many important issues that resonate in today's policy debate over what to do about the specter of deflation. These include the zero nominal bound problem—that very low inflation that comes from reducing nominal interest rates makes it difficult to conduct monetary policy by conventional means (Orphanides 2001). In contrast to today, in the pre-1914 era, little emphasis was placed by the policymakers in countries such as the United Kingdom and Germany, which had central banks, in using monetary policy to stimulate the real economy. Hence, the zero nominal bound was not viewed as a problem.

We also do not explicitly distinguish between the effects of actual versus expected price-level changes. It is unexpected deflation that produces negative consequences. However, the steep slope of the aggregate supply curve revealed in our work suggests that price-level changes were largely anticipated. We also do not consider the efficiency aspects of deflation. According to Friedman (1969), the optimum holding of money would occur at a rate of deflation equal to the long-run growth rate of real output.

Finally, although we find that pre-1914 deflation was primarily of the good variety, that does not mean that people *felt* good about it. The common perception of the 1880s and 1890s in all three countries was that deflation was depressing. This, in turn, may reflect the fact that deflation was largely unanticipated. It may also have reflected money illusion.[13] This was reflected in labor strife and political turbulence. This perception can be seen in the views of U.S. farmers, who believed that the terms of trade had turned against them, and workers in all three countries, who did not view falling money wages as being compensated by even more rapidly falling commodity prices. It is doubtful that a *true* deflation today would be any less unpopular.

### ACKNOWLEDGMENTS

For helpful comments, we thank Tam Bayoumi, Jon Faust, Dale Henderson, Ulrich Kohli, Andy Levin, Marc Wiedenmeir, and our discussants, Larry Christiano and Francois Velde. For able research assistance, we thank Sonal Dhingra.

### REFERENCES

[13] Friedman and Schwartz (1963, 41–42) compare the U.S. experience of the 1870s, when money growth exceeded the growth of the labor force but not the growth of real output (so that nominal wages were rising), with the 1880s, when money growth was less than the growth of the labor force and real growth and money wages declined. They then relate these facts to the increase in labor unrest and agitation over the monetary standard.

Amisano, G., and C. Giannini. 1997. *Topics in Structural VAR Econometrics.* Berlin: Springer-Verlag.

Balke, N., and R. Gordon. 1986. Historical Data. In *The American Business Cycle,* ed. Robert J. Gordon. Chicago: University of Chicago Press.

Barro, R. 1979. Money and the Price Level under the Gold Standard. *Economic Journal* 89: 13–33.

Bergman, U., M. Bordo, and L. Jonung. 1998. Historical Evidence on Business Cycles: The International Experience. In *Beyond Shocks: What Causes Business Cycles?* ed. J. Fuhrer and S. Schuh, 65–113. Boston: Federal Reserve Bank of Boston.

Bernanke, B. 1983. Nonmonetary Effects of the Financial Crisis in Propagation of the Great Depression. *American Economic Review* 73(3): 257–76.

Blanchard, O. J., and D. Quah. 1989. The Dynamic Effect of Aggregate Demand and Supply Disturbances. *American Economic Review* 79(4): 655–73.

Bordo, M. 1981. The Classical Gold Standard: Some Lessons for Today. *Federal Reserve Bank of St. Louis Review* 63(5): 2–17.

Bordo, M., and R. W. Ellson. 1985. A Model of the Classical Gold Standard with Depletion. *Journal of Monetary Economics* 16: 109–20.

Bordo, M., and A. Redish. 2004. Is Deflation Depressing? In *Deflation: Current and Historical Perspectives,* ed. Richard Burdekin and Pierre Siklos. New York: Cambridge University Press.

Bordo, M., C. Erceg, and C. Evans. 2000. Money, Sticky Wages and the Great Depression. *American Economic Review* 90(5): 1447–63.

Borio, C., and A. J. Filardo. 2003. Back to the Future? Assessing the Threat of Deflation. Working Paper No. 152, Bank for International Settlements.

Canova, F., and M. Ciccarealli. 1999. Forecasting and Turning Point Predictions in a Bayesian Panel VAR Model. Unpublished manuscript.

Craig, L., and D. Fisher. 2000. *The European Macroeconomy: Growth and Integration,* 1500–1913. London: Edward Elgar.

Deutsche Bundesbank. 1976. *Deutsches Geld-und Bankwesen in Zahlen, 1876–1975.* Frankfurt: Herausgeber Deutsche Bundesbank.

Dowd, K., and D. Chappell. 1997. A Simple Model of the Gold Standard. *Journal of Money, Credit, and Banking* 29(1): 94–105.

Friedman, M. 1969. The Optimum Quantity of Money. In *The Optimum Quantity of Money and Other Essays,* ed. Milton Friedman. Chicago: Aldine.

Friedman, M., and A. Schwartz. 1963. *A Monetary History of the United States, 1867–1960.* Princeton, NJ: Princeton University Press.

Holtz-Eakin, D., W. Newey, and H. S. Rosen. 1988. Estimating Vector Autoregressions with Panel Data. *Econometrica* 56(6): 1371–95.

International Monetary Fund (IMF). 2002. *World Economic Outlook*. Washington, DC: IMF.

Kehoe, T., and E. Prescott. 2002. Great Depressions of the 20th Century. *Review of Economic Dynamics* 5(1): 1–18.

Kumar, M., S. T. Baig, J. Decressin, C. Faulkner-MacDanagh, and Tarhan Feyziogulu. 2003. Deflation: Determinants, Risks, and Policy Options. Occasional Paper No. 221, International Monetary Fund.

McCloskey, D., and J. R. Zecher. 1976. How the Gold Standard Worked, 1880–1913. In *The Monetary Approach to the Balance of Payments*, ed. J. A. Frenkel and H. G. Johnson. Toronto: University of Toronto Press.

Mitchell, B. 1998. *International Historical Statistics: Europe, 1750–1993*. 4th ed. New York: Stockton Press.

Orphanides, A. 2001. Monetary Policy Rules, Macroeconomic Stability and Inflation: A View from the Trenches. Finance and Economics Discussion Paper No. 2001–62, Federal Reserve Board of Governors.

Pesaran, M. H., and R. Smith. 1995. Estimating Long-Run Relationships from Dynamic Heterogeneous Panels. *Journal of Econometrics* 68: 78–113.

Rockoff, H. 1984. Some Evidence on the Real Price of Gold, Its Costs of Production, and Commodity Prices. In *A Retrospective on the Classical Gold Standard, 1821–1931*, ed. M. D. Bordo and A. J. Schwartz. Chicago: University of Chicago Press.

Sommariva, A., and G. Tullio. 1987. *German Macroeconomic History, 1880–1970: A Study of the Effects of Economic Policy on Inflation, Currency Depreciation and Growth*. New York: St Martin's Press.

U.S. Gold Commission. 1982. *Report to the Congress of the Commission on the Role of Gold in the Domestic and International Monetary Systems*. Washington, DC: U.S. Gold Commission.

# Commentary

*François R. Velde*

## 1. INTRODUCTION

Central bankers are wont to ask their staff questions such as, "Is deflation good or bad?" Economists are wont to respond that the question is not well posed. Prices, they like to say, are endogenous, like quantities. Whether a fall in prices is good or bad depends on what causes it and what that cause does to quantities. Thus, the central banker's worry about deflation needs to be formulated as, "So what causes deflation, and what does it do to GDP?"

Why are central bankers (and the public in general) so worried about deflation? Modern economies offer few examples, and two are particularly well known. One is the Great Depression in the United States in the 1930s, which saw prices fall by 24% and GDP fall by 25% from 1929 to 1932. The other is Japan between 1998 and 2002, when prices fell by 1.6% on average while GDP grew only 1%. Because two points are enough to draw a line, these two instances probably account for deflation's bad reputation. But there are other examples, without having to reach far back into a past plagued by a scarcity of data. The period of the classical gold standard, from 1873 to 1913, in fact provides us with worldwide deflation followed by worldwide inflation—not quite a controlled experiment, but at least the economies were comparable if not identical in these adjacent time periods. And, at first blush, there does not seem to be much evidence for the malign effects of deflation compared to inflation.

## 2. THIS PAPER

This paper examines in more detail the four economies of table 1 during this period using an identified VAR approach. The three variables in the VAR are output, money, and prices. The approach consists of identifying the exogenous causal factors with (linear combinations) of the forecast errors in the VAR, examining whether the shock that moves around prices also moves around output (by looking at impulse responses), and estimating how much of output variation is explained by that shock (looking at historical decompositions).

**Table 1. Average Annual Growth Rates of Prices, GDP, and GDP per Capita**

|  | Prices | | GDP | | GDP per Capita | |
|---|---|---|---|---|---|---|
|  | 1880–96 | 1897–1913 | 1880–96 | 1897–1913 | 1880–96 | 1897–1913 |
| United States | –1.6% | 1.9% | 3.3% | 4.5% | 1.2% | 2.6% |
| United Kingdom | –0.6% | 0.8% | 1.6% | 1.7% | 0.8% | 0.9% |
| Germany | –0.3% | 1.2% | 3.0% | 2.7% | 2.0% | 1.3% |
| France | –0.8% | 0.8% | 1.7% | 1.8% | 1.5% | 1.6% |

The identification strategy is based on the very nature of the gold standard and a "small, open economy" view of each of the economies in the sample. It follows that, in each one, the price level is pegged by the world price of gold and is not affected by either domestic output or domestic money supply. This leads to the following identification of the three shocks in the three-variable VAR: (1) Shock A is the only source of long-run forecast error for $p$; (2) shock B is orthogonal to A, and A and B are only sources of long-run forecast error for output; and (c) shock C is orthogonal to both A and B (and has no long-run impact on prices and output by construction). The authors label A, B, and C as "money supply shock," "aggregate supply shock," and "aggregate demand shock."

To summarize their results, Bordo, Landon-Lane, and Redish find the following:

- Shock A, which drives $p$ in the long run, drives $p$ in the short run, too; this allows us to call it the cause of deflation.
- Shock A does affect $Y$, even in the long-run.
- Shock A effects $Y$, but quantitatively, Shock A explains little of the variation in $Y$.

The conclusion that follows is that deflation (and inflation as well, because the effect of the shocks is symmetric) is benign for output.

### 3. MINOR REMARKS

As a matter of presentation, I would have liked to see more numbers than what the authors provide. For example, the authors say that "the money supply shocks are correlated across the three countries, as are the supply shocks. The demand shocks are uncorrelated." Table 2 suggests that statement is a little sweeping.

Table 2. Correlations between Identified Shocks

|  | Money Supply | Aggregate Supply | Aggregate Demand |
|---|---|---|---|
| U.S.–U.K. | .31 | .22 | –.34 |
| U.S.–Germany | .40 | –.45 | .20 |
| U.K.–Germany | .47 | –.08 | –.15 |

It would also have been instructive to plot the impulse response function for real balances, *M/p*, as a function of the various shocks and to provide a quantitative measure of how much each single shock explains. It is also a little puzzling that the authors did not use per capita data.

Some robustness checks could have been carried out—for example, using per capita series, using M0 instead of M2, and estimating individual country VARs. However, the authors kindly lent me their data, and I have convinced myself that the results are qualitatively robust, although there are some quantitative changes (particularly in the response of output to money supply and aggregate demand shocks).

### 4. THE IDENTIFICATION

What about the identification? The basic assumption of small, open economies on the gold standard implies that domestic shocks (aggregate demand and aggregate supply shocks) do not affect price level in the long run: Gold flows will see to that. Is this reasonable? A first question is whether the economies were small. Table 3 suggests that they were not: The three economies in the sample amount to a third of the world in 1913, and the United States alone represents a fifth.

Are they open? This deserves to be documented. Finally, are they on the gold standard? The United States has a peculiar history in this respect until 1900. Until 1879 (before the sample starts in the paper), it was transitioning from the fiat money regime of greenbacks to a return on a metallic standard. In 1873, it was decided that this regime would be the gold standard, but political

Table 3. Share of World Output

|  | 1870 | 1900 | 1913 |
|---|---|---|---|
| United States | 8.7% | 15.8% | 19.0% |
| United Kingdom | 8.8% | 9.3% | 8.2% |
| Germany | 6.3% | 8.5% | 9.0% |
| Total | 23.9% | 33.6% | 36.1% |

Source: Maddison (1995).

pressures between 1878 and 1896 resulted in some uncertainty as to whether silver might not also be made legal tender, and from 1878 to 1896 (under the Bland-Allison Act and later the Sherman Act), the United States was actively engaged in purchasing and minting silver (or issuing paper backed by silver). Aside from the runs on the dollar in the early 1890s, however, it is unlikely that this materially affected the determination of the price level.

What are those identified shocks?

- A is called *money supply shock*
- B is called *aggregate supply shock*
- C is called *nonmonetary demand shock, aggregate of money demand shocks and temporary spending shocks*, and *dominated by velocity shocks* (drives up $M/p$, leaving $Y$ flat)

As for the identity of shock C, it is rather surprising to see that it completely fails to account for the panics of 1893 and 1907 (see Figure 6B in the paper).

But the most important shock, naturally, is the first one, the so-called money supply shock. Does its impact on the variables correspond to what one would expect from a money supply shock in a gold standard, where such a shock would be related to gold?

This shock drives up $Y$ in the long run in the United States and United Kingdom; this finding is robust, even quantitatively, for the United States, although somewhat less so for the United Kingdom. It is hard to see why that would be so. The shock also drives $M/p$ down (except in the United States). But in a commodity standard, shocks to the commodity should have no long-run effects on $M/p$: the value of resources held as cash balances is not a function of the commodity used for that purpose. Finally, in response to this shock, $M$ moves immediately and $p$ more slowly, whereas the price–specie flow mechanism suggests the reverse, if anything.

Adding gold supply shocks (using the admittedly questionable data from Ridgway) does not soak up this mystery shock. But replacing M2 with M0 and adding gold supply shocks does make $M/p$ unresponsive to the shock. This suggests that the shock may not be related to gold but to other aspects of the monetary system (what the authors call *intermediation shocks*), or else the gold standard/small, open economy assumption needs revisiting.

## 5. THE ANSWER TO THE QUESTION

The answer is that the sources of forecast errors to prices (conditional on a trend break in 1896) don't affect the forecast of output. That is an interesting answer: Surprise inflation or deflation does not lead to surprise booms or busts. It's not clear that this is what the central bankers have in mind when they worry about a deflation that they clearly expect (although they might not know its exact extent). It's not clear either that the negative effects that William Jennings Bryan and assorted inflationists of the late nineteenth century had in mind were purely those coming from surprise deflations. That said, the answer the authors bring is an important and useful one.

## ACKNOWLEDGMENTS

The views expressed herein do not necessarily represent those of the Federal Reserve Bank of Chicago or the Federal Reserve System. I thank the authors for providing me with their data and code.

## REFERENCES

Maddison, A. 1995. *Monitoring the World Economy, 1820–1992.* Paris: Organisation for Economic Co-operation and Development.

# 6

# Monetary Policy Orientation in Times of Low Inflation

*Jürgen von Hagen and Boris Hofmann*

## 1. INTRODUCTION

The past 20 years have seen a general reduction in inflation rates to very low levels everywhere in the OECD (Organisation for Economic Co-operation and Development). The general return to (almost) price stability reflects a shift in monetary policy philosophies from an attitude of actively exploiting the Phillips curve to manage the macroeconomy to a more modest one aimed at stable monetary conditions and low inflation. This shift in monetary policy philosophies has had its repercussions in the move to more independent central banks and the adoption of rules-based regimes such as inflation targeting.[1] In Europe, it has its visible reflection in the European Union (EU) Treaty of 1997 and in the charter of the European Central Bank (ECB), which, for now, has made price stability the principal goal of monetary policy.

The changing pattern of monetary policy has been accompanied by a change in the view most economists take on the inflationary process and the role of monetary policy in it. Twenty years ago, it was widely accepted that the main cause of inflation was excessive money growth and that to keep inflation down, the central bank had to control the growth rate of money. Today's New Keynesian consensus model of monetary policy transmission does not even make the role of money in determining the rate of inflation explicit. Instead, it sees the main role of the central bank as setting an interest rate that affects the output gap, which, in turn, determines the rate of inflation through the Phillips curve. Much of that shift in the consensus view on monetary policy transmission is the result of the empirical observation that, both in the United States and in Europe, the correlation between money growth and inflation seems to have all but vanished. Based on this observation, many economists have criticized the ECB's original monetary policy framework, which

---

[1] For a review of the experience with inflation targeting, see Neumann and von Hagen (2002).

assigned the growth rate of money the first of "two pillars" of its monetary analysis for being outdated and, hence, inappropriate.[2] Responding to these critics, the ECB recently downgraded the role of money in its policy framework.[3]

This critique and the actions taken by the central bank, however, may be seen as rushing to unfounded conclusions. The general reduction in inflation rates of the past 30 years has come with a general decline in the volatility of inflation, too. If this is the result of less expansionary and less volatile money growth rates, it could be the result of monetary policies aimed at lower and less volatile inflation. Furthermore, as we will show here, the empirical correlation between inflation rates and the output gap has also decreased in the euro area in recent years. This implies that the empirical performance of the consensus model has deteriorated as well.

An important policy implication of these observations is that the traditional signals central banks look at to assess future inflation—namely, money growth and output gaps—become less informative when the level of inflation is low. In this paper, we explore this point and its consequences in more detail. Our main point is that in times of low inflation, central banks should focus mainly on the underlying inflation trend rather than on high-frequency changes in inflation. Empirically, this means that they should use information from long-run movements in the determinants of inflation. In principle, they can do that by looking at long-run movements in money, real output, and interest rates, or long-run movements in the output gap. However, long-run movements in the output gap are uninformative because, by construction, the output gap is zero on average over the business cycle. The implication is that, despite the lower correlation between money growth and inflation at high frequencies, central banks should watch monetary trends, especially when inflation is low.

The remainder of this paper is organized as follows: Section 2 reviews the development of monetary and inflation trends over the past 30 years. Section 3 presents a version of the consensus model to interpret these observations. Section 4 reports our empirical estimates, which show that the empirical correlation between money growth and inflation has declined as inflation rates have come down and that the same is true for output gaps and inflation.

---

[2] See, for example, Alesina et al. (2001), De Grauwe and Polan (2001), Galí (2001), and Svensson (1999).

[3] Specifically, in a statement of May 2003, the ECB (2003) reversed the roles of the first and the second pillar and renounced the regular assessment of the monetary reference in the future.

Furthermore, we develop a model of trend inflation and show that this model continues to predict inflation well even in times of low inflation. Section 5 concludes.

## 2. INFLATION AND MONETARY VOLATILITY: EMPIRICAL TRENDS

Several recent studies have reconsidered the empirical correlation between money growth and inflation standing behind Friedman's famous dictum that inflation is always and everywhere a monetary phenomenon. McCandless and Weber (1995) show the high correlation between money growth and inflation in a sample of 110 countries over the period from 1960 to 1990 (figure 1). According to their evidence, high money growth rates are coupled with high inflation rates, whereas low money growth rates are tied to low inflation. Their results are robust to variations in the definition of money and changes in the sample countries. However, figure 1 reveals that the strength of the correlation is higher for high rates of inflation than for low rates. King (2001) replicates their study for 116 countries from 1968 to 1998. His basic result is the same. In addition, he shows that the correlation between inflation and money growth becomes visible only if both are averaged over more than 10 years.[4] Lucas (1980) finds a strong positive correlation between U.S. annual inflation and money growth rates and shows that this correlation increases when short-run fluctuations are filtered out of the data. Tanner (1993) shows that the correlation between annual U.S. inflation and money growth rates declines in the 1980s compared to the 1970s. Christiano and Fitzgerald (2003) find that the correlation between these two variables is positive and stable for long frequencies in U.S. data spanning the 20th century. After 1960, this correlation declined for short frequencies.

However, turning from simple correlations to Granger causality tests, Friedman and Kuttner (1992) show that monetary aggregates have no marginal information value for U.S. inflation after 1980. Estrella and Mishkin (1997) even ask, "Is there a role for money in monetary policy?" and conclude that, based on VAR evidence, the answer must be unambiguously no. Similarly, Stock and Watson (1999) find that the information value of monetary aggregates in inflation forecasts is negligible if not even negative. For the euro area, Gerlach (2004) and Svensson (1999) demonstrate that growth rates of the ECB's broad monetary aggregate, M3, do not result in Granger causality concludes.

---

[4] Further results supporting the same conclusions are found in Barro (1990), Dwyer and Hafer (1988, 1999), and Poole (1994).

**Figure 1.  Average Annual Rates of Growth in M2 and in Consumer Prices During 1960–90 in 110 Countries**

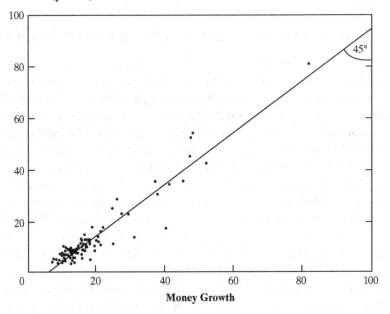

Source: International Monetary Fund.

inflation. Nicoletti Altimari (2001) follows the Stock and Watson methodology to estimate the marginal information content of money for euro-area inflation. He finds little or no information value for short forecast horizons. Trecroci and Vega (2002) estimate a multivariate VAR with money, output, inflation, and short- and long-term interest rates and find no Granger causality of money growth for inflation.

DeGrauwe and Polan (2001) are among the most forceful critics of Friedman's dictum that inflation is always a monetary phenomenon. Using data spanning 30 years from 165 countries, they show that the strength of the correlation depends critically on the level of the inflation rate. They report that regressions of inflation on money growth are significant only for inflation rates above 17.4%. De Grauwe and Polan conclude that central banks should pay no attention to monetary developments as long as inflation is low or moderate. Similarly, Svensson (1999) argues that money or monetary growth rates are irrelevant for monetary policy in times of low inflation.

But this conclusion seems premature. Consider the following simple statistical representation of money and the price level:

$$\begin{aligned}
P_t &= P_t^* + \mu_t, \\
P_t^* &= M_t^* \\
M_t &= M_t^* + \xi_t \\
\Delta M_t^* &= \pi^* + \varepsilon_t.
\end{aligned}$$

(1)

Here, $P$ is the logarithmic price level and $M$ is the logarithmic money supply. The price level fluctuates randomly around its trend value, $P^*$, for example, because of temporary shocks to food prices or cost shocks. Similarly, the money supply fluctuates around its trend level, $M^*$. Here, the price-level trend and the monetary trend are assumed to be proportional to each other. Trend money grows with the permanent (drift) term, $\pi^*$, and a random shock, $\varepsilon$.

Assume, for simplicity, that the two temporary-level shocks, $\mu$ and $\varepsilon$, are uncorrelated. Then the correlation between the average inflation rate and the average money growth rate over $T$ periods is

(2) $\quad \rho_T = \dfrac{\text{var}(\varepsilon)}{\sqrt{\text{var}(\varepsilon) + 2T^{-1}\,\text{var}(\xi)} \ \ \sqrt{\text{var}(\varepsilon) + 2T^{-1}\,\text{var}(\mu)}}.$

This says, first, that the estimated correlation coefficient increases with the length of the period, $T$, over which we compute the averages. The reason is that the temporary-level shocks wash out as we consider longer and longer periods. This reproduces King's (2001) observation mentioned earlier. Second, periods characterized by a series of large money growth shocks, $\varepsilon$, are characterized by a larger correlation between money growth and inflation. In contrast, when money growth shocks are small, the correlation becomes weaker. Thus, if declining and low money growth rates have reduced volatility, the correlation of money growth and inflation becomes weaker. Finally, suppose that the central bank aims for a constant monetary policy in the sense that growth rate shocks completely disappear. In this situation, the correlation between money growth and inflation disappears altogether. However, the trend inflation rate is given by $\pi^*$, the trend money growth rate set by the central bank. Obviously, to conclude that money growth has no information about inflation would be completely unwarranted in this situation.

In table 1, we provide some background data for this reasoning. The first part of this table collects the standard deviations and averages of monthly series of annual inflation rates in 14 OECD countries from 1966 to 2002. Inflation is measured on the basis of consumer price indexes. We consider five subperiods: The final years of the Bretton Woods system, 1966–72; the years of the oil price shocks and the European "snake" (an exchange rate peg of several European countries to the deutsche mark), 1973–78; the years of the European Monetary System, 1979–91; the early 1990s, 1992–96; and the late 1990s, 1997–2002. The early 1990s are interesting because this is the period when several OECD countries started a new regime of inflation targeting. The table shows that inflation rates became much more volatile after the end of the Bretton Woods system. Average inflation rates went up at the same time. Inflation volatility peaked during the 1980s, when inflation rates came down everywhere. The 1990s featured low inflation rates and low volatility.

The second part of the table collects the averages and standard deviations of monthly series of annual money growth rates in the same countries and years. Here, the development of average growth rates is not as clear cut. But with regard to volatilities, we observe a very similar tendency. The volatility of money growth rates generally increased substantially during the 1970s and declined substantially in the 1990s. Interestingly, this is also true for the inflation-targeting countries—Sweden, the United Kingdom, Canada, and Australia. Thus, at first glance, the data are consistent with the notion that the observed correlation between money growth and inflation may have declined because of the fall in the volatility of money growth shocks and, hence, inflation. We will explore this relationship further later. At this point, we simply note that the data do not justify the conclusion that monetary developments have become irrelevant for monetary policy.

Table 1. Part 1: Inflation: Average and Volatility

| | Average Inflation | | | | | Standard Deviation of Inflation | | | | |
|---|---|---|---|---|---|---|---|---|---|---|
| | 1966–72 | 1973–78 | 1979–91 | 1992–96 | 1997–2002 | 1966–72 | 1973–78 | 1979–91 | 1992–96 | 1997–2002 |
| USA | 4.1 | 7.7 | 5.9 | 2.9 | 2.3 | 1.2 | 2.2 | 3.5 | 0.3 | 0.8 |
| CAN | 3.8 | 9.0 | 6.5 | 1.5 | 2.0 | 0.9 | 1.7 | 3.0 | 0.8 | 0.9 |
| JPN | 5.5 | 11.4 | 2.7 | 0.8 | 0.0 | 1.5 | 6.2 | 2.0 | 0.8 | 1.1 |
| AUS | 3.9 | 7.0 | 3.7 | 2.9 | 1.6 | 1.6 | 2.1 | 1.8 | 0.9 | 0.8 |
| AUT* | 3.9 | 12.2 | 10.9 | 2.2 | 0.8 | 1.6 | 3.2 | 2.5 | 1.4 | 2.0 |
| CH | 4.4 | 4.9 | 3.7 | 2.2 | 0.8 | 1.8 | 3.8 | 1.9 | 1.4 | 0.6 |
| D | 3.3 | 5.1 | 2.9 | 3.1 | 1.5 | 1.6 | 1.7 | 2.0 | 1.6 | 0.8 |
| DK* | 6.5 | 10.7 | 6.5 | 1.9 | 2.4 | 2.4 | 3.0 | 3.5 | 0.4 | 0.4 |
| E | 6.0 | 17.7 | 10.1 | 4.7 | 2.7 | 2.3 | 4.6 | 4.3 | 0.8 | 0.8 |
| I | 3.3 | 15.7 | 10.9 | 4.6 | 2.2 | 2.0 | 4.5 | 5.7 | 0.8 | 0.4 |
| IRE* | 6.2 | 14.8 | 8.7 | 2.2 | 3.4 | 2.6 | 4.9 | 6.5 | 0.7 | 1.8 |
| NL | 5.6 | 7.9 | 3.4 | 2.5 | 2.8 | 2.0 | 2.2 | 10.1 | 0.6 | 1.0 |
| NZ* | 6.0 | 12.9 | 10.9 | 2.2 | 1.7 | 2.5 | 3.1 | 5.4 | 1.4 | 2.0 |
| SE | 5.1 | 9.7 | 8.2 | 2.5 | 1.1 | 2.1 | 2.1 | 2.9 | 1.5 | 1.1 |
| UK | 5.7 | 15.0 | 7.9 | 2.7 | 2.4 | 2.3 | 5.7 | 4.4 | 0.8 | 0.9 |

* Based on quarterly data.
Source: *International Financial Statistics.*

Table 1. Part 2: Money Growth: Average and Volatility

|  | Average Inflation | | | | | Standard Deviation of Inflation | | | | |
|---|---|---|---|---|---|---|---|---|---|---|
|  | 1966–72 | 1973–78 | 1979–91 | 1992–96 | 1997–2002 | 1966–72 | 1973–78 | 1979–91 | 1992–96 | 1997–2002 |
| USA | 4.1 | 7.7 | 5.9 | 2.9 | 2.3 | 1.2 | 2.2 | 3.5 | 0.3 | 0.8 |
| CAN | 5.3 | 8.3 | 10.0 | 8.3 | 10.0 | 8.1 | 3.8 | 9.1 | 3.5 | 3.9 |
| JPN | 18.6 | 13.8 | 5.4 | 7.4 | 11.7 | 5.0 | 6.7 | 4.3 | 4.6 | 7.6 |
| AUS | 7.4 | 12.0 | 11.5 | 13.7 | 11.9 | 2.9 | 7.8 | 7.9 | 5.9 | 4.1 |
| AUT | 8.9 | 9.1 | 5.2 | 8.8 | 5.3 | 4.4 | 3.4 | 5.6 | 2.8 | 0.8 |
| CH | 11.6 | 3.4 | 2.6 | 5.7 | 6.0 | 5.1 | 7.9 | 8.1 | 5.4 | 5.4 |
| D | 8.7 | 9.6 | 7.4 | 8.1 | 7.4 | 3.9 | 4.7 | 5.9 | 2.8 | 2.0 |
| DK | 9.5 | 10.7 | 12.1 | 4.4 | 6.1 | 4.9 | 6.9 | 7.3 | 6.8 | 3.2 |
| E | 14.1 | 20.4 | 14.3 | 4.1 | 12.3 | 6.5 | 3.4 | 4.4 | 4.1 | 2.0 |
| I | 19.2 | 17.8 | 12.2 | 4.3 | 10.0 | 5.0 | 7.3 | 4.6 | 3.8 | 2.4 |
| IRE | 10.3 | 19.4 | 16.3 | 18.1 | 0.5 | 9.2 | 22.5 | 27.6 | 25.9 | 20.5 |
| NL | 11.6 | 10.3 | 5.9 | 7.7 | 9.9 | 4.4 | 7.7 | 3.3 | 4.2 | 1.6 |
| NZ | 5.2 | 12.7 | 13.1 | 3.7 | 8.6 | 6.9 | 11.0 | 12.6 | 4.4 | 6.7 |
| SE | 12.3 | 10.7 | 10.1 | 3.4 | 4.4*** | 3.1 | 3.2 | 6.6 | 4.4 | 3.0*** |
| UK | 10.3 | 21.4 | 14.3*** | 6.3** | 7.8** | 6.7 | 7.2 | 4.1*** | 3.2** | 3.4** |

* 1982–91; ** annualized six-month growth rates from the Bank of England; *** 1997–2000.
Source: *International Financial Statistics.*

A convenient way to judge the indicator property of money for the inflation rate is the $P^*$ approach of Hallman, Porter, and Small (1991).[5] It inverts the quantity equation to derive a long-run equilibrium price level, $P_t^* = M_t - y_t - v_t$, where $v_t$ is the log of the velocity of money and $y_t$ is log of output. The $P^*$ approach assumes the existence of a stable long-run money-demand function, which we interpret as the existence of a stable, cointegrating relationship between the price level, money supply, and real output. The main determinant of the velocity of money is the opportunity cost of holding money, which we approximate by the government bond yield.[6] We estimate the long-run money-demand function in the euro area based on a cointegrating VAR over the period 1980:IQ–2002:IVQ. The VAR includes real M3 (currency in circulation; checkable, time, and savings deposits; and certificates of

[5] Von Hagen and Hayo (1999) were the first to show that this approach yields a good empirical representation of euro-area inflation in the 1980s and 1990s.

[6] Euro-area money demand models using short-term interest rates as the opportunity-cost variable often exhibit parameter instability and non-homogeneity with respect to real income.

deposits issued by banks), real gross domestic product (GDP), and the nominal 10-year government bond yield, *Rl*. Real M3 is defined by nominal M3 deflated by the euro-area consumer price index, the harmonized index of consumer prices (HICP). The VAR contains a centered impulse dummy for 1990:IIIQ, dummying out a large outlier in the money equation associated with German reunification.

The results are reported in table 2. The Johansen trace test suggests a single long-run relationship, which we identify by normalizing on the real money coefficient. The restriction that the coefficient has on real GDP is one that could not be rejected and was therefore imposed. The estimated cointegrating vector states that long-run money demand is homogenous in real GDP and the price level and depends negatively on the government bond yield. Thus, the long-run velocity of money is a positive function of the long-term interest rate.

The long-run money demand relationship yields a solution for $P^*$ of

(3)  $P_t^* = M_t - y_t + 0.038 Rl_t.$

The $P^*$ model is a forward-looking model of inflation in the sense that it considers the long-run price level, $P^*$, to be the price level that would prevail if all prices had already adjusted to the current levels of output, the money supply, and the interest rate. The model assumes that the actual price level adjusts gradually to this equilibrium price level, so that the inflation rate will rise if the price gap—that is, the difference between $P^*$ and $P$—is positive and will fall if it is negative,

**Table 2. Estimating a Long-Run Money-Demand Function for the Euro Area**

**Unrestricted Cointegration Rank Test**

| Hypothesized No. of CE(s) | Eigenvalue | Trace Statistic | 5% Critical Value | 1% Critical Value |
|---|---|---|---|---|
| None* | 0.206156 | 33.07013 | 29.68 | 35.65 |
| At most 1 | 0.134700 | 12.75370 | 15.41 | 20.04 |
| At most 2 | 0.000249 | 0.021905 | 3.76 | 6.65 |

*(**) denotes rejection of the hypothesis at the 5% (1%) level.
Trace test indicates one cointegrating equation(s) at the 5% level.
Trace test indicates no cointegration at the 1% level.

Estimated co-integrating vector:
$M / P = Y - 0.038 irl$
    (−9.24)

Test of homogeneity restriction: Chi-square 1 = 2.19 (0.14)

| Error Correction: | D(LNRM3) | D(LNGDPR) | D(IRL) |
|---|---|---|---|
| CointEq1 | −0.033403 | −0.041891 | −0.897962 |
| | (0.01332) | (0.01231) | (0.78605) |
| | [−2.50849] | [−3.40401] | [−1.14238] |
| D(LNRM3(−1)) | 0.155890 | −0.063314 | −5.359175 |
| | (0.10103) | (0.09337) | (5.96373) |
| | [1.54305] | [−0.67812] | [−0.89863] |
| D(LNRM3(−2)) | 0.055251 | −0.016947 | 3.990832 |
| | (0.09891) | (0.09142) | (5.83904) |
| | [0.55857] | [−0.18539] | [0.68347] |
| D(LNGDPR(−1)) | −0.018760 | −0.059016 | 11.16043 |
| | (0.12519) | (0.11570) | (7.39029) |
| | [−0.14985] | [−0.51007] | [1.51015] |
| D(LNGDPR(−2)) | 0.190490 | −0.101837 | −0.641314 |
| | (0.12261) | (0.11332) | (7.23802) |
| | [1.55357] | [−0.89869] | [−0.08860] |
| D(IRL(−1)) | −0.001410 | 0.003980 | 0.632798 |
| | (0.00182) | (0.00168) | (0.10728) |
| | [−0.77591] | [2.36977] | [5.89841] |
| D(IRL(−2)) | 0.000396 | −0.000785 | −0.180336 |
| | (0.00193) | (0.00178) | (0.11372) |
| | [0.20572] | [−0.44074] | [−1.58577] |
| C | 0.005555 | 0.007162 | −0.101495 |
| | (0.00146) | (0.00135) | (0.08595) |
| | [3.81507] | [5.32224] | [−1.18082] |
| D903 | 0.024250 | 0.006176 | 0.352946 |

$$(4) \quad P_t - P_{t-1} = \lambda_0 + \lambda_1 (P_t^* - P_t),$$

where $0 < \lambda_1 \leq 1$. Consistency of the model requires that $\lambda_0$, the trend inflation rate when the price level equals its long-run value and the long-run interest rate is constant, be equal to the difference between the trend growth rates of money and output.[7]

Figure 2 shows the development of the price gap and the inflation rate in the Euro area over the period from 1980 to 2002. Three observations stand out. First, during the period of the relatively high and volatile inflation rates

---

[7] Hallman, Porter, and Small (1991) refer to Mussa (1982) as a theoretical basis for their model. Mussa proposes the price adjustment equation, $P_1 - P_{t-1} = \alpha(p_t^* - p_t) + \pi_t^*$, where $\pi^*$ is a forward-looking expectation of the trend inflation rate. In empirical implementations of the $P^*$ model, including Hallman, Porter, and Small, this term is usually omitted.

Figure 2.  Inflation and the Price Gap in the Euro Area

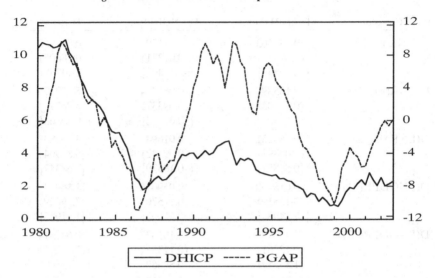

of the 1980s, the price gap tracks euro-area inflation quite well. When inflation accelerated again in the late 1980s, the price gap overshoots by a large
amount, but this is compatible with the idea that it leads observed inflation,
and there is gradual adjustment between the two. Second, the relationship
between the price gap and inflation seems to become more tenuous in the
1990s, when inflation reached low levels and was much less volatile than
before. Third, the inflation rate features a long-run, downward trend over the
entire sample period, which is not visible in the price gap. The inability of the
price gap to track the long-run trend is implied by its construction from a
co-integrated relationship between money, output, and prices.

The New Keynesian model of the monetary transmission mechanism
focuses on the Phillips-curve relation between inflation and the output gap. In
figure 3, we show the two key variables of this relation for the euro area from
1980 to 2002. The figure shows the HICP (consumer price) inflation rate and
the output gap. Here, output is measured by log real GDP, and the output gap
is the log difference between actual output and trend output derived from a
conventional HP filter. This figure, too, reveals three main observations. First,
the output gap tracks inflation quite well until the mid-1980s and, disregarding
some overshooting, even into the early 1990s. Second, the relationship
between the output gap and the inflation rate appears to have weakened after
1990, when inflation in the euro area is relatively low and much less volatile.
Third, like the price gap, the output gap cannot reproduce the long-run, downward trend of inflation during this period. Again, this is because of the cyclical
nature of this indicator. The figure thus suggests a very similar stylized fact for

the link between inflation and the output gap: As inflation becomes low and stable, changes in the output gap become less informative for inflationary developments.

**Figure 3. Inflation and the Output Gap in the Euro Area**

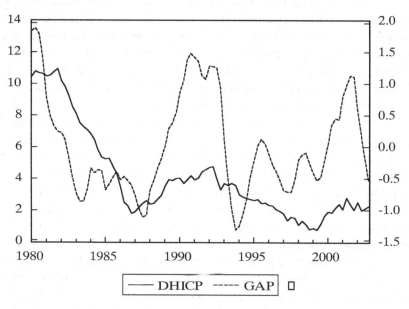

3. INFLATION, OUTPUT, AND MONEY: A MODEL

The consensus model of monetary policy transmission can be summarized in the following equations:[8]

(5)   $y_t = b_0 - b_1 (R_t - E_t \Delta P_{t+1}) + E_t y_{t+1} + v_t$

(6)   $\Delta P_t = (1 - c_1) \Delta P_{t-1} + c_1 E_t \Delta P_{t+1} + c_2 (y_t - y^*) + \phi_t,$

   $0 < c_1 < 1$

(7)   $R_t = r^* + E_t \Delta P_{t+1} + d_1 (E_t \Delta P_{t+1} - \pi^*) + d_2 (y_t - y^*) + \theta_t$

(8)   $M_t - P_t = y_t - a_1 R_t + \varsigma_t.$

Here, $y_t$ is the log of real output, $y^*$ is its trend value, and $(y_t - y^*)$ is the output gap. The variable $P_t$ denotes the log of the price level, $R_t$ an interest rate, $r^*$ the equilibrium real interest rate, and $M_t$ the log of the money stock.

---

[8] See, for example, McCallum (2001), Nelson (2003a, 2003b), or King (2001).

Finally, $\pi^*$ is the central bank's target rate of inflation; $E_t$ stands for an expectation based on information available at time $t$; and $v_t$, $\varphi_t$, $\theta_t$, and $\zeta_t$ are random shocks with zero expectation. Equation (5) is a forward-looking IS derived from optimizing consumer behavior. Equation (6) is a New Keynesian Phillips curve derived from Calvo price setting by firms operating under imperfect competition. Equation (7) is a standard Taylor rule, and equation (8) a standard money-demand function. Although most representations of the model today skip the latter, it is compatible with the rest of the model to retain it, and it will be important for our subsequent analysis. Assuming that the nominal interest rate is the central bank's policy instrument, the money stock is endogenously determined by equation (8).

The model describes a long-run equilibrium as a situation in which the output gap is zero and the real interest rate equals the Wicksellian rate $r^* = (b_0+\mu)/b_1$, where $\mu$ is the long-run growth rate of trend output. Given that the central bank knows what $r^*$ is and sets the nominal interest rate accordingly, the long-run equilibrium has $E_t\, \Delta P_{t+1} = \pi^*$—that is, the equilibrium inflation rate equals the central bank's target rate. This implies that the money growth rate equals $E_t\Delta M_{t+1} = \mu + \pi$ in the long-run equilibrium. Thus, although most presentations focus on the Phillips curve (6) as the transmission channel of monetary policy, the consensus model embeds a link between inflation and money growth in the long run that is entirely consistent with the traditional quantity equation. Saying that the central bank has kept inflation in the long run at a rate equal to $\pi^*$ or that the central bank has kept money growing at a long-run rate of $\mu + \pi^*$, and saying that either has produced an inflation rate of $\pi^*$ are equivalent statements in the context of this model—they just look at the long-run equilibrium from two different angles. Furthermore, comparing a long-run equilibrium with a low inflation rate to a long-run equilibrium with a higher inflation rate is equivalent to comparing a long-run equilibrium with low money growth to one with higher money growth. Thus, trend money growth rates contain information about trend inflation rates. The same is obviously not true for long-run output gaps, which are zero in all long-run equilibria.

Furthermore, the model also embeds a correlation between changes in the money stock and inflation in the short run, which operates through the impact of monetary policy shocks on aggregate demand and the Phillips curve. Consider a negative interest rate shock, $\theta_t < 0$. This leads to an immediate increase in the output gap and an increase in inflation. At the same time, the money stock increases. Thus, inflation and money growth are positively correlated. This correlation is muted, however, by money-demand shocks, $\zeta_t$. The smaller the variance of monetary policy shocks latter relative to the variance of money-demand shocks, the smaller the short-run correlation between money growth and inflation. As a result, the model generates an interpretation of the statistical argument made in the preceding section. After the end of the Bretton Woods system, monetary policy became more expansionary and more volatile in OECD countries, leading to higher variances in money growth and inflation as well higher inflation rates. In contrast, the 1990s saw a return to less volatile monetary policies. Though the first change increases the correlation between money growth and inflation, the second one reduces this correlation.

To pursue this argument further, we calibrate a solution of the model. By substituting equation (7) into equations (5) and (6) and taking linear approximations around the steady state, we obtain

(9)   $b_1 d_1 E_t \tilde{\pi}_{t+1} - E_t \tilde{y}_{t+1} + (1 + b_1 d_2) \tilde{y}_t = v_t - b_1 \theta_t,$

(10)   $-c_1 E_t \tilde{\pi}_{t+1} + \tilde{\pi}_t - c_2 \tilde{y}_t - (1 - c_1) \tilde{\pi}_{t-1} = \phi_t,$

where the tilde denotes a small percentage deviation from the steady state. Note that this system does not depend on the money-demand shock. Substituting (10) into (9), we can eliminate output from the system and derive the solution for inflation,

(11)   $AE_t \tilde{\pi}_{t+2} + BE_t \tilde{\pi}_{t+1} + C \tilde{\pi}_t + D \tilde{\pi}_{t-1} = v_t - b_1 \theta_t + \dfrac{1 + b_1 d_2}{c_2} \phi_t,$

where $A, B, C,$ and $D$ are composite parameters. This yields a rational-expectations solution for inflation, which we use to obtain the solution for aggregate output. We then substitute both solutions into the money-demand function to obtain the equilibrium solution for money demand.

To calibrate this model, we chose a set of parameters that are conventional in a quarterly model. The parameter $b_1$ is inessential and can be ignored. We chose the inverse of the risk-aversion parameter $b_1 = 1/6$ (Woodford 2003), $c_1 = 0.8$ (Galí and Gertler 1999; Steinsson 2003), and $c_2 = 0.04$. For the Taylor rule, we chose both the standard parameter $d_1 = d_2 = 0.5$ (Taylor 1993; Woodford 2001) and, alternatively, $d_1 = 0.01$ (weak inflation targeting) and $d_1 = 10$ aggressive inflation targeting. Finally, we set the interest rate elasticity of money demand, $a_1 = 0.1$ (Hayo 1999).

We use this calibration to simulate a "taste shock" to the IS curve, a cost-push shock to the Phillips curve, and a monetary policy shock to the Taylor rule. Although the first two shocks are assumed to be positive, the policy shock is negative. Figures 4A–D plot the impulse-response functions for the nominal interest rate, inflation, output, and nominal balances for the standard

Taylor rule. A taste shock, which corresponds to an exogenous increase in aggregate demand for output, raises output and inflation. The central bank reacts with an increase in the nominal interest rate. The nominal money supply increases as the demand for money goes up. With a cost-push shock, we get a large increase in the rate of inflation and, simultaneously, a decline in the level of output. The interest rate increases. As the figures indicate, nominal balances also increase. With a monetary policy shock, output and inflation decline, and so does the nominal money supply. Finally, we can also simulate the effect of a money demand shock. Naturally, this shock has no impact on the economy other than an increase in nominal balances. This basic pattern is the same for all choices of the policy parameter, $d_1$—that is, weak, standard, and strong inflation targeting.

In table 3, we report the correlation between money and inflation and money and output together with the standard deviations of inflation, output, and money under various scenarios. Here, we set the standard deviation of taste shocks equal to 0.316 and the standard deviation of cost-push shocks equal to 0.1. To simplify, we ignore money-demand shocks. We compare the results of highly volatile monetary policy, where the standard deviation of policy shocks is 10, and a less volatile monetary policy with a standard deviation of policy shocks equal to 3.16. We obtain the highest correlation of money and inflation with weak inflation targeting and a highly volatile policy and the lowest correlation with strong inflation targeting and low policy volatility. Similarly, the volatility of inflation and money is higher with weak inflation targeting and highly volatile monetary policy than with strong inflation targeting and less policy volatility. Finally, table 3 shows that the correlation between output and inflation is also affected by this shift in policy. The correlation is positive under a high policy volatility. As policy becomes less volatile, the negative correlation induced by the cost-push shock dominates.

These simulations show that the new consensus model can reproduce the empirical observations noted previously. Note that we do not assume any change in the structural parameters of the model other than changes in monetary policy. That is, we need not assume a structural break in the transmission mechanism of monetary policy to understand why money has become "less informative" for inflation. Instead, this can be interpreted as a consequence of a less erratic monetary policy and a stronger commitment to low inflation.

Table 3. Correlations of Money, Inflation, and Output in the Consensus Model

|  | $\sigma_\theta = 10$ | $\sigma_\theta = 10^{1/2}$ |
|---|---|---|
|  | **Weak Inflation Targeting** | |
| Corr. money and inflation | 0.56 | 0.31 |
| Corr. money and output | 0.88 | 0.17 |
| Corr. output and inflation | 0.12 | −0.62 |
| Std. inflation | 0.0821 | 0.0704 |
| Std. output | 0.0539 | 0.0259 |
| Std. money | 1.0868 | 0.1978 |
|  | **Standard Taylor Rule** | |
| Corr. money and inflation | 0.55 | 0.30 |
| Corr. money and output | 0.89 | 0.19 |
| Corr. output and inflation | 0.13 | −0.63 |
| Std. inflation | 0.0872 | 0.0704 |
| Std. output | 0.0539 | 0.0259 |
| Std. money | 1.0847 | 0.1968 |
|  | **Strong Inflation Targeting** | |
| Corr. money and inflation | 0.50 | −0.04 |
| Corr. money and output | 0.91 | 0.48 |
| Corr. output and inflation | 0.13 | −0.62 |
| Std. inflation | 0.0824 | 0.0707 |
| Std. output | 0.0537 | 0.0256 |
| Std. money | 1.0444 | 0.1881 |

## 4. INFLATION, THE OUTPUT GAP, AND MONEY IN THE EURO AREA

In this section, we develop an empirical model of inflation in the euro area. We take the New Keynesian Phillips curve as a starting point and show that it does not yield a satisfactory empirical model in times of low inflation. We then show that a Phillips curve augmented by trend inflation, modeled as a function of the low-frequency component of M3 growth, performs better.[9]

Our empirical version of the New Keynesian Phillips curve takes the following form:

---

[9] For similar approaches, see Gerlach (2004) and Neumann (2003).

(12)   $\pi_t = \sum_{i=1}^{4} \alpha_i \, \pi_{t-i} + \beta y_{t-1} + \delta \Delta p_t^{oil}.$

Here, $p^{oil}$ is the world price of crude oil. The empirical specification approximates the expected inflation term of equation (6) by a distributed lag over past inflation rates and includes a lagged instead of a current output gap. The output gap is derived from real GDP subtracting trend output determined by using an HP filter. Estimating the empirical Phillips curve over the period from 1980 to 2002 in quarterly data yields the model reported in table 4. Over the entire time period, inflation responds to the output gap with a coefficient for the output gap of 0.36 with a $t$ statistic of 2.59.

In order to assess whether the relationship between the inflation rate and the output gap has indeed weakened, as figure 3 suggests, we estimate this Phillips curve recursively over the sample period. Figure 5 plots the coefficient on the output gap together with its two-standard-error confidence bands. The graph indicates that the output gap elasticity drops substantially in the second half of the 1980s. Furthermore, the lower bound of the confidence almost touches zero towards the end of the sample period. Thus, the estimate

Table 4. A New Keynesian Phillips Curve for the Euro Area

| Variable | Coefficient | Std. Error | $t$ Statistic | Prob. |
|---|---|---|---|---|
| DHICP(–1) | 0.354826 | 0.096669 | 3.670518 | 0.0004 |
| DHICP(–2) | –0.053469 | 0.099889 | –0.535282 | 0.5939 |
| DHICP(–3) | 0.173041 | 0.103339 | 1.674492 | 0.0977 |
| DHICP(–4) | 0.435977 | 0.100113 | 4.354859 | 0.0000 |
| DOIL | 0.006531 | 0.002198 | 2.972039 | 0.0038 |
| GAP(–1) | 0.356075 | 0.137298 | 2.593442 | 0.0112 |
| C | 0.161383 | 0.205422 | 0.785619 | 0.4343 |
| Adjusted $R^2$ | 0.861676 | | DW | 1.880418 |

has lost significance compared to the earlier part of the sample period. This confirms the notion that, in the low-inflation 1990s, the output gap has lost information content for inflation in the Euro area.

### Figure 4. Standard Taylor Rule, $d_1 = 0.5$

#### A. Impulse Responses of Taste Shock

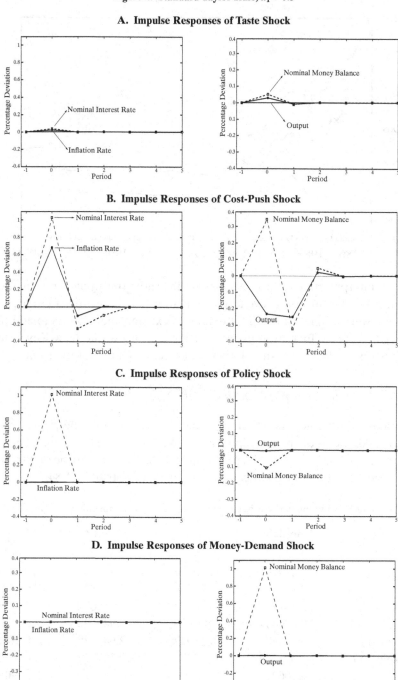

#### B. Impulse Responses of Cost-Push Shock

#### C. Impulse Responses of Policy Shock

#### D. Impulse Responses of Money-Demand Shock

**Figure 5. Recursive Estimates of the Output-Gap Coefficient**

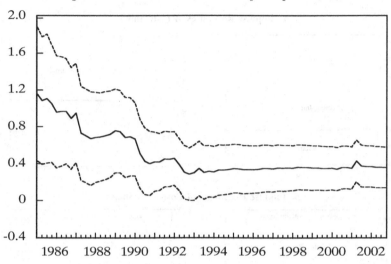

One interpretation of this result is that the short-run, cyclical information contained in the autoregressive term in equation (12) is insufficient to predict inflation well in times of low inflation. Our next step, therefore, is to add the price gap as more forward-looking inflation forecast to the New Keynesian Phillips curve. This yields an inflation adjustment equation of the form

$$(13) \quad \pi_t = \sum_{i=1}^{n} \alpha_i \pi_{t-i} + \beta y_{t-1} + \lambda (p^* - p)_{t-1} + \delta \Delta p_t^{oil}.$$

Estimating the new inflation adjustment equation over the period from 1980 to 2002 yields the results reported in table 5. Over the entire time period, the estimated coefficient for the price gap of 0.003 with a *t* statistic of 0.16 and an estimated output gap coefficient of 0.24 with a *t* statistic of 1.84.

**Table 5. An Empirical New Keynesian Phillips Curve Including the Price Gap**

| Variable | Coefficient | Std. Error | *t* Statistic | Prob. |
|----------|-------------|------------|---------------|-------|
| DHICP(–1) | 0.354874 | 0.097044 | 3.656855 | 0.0004 |
| DHICP(–2) | –0.049181 | 0.100540 | –0.489168 | 0.6260 |
| DHICP(–3) | 0.175791 | 0.103845 | 1.692821 | 0.0942 |
| DHICP(–4) | 0.441757 | 0.100980 | 4.374680 | 0.0000 |
| DOIL | 0.006497 | 0.002207 | 2.943992 | 0.0042 |
| GAP(–1) | 0.368721 | 0.139499 | 2.643178 | 0.0098 |
| PGAP(–1) | –0.013933 | 0.023705 | –0.587774 | 0.5583 |
| C | 0.106213 | 0.226575 | 0.468776 | 0.6404 |
| Adjusted $R^2$ | 0.871325 | | DW | 1.892062 |

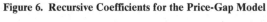

**Figure 6. Recursive Coefficients for the Price-Gap Model**

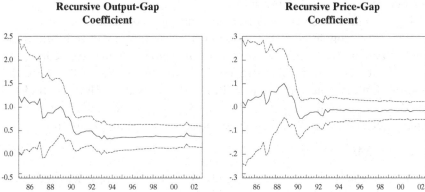

Recursive estimates of the price gap and the output gap coefficient, reported in figure 6, suggest that the relationship between the inflation rate and both the price gap and the output gap has weakened since the second half of the 1980s. Thus, both variables provide less guidance for central bank policy in the low-inflation period.

Compared to the theoretical model above, the empirical specification of the Phillips curve considered so far makes no use of the trend inflation rate, $\pi^*$. As indicated previously, this trend inflation rate must be consistent with the long-run money-demand function. By first differencing the quantity equation and inserting trend values, we can derive the long-run trend inflation rate as

(14) $\pi^* = \Delta M^* - \Delta Y^* - \Delta v^*$.

The trend inflation rate is therefore given by the trend growth rate of money less trend output growth and less trend velocity. A velocity trend could result from wealth effects or an income elasticity above 1 in the long-run money-demand function. In this vein, the ECB argues that the velocity of money in the euro area exhibits a negative trend of around –1.0% annually. Note, however, that over the 23 years considered in our sample, we observe a gradual decline in long-term interest rates, which is the result of the gradual disinflation in the euro area. Given our estimates of the long-run money-demand function, this also gives rise to a secular decline in the velocity of money. Over the sample period, the long-term nominal interest rate fell by an average of 7 basis points per quarter. From the estimated long-run money-demand equation, this implies a lasting decline in the velocity of money of about 1% per year. Thus, the estimated money-demand function yields exactly the same trend inflation rate as the one calculated based on the assumption of a deterministic trend in the velocity.[10]

Figure 8 plots the velocity of money and the long-term nominal interest rate over the sample period. The graph suggests that a deterministic trend would track the long-run development of the velocity similar to the long-run interest rate. However, there are several episodes in the 1990s where the long-run interest rate moves up and the velocity with it. Thus, we find the specification using the interest rate more satisfactory than the specification using a deterministic trend. This yields our estimate of trend inflation:

$$(15) \quad \pi^* = \Delta M^* - \Delta Y^* + 0.0387^* \, \Delta i^*,$$

where trend money growth and trend GDP growth were calculated using standard HP filters. Furthermore, $\Delta i^*$ is the trend in the long-term nominal interest rate over the sample period. Long-term interest rates declined on average by 7 basis points per quarter, which implies a trend decline of velocity of about 1% annually.

**Figure 8. Velocity and the Long-Run Interest Rate in the Euro Area**

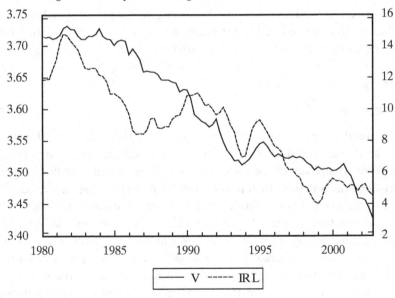

**Figure 9. Inflation and Trend Inflation in the Euro Area**

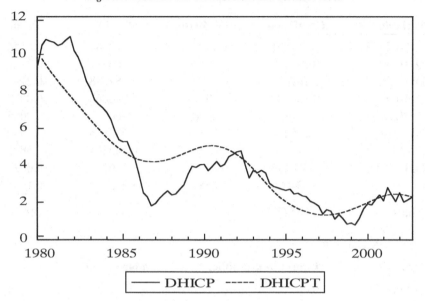

In figure 9, we show the development of the inflation rate and the trend inflation rate $\pi^*$ estimated in this way. The trend inflation rate implied by the quantity equation describes the long-run development of the actual inflation rate well. Importantly, our estimated trend inflation rate is leading turning points of the actual inflation rate in the mid-1980s, early 1990s, and also in the low-inflation period of the mid-1990s. Adding the trend inflation rate to the inflation adjustment equation yields the following equation:

$$(16) \quad \pi_t = \sum_{i=1}^{n} \alpha_i \pi_{t-i} + \beta \pi_{t-1} + \lambda (p^* - p)_{t-1} + \gamma \pi^*.$$

In table 6, we report estimates of this equation over the entire time period. The table shows the elasticities of the output gap, the price gap, and the trend inflation rate, together with their long-run multipliers, calculated as the estimated elasticity divided by 1 less the sum of the coefficients of the auto-regressive inflation terms. The results show that the output gap elasticity is significant at the 10% level, whereas the price gap is again not significantly different from zero.

Table 6. A New Keynesian Phillips Curve Including Trend Inflation

| Variable | Coefficient | Std. Error | t Statistic | Prob. |
|---|---|---|---|---|
| DHICP(–1) | 0.243801 | 0.098591 | 2.472844 | 0.0154 |
| DHICP(–2) | –0.123969 | 0.098364 | –1.260311 | 0.2111 |
| DHICP(–3) | 0.109658 | 0.100816 | 1.087698 | 0.2799 |
| DHICP(–4) | 0.384609 | 0.097595 | 3.940866 | 0.0002 |
| DOIL | 0.006305 | 0.002097 | 3.006309 | 0.0035 |
| GAP(–1) | 0.235438 | 0.138995 | 1.693855 | 0.0940 |
| PGAP(–1) | 0.013050 | 0.024066 | 0.542264 | 0.5891 |
| DHICPT | 0.429297 | 0.135137 | 3.176752 | 0.0021 |
| C | –0.334095 | 0.255994 | –1.305087 | 0.1955 |
| Adjusted $R^2$ | 0.885274 | | DW | 1.859912 |

Long-run multipliers:

| Variable | Long-run multiplier | Standard error |
|---|---|---|
| GAP(–1) | 0.60 | 0.43 |
| PGAP(–1) | 0.01 | 0.04 |
| DHICPT | 1.11 | 0.15 |

Table 7. A New Keynesian Phillips Curve Including Trend Inflation, 1990–2002

| Variable | Coefficient | Std. Error | *t* Statistic | Prob. |
|---|---|---|---|---|
| DHICP(–1) | –0.190740 | 0.142574 | –1.337832 | 0.1880 |
| DHICP(–2) | –0.328433 | 0.144873 | –2.267043 | 0.0285 |
| DHICP(–3) | –0.035015 | 0.136486 | –0.256545 | 0.7988 |
| DHICP(–4) | 0.165337 | 0.138752 | 1.191604 | 0.2400 |
| DOIL | 0.003406 | 0.002281 | 1.493398 | 0.1426 |
| GAP(–1) | 0.127286 | 0.184329 | 0.690536 | 0.4936 |
| PGAP(–1) | 0.096774 | 0.044196 | 2.189665 | 0.0340 |
| DHICPT | 0.763268 | 0.237746 | 3.210435 | 0.0025 |
| C | 1.448568 | 0.633744 | 2.285731 | 0.0273 |
| Adjusted $R^2$ | 0.605176 | | DW | 2.052629 |

Long-run multipliers:

| Variable | Long-run multiplier | Standard error |
|---|---|---|
| GAP(–1) | 0.09 | 0.13 |
| PGAP(–1) | 0.07 | 0.02 |
| DHICPT | 0.55 | 0.12 |

The trend inflation rate is significant at the 1% level. Thus, the monetary trend inflation rate appears to be the most important determinant of the inflation rate. The long-run multipliers of the output gap and price gap are both not significantly different from zero; the long-run multiplier of the monetary trend inflation rate is significant at the 1% level, and the hypothesis that the inflation rate fully adjusts in the long run to the trend inflation rate—that is, that the long-run multiplier of the trend inflation rate is not significantly different from one—cannot be rejected.

Figure 7 presents the recursive estimates of the coefficients on the output gap, the price gap, and the inflation trend for this model. The coefficients for the output gap and the price gap are positive in the 1980s but come close to zero in the 1990s and lose significance. The coefficient on the inflation trend falls, but it remains positive and significant overall. The decline in the trend coefficient is consistent with the notion that trend shocks were more important in the early than in the later part of the sample. Thus, the two more cyclically oriented indicators lose information value for inflation, whereas the inflation trend remains important in the low-inflation period. As a test of the robustness of this finding, we estimate the model of equation again using data only for

*Jürgen von Hagen and Boris Hofmann*

**Figure 7. Recursive Coefficients for the Inflation-Trend Model**

Recursive
Output-Gap
Coefficient

Recursive
Price-Gap
Coefficient

Recursive
Inflation-Trend
Coefficient

the low-inflation period starting in 1990. As shown in table 6, the output gap is not significant for explaining euro-area inflation in this period. In contrast, the inflation trend is important and highly significant.

## 5. CONCLUSIONS

Numerous authors have claimed that under conditions of low inflation, monetary and money growth are irrelevant for inflation. This claim is based on the observation that the correlation between money growth and inflation has become weak, if not vanished, in recent years.

In this paper, we argue that the policy conclusion drawn from this observation is unwarranted. A general feature of the move to low inflation is that the volatility of inflation has declined, too. Our interpretation is that this reflects the move to a less activist and erratic conduct of monetary policy. As monetary policy shocks become less important, other shocks affecting inflation temporarily move to the forefront and dampen the correlation between money and inflation. We show that a similar argument holds for the output gap.

Thus, with low and less volatile inflation, the traditional indicators that central banks look at to assess the inflation outlook become less informative. This leaves the central bank with less orientation. However, we show that trend inflation still provides good guidance for monetary policy under low inflation. For the euro area, trend inflation can be estimated from monetary and output trends. Thus, despite the declining correlation of money growth rates and inflation at high frequencies, monetary aggregates remain important as an orientation for monetary policy.

ACKNOWLEDGMENTS

The views expressed in this paper do not necessarily represent the views of the institutions the authors are affiliated with.

REFERENCES

Alesina, A., O. Blanchard, J. Galí, F. Giavazzi, and H. Uhlig. 2001. *Defining a Macroeconomic Framework for the Euro Area.* Monitoring the European Central Bank 3. London: Centre for Economic Policy Research.

Altimari, Nicoletti S. 2001. Does Money Lead Inflation in the Euro Area? Working Paper No. 63, European Central Bank.

Barro, R. J. 1990. Macroeconomics. 3rd ed. New York: Wiley.

Christiano, L. J., and T. Fitzgerald. 2003. Inflation and Monetary Policy in the 20th Century. *Federal Reserve Bank of Chicago Economic Perspectives* 27(1): 21–45.

De Grauwe, P., and M. Polan. 2001. Is Inflation Always and Everywhere a Monetary Phenomenon? Discussion Paper No. 2841, Centre for Economic Policy Research.

Dwyer, G., and R. W. Hafer. 1988. Is Money Irrelevant? *Federal Reserve Bank of St. Louis Review* 70: 3–17.

Dwyer, G., and R. W. Hafer. 1999. Are Money Growth and Inflation Still Related? *Federal Reserve Bank of Atlanta Economic Review* 84(2): 32–43.

Estrella, A., and F. Mishkin. 1997. Is There a Role for Money in Monetary Policy? *Journal of Monetary Economics* 40: 279–304.

European Central Bank (ECB). 2003. The ECB's Monetary Policy Strategy. News release, May 2003.

Friedman, B. M., and K. N. Kuttner. 1992. Money, Income, Prices, and Interest Rates. *American Economic Review* 82: 772–92.

Galí. J. 2001. Monetary Policy in the Early Years of EMU. In *The Functioning of EMU: Challenges of the Early Years,* edited by M. Buti and A. Sapir. Oxford: Oxford University Press.

Galí, J., and M. Gertler. 1999. Inflation Dynamics: A Structural Econometric Analysis. *Journal of Monetary Economics* 44: 195–222.

Gerlach, S. 2004. *The ECB's Two Pillars. Economic Policy* 40: 389–439.

Hallman, J. J., R. D. Porter, and D. H. Small. 1991. Is the Price Level Tied to the M2 Monetary Aggregate in the Long Run? *American Economic Review* 81: 841–58.

Hayo, B. 1999. Estimating a European Demand for Money. *Scottish Journal of Political Economy* 46: 221–44.

King, M. 2001. No Money, No Inflation—The Role of Money in the Economy. *Bank of England Quarterly Bulletin* Summer: 162–77.

Lucas, R. E. 1980. Two Illustrations of the Quantity Theory of Money. *American Economic Review* 70: 1005–14.

McCallum, B. T. 2001. Monetary Policy Analysis in Models Without Money. *Federal Reserve Bank of St. Louis Review* 83(4): 145–64.

McCandless, G. T. Jr., and W. E. Weber. 1995. Some Monetary Facts. *Federal Reserve Bank of Minneapolis Quarterly Review* 19(3): 2–11.

Mussa, M. 1982. A Model of Exchange Rate Dynamics. *Journal of Political Economy* 90: 74–104.

Nelson, E. 2003a. The Future of Monetary Aggregates in Monetary Policy Analysis. Discussion Paper No. 3897, Centre for Economic Policy Research.

Nelson, E. 2003b. Money and the Transmission Mechanism in the Optimizing IS-LM Specification. Unpublished manuscript, Bank of England.

Neumann, M. J. M. 2003. The European Central Bank's First Pillar Reassessed. Working paper, IIW Bonn University.

Poole, B. 1994. Keep the M in Monetary Policy. *Jobs and Capital* 3: 2–5.

Steinsson, J. 2003. Optimal Monetary Policy in an Economy with Inflation Persistence. *Journal of Monetary Economics* 50: 1425–56.

Stock, J., and M. Watson. 1999. Forecasting Inflation. *Journal of Monetary Economics* 44: 293–335.

Svensson, L. E. O. 1999. How Should Monetary Policy Be Conducted in an Era of Price Stability? In *New Challenges for Monetary Policy*, 195–259. Kansas City, MO: Federal Reserve Bank of Kansas City.

Tanner, J. E. 1993. Did Monetarism Die in the 1980s? *Journal of Economics and Business* 45: 213–29.

Taylor, J. B. 1993. Discretion Versus Policy Rules in Practice. *Carnegie–Rochester Conference Series on Public Policy* 39: 195–214.

Trecroci, C., and J. L. Vega. 2002. The Information Content of M3 for Future Inflation. *Weltwirtschaftliches Archiv* 138: 22–53.

von Hagen, J. 2004. Hat die Geldmenge ausgedient? *Perspektiven der Wirtschaftspolitik* 5(4): 423–53.

von Hagen, J., and B. Hayo. 1999. Monetary Conditions in the Euro Area. EMU Monitor Working Paper, ZEI University of Bonn.

Woodford, M. 2001. The Taylor Rule and Optimal Monetary Policy. Working paper, Princeton University.

Woodford, M. 2003. Optimal Interest-Rate Smoothing. *Review of Economic Studies* 70(4): 861–86.

# Commentary

*Jack Selody*

It is well known that a variable that is the subject of control—in this case, inflation—loses its ability to be predicted by the variable being manipulated to effect that control—either the output gap or fluctuations in money around its trend, depending on your preferred model. In other words, the correlation between the two variables is destroyed by the process of control.

The reason for this is straightforward. Without control, a shock that causes the output gap or money to move will result in a subsequent move in inflation. With control, a shock that would otherwise cause the output gap or money to move will either be offset by a preceding monetary policy action, leaving both inflation and the output gap or money unchanged, or result in a policy-induced offsetting move in the output gap or money, leaving inflation alone unchanged. In either case, inflation will be uncorrelated with money or the output gap because it remains largely unaffected.

There are two caveats to this loss of correlation. First, imperfect offsets by monetary policy to shocks will show up in the output gap, money, and inflation. If such policy errors are frequent, the correlation will be reduced but not destroyed. Second, a change in the trend growth rate of money will still be reflected in the trend inflation rate.

In their paper, Jürgen von Hagen and Boris Hofmann do an excellent job of demonstrating this reduction in correlation with a real-world example from Europe. They build two standard models of the monetary transmission process—one in which money is the proximate cause of inflation and another in which the output gap is the proximate cause of inflation—and show that the correlation between inflation and both money and the output gap vanishes during periods of effective inflation control. They are careful about how they parameterize the models, and as a result, the results are convincing.

The authors also report data from 14 OECD (Organisation for Economic Co-operation and Development) countries to show that the volatility of both inflation and money is lower during periods of rigorous inflation control, consistent with the results of the model simulations. More importantly, however, they show that the long-run relationship between money and prices remains intact during periods of rigorous inflation control. The stability of this long-run relationship is important because it suggests that a change in the trend of money will show up as a change in the trend of prices even when inflation is targeted rigorously.

This paper is important in that it reminds us that moving to a regime of inflation control will change the properties of the indicators of monetary policy. Consequently, monetary policy must find new indicators or new ways to use its traditional indicators.

It is significant that the indicators that are traditionally used by monetary policy to foresee future inflation have lost their predictive ability in recent times. That inflation has remained on target during this time, despite this loss, is a testament to the robustness of the current monetary policy framework. Yet the loss of information content in the traditional indicators should leave monetary policymakers somewhat uneasy.

The authors suggest that trend inflation still provides good guidance for monetary policy under low inflation. This is true in theory. However, in practice, I find this cold comfort because if trend inflation is constructed from past inflation, inflation will undoubtedly be out of control by the time a new trend is unambiguously identified.

Alternatively, inflation expectations may be a reliable indicator of trend inflation, and these expectations may give monetary policy the lead time it needs. Indeed, the increasing focus of monetary policymakers on monitoring inflation expectations may explain why monetary policy has been so successful in recent years. Further exploration of this issue is warranted.

It may be that central bank economists are using models that are capable of identifying shocks with the potential to affect inflation with enough lead time that monetary policy can effectively offset the shocks. If so, central banks should continue to invest heavily in these models because it is imperative that they keep pace with economic developments. Further research into what makes these models effective at identifying relevant shocks would be beneficial.

Finally, it may be that money and the output gap are good indicators of inflation when monetary policy makes mistakes, but we have been fortunate in recent years that monetary policy has not been prone to error. In this case, it is business as usual on the monetary policy front because the information content of the traditional indicators will return when needed. Nevertheless, further research into methods that would improve the measurement of money and the output gap would be helpful.

No doubt all the above are part of the story of why monetary policy has been successful in recent times despite the decline in the information content of the traditional indicators. Thus, I encourage work to proceed on all fronts.

# Commentary

*Pierre L. Siklos*

I have a great deal of sympathy with the main message of von Hagen and Hofmann's paper, namely that central banks, to paraphrase Laidler (1988), should take money seriously. The authors point out that, in debates over the conduct of monetary policy, the role of money has been downgraded in recent years, largely because the empirical evidence about the size of the correlations between short-run variations in money growth and inflation appears mixed to unfavorable. To make matters possibly worse for the "monetarists," the correlation between money growth and inflation disintegrates when the level of inflation and its volatility fall to "low" levels. As a result, even the fledgling European Central Bank (ECB) has relegated the role of monetary aggregates to the background in conducting monetary policy.[1]

Indeed, a summary of the debate over the extent to which inflation is a monetary phenomenon suggests at least four factors that have produced a certain amount of dissatisfaction about the usefulness of monetary indicators of inflation. Not in any particular order of importance, these factors include
- the choice of the sample period
- country-specific factors
- data frequency and the span of the data set
- the definition of the monetary aggregate in empirical work.

Although it is generally agreed that the full impact of monetary policy occurs with long and variable lags, a central bank is naturally expected to take the view that, in the long run, inflation is primarily a monetary phenomenon.

One might expect little or no controversy over the authors' contention that one should not ignore the quantity of money. Yet, as the authors correctly point out, money seems to be out of the monetary policy picture even among some central bankers. Hence, an attempt to rehabilitate the role of money in monetary policy is welcome. However, the case made by von Hagen and Hofmann for making money once again a "pillar" of monetary policy is not always convincing. My comments will focus on conceptual and empirical questions that arise from the results presented in the paper.

First, as Laidler (1999) points out, by treating money as passive in models such as the authors' equations (5)–(8), one is unlikely to conclude that money plays an empirically meaningful role. Yet, this is essentially what the authors

---

[1] Relegating money targets to a lesser role is only partly the result of their poor performance as indicators of future inflation. The main impetus, I believe, is the general view that the ECB has been less than clear about how monetary policy has been or ought to be conducted in the euro area.

do in order to avoid any inconsistencies with a model consisting of an IS curve, a Phillips curve, and a Taylor rule. Instead, the point the authors should be emphasizing is that money should have an "active" role in macro models. Nevertheless, even Laidler (1999) might admit that this is easier said than done. He points out, for example, that changing definitions of monetary aggregates pose a serious problem, but the solution to monitor and revise such definitions is appropriate.[2] This effectively implies that the $P^*$ approach, driven by the behavior of monetary aggregates, though a useful way to measure the indicator properties of money as the authors contend, ends up being a backward-looking inflation indicator even if, in theory at least, it is meant to be a forward-looking indicator. Indeed, there is a rich literature that readily points out the failings of the $P^*$ model (e.g., Christiano 1989; Gerlach and Svensson 2003). The $P^*$ in von Hagen and Hofmann's equation (3), derived from a test for cointegration between real M3, real GDP, and a long-run interest rate, is far more fragile than the authors let on.[3] Indeed, the finding of cointegration is easily overturned unless the long-run interest rate is omitted from the cointegrating relationship. The price gap, which can be likened to an error-correction term, is, therefore, sensitive to the hypothesized specification. An example is shown in figure 1.

Figure 1 plots the price gap version derived by von Hagen and Hofmann, which I was able to replicate, as well as one based on an alternative estimate of the underlying long-run relationship. Indeed, the alternative measure of the price gap suggests a very different picture for the relationship with inflation in the harmonized index of consumer prices (HICP), as shown in figure 2. Hence, as a *long-run* indicator, the $P^*$ model tracks rather well, but it is unclear whether the version used by von Hagen and Hofmann is "best" in some statistical sense. For example, I would argue that the version presented below is a relatively better representation of the relationship between the price gap and inflation in the euro area than in figure 2 of von Hagen and Hofmann.

Von Hagen and Hofmann not only try to produce evidence that is favorable to raising the profile of a monetary aggregate, they also go on to contend that the output gap loses its informational content for monetary policy in the 1990s. However, their conclusion is based only on the impact of the output

---

[2] The forecasting ability of monetary aggregates in countries such as the United States and Canada improves once we create "composite" monetary aggregates that are linear combinations of existing monetary aggregates (see Feldstein and Stock 1996; Siklos and Barton 2001). The proliferation of money-supply definitions in North America (and elsewhere) reflects the impact of frequent financial innovations. The role of these innovations, not as important in the euro-area context as far as I am aware, is a practical point that von Hagen and Hofmann do not explicitly address and yet may prove to be a problematic one in future.

[3] A point made already by Söderlind and Vredin (1996).

### Figure 1. Alternative Price Gap Measures

Alternative Price Gap measure
Replicating Von Hagen Hofmann

**Note:** The dashed line replicates the price gap reported in von Hagen and Hofmann using their data. The solid line is based on a price gap evaluated from the co-integrating relationship between the logarithm of M3 and real GDP for the euro area, including a constant in the co-integrating equation as well as an exogenous dummy variable for the period since German reunification in 1990.

### Figure 2. Actual Inflation and the Price Gap

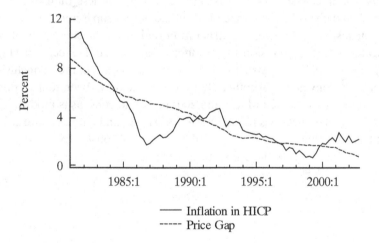

Inflation in HICP
Price Gap

**Note:** The price gap is the difference between $P$ and $P^*$ as defined in von Hagen and Hofmann using the $P^*$ values generated previously.

gap in their Phillips curve specification (estimated using ordinary least squares) and not on its ability to explain the monetary authority's reaction function. If we are to take seriously the role of money, then an additional way to test this hypothesis is to ask, for example, whether money growth represents a useful instrument in a Taylor rule. As shown in table 1, using their data, the test for overidentifying restrictions shows that $p$ values are improved with the addition of money growth in the set of instruments, although a specification that includes the conventional set of instruments performs just as well.[4] Part of the difficulty, of course, is that it is unclear what we are to make of euro-area data prior to 1999, when the ECB came into being. Moreover, the coefficients in the Taylor suggest a potential misspecification, as there is clearly near unit root behavior in the nominal interest rate in both samples when money growth is an added instrument, especially in the post-1990 sample— that is, once we consider the period since German reunification. Hence, it is far from clear that their equation (7) is properly specified. Also, notice that the output gap is generally significant in all specifications except again for the post-1990 sample when inflation is significant (though less than one would have predicted given Taylor's principle), but the output gap is not. This evidence is only suggestive, of course, of a structural break or of the sensitivity of such specifications to the inclusion of a monetary aggregate. Hence, von Hagen and Hofmann's claim that structural breaks would not affect their conclusions is not entirely convincing.[5] Another alternative would have been to incorporate a McCallum-type rule (see McCallum 2001) into the consensus model.

In spite of the objections raised above, von Hagen and Hofmann are correct in emphasizing that "money" ought to be taken seriously. To do otherwise would be to ignore one of the arguably few clear lessons from monetary history.

---

[4] The results were quite robust to the number of instruments used. When I added one-year-ahead money growth to the Taylor rule, the $J$ test could not reject the overidentifying restrictions for either sample although expected money growth was highly insignificant.

[5] Indeed, if one estimates their New Keynesian Phillips curve using GMM, the output gap is significant, as is $P^*$, though the coefficient is arguably economically small.

Commentary                                    213

Table 1. Selected Taylor Rule Estimates for the Euro Area

| Variables | Samples | | | |
|---|---|---|---|---|
| | 1982–2001 | 1990–2001 | 1982–2001 | 1990–2001 |
| Constant | .005 (.033)* | .14 (1.51) | −.29 (−1.94) | .02 (.23) |
| One-period lagged nominal interest rate | .92 (18.04) | .99 (31.40)* | .88 (15.27)* | .94 (25.27)* |
| One-year-ahead inflation rate | 0.11 (1.06) | −.05 (−.74) | .45 (2.45)* | .14 (1.09) |
| One-year-ahead output gap | 0.55 (5.28)* | .41 (8.36)* | .08 (.81) | .29 (3.26)* |
| J statistic | 7.20 (.78) | 10.40 (.49) | 7.15 (.79) | 9.46 (.58) |
| Instrument list includes lagged money growth? | No | Yes | No | Yes |

Note: Estimated using GMM with fixed bandwidth. Inflation is the HICP, and the output gap is the HP-filtered real GDP for the euro area. Data are from von Hagen and Hofmann. The $J$ statistic is the test for overidentifying restrictions with $p$ values in parenthesis. Four lags of each of the right-side variables (except the constant) and includes money growth (M3 growth) only in the cases shown. The $t$ statistic for each coefficient is shown in parenthesis.

## ACKNOWLEDGMENTS

I am grateful to Jürgen von Hagen and Boris Hofmann for making available the data used in their paper.

REFERENCES

Christiano, L. 1989. *P\**: Not the Inflation Forecaster's Holy Grail. *Federal Reserve Bank of Minneapolis Quarterly Review* 13: 3–18.

Feldstein, M., and J. H. Stock. 1996. Measuring Money Growth When Financial Markets Are Changing. *Journal of Monetary Economics* 37: 3–27.

Gerlach, S., and L. E. O. Svensson. 2003. Money and Inflation in the Euro Area: A Case for Monetary Indicators? *Journal of Monetary Economics* 50: 1649–72.

Laidler, D. E. W. 1988. Taking Money Seriously. *Canadian Journal of Economics* 21: 687–713.

Laidler, D. E. W. 1999. The Quantity of Money and Monetary Policy. Working Paper No. 99-1, Bank of Canada.

McCallum, B. T. 2001. Monetary Policy Analysis in Models without Money. Federal Reserve Bank of St. Louis, *Review* 83(4): 145–64.

Siklos, P. L., and A. Barton. 2001. Monetary Aggregates as Indicators of Economic Activity in Canada: Empirical Evidence. *Canadian Journal of Economics* 34: 1–17.

Söderlind, P., and A. Vredin. 1996. Applied Cointegration Analysis in the Mirror of Macroeconomic Theory. *Journal of Applied Econometrics* 11: 363–81.

# 7

## Observations on Disinflation in Transition Economies

### Paul Wachtel and Iikka Korhonen

The transition to market-based economies began just a little more than a decade ago in 27 countries of central Europe and the former Soviet Union. Most observers in the early 1990s thought that the transition process would be long and tedious. Early transition experiences seemed to support that expectation. Most of the transition countries experienced sharp initial declines in output, periods of rapid inflation—including many hyperinflations—and enormous political obstacles to reform. There was ample reason to believe that transition would be a specific area of concern to economists for many years to come. However, the unique transition experiences are largely past in most countries, and the term "transition economics" might even be disappearing from view. At the very least, the term is barely relevant in much of central Europe, although it is still applicable in the republics of the former Soviet Union and possibly China. That is not to say these countries are trouble free, but that they share problems that are common to other emerging market economies. However, some of the advanced transition countries are quickly leaving that status. Nothing symbolizes this more than the accession of eight formerly planned economies from the Baltics, central Europe, and the Balkans to the European Union in the spring of 2004.

The rapidity of the transition experience is well illustrated by the path of inflation in these countries. Not surprisingly, one of the first manifestations of transition was high inflation. The causes of these inflationary outbursts were classical. First, the removal of price controls and quantity allocations, which repressed demand, led to rapid adjustments to free-market prices. Second, fiscal and financial crises resulted in periods of rapid monetary expansion as governments relied on seigniorage to support budgets as well as state-owned enterprises. In the early 1990s, more than half of the transition countries experienced at least one year with annual inflation in excess of 1,000% or close to it. However, stabilization policies were in place in virtually every transition country by 1995, and the policies were remarkably successful. Since 1997, only three countries have experienced annual inflation in excess of 100%. By 2002, annual inflation rates were below 15% in all but five countries and below 5%

in just half.[1] The transition experience with inflation has been nothing short of remarkable.

Why did the transition economies do so well so quickly in bringing inflation under control? One answer is that the consensus view of stabilization policy had just come into its own in the policy world by the 1990s. Approaches to macroeconomics and policymaking that were not self-evident to the leaders and intellectuals of the less developed world during the 1960s, 1970s, and 1980s were learned quickly in the transition world of the 1990s. Thus, the Latin American experiences of generations who repeatedly fought inflation without a political consensus that accepted macroeconomic realities were not repeated in central Europe.

Another answer, based on the political economy of transition, was suggested early on by Havrylyshyn (1997). Policymakers were able to introduce disinflation policies that coincided with the interests of powerful oligarchs. At the start of transition, the elite took advantage of inflation, low interest rates, and poor institutional structure to transfer capital from the state to private interests. Once established as capitalists, the elite had an interest in disinflation. There are countries where disinflation did not take hold so quickly. Russia seemed to follow the Latin American experience for much of the 1990s: High and persistent fiscal deficits ultimately led to a financial crisis and the reemergence of high inflation in 1998. However, this might be explained by continued tension between the interests of the oligarchs and the government in Russia.

The experience with disinflation does not imply that transition economics is a complete success. Although the lessons of stabilization policy were largely learned, there are other economic issues for which transition problems are still extant. In particular, health, education, and pension systems remain largely unchanged, and subsidies to government-owned enterprises are still common. Important institutional reforms are still needed—for example, so that property rights are clearly defined and fairly enforced. Confidence in the rule of law is far from perfect, and corporate governance needs to be improved. Moreover, liberalization of the economies and support for a competitive environment might face opposition from private-sector monopolist interests.

The influence of Western investors and institutions in the transition economies may be another important reason why the transition economies were able to adopt stabilization policies rapidly. Relatively large flows of foreign direct investment and portfolio investment into the fast-track transition economies of Europe (Poland, Hungary, and the Czech Republic) started immediately after the transition. Pressures for institutional reform accompanied

---

[1] For data from the European Bank for Reconstruction and Development on the annual average consumer price level, see table 1.

these flows. In addition, reform elements in these countries found an environment with an institutional memory of market institutions and the human capital to jump-start the process. Furthermore, some countries, Hungary in particular, had already started tentative market reforms in the 1980s, making the subsequent transition process easier. As a result, policy and regulatory abuses in these countries were rather short-lived. By the mid-1990s, the fast-track transition economies had reformed the financial sector and established sound institutional structures for monetary policy. With these accomplishments, it is not surprising that stabilization policy fell into place.

Another important answer is the pull of Europe. For a variety of political and social reasons, the nations of central Europe have an overwhelming desire to be part of Europe and the institutions of the European community. So, a consensus commitment to join Europe led to a willingness to adopt stringent economic policies and structural reforms in the countries chosen for accession. This has also influenced policy in other Balkan countries that do not want to be left out of the second wave and some of the other countries (e.g., Ukraine) that do not want to appear un-European.

We begin the discussion with an overview of the inflation experience in transition. Only a brief overview is needed because this is far from the first essay to take note of the remarkable inflation history in the region. Koen and De Masi (1997) surveyed the initial experiences of transition, and Dabrowski (1999) and Cottarelli and Doyle (1999) looked at the phenomenon in the late 1990s. Table 1 shows annual consumer price index (CPI) inflation rates for the transition countries, separated into three regional groups. In all groups, the median inflation rates declined steadily. For the central and eastern European (CEE) countries, the median dipped below 50% per year in 1993; in the Commonwealth of Independent States (CIS), that milestone was passed in 1996. The 10% threshold for the median was passed in 1997 in the CEE; the median inflation rate in the former Soviet Union (FSU) almost reached that level in 1998 and again in 2001 but did not fall below 10% until 2002. The strongest efforts to bring inflation down to European levels were in the countries selected for accession to the European Union (EU). The reference rate for inflation using the Maastricht convergence criteria was between 3% and 3.5% in the three years 2000–02.[2] The median accession country inflation rate reached this threshold in 2002. In 2002, the median inflation rate in the eight countries that entered the EU in 2004 was 2.6%, not much more than the euro-area inflation rate of 2.3%.

---

[2] The Maastricht Treaty set the reference rate for inflation convergence as the average of the three lowest inflation rates in the EU plus 1.5%. If this rule is applied to the countries in the euro area, the reference rates are 3.2%, 3.5%, and 3.0% in 2000–02.

**Table 1. Inflation in Central and Eastern Europe and the CIS**

| | 1991 | 1992 | 1993 | 1994 | 1995 | 1996 | 1997 | 1998 | 1999 | 2000 | 2001 | 2002 | 2003 |
|---|---|---|---|---|---|---|---|---|---|---|---|---|---|
| **Central and Eastern Europe and the Baltic States** | | | | | | | | | | | | | |
| Croatia | 123 | 665.5 | 1,517.5 | 97.6 | 2 | 3.5 | 3.6 | 5.7 | 4.2 | 6.2 | 4.9 | 2.4 | 2.4 |
| Czech Republic | 52 | 11.1 | 20.8 | 9.9 | 9.1 | 8.8 | 8.5 | 10.7 | 2.1 | 3.9 | 4.7 | 1.8 | 0.2 |
| Estonia | 210.5 | 1,076.0 | 89.8 | 47.7 | 29 | 23.1 | 11.2 | 8.1 | 3.3 | 4 | 5.8 | 3.6 | 1.4 |
| Hungary | 35 | 23 | 22.5 | 18.8 | 28.2 | 23.6 | 18.3 | 14.3 | 10 | 9.8 | 9.2 | 4.8 | 4.7 |
| Latvia | 172.2 | 951.2 | 109.2 | 35.9 | 25 | 17.6 | 8.4 | 4.7 | 2.4 | 2.6 | 2.5 | 1.9 | 3.3 |
| Lithuania | 224.7 | 1,020.5 | 410.4 | 72.1 | 39.6 | 24.6 | 8.9 | 5.1 | 0.8 | 1 | 1.3 | 0.3 | -0.8 |
| Poland | 70.3 | 43 | 35.3 | 32.2 | 27.8 | 19.9 | 14.9 | 11.8 | 7.3 | 10.1 | 5.5 | 1.7 | 0.5 |
| Slovak Republic | 61.2 | 10 | 23.2 | 13.4 | 9.9 | 5.8 | 6.1 | 6.7 | 10.6 | 12 | 7.1 | 3.3 | 8.5 |
| Slovenia | 117.7 | 207.3 | 32.9 | 21 | 13.5 | 9.9 | 8.4 | 7.9 | 6.1 | 8.9 | 8.4 | 7.5 | 6.1 |
| *Median* | *117.7* | *207.3* | *35.3* | *32.2* | *25* | *17.6* | *8.5* | *7.9* | *4.2* | *6.2* | *5.5* | *2.4* | *2.4* |
| **Southeastern Europe** | | | | | | | | | | | | | |
| Albania | 35.5 | 226 | 85 | 22.6 | 7.8 | 12.7 | 33.2 | 20.6 | 0.4 | 0.1 | 3.1 | 5.4 | 3.5 |
| Bulgaria | 333.5 | 82 | 73 | 96.3 | 62 | 123 | 1,082.0 | 22.2 | 0.7 | 9.9 | 7.4 | 5.9 | 2 |
| FYR Macedonia | 114.9 | 1,664.4 | 338.4 | 126.5 | 16.4 | 2.5 | 0.8 | 2.3 | -1.3 | 6.5 | 5.3 | 2.4 | 1.5 |
| Romania | 170.2 | 210.4 | 256.1 | 136.7 | 32.3 | 38.8 | 154.8 | 59.1 | 45.8 | 45.7 | 34.5 | 22.5 | 14.5 |
| Serbia and Montenegro | 121 | 9,237.0 | $16.5 \times 10^{12}$ | 3.3 | 78.6 | 94.3 | 21.3 | 29.5 | 37.1 | 60.4 | 91.3 | 21.4 | 12 |
| *Median* | *121* | *226* | *170.6\** | *96.3* | *32.3* | *38.8* | *33.2* | *22.2* | *0.7* | *9.9* | *7.4* | *5.9* | *3.5* |
| **Commonwealth of Independent States** | | | | | | | | | | | | | |
| Armenia | 274 | 1,346.0 | 1,822.0 | 4,962.0 | 175.8 | 18.7 | 14 | 8.7 | 0.7 | -0.8 | 3.2 | 1.2 | 6.1 |
| Azerbaijan | 107 | 912 | 1,129.0 | 1,664.0 | 412 | 19.7 | 3.5 | -0.8 | -8.5 | 1.8 | 1.5 | 2.8 | 2.1 |
| Belarus | 94.1 | 970.8 | 1,190.2 | 2,221.0 | 709.3 | 52.7 | 63.8 | 73.2 | 293.8 | 168.9 | 61.4 | 42.6 | 29 |
| Georgia | 79 | 887.4 | 3,125.4 | 15,606.5 | 162.7 | 39.4 | 7.1 | 3.6 | 19.2 | 4.1 | 4.6 | 5.6 | 5 |
| Kazakhstan | 78.8 | 1,381.0 | 1,662.3 | 1,892.0 | 176.3 | 39.1 | 17.4 | 7.1 | 8.3 | 13.2 | 8.4 | 5.8 | 6.1 |
| Kyrgyz Republic | 85 | 855 | 772.4 | 180.7 | 43.5 | 31.9 | 23.4 | 10.5 | 35.9 | 18.7 | 6.9 | 2.1 | 2.4 |
| Moldova | 98 | 1,276.4 | 1,184.0 | 487 | 30.2 | 23.5 | 11.8 | 7.7 | 39.3 | 31.1 | 9.6 | 5.2 | 10 |
| Russia | 92.7 | 1,526.0 | 875 | 311.4 | 197.7 | 47.8 | 14.7 | 27.6 | 86.1 | 20.8 | 21.6 | 15.7 | 13.9 |
| Tajikistan | 112 | 1,157.0 | 2,195.0 | 350 | 609 | 418.8 | 43.2 | 27.6 | 32.9 | 38.6 | 12.2 | 16 | |
| Turkmenistan | 103 | 493 | 3,102.0 | 1,748.0 | 1,005.3 | 992.4 | 83.7 | 16.8 | 24.2 | 8.3 | 11.6 | 10.6 | 9.6 |
| Ukraine | 91 | 1,210.0 | 4,734.0 | 891 | 377 | 80 | 15.9 | 10.6 | 22.7 | 28.2 | 12 | 0.8 | 5.1 |
| Uzbekistan | 109.7 | 645.2 | 534.2 | 1,568.3 | 304.6 | 54 | 70.9 | 29 | 29.1 | 25 | 27.2 | 27.6 | 12.4 |
| *Median* | *96.1* | *1,063.9* | *1426.3* | *1,616.2* | *251.2* | *43.6* | *16.6* | *10.5* | *25.9* | *19.8* | *10.6* | *5.7* | *7.9* |
| **2004 and 2007 EU Accession Countries** | | | | | | | | | | | | | |
| *Median* | *144* | *62.5* | *54.2* | *34.1* | *28* | *21.5* | *8.9* | *9.4* | *4.7* | *9.4* | *6.5* | *3.4* | *2.7* |

Source: EBRD, Transition Report 2003, table A.3.3, p. 58.

Note: Data are the change in annual average retail/consumer price level in percent. Data for 1991–2001 represent the most recent official estimates of outturns as reflected in publications from the national authorities, the IMF, the World Bank, and the OECD. Data for 2002 are preliminary actuals, mostly official government estimates. Data for 2003 are EBRD projections. Eight 2004 EU accession countries are central and eastern Europe and the Baltics (top panel) except Croatia. The 2007 EU accession countries are Romania and Bulgaria. The figure for Albania for 1997 is based on the limited country data available.

* The value for Serbia and Montenegro is not included in the median.

A good measure of the success of disinflation is a sustained low inflation, for which we use the average inflation rates for the five-year period 1998–2002. The five-year average was below 5% in the Baltics, Croatia, Czech Republic, and three additional countries (Macedonia, Armenia, and Azerbaijan) for which an observer might question the quality of the data. The five-year average was above 10% in Romania, Serbia, and the larger FSU countries (Russia, Belarus, and Ukraine), as well as most of central Asia (except Kazakhstan) and a few other small FSU republics.

There is, of course, some variation in inflation experience among the 26 countries for which data are reported in table 1. A few countries, which started some economic reforms in advance of the political transition, were able to avoid hyperinflation (Hungary, Czech Republic, and Slovak Republic). In some countries, the disinflation was dramatic: Croatia went from over 1,000% inflation to almost none in two years. In others, the process was more gradual: The inflation rate in Hungary declined from 35% to 10% over the course of a decade.[3] In still others, reforms were not immediately successful: In Bulgaria, initial efforts at reform were unsuccessful, and inflation returned with vengeance in 1997. However, the introduction of a currency board and the accompanying fiscal adjustment brought inflation down fairly quickly.

Aggregating the data across the transition countries, many of which are very small, obscures the fact that inflation remains a problem in several large and important countries where fiscal discipline, financial reforms, extensive restructuring, and genuine privatization have lagged. Specifically, the 2002 inflation rate was 16% in Russia, 22% in Romania, 28% in Uzbekistan, and 43% in Belarus, with only modest amounts of disinflation anticipated for 2003.

Another useful way to examine the disinflation is to look at the experiences that followed stabilization policies. Cottarelli and Doyle (1999) use the dating of transition stabilizations prepared by Fischer, Sahay, and Vegh (1998) and show how long it took to reach disinflation mileposts. Table 2 updates this table with data on monthly inflation rates from the European Bank for Reconstruction and Development (EBRD). There are two broad observations from the table. First, stabilization programs usually take hold very quickly. Second, after an initial burst, the pace of disinflation slows down. A stabilization program brings inflation below 60% in about a year (the median for successful stabilizations is 13 months). The median time for inflation to fall from 60% to 30% is about four months. However, further

---

[3] There is much debate concerning the speed of disinflation in Hungary; see Olivier Blanchard (pro faster disinflation) and Kornai (con) in Cottarelli and Szapary (1998).

Table 2. Disinflation Thresholds

| Country | Peak Inflation (1990–2002) | Peak Inflation Date | Stabilization Program Date | Months to | Inflation < 60 | Months to | Inflation < 30 | Months to | Inflation < 15 | Months to | Inflation < 7 |
|---|---|---|---|---|---|---|---|---|---|---|---|
| Albania | 336.80 | 1992, Oct. | 1992, Aug. | 14 | 1993, Oct. | 3 | 1994, Jan. | 15 | 1995, Apr. | 2 | 1995, Jun. |
| Armenia | 29600.90 | 1994, May | 1994, Dec. | 13 | 1996, Jan. | 4 | 1996, May | 25 | 1998, Jun. | 2 | 1998, Aug. |
| Azerbaijan | 1899.00 | 1994, Nov. | 1995, Jan. | 13 | 1996, Feb. | 3 | 1996, May | 5 | 1996, Oct. | 4 | 1997, Feb. |
| Belarus | 2809.60 | 1994, Aug. | 1994, Nov. | 18 | 1996, May | NA | NA | NA | NA | NA | NA |
| Bulgaria (I) | 304.50 | 1992, Jan. | 1994, Dec. | 8 | 1995, Aug. | NA | NA | NA | NA | NA | NA |
| Bulgaria (II) | 2040.40 | 1997, Mar. | 1997, Apr. | 12 | 1998, Apr. | 0 | 1998, Apr. | 3 | 1998, Jul. | 2 | 1998, Sep. |
| Croatia | 1944.90 | 1993, Jun. | 1993, Oct. | 12 | 1994, Oct. | 1 | 1994, Nov. | 1 | 1994, Dec. | 0 | 1994, Dec. |
| Czech Republic | 67.60 | 1991, Jun. | 1991, Jan. | 3 | 1991, Apr. | 1 | 1991, Jul. | 2 | 1991, Oct. | 86 | 1998, Dec. |
| Estonia | 1241.90 | 1992, Sep. | 1992, Jun. | 16 | 1993, Oct. | 18 | 1995, Apr. | 21 | 1997, Jan. | 20 | 1998, Sep. |
| Georgia | 50654.00 | 1994, Sep. | 1994, Sep. | 14 | 1995, Nov. | 12 | 1996, Nov. | 2 | 1997, Jan. | 4 | 1997, May |
| Hungary | 31.00 | 1995, Jun. | 1990, Mar. | 10 | 1991, Jan. | 13 | 1992, Feb. | 77 | 1998, Jul. | 41 | 2001, Dec. |
| Kazakhstan | 3033.30 | 1994, Jun. | 1994, Jan. | 25 | 1996, Feb. | 11 | 1997, Jan. | 9 | 1997, Oct. | 10 | 1998, Aug. |
| Kyrgyz Republic | 1257.00 | 1992, Dec. | 1993, May | 23 | 1995, Apr. | 23 | 1997, Mar. | 10 | 1998, Jan. | 44 | 2001, Sep. |
| Latvia | 1444.60 | 1992, Nov. | 1992, Jun. | 16 | 1993, Oct. | 15 | 1995, Jan. | 23 | 1996, Dec. | 12 | 1997, Dec. |
| Lithuania | 1412.60 | 1992, Nov. | 1992, Jun. | 28 | 1994, Oct. | 20 | 1996, Jun. | 7 | 1997, Jan. | 13 | 1998, Feb. |
| Macedonia, FYR | 2100.30 | 1992, Oct. | 1994, Jan. | 12 | 1995, Jan. | 2 | 1995, Mar. | 4 | 1995, Jul. | 7 | 1996, Feb. |
| Moldova | 2198.40 | 1992, Dec. | 1993, Sep. | 9 | 1994, Jun. | 9 | 1995, Mar. | 14 | 1996, Jun. | 62 | 2001, Aug. |
| Poland | 1173.00 | 1990, Feb. | 1990, Jan. | 24 | 1992, Jan. | 43 | 1995, Aug. | 23 | 1997, Jul. | 44 | 2001, Mar. |
| Romania (I) | 317.00 | 1993, Nov. | 1993, Oct. | 16 | 1995, Feb. | NA | NA | NA | NA | NA | NA |
| Romania (II) | 177.41 | 1997, Jun. | 1998, Mar. | 3 | 1998, Jun. | 19 | 2002, Jan. | NA | NA | NA | NA |
| Russia (I) | 2321.60 | 1992, Dec. | 1995, Apr. | 14 | 1996, Jun. | 5 | 1996, Nov. | 7 | 1997, Jun. | NA | NA |
| Russia (II) | 126.52 | 1997, Jul. | 1999, Sep. | 2 | 1999, Nov. | 4 | 2000, Mar. | NA | NA | NA | NA |
| Slovak Republic | 73.70 | 1991, Jun. | 1991, Jan. | 3 | 1991, May | 1 | 1991, Jun. | 2 | 1991, Oct. | 51 | 1996, Jan |
| Slovenia | 88.20 | 1992, Dec. | 1992, Feb. | 3 | NA | 3 | 1992, Oct. | 32 | 1995, Jun. | 39 | 1998, Sep. |
| Ukraine | 10155.00 | 1993, Dec. | 1994, Nov. | 24 | 1996, Nov. | 4 | 1997, Mar. | 6 | 1997, Sep. | 50 | 2001, Nov. |

**Sources:** Cottarelli and Doyle (1999); European Bank for Reconstruction and Development.

**Note:** This table reproduces and extends the results obtained by Cottarelli and Doyle (1999) in table 2 using an updated data set. Periods between thresholds were defined using the three-month moving averages of annualized monthly inflation rates. When these first fell below a threshold, and remained there for a year, the country was deemed to have crossed the threshold.

progress in inflation reduction takes more time. The median time for inflation to fall from 30% to 15% is eight months, and from 15% to 7.5%, one year. The initial disinflation experiences are almost all rapid. Stabilization programs always bring inflation below 60% in about two years or less. Further progress is sometimes delayed. In Belarus, Bulgaria, Romania, and Russia, stabilization programs failed, and in Poland, it took almost four years to bring inflation under 30%. In Hungary, an early successful stabilization program was followed by a slow disinflation, and it took eight years for inflation to reach 15%. Inflation less than 7.5% was not reached until developed-country inflation levels consistently dropped below that level. So, the length of time to this final milestone depends largely on the date when the 15% milestone is passed.

The inflation experiences in transition countries have been extensively summarized in the International Monetary Fund (IMF) working paper by Cottarelli and Doyle (1999) and the CASE (Warsaw) report by Dabrowski (1999). Both of these papers reflect the amazement with which the successful disinflation programs were received. With a perspective of several more years, we both echo the amazement and note that the success of disinflation programs around the world has been taken for granted. In addition to bringing some of the relevant observations up to date, it will be useful to evaluate the disinflation experience and comment on some relevant issues, including whether low inflation is sustainable.

In the following sections, we describe how the transition countries achieved disinflation. Next, we argue that inflation may have contributed positively to the necessary changes in relative prices. The third section argues that the recorded inflation may overstate true inflation, and this problem was probably quite severe in the early years of transition. The fourth section has country studies for a small country with a rapid disinflation, Estonia; a rapidly growing transition country that disinflated gradually, Poland; a less successful disinflation story, Romania; and the largest transition country, Russia. Disinflation stories emphasize the choice of exchange rate regime and fiscal policy. We conclude that successful disinflation can occur with different approaches to the exchange rate, but fiscal discipline is a necessary condition for success. In the fifth section, we examine the evidence on the Balassa-Samuelson effect in the transition countries. Empirical studies suggest that the transition countries are likely to experience real exchange rate appreciation as their income levels increase. However, the resulting inflation differentials with the rest of the world will not be very large. The sixth section offers concluding remarks.

## 1. HOW DID THE TRANSITION COUNTRIES DISINFLATE?

A discussion of disinflation in transition countries has to be divided into two parts: the end of high inflation and the end of moderate inflation. As noted already, there are several studies of the former. Not surprisingly, control of the fiscal deficit is given the strongest credit in econometric studies and case analyses of high-inflation episodes. There has been less analysis of the more recent experience with disinflation, with the notable exception of Brada and Kutan (2002).

The initial stages of transition were accompanied by large fiscal deficits. Peak deficits in the general government balance were typically over 5% of gross domestic product (GDP) in the advanced transition countries and often much more in the FSU countries.[4] For example, the balance was over –10% in Bulgaria in 1993 and 1996, –7.5% in Hungary in 1994, and –11.9% in the Slovak Republic in 1992. In the FSU countries, where the collapse of output was larger and tax collections broke down, the deficits were even larger, almost 20% of GDP in Russia in 1992 and more in Ukraine. There were some exceptions: The peak deficit reported for the Czech Republic was –3.1% of GDP in 1992, and Slovenia maintained a budget surplus in the early transition years. All of these figures understate the true burden because quasi-fiscal deficits in the form of government support to enterprises through central bank credit were large as well. Nevertheless, a hallmark of the disinflation era was that the deficits were reduced significantly. In most countries, by 1997, the deficits were less than 3% of GDP for several years running, with the exception of Hungary.

Improved fiscal balances in the mid-1990s reduced the expectation that deficits would be monetized and helped to lower inflationary expectations. The data on deficits understate the extent of progress on fiscal reform because quasi-fiscal deficits are not measured. Subsidies through directed credits and distorted prices (importantly, the price of energy) disappeared as well. Perhaps equally important was the development of a capacity for government deficit financing other than monetization. Treasury bills were introduced in the advanced transition countries during the early 1990s and in the former Soviet Union during the mid-1990s. In addition, several countries were able to introduce government bonds with longer maturities by the end of the decade. Revenue from privatization has also been a relatively large

---

[4] Measurement of the deficit is often imprecise, particularly in the early transition years, when accounting standards change. For example, the government balance in Poland was reported to be –6.7% of GDP in 1991 and 1992 until recently, when government figures were revised to –2.1% and –4.9%, respectively.

source of financing. Even though large-scale privatization was completed in many transition countries by the mid-1990s, sales of large infrastructure companies and banks continued after that.

Although the capacity to absorb deficits without monetization has increased, the deficits have begun to increase as well. By the end of the 1990s, most of the countries of central Europe were running fiscal deficits in excess of 5% of GDP. In 2003, the deficit reached –6.7% of GDP in both Poland and the Czech Republic and –9.2% in Hungary. Although there is no apparent inflationary impact, it may well emerge suddenly and powerfully. Large deficits have not reemerged in the countries of the FSU. Russia has a fiscal surplus, which is as much the result of improving world commodity and energy prices as policy changes.

The other pillar of disinflation is monetary policy itself. Of course, fiscal and monetary policies are related, and an early review of disinflation in transition (Begg 1997) notes that monetary policy rarely succeeds if sound fiscal policy has not been established. A money-supply-based disinflation to stop hyperinflation works because it is also a fiscal-based disinflation when seigniorage is the most important source of government revenue.

Needless to say, disinflation was accompanied by reduced money expansion. The interesting issue is how money expansion was kept under control. Macro conditions were far too chaotic in the prestabilization period to adopt either money aggregate targets or interest rate targets. Large overhangs of forced saving meant that the initial money stocks were large. Although early high inflation eroded the value of these stocks, support of both enterprises and the government through money creation led to rapid growth of money. Furthermore, successful disinflation led to a rebound in real money demand and increased intermediary activity. Thus, money multipliers are variable and difficult to predict. It would have been impossible to target money aggregates in this environment. Any attempt to do so would not have been credible. Similarly, high and variable inflation made interest rate targets equally impractical. Moreover, money market institutions and instruments for the application of interest rate targets did not exist at first.

So, the exchange rate is the most obvious choice as a target for monetary policy. Although policymakers kept a careful watch on the exchange rate as the only reliable indicator of the success of efforts to disinflate, only a few countries adopted formal exchange rate targets. For example, Poland adopted a crawling peg exchange rate target in order to influence both policy and expectations. Russia used a crawling peg from 1996 to 1998 while it tried, ultimately unsuccessfully, to maintain an overvalued currency. Estonia is exceptional: It adopted a hard peg early on (June 1992), and it was followed by the other two Baltic countries, Latvia and Lithuania, in 1994. Many countries avoided a formal peg and many have moved toward floating exchange rates.

This is surprising because formal exchange rate targets that are highly visible and that effect prices directly through inflation pass-through can be very helpful in implementing a credible disinflation policy. There are difficulties in choosing an appropriate exchange rate path that complicate the use of formal exchange rate targets. First, capital flows can influence the nominal exchange rate, and second, transition structural adjustments lead to changes in real exchange rates. Thus, an explicit target might have as many advantages as disadvantages. The number of transition countries with floating exchange rates increased over the 1990s.

Monetary policy management of the inflation rate in many of the transition countries was complicated by the role of capital inflows. Central banks usually absorb capital inflows in order to avoid currency appreciation and then sterilize the impact on the domestic monetary base. However, there are limits on the ability of a central bank to sterilize. First, sterilization is costly to a central bank that holds low-interest-earning foreign assets. Second, it constrains the central bank balance sheet and might make it difficult to react to domestic financial-sector shocks.

A comparison of Hungary, Poland, and the Czech Republic during the mid-1990s is instructive (see Roubini and Wachtel 1999). The commitment to a pegged exchange rate was strongest in the Czech Republic (the *koruna* was pegged from 1991 to 1997); weakest in Hungary, which had repeated devaluations; and somewhat stronger in Poland, where the crawling peg was carefully managed. Inflation was highest in Hungary and lowest in the Czech Republic. The Czech Republic had used a fixed exchange rate as a nominal anchor and cornerstone for its initial stabilization program. However, real appreciation and problems financing the external imbalance inhibited Czech growth toward the end of the decade, and the exchange rate peg had to be abandoned in 1997 after a speculative attack.

Thus, the surprising conclusion is that disinflation in transition economies took place while the predominant form of monetary targeting was policy judgment. At the same time, a new approach to policy targeting was taking hold among the developed countries. In the course of the 1990s, inflation targeting became all the rage and was picked up in the transition world as well. At first, the use of inflation targets was informal, but by the end of the decade, several transition countries formally had adopted inflation targets. This was only possible once inflation rates had subsided, so that inflation forecasts over a medium-term horizon could be taken seriously. Jones and Mishkin (2003) describe the use of inflation targets in Hungary, Poland,

and the Czech Republic. The Czech Republic dropped its nominal anchor for a floating exchange rate in 1997. This left monetary policy without any target to help reduce the inflation rate, and at the end of the year, the central bank formally adopted inflation targets.

Inflation targets have the distinct advantage of avoiding the pitfalls of traditional monetary targets—interest rates, exchange rates, or monetary aggregates. Moreover, the few years of experience with inflation targets around the world are promising. In addition, adopting inflation targets can lead to more transparent and more consistent communication from the central bank about policy, which helps to establish credibility. However, there are two observations to bear in mind: First, missed inflation targets can lead to abrupt and perhaps ill-advised changes in policy.[5] Although everyone agrees that inflation targets should not be a straightjacket, there might be a loss of credibility to a transition-country central bank that ignores overshooting beyond its stipulated policy horizon. Second, the apparent success of inflation targeting by transition countries cannot easily be distinguished from the influence of EU accession because all of the transition inflation targeters are also accession countries.

Transition central bankers, particularly in Poland, may soon encounter the pitfalls that result from rigid targets that are missed. Poland adopted inflation targets in 1998 and continued to utilize a crawling band exchange rate target for policy operations until April 2000, when a floating regime was announced. The original short-term inflation targets were 2 percentage points wide, but in 2002, the bank specified a target of 5%, with a permissible fluctuation band of 1 percentage point. According to the Organisation for Economic Co-operation and Development (OECD), "The Bank hopes that by empha-sizing its desire to achieve a specific level of inflation as opposed to an outcome within a range, its communications will be better able to affect expectations" (2002a, 41). This seems to be a dangerous strategy for a transition economy in which nonmarket structural forces continue to affect inflation and for a small, open economy in which external shocks have large effects (although Poland is clearly the largest and least open of the accession countries). The bank does say that in the event of a missed target, policy will be aimed at moving toward the medium-term rather than the short-term target.

As noted already, all of the transition countries that have adopted inflation targets are accession candidates, and the influence of expectations about accession probably has been more important than the use of a particular policy

---

[5] This is basically the reason the Greenspan Fed resisted the formal use of inflation targets.

approach over the last few years. It is too early to disentangle these simultaneous developments. Success in seeking EU membership is also probably correlated with a further prerequisite for inflation targeting, that is, institutional capability. For inflation targeting to be effective, the central bank must be able to forecast inflation and gauge the effects of its own actions. This requires an adequate number of highly skilled staff, which simply was not available in the early years of transition, but EU accession has led to the rapid development of institutional capabilities with support from international institutions and without domestic political resistance.

For many years, it has been fashionable to attribute successful macroeconomic outcomes to central bank independence. Although the original econometric evidence has been criticized, it is still an interesting indicator. Cukierman, Miller, and Neyapti (2002) look at the characteristics of central banks in transition economies. The central banks established in the transition economies score very well on various indexes of institutional, policy, and legal independence when compared to other developing countries and even when compared to developed-country central banks in the 1980s. Moreover, the central banks established later are institutionally stronger. Some early studies concluded that central bank independence is associated with lower inflation rates (Dabrowski 1999), but Cukierman, Miller, and Neyapti indicate that the relationship is weak in the initial stages of transition, when price decontrol dominates. However, in later stages, when liberalization is sustained, there is somewhat less inflation with a more independent central bank. Improvements in institutional structure and disinflation take place simultaneously. In the transition countries and probably elsewhere as well, central bank independence is endogenous.

Since 1999, inflation rates in a majority of transition countries have been at developed-country levels. One explanation is that monetary and fiscal discipline and improvements in institutional structure (e.g., inflation targets and independent central banks) have convincingly established the disinflation bona fides of transition policymakers. An alternative explanation might attribute this to positive external shocks that are specific to this episode. Brada and Kutan (2002) conclude that the most recent disinflation was the result of positive shocks rather than the development of sound monetary and fiscal institutions and policies.

In this view, tight monetary policy throughout the 1990s only served to offset the lack of progress on true fiscal reform. Even if measured fiscal deficits declined, off-balance-sheet subsidies and unfunded liabilities constitute large longer-run fiscal problems. Moreover, monetary policy in the advanced transition economies in the mid- and late 1990s was inherently unstable.

As noted previously, the Czech Republic quickly moved from various exchange rate pegs to floating to inflation targeting as it groped for an effective policy tool. As a result, the reduction in inflation in the late 1990s was the result of something other than the influence of a credible and stable monetary policy target. Brada and Kutan conclude that an external shock—a decline in import prices, particularly energy—rather than any shift in monetary regime was the source of the later disinflation. Because tradables can account for as much as two-thirds of the components of the CPI, a shock can have a major influence on inflation rates.

This discussion serves to temper our amazement with the extent of disinflation in transition. It might well be premature to declare victory over inflation in the advanced transition countries, for several reasons. First, the external shock from import prices is transitory. Second, the fiscal deficits in these countries have been worsening and, in several places, are as large as they have ever been. Finally, there has not been a long enough period of managing inflation targets to create an environment in which inflation expectations are really quiescent.

However, there is one wildcard in this discussion: the influence of EU accession. In 1993, the EU's Copenhagen Declaration stated that CEE transition countries "that so desire shall become members of the EU." This vague commitment to expansion became a reality in 1998, when negotiations with the accession countries started, culminating with the announcement in October 2002 of the first-round accession countries. Eight transition countries were to become part of the EU in May 2004, and two more expect to finish negotiations and join in 2007. In addition, most of these countries expect to be part of the euro area as well.[6] Several countries of central Europe that were left out of the first round of accession talks (e.g., Croatia) and some countries of the FSU (e.g., Ukraine) expect to be included in a second round of EU enlargement. Among the countries already in and the transition candidates, the consensus is that the economic and monetary integration of Europe will go forward rapidly. Monetary integration poses additional problems because price-level convergence might generate inflation in some parts of the euro area.

The anticipation of European integration had a strong influence on inflation, particularly after negotiations commenced in 1998. First, the high and increasing likelihood of accession led to the expectation that inflation would move

---

[6] For example, Estonia has indicated that it will join the monetary union at the earliest possible date, 2007. The Czech authorities have acknowledged that their membership in the monetary union will be delayed by some years because of the current high fiscal deficit.

toward European levels. This effect of European integration may well be the single most important influence on inflation. Second, the enormous emphasis on accession enabled policymakers to maintain a tight monetary policy in order to adjust to standards in the euro area. Any slowdown in future accession plans or decisions to limit the extent of the EU could result in inflation problems for those countries that are affected. Similarly, Russia and the other republics of the FSU that do not expect to become part of the EU and still have double-digit inflation rates will have to rely on domestic policies and institutions to reduce inflation expectations. In addition, these countries may not have the same incentives to bring inflation to single-digit levels and may choose to emphasize other domestic priorities.

A successful disinflation should not just result in low inflation, it should also be credible and accompanied by long-term expectations that inflation will not recur. An indication of long-term credibility is a willingness to hold domestic money, that is, liquid assets denominated in the local currency. Monetization ratios are low throughout the region because of weakly developed financial systems (Bonin and Wachtel 2003), but increases in this ratio are an indicator of confidence in the financial system and the stability of prices. Table 3 shows monetization ratios (M2/GDP) in 1995 and 2001 for the transition countries. They were increasing except in countries where successful stabilization had not occurred by 1995 (Bulgaria, Belarus, and Romania). Higher monetization ratios are found in the more advanced transition countries, which stabilized earlier on, although the increases in the late 1990s varied. The ratio in the Czech Republic declined a bit, and in Hungary, it went up by about one-tenth; in Estonia and Slovenia, the increases were quite large.

## 2. DID INFLATION DO ITS JOB?

Perhaps one of the most important distinguishing characteristics of the formerly planned economies was the extent to which prices were distorted. Restrictions on trade and domestic-allocation mechanisms kept the prices of even internationally traded commodities from reaching their world-market prices. And the prices of domestically produced goods were set administratively and could venture far from what they would be if allowed to follow market forces. Thus, the removal of controls and price-setting arrangements led to a rapid change in prices. The removal of price restraints and the large overhang of liquid balances led to the immediate outbreak of inflation.

Table 3. Monetization Ratios

|  | 1995 | 2001 |
|---|---|---|
| Albania | 46.8 | 64.4 |
| Armenia (M3) | 7.7 | 13.4 |
| Azerbaijan | 12.3 | 12.9 |
| Belarus | 15.0 | 15.2 |
| Bosnia | 14.8 | 44.6 |
| Bulgaria | 65.4 | 40.9 |
| Croatia (M4) | 25.0 | 65.1 |
| Czech Rep | 75.3 | 73.4 |
| Estonia | 26.5 | 41.7 |
| FYR Macedonia | 11.0 | 29.8 |
| Georgia (M3) | 5.0 | 11.1 |
| Hungary | 41.9 | 46.9 |
| Kazakhstan | 11.4 | 17.7 |
| Kyrgyz Republic (M3) | 17.2 | 11.1 |
| Latvia | 22.5 | 32.0 |
| Lithuania | 22.7 | 26.7 |
| Moldova (M3) | 16.5 | 23.3 |
| Poland | 36.1 | 43.8 |
| Romania | 25.3 | 23.2 |
| Russia | 15.5 | 17.7 |
| Serbia | — | 14.0 |
| Slovak Republic | 65.4 | 70.5 |
| Slovenia | 27.8 | 41.2 |
| Tajikistan | 19.1 | 9.5 |
| Turkmenistan (M3) | 18.9 | 17.6 |
| Ukraine (M3) | 12.7 | 22.3 |
| Uzbekistan (M3) | 18.2 | 12.4 |

**Source:** European Bank for Reconstruction and Development.
**Note:** Ratios of M2 to GDP are percentages unless otherwise noted in parentheses.

Generally, the initial outburst of inflation was the result of the following causes:
- Removal of price controls, constraints, and administered price setting
- Seigniorage financing of government
- Credit expansion to support government enterprises
- Spending of forced saving, that is, monetary overhang

Initial outbursts of high inflation, often at hyperinflation rates, impose large economic costs. First, the value of financial savings erodes. Second, the support of inefficient enterprises continues. Third, hyperinflation inhibits the effective operation of the payments system. But there is also one possible way in which inflation, even at relatively high levels, can be beneficial. The inflationary environment allows and encourages the adjustment of relative prices. In discussions of moderate inflation in developed countries, the costs and benefits of inflation have been called the "sand" and "grease" effects (Groshen and Schweitzer 1997). The sand in the wheels of the price system occurs because inflation is associated with forecast errors, so that even in a competitive system, there are mistakes in price setting and distortions to relative prices. The grease effect occurs because inflation reduces the costs of making price adjustments and facilitates changes in relative prices when some prices are rigid downward.

The "job" of inflation in transition is to provide the grease for price setting and bring about adjustments in relative prices. Is there evidence that relative price adjustments took place and that the structure of prices became less distorted? Did inflation do its job?

There are only a few studies that have looked at this issue indirectly by examining the degree of price variability or the extent of price-level convergence. The thrust of the evidence is that a large amount of price-level adjustment took place early in the transition process, but the amount of adjustment has slowed down, and there are still large differences in the structure of prices between the transition economies and the developed economies. The differences that persist are related to both nonmarket determinants of prices and productivity differentials between the traded and nontraded goods sectors (the Balassa-Samuelson effect, which will be discussed later).

Coorey, Mecagni, and Offerdal (1998b) look at relative price variability measures such as the variance and skewness of inflation rates across price-index components. They find that relative price variability is associated with the level of inflation, a finding that has been established for developed countries already. Although it is difficult to disentangle the direction of causality between inflation rates and relative price variability, there are some inferences that can be drawn for the transition economies. First, the data suggest that the variance among price-index components is both particularly high in transition countries relative to developed economies and higher early in the transition process. In particular, there are spikes in relative price variability when the initial price liberalizations occur, and there is evidence of causality from relative price variability to inflation.[7] Although inflation in the transition countries was clearly the result of standard causes as well (money growth, wage pressures, etc.), price shocks from liberalization seem to play a significant role.

Wozniak (chapter 10 in Dabrowski 2003) looks at disaggregated price movements in Poland, Hungary, and the Czech Republic and reaches very similar conclusions. Relative price changes had an impact on initial inflation

---

[7] A disaggregated analysis of price changes in Poland (Wozniak 1998) confirms this.

rates, particularly in Poland, where the initial distortions were greatest. Through the mid-1990s, the gradual relaxing of administered price adjustments influenced inflation rates in all countries, with the biggest effects in Hungary. There continues to be considerable debate among policymakers about the optimal speed and magnitude of price liberalization.

An association between spikes in price changes due to liberalization and the overall inflation rate has an interesting implication. Efforts to disinflate with standard policy tools might be a mistake if low inflation will delay relative price changes, which suggests that there is an added cost to disinflation in transition economies. That is, disinflation might have real costs if it delays relative price adjustments. Recall that most transition economies ended hyperinflation very quickly but then took several years to bring inflation below 10%. At the time, this was faulted as the result of an unwillingness to maintain a credibly tight monetary and fiscal policy. However, it may well have been the correct strategy to follow because a moderately high inflation rate allows relative price adjustments to continue. Thus, in retrospect, the long periods of time required to bring inflation from 60% to 15% per year in many advanced transition countries (e.g., Poland, Hungary, and the Baltics) may have been a better policy than the very rapid disinflations in some countries. Of course, this argument assumes that at least some prices are rigid downward.

There is some indication from table 4A that countries with slower disinflations have undergone a greater overall price-level adjustment. The price levels relative to OECD averages are higher in Poland and Hungary than in the Czech and Slovak republics, although the Czech Republic has the highest GDP per capita.[8] The latter two countries did not experience enough inflation to make as much overall price adjustment. However, the extent to which price levels in the transition countries are still very different from the OECD averages is shown in table 4B. In particular, goods prices have adjusted much more than service prices, particularly government services. There are also large country-to-country differences in the adjustments.

Thus, the answer to the question posed—did inflation do its job?— is probably "somewhat." Although liberalization of controlled prices contributed to inflation early on, not all prices were liberalized in the initial phases. Many prices are yet to be liberalized. As a result, for the implementation of inflation targeting, the Czech National Bank uses a measure called "net inflation" that removes the influence of administered prices until they

---

[8] In 2002, Czech per capita GDP on a purchasing power parity basis was 62% of the EU-15 average. Corresponding figures for Hungary, the Slovak Republic, and Poland were 53%, 47%, and 41%, respectively. Relative price levels and per capita income are usually closely correlated.

Table 4A. Price Levels Relative to the OECD or the United States

| | Relative to OECD 29 | | | | Relative to OECD 30 | | | Relative to the U.S. |
|---|---|---|---|---|---|---|---|---|
| | 1990 | 1993 | 1996 | 1998 | 1999 | 2000 | 2001 | 2003 |
| Czech Republic | 23 | 30 | 39 | 41 | 39 | 36 | 39 | 55 |
| Hungary | 38 | 43 | 44 | 45 | 42 | 39 | 43 | 54 |
| Poland | 29 | 38 | 46 | 49 | 45 | 45 | 51 | 53 |
| Slovak Republic | — | — | — | — | 33 | 32 | 33 | 37 |

**Source:** Organisation for Economic Co-operation and Development, *Main Economic Indicators,* February 1999 and October 2003.

Table 4B. Price Levels Relative to the OECD, 1999, by Type of Goods

| | Bu | Cr | Cz | Es | Hu | La | Li | Po | Ro | Ru | Sk | Sl | Uk |
|---|---|---|---|---|---|---|---|---|---|---|---|---|---|
| Consumer nondurables | 42 | 77 | 58 | 60 | 60 | 63 | 59 | 61 | 43 | 40 | 51 | 87 | 34 |
| Consumer semidurables | 43 | 90 | 65 | 72 | 62 | 93 | 74 | 68 | 32 | 53 | 54 | 85 | 45 |
| Consumer durables | 48 | 90 | 70 | 64 | 73 | 79 | 69 | 81 | 63 | 69 | 63 | 79 | 71 |
| Producers goods | 40 | 66 | 60 | 77 | 66 | 74 | 71 | 64 | 43 | 31 | 59 | 80 | 37 |
| Consumer services | 19 | 39 | 26 | 31 | 30 | 29 | 24 | 34 | 24 | 13 | 20 | 51 | 11 |
| Government services | 12 | 39 | 23 | 23 | 24 | 19 | 19 | 27 | 13 | 8 | 17 | 47 | 5 |
| GDP | 24 | 54 | 39 | 43 | 42 | 42 | 38 | 45 | 29 | 22 | 33 | 64 | 17 |

**Source:** Organisation for Economic Co-operation and Development, Purchasing Power Parities and Real Expenditures, table 11, 2002.

are liberalized. Even in this advanced transition economy, about one-fifth of the CPI is netted out. Finally, price levels are still very far away from developed-country experience. So, even in the most advanced transition countries, there is still a lot of adjustment to go.

Disaggregated price movements in transition countries are clearly relevant to understanding the future of moderate inflation in transition countries. Stabilization policies are important, but they do not tell the whole story. Some recent research on Albania, where conventional stabilization policy reduced inflation in the mid-1990s, presents a cautionary tale (Domac and Elbirt 1998; Rother 2000). Monetary restraint, exchange rate pass-through and, to a lesser extent, fiscal restraint led to rapid disinflation (Domac and Elbirt 1998). However, the disinflation path was not smooth, and hyperinflation almost returned in 1997 as a result of political pressures for looser policies in 1996 and the affect of pyramid schemes on the financial sector. There is another part of the inflation story in Albania: the influence of price controls and dis-aggregated price movements. Although about one-half of prices were liberalized in 1992, many controls still exist. Rother's VAR analysis shows that the skew-ness of the distribution of price increases influences inflation. Thus, with very low inflation rates, further price liberalizations can introduce significant infla-tionary shocks. Thus, Albania may find itself in a quandary in which it can maintain low inflation (the 1999–2002 average was about 2%) or complete the process of market liberalization but cannot do both simultaneously.

Inflation targets can be too low if they do not allow for the accommoda-tion of inflation shocks from liberalization or other sources. These observations could apply to many of the less advanced transition economies, in which disinflation may have been too successful. Aggregate policy and external shocks may have brought inflation down to levels that cannot accommodate the price liberalizations that still need to occur.

### 3. CAN WE BELIEVE THE NUMBERS?

Inflation mismeasurement and biases in calculated inflation rates are frequent topics of discussion in developed countries. The 1996 Boskin Commission report in the United States provided explicit estimates of the biases in the CPI. Since that time, the U.S. Bureau of Labor Statistics has improved both the measurement of prices and the calculation of inflation rates. Improvements include obtaining prices from new discount outlets. In addition, the index calculation now allows for regular changes in expenditure weights. In the euro area, there were similar concerns and efforts to improve price measurement with the establishment of the harmonized index of consumer prices (HICP). However, mismeasurement of prices in the less developed economies is rarely discussed. As long as the focus of interest is disinflation that brings inflation from, for example, 1,000% to 10%, the quality of the data is not a central concern. But, with inflation rates consistently below 10% and with increased interest in cross-country comparisons and small changes in the inflation trend, the quality of the data being examined is worth considering. Moreover, reliable measures of price indexes are essential for determining changes in real income.

Not surprisingly, there are some important reasons why inflation measures in the transition economies might be subject to serious mismeasurement. Filer and Hanousek (2003) summarize their extensive project on inflation bias in the Czech Republic and some other transition countries. In the Czech Republic, the major source of bias is the failure to account for quality improvements in goods sold and the entrance of new goods onto the market. Substitution bias from the use of fixed-weight indexes and outlet substitution resulting from new markets also contribute to the measured bias. Their estimates change somewhat over time and with different assumptions but seem fairly robust. At least one-third of the measured average inflation rates in the Czech Republic (about 10% per year) are the result of measurement bias.[9] The implications of this are large. Real growth (with GDP deflated by the measured CPI) over the decade was –0.7% per year. With inflation properly measured to correct for the estimated biases, the growth rate was 3.6%.

A common way of measuring transition progress is to look at real GDP relative to its pretransition (1989) level. In 1999, the EBRD data indicated that only three transition countries had regained their 1989 levels: Poland, the Slovak Republic, and Slovenia. By 2001, the Czech Republic, Hungary, Albania, and Uzbekistan had been added to the list. With substantial price changes compounded over 10 or more years, small errors in index measurement can lead to substantially different conclusions. The story might be substantially different with more accurate measurement of price changes.[10]

Filer and Hanousek provide some direct evidence that economic well-being has improved more than the real GDP data suggest because inflation has been overstated. They conducted focus groups to determine how consumers would allocate price changes to inflation as opposed to quality changes. They

---

[9] The Boskin Commission report in the United States provided similar results. The overall bias in the inflation rate is about 1.2% per year with an average inflation rate of 2.8%.

[10] Of course, the measurement of real GDP is fraught with difficulties as well. In the pretransition era, it was probably overstated, and in the early transition years, the output declines were very large because activity in the informal sector was overlooked.

did this by asking Czech consumers how much they would pay at the current time for a brand new 1990 good. Their results indicate that much more of the observed price changes should be attributed to quality changes than the official CPI does. For example, clothing prices went up more than two and half times over the decade. The index attributes about 30% of this to quality change, so that the CPI for clothing more than doubled. However, when consumer perceptions are used to measure quality improvements, the price increase is only about 50%.

The measurement problems will in all likelihood diminish with time as national authorities follow internationally accepted norms and improve their data-collection procedures. In addition, with moderate inflation, the biases do not create such large distortions. However, economic historians looking back on the transition decade will be well advised to keep this discussion in mind.

## 4. DISINFLATION: CASE STUDIES

The experience with disinflation in the two dozen or so transition countries, all in the same decade, provides a useful laboratory to study disinflation policies. Are there particular types of policies that worked better? Which policies seemed to have generated successful disinflations? In other words, how did they do it?

A convenient way of addressing these issues is to look at policy history in a few countries. Following de Menil (2003), we will look at Poland and Romania, as well as Estonia and Russia.

### 4.1 Disinflation in Poland

The Polish government introduced a stabilization program, the Balcerowicz Plan, on New Year's Day 1990 in an economy already suffering from high inflation (the monthly inflation rate peaked at about 50% in 1989). The Polish *zloty* was devalued to half its initial exchange rate and pegged to the dollar. Both monetary and fiscal policies were drastically tightened and credit creation stopped immediately. State subsidies were withdrawn, price controls removed, foreign direct investment encouraged, and privatization programs started. A large decline in production followed, forcing the National Bank of Poland (NBP) to ease monetary policy later in 1990, only to retighten it a few months later. Inflation shot up and the recession intensified. The zloty was devalued again and a crawling peg was adopted. The hyperinflation had abated, but inflation was still high. The intention was to gradually reduce the rate of crawl in order to control inflation expectations.

Over the next several years, monetary and fiscal policy alternated between expansionary and contractionary episodes as the government tried to cope with unemployment problems, impose hard budget constraints on the government and enterprises, and recapitalize the banking system. Although there were fits and starts to the stabilization, the commitment to the crawling peg as a form of inflation target was deliberate and purposeful. From 1991 to 1998, the crawl was reduced from a monthly rate of 1.8% to 0.5%, the bands were widened, and inflation came down gradually. The nominal peg decreased in importance as a result of the widening of fluctuation bands, and the NBP adopted inflation targeting in 1998, aiming for around 7% inflation. The targets were not met in 1998 and 1999, and the NBP risked losing its hard-earned credibility. Monetary policy was eased slightly, and the gains from disinflation dissipated as inflation reached double digits again.

In April 2000, the monetary authorities adopted a floating exchange rate regime and set out a goal of bringing inflation below 4% by the end of 2003. During the second half of 2000, real interest rates rose as the zloty appreciated against the euro and the dollar. The September 2001 terrorist attacks against the United States further contributed to the appreciation of the zloty. The strong real appreciation of the currency had led the central bank to substantially tighten monetary policy. This environment of tight money and a slowdown in European demand led to a sharp fall in investment activity, causing to an overall slowdown of the economy. It did bring about a reduction in inflation to about 5% in 2001.

The story of Polish transition and stabilization can be read in several ways. First, the disinflation was extremely slow; it took a full decade to bring inflation below 5%. Second, although growth in most recent years has been robust and Poland is often viewed as the most successful transition country, there is still substantial unemployment. Although recent GDP growth is strong, there are persistent problems such as high wages in state-owned industries and persistent unemployment. The NBP has had more than a decade of experience with nominal anchors. It began with a fixed peg, changed to a credible crawling peg, and finally switched to an inflation target as the anchor. The rapid decline in inflation at the very end of the 1990s might have been the result of the credibility of the NBP's inflation targeting program or the influence of EU accession on inflation expectations.

An evaluation of the experience with inflation targets must be mixed. Inflation overshot the target bands as soon as they were introduced and then undershot them for two years in succession. As the OECD notes, "[T]he principal advantage of an inflation targeting regime over alternative anchors for monetary policy is its capacity to affect expectations" (2002a, 43). The NBP backs up its inflation target regime with a regular reporting of inflation developments by the policy council, an admirable degree of transparency.

Inflation expectations may well have come down considerably, but recent macroeconomic developments do not support the sustainability of very low inflation rates. In response to a weak economy, monetary policy was significantly looser in 2002 than earlier. Short-term interest rates went from a peak of 19% in early 2001 to 8% in mid-2002 while the inflation rate went from around 7% to 2%. Moreover, the fiscal deficit is almost 7% of GDP, and the structural reforms that are needed to change the fiscal stance have slowed down. Finally, the zloty has depreciated against the euro, which will inevitably affect inflation in the future. Although Poland has had access in the international financial markets since the mid-1990s, its Standard and Poor's long-term foreign currency credit rating has been BBB+ since 2000. The macroeconomic fundamentals are strong enough to make the future for inflation in Poland uncertain.

**Figure 1. Poland 1990–2002**

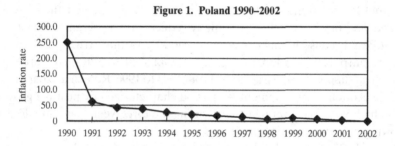

**Figure 2. Poland 1997–2002**

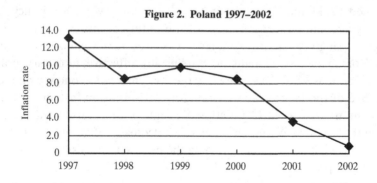

## 4.2 Disinflation in Romania

The history of transition in Romania contrasts with that of Poland. As de Menil comments, "[T]he dominant impression...of the first ten years of transition in Romania...is one of difficulty. The period was marked by a succession of crises" (2003, 283). Romania is the only central European transition country that has not accomplished an effective disinflation program. There are two features of macro policy that have resulted in this outcome. First, although the formal structure of a reformed banking system dates to 1991, Romanian monetary and banking policy made banks the automatic supplier of financial resources for state-owned enterprises. Second, controls over domestic prices and control over foreign exchange transactions continued to be significant influences throughout the decade.

A stabilization program was introduced in 1993 as inflation reached 290% and output fell by 30%. Although monetary policy was tightened, the currency devalued, and price controls substantially reduced, the program was a short-lived success because it was not accompanied by further structural reforms. Romania purposefully adopted a gradual approach to reform in order to ensure social support for the transition. From 1994 to 1996, Romania experienced a volatile economic environment—a period characterized by positive growth but also high inflation (averaging 50% during the three-year span), in addition to growing macroeconomic imbalances.

The gradualist approach did nothing to reduce subsidies to the unprofitable agriculture and energy sectors. The central bank provided liquidity to the state-owned banks that lent heavily to these sectors. Monetary policy was inherently accommodating because of the deterioration of the financial situation, causing persistent inflationary pressures. It was almost impossible for the Romanian central bank to pursue any effective monetary policy because its actions were constrained by the government's economic policy.

Because of the lack of any meaningful anti-inflation instruments, the government tried to control inflation through price controls and foreign exchange transactions. Although it helped to decrease inflation from 61% to 27% between 1994 and 1995, postponing the necessary prices adjustments to stem inflation proved unsustainable in the long run. In the absence of any significant enterprise restructuring or change in bank behavior, unsustainable fiscal deficits continued and the country was back in crisis by 1996.

At the end of 1996, a new government came to power, set on implementing a bolder approach to reform. It broke with the gradualist approach and dramatically accelerated the process of structural reforms. Prices and the foreign exchange market were fully liberalized. Tariffs were reduced, and subsidies for loss-making state enterprises were removed. The reforms also gradually reduced directed credits to the agricultural sector. The government sold 60% of the companies from the State Ownership Fund in one year to drastically accelerate privatization. The policy of using the central bank as the main provider of credit to the real sector ended immediately.

The transition shock in Romania really occurred in early 1997. Output fell sharply, and inflation soared to 150%. Large state-owned enterprises were among the most affected, as they had previously benefited from easy financing. The government postponed its planned large-scale restructuring of large state-owned enterprises and the National Bank of Romania (NBR) relaxed monetary policy.

Although the 1997 stabilization program failed in its primary objectives, it did free up prices and correct the exchange rate. The conduct of monetary policy had been complicated by very high interest rate volatility driven by fluctuations in Treasury bill issuance, the occasional need to act as a lender of last resort to state banks, the country's weak balance-of-payments position, and the need to build up foreign reserves. The NBR pursued a moderate real exchange rate appreciation to temporarily help disinflation.

By the end of 1998, inflation was down to 41%, largely driven by real appreciation of the exchange rate. However, the East Asian and Russian financial crises inhibited further progress. Romania had difficulty financing its external deficit and, in early 1999, came close to a payment crisis as a result of excessively low foreign reserves and an inability to refinance debts. Exchange rate depreciation and fear of sovereign default kept interest rates high.

The NBR continued to focus on exchange rate policy in 2000 because it feared productivity gains would be lost through excessive real exchange rate appreciation. Inflation fell below its 1998 level yet remained stubbornly high at 40%. In July, the central bank, finally free from budget and real-sector financing, announced a tighter monetary policy stance. Fiscal reforms reduced off-budget spending and improved tax collections; the deficit in 2002 was only 3% of GDP, relatively low for the transition countries. Inflation went down to 17% by the end of 2002 and has continued to decline slowly. Romania was as a latecomer to transition reforms because two tries at stabilization were needed. As a consequence, the fundamentals point to further reduction in inflation rates.

The Romanian experience illustrates the pitfalls of half-hearted reforms. Disinflation was extremely slow and uneven because fiscal policy was not brought under control; enterprise subsidies continued for a longer time in Romania than elsewhere.

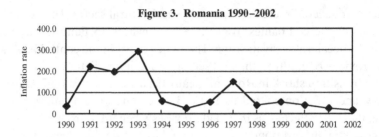

Figure 3. Romania 1990–2002

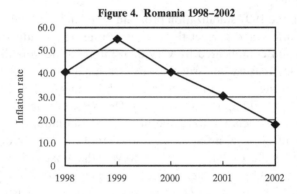

Figure 4. Romania 1998–2002

### 4.3 Disinflation in Estonia

Inflation reached 1,000% soon after Estonia declared its independence from the Soviet Union in October 1991 and began its national existence under very precarious circumstances. The national currency, the *kroon*, was introduced in June 1992, and a currency board arrangement was put in place. At the same time, an ambitious program of price liberalization began. Furthermore, 80% of the country's state-owned small businesses were sold off in two years, and there were three rounds of large-scale privatization with foreign participation for major enterprises.

The currency board fixed the kroon exchange to the German deutsche mark. The kroon was fully convertible, and central bank liabilities were fully backed by foreign exchange reserves. Loans to the government by the Bank of Estonia were prohibited, and the bank was not to be liable for the state's financial obligations. The currency board arrangement was chosen to gain credibility and to provide a solid nominal anchor for restructuring.

After the monetary reform, hyperinflation continued for a few months before the first effects of the reform were seen in a rapidly declining inflation level. By the end of 1993, inflation had drastically declined from four digits in

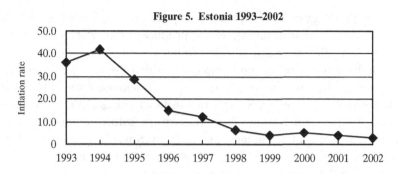

Figure 5. Estonia 1993–2002

the past year to 41%. Inflation rates continued to decline steadily over the next five years, but it was not until May 1998 that inflation reached single-digit levels. Inflation has averaged less than 4% over the last five years.

The currency board provided a credible nominal anchor and enforced fiscal discipline. As a result, it is responsible for the successful disinflation. However, the currency has appreciated in real terms, which can create problems for any fixed exchange rate regime. A very large current account deficit may threaten the stability of the regime, although the economy has been able to finance them without difficulty.

Price increases are somewhat higher in Estonia compared to those in advanced economies because of the Balassa-Samuelson effect. That is, higher productivity growth in Estonia resulting from real convergence yielded convergence of the structure and level of prices as well. Thus, the Balassa-Samuelson effect is estimated to have caused an inflation difference of about 2 percentage points compared to inflation in advanced economies (Randveer 2000). Thus, it is unclear whether there has been too much real appreciation. Also, the initial value of the kroon was probably undervalued by design.

The currency board arrangement has been the cornerstone of successful disinflation in Estonia. Nevertheless, fixed exchange rate regimes inhibit responses to shock, and it is well known that the time to exit such a regime is well before any shock occurs. So far, the Estonian economy has proven to be very flexible. For example, the 1998 Russian crises caused only a temporary fall in output.

### 4.4 Disinflation in Russia

As the Soviet Union was disintegrating, the old command structure of the economy deteriorated. This led to disruption of deliveries and distribution and consequently, production had already started to decline under Gorbachev. The decline was further exacerbated after the abortive coup of August 1991 and the breakup of the Soviet Union. Russia began a stabilization program with a large-scale liberalization of prices, which, it was hoped, would quickly lead to improved incentives for producers. Other reform measures such as privatization were slated to follow later.

When the majority of consumer prices were liberalized at the beginning of January 1992,[11] the Russian price level jumped immediately upward. This was not surprising because many Soviet-era consumer prices did not even cover production costs, and Russian consumers were willing spend their large accumulated stock of monetary assets from Soviet-era forced savings. Liberalization worked as predicted: Consumer goods reappeared, prices increased, and the value of the money overhang fell.

Monthly inflation rates in early 1992 oscillated between 10% and 35%, and relative prices changed drastically. A stabilization of sorts seemed to be working as monthly inflation rates declined to below 10% in the summer of 1992. However, at the same time, production continued its fall, and public finances were in disarray.

Political pressures to halt the decline in production increased. Also, a new central bank management was much more sympathetic toward central bank financing of public deficits, and credits both to the government and to enterprises accelerated. This had an almost immediate effect on inflation, and by the end of 1992, the monthly inflation rate was again over 25%.

Monetary policy in Russia was complicated by the existence of the *ruble* zone. After the Soviet Union disintegrated, the ruble continued to be the currency in most of its successor states for some time, and rules concerning the issuance of money were unclear at best. In practice, most former Soviet Union republics expanded the ruble money supply at a rapid pace to cover their budget deficits, which affected inflation in the entire ruble area. The ruble area dissolved mainly during 1993, when most successor states introduced their own national currencies (Odling-Smee and Pastor 2001).

An effort at restabilization occurred in 1994 when the Russian parliament approved a budget with a clearly smaller deficit, and Russia was able to restart its program with the IMF. Inflation expectations abated and the ruble stabilized. In the summer of 1994, monthly inflation was under 5% for the first time since the start of the transition. However, by the autumn, it had become apparent that the government would be unable to resist demands for budget financing. Currency markets recognized this, and in October 1994, the ruble depreciated approximately 20% in one day. Consequently, inflation jumped again to more than 15% per month. In the end, the federal govern-

---

[11] Prices for most public goods, such as energy, were not liberalized, and rents remained administratively set.

ment deficit for 1994 was more than 10%, much larger than in 1993. Although inflation was lower, it was still around 300% for the year.

At the beginning of 1995, the Russian authorities were ready for another stabilization attempt. Structural reforms were started and authorities were willing to cut expenditures in order to reduce the public-sector deficit. Again, the IMF was ready to provide financing under a new program. The Central Bank of Russia adopted an informal crawling peg policy, and the rate of depreciation was chosen to be smaller than the prevailing inflation rate. Therefore, gradual real appreciation of the ruble would be used as a tool for disinflation. Because Russia was dollarized to such a high degree, an external anchor was deemed important for influencing inflationary expectations. Russia cut the federal government deficit almost in half 1995. By the end of 1995, the monthly inflation rate was consistently below 5%. However, in the run-up to the presidential elections in the summer of 1996, public expenditures were increased again, and tax evasion accelerated. But this time, the central bank was not forced to finance the deficit because the Russian government had gained access to capital markets. Russia was able to sell bonds, denominated both in rubles and dollars, to both foreign and domestic investors. In 1996, although the federal government deficit was 9.4% of GDP, the inflation declined to under 50% and fell into the teens in 1997. It seemed that the transition adjustments had taken place successfully.

Russia's fiscal difficulties reemerged in 1998, for two related reasons. First, tax collections lagged as domestic reforms faltered. Second, the Asian emerging markets crisis made investors more cautious and financing of the deficit increasingly difficult. Russia's risk premium in the international bond markets shot up and, although a new program with the IMF was agreed upon in July, it soon proved to be inadequate. In August, Russia had to let the ruble float and declare a moratorium on its debts. Monetary and exchange rate policies had been unable to contain inflation because fiscal policy was not on sustainable path. Following the large devaluation of the ruble, inflation shot up again, and immediately after the crisis, monthly inflation was over 35%.

However, the reversal was short-lived, and surprisingly, by the beginning of 1999, monthly inflation was again clearly below 5%. There are several reasons for this favorable development. After the devaluation, the Russian authorities were fairly quick in stabilizing the external value of the ruble, partly with the help of capital controls. Capital controls prevented the reemergence of foreign lending to Russian banks and thus helped to curb the growth of domestic credit. Also, the fiscal deficit was curtailed dramatically, as Russia had stopped servicing almost all of its debt. Later in 1999 (and beyond), sharply higher oil prices improved Russia's terms of trade substantially. Because the Russian government derives a substantial part of its tax revenue from the energy sector,[12] this terms-of-trade shock had a very positive effect on Russia's fiscal position. Fiscal surpluses beginning in 2000 have helped to keep annual inflation rates below 20% in recent years. Also, Russia has returned to a crawling peg policy, whereby the ruble depreciates fairly steadily against the dollar. The crawling peg regime provides a nominal anchor, and this time, fiscal policy is consistent with the exchange rate regime.

Although inflation is now low by Russia's historical standard and fairly stable as well, Russia is the one transition country in which a successful stabilization program has not brought inflation down to developed-country levels. Although high oil prices have contributed to a substantial current account surplus, the Central Bank of Russia has not been willing to let the ruble appreciate because this would make many Russian manufacturers less competitive. Also, the central bank does not have adequate monetary policy tools to sterilize the capital inflows, and therefore persistent inflation is the natural response. The Central Bank of Russia will probably try to push down inflation only gradually. And as long as the Russian government is able to maintain its present fiscal stance, the central bank will not face substantial pressures to alter its own policies.

**Figure 6. Russia 1990–2002**

**Figure 7. Russia 1996–2002**

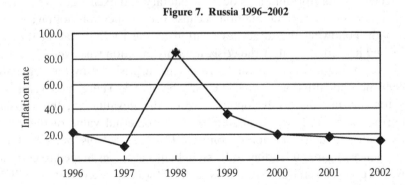

---

[12] Tax evasion is more difficult in this sector than elsewhere because oil flows through pipelines owned by Transneft, which is, in turn, owned by the Russian government.

## 5. IS INFLATION INEVITABLE IN TRANSITION?

The story of inflation in transition countries is not just a tale of wild hyperinflation following a structural change, followed by an astounding ability to disinflate. There are aspects of the transition process that inevitably lead to inflation. These issues are becoming more important now that the overall disinflation has been so successful. As we have seen, inflation rates are at Western levels in many transition countries. Now, an important issue faced by policymakers is whether the euro inflation rate is the appropriate target or whether inflation somewhat greater than in Europe is the appropriate and realistic target. In this event, efforts to maintain too low an inflation rate can lead to recession. In this section, we will examine the reasons why some inflation is inevitable and appropriate in transition.

Inflation might be inevitable in transition because of structural adjustments, income convergence, and Balassa-Samuelson effects. The size of the inflation differential is particularly important in countries that want to join the euro area in the near future. In principle, higher inflation resulting from income convergence could threaten the attainment of the Maastricht criterion on inflation. This could, in turn, delay the countries' entry into the euro area.

Following the seminal contributions of Balassa and Samuelson just 40 years ago, the Balassa-Samuelson effect is understood to explain the often-observed tendency of prices for nontraded goods to increase faster than the prices of traded goods. The Balassa-Samuelson effect offers an explanation of the differences in productivity growth between the traded and nontraded sectors. The starting point for the analysis is the observation that productivity growth in the traded goods sector is usually faster than in the nontraded goods sector. The reasons for this in the transition countries are straightforward. With the freeing up of market controls and the opening of the economies, the sectors that were most quickly exposed to competitive pressures were the traded goods sectors. That is, it is assumed that the law of one price holds for traded goods (but not for nontraded goods). As productivity in the traded goods sector increases, wages in that sector go up as well. It is assumed that labor is to some extent mobile across sectors, and therefore wages rise in the non-traded goods sector (such as the service sector and government) as well. Higher wages in the nontraded sector are possible only if the relative prices of nontraded goods increase. Because wages increase throughout the economy more rapidly than average productivity, the overall price level increases as well.[13] The resulting inflation leads to an increase in the real exchange rate.

---

[13] The appendix includes a formal presentation of the Balassa-Samuelson effect on inflation in the traded and nontraded goods sectors and on inflation differentials between countries (i.e., real exchange rate changes).

Figure 8. Real Effective Exchange Rate in Selected Transition Countries, January 1994–April 2002 (1995 = 100)

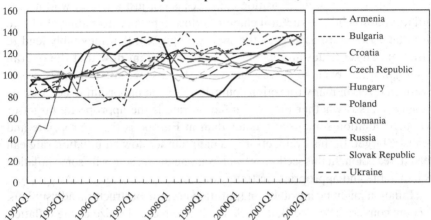

In fact, interest in the Balassa-Samuelson effect stems from the observation of real exchange rate appreciation in transition countries. Figure 8 depicts the evolution of the real effective exchange rate in a number of transition countries between 1994 and 2002. We can see that there has been a general tendency for the real effective exchange rates to appreciate, although there have been reversals in the trend in some countries (e.g., in Russia after the August 1998 crisis).

The enormous interest in EU accession and convergence has led to a large number of studies that have tested and measured the magnitude of the effect in the transition countries. Recent reviews are provided by Mihaljek (2002) and Égert (2003). This strand of literature has been partly prompted by the EU accession countries' desire to enter the euro area. As the entry criteria to the euro area include exchange rate stability[14] and inflation convergence,[15] a strong tendency toward high inflation rates as the pace of structural adjustment in the traded and nontraded goods sectors diverge could endanger the simultaneous attainment of both criteria. As the accession countries have grown faster than the current EU members, convergence in income levels is taking place, although there are still considerable gaps between per capita

---

[14] Exchange rate stability is defined as participation in the exchange rate mechanism for at least two years without devaluation of the central parity and without significant tensions in the foreign exchange market. Also, the exchange rate must be close to the central parity for the two-year period.

[15] Inflation cannot exceed the average inflation of the three EU countries with the *lowest* inflation by more than 1.5 percentage points.

GDP in the current EU countries and the accession countries.[16] Therefore, higher inflation resulting from Balassa-Samuelson effects is at least a possibility if the nominal exchange rate is fixed. Also, as noted earlier, price levels in the accession countries are clearly lower than in the EU countries, and in this respect there is room for catching up, that is, higher inflation.

Typically, empirical efforts to measure the Balassa-Samuelson effect regress the relative price of nontraded to traded goods on indicators of labor productivity in both sectors. Some recent contributions include Arratibel, Rodriguez-Palenzuela, and Thimann (2002), Coricelli and Jazbec (2001), Mihaljek (2002), and Égert (2003).

Arratibel, Rodriguez-Palenzuela, and Thimann (2002) use monthly data between 1990 and 2001 (when available) for 10 accession countries and include a large number of control variables in their estimations. They find that the Balassa-Samuelson effect is "relatively insignificant" in explaining inflation developments in the accession countries. Coricelli and Jazbec (2001) also include countries of the former Soviet Union in their estimation with data for 1990–1998. They find that in the early years of transition, structural reforms were more important in explaining relative price movements. Their estimate of the contribution of the Balassa-Samuelson effect is approximately 1 percentage point per annum. Mihaljek (2002) explains inflation differentials between the euro area and six transition countries with differential growth of productivity across sectors. The quarterly data start from the mid-1990s and therefore avoid using observations from the early years of transition. With the exception of Slovenia, the contribution of the Balassa-Samuelson effect to the annual inflation differential is less than 1 percentage point.

One recurring problem in estimating relative prices is the definition of traded and nontraded sectors. Many studies proxy traded goods prices with the producer price index and nontraded goods prices with the consumer price index. Some others divide, for example, the GDP deflator into traded and nontraded parts. Sometimes everything except manufacturing is deemed nontraded, and sometimes agriculture is traded and sometimes not. Égert (2003) uses a very detailed dataset[17] that allows better distinction between the traded and nontraded sectors. Although the study concerns only Estonia, it can also shed light on the evolution of the Balassa-Samuelson effect in other transition countries. Although the Balassa-Samuelson effect is estimated to have averaged between 2% and 3% for the whole sample period (1993–2002), it is shown to

---

[16] In 2002, the average per capita GDP in the 10 countries slated to join the EU in May 2004 was 46% of the EU average.

[17] The CPI is disaggregated into 260 items and GDP is disaggregated into 15 sectors.

decline quite clearly over the decade in question. At the end of the period, the inflation contribution is less than 1 percentage point.[18] This is quite understandable, as Estonia has rapidly converged toward the EU level, both in per capita income and in productivity.

In addition, empirical studies on the Balassa-Samuelson effect have concentrated on the behavior of the real exchange rates. De Broeck and Sløk (2001) examine the effect of sectoral productivity growth on real exchange rate movements in a sample of 26 transition countries and 17 OECD countries. They find that differential productivity growth exerts a different influence on the real exchange rate in the accession countries compared to the other transition countries. In the EU accession countries, the Balassa-Samuelson effect appears to have its predicted influence on real exchange rate, but in the other transition countries, there appears to be very little connection between the two. In the accession countries of central and eastern Europe, De Broeck and Sløk estimate that the Balassa-Samuelson effect had raised annual inflation by 1 percentage point at the end of the sample period.

The empirical research on the Balassa-Samuelson effect confirms that it has had an influence on inflation and real exchange rate developments in the transition countries. However, the estimated magnitude of the Balassa-Samuelson effect is relatively small, generally around 1 percentage point per annum. Moreover, the size of the Balassa-Samuelson effect is supposed to decrease as income convergence takes place. This is also what has been found in the empirical studies. Policymakers in the accession countries can rest easy. The thrust of the research on the Balassa-Samuelson effect suggests that inflation differentials are no more than 1%–2% and will diminish over time.

## 6. CONCLUSIONS

Disinflation in the transition economies has been, as we noted at the outset, remarkable. It is easy to look at the equally remarkable monetary reforms and attribute the disinflation success to them. Indeed, inflation is a monetary phenomenon, and the institutions for responsible monetary policy did not exist in these countries 15 years ago. Central banks as responsible and independent keepers of monetary discipline are a new phenomenon. Moreover, the entire financial structure was geared to soft budget constraints that exacerbated inflation pressures. So, one concluding observation is that

---

[18] As Estonia has a rigidly fixed exchange rate, the Balassa-Samuelson effect should manifest itself as higher inflation.

disinflation is the result of rapid institution building and important government-sector structural reforms in many transition countries. Inflation continues to be a problem where institutional development lags.

Proponents of specific monetary policy approaches will look to the transition countries for evidence that favors a particular policy stance. However, there has been substantial disinflation with every imaginable exchange rate regime[19] and approach to monetary policy. We do not see evidence to support a specific approach in the transition experience. Instead, the transition experience argues in favor of good macroeconomic fundamentals. In particular, fiscal constraint may be more important because it is a necessary precursor to appropriate monetary policy.

Finally, although the disinflation has been remarkable, there can be too much of a good thing. The very low inflation rates attained in 2001 and 2002 throughout the region may not be sustainable. First, there are large relative price adjustments still to be made. These adjustments are similar to an external shock that can influence inflation rates. Similarly, the recent disinflation might be largely the result of transitory global shocks that have masked some of the remaining problems in the transition countries. Second, any acceleration of inflation that results can easily erode confidence in policymakers and affect inflation expectations. Similarly, any slowdown in the pace of EU expansion could lead to altered inflation expectations. Third, the very low inflation rates divert attention from some of the macro fundamentals that could be problematic. In particular, recent increases in government deficits are surprisingly large. Moreover, remaining structural reforms need to affect some hard-to-reach sectors such as health care and pension systems.

Contrary to our original thoughts, perhaps the roller coaster ride called *transition* is not over. Inflation rates might well diverge from developed-country levels in many of the transition economies, and it is not obvious how policy will respond.

### APPENDIX: THE BALASSA-SAMUELSON EFFECT

More formally, we can briefly sketch a version of the Balassa-Samuelson effect. A similar exposition can be found in Obstfeld and Rogoff (1996). It is assumed that a small, open economy produces two composite goods: tradables and nontradables. If we let the subscript $T$ denote the traded sector and $NT$

---

[19] For a recent overview of exchange rate regimes in the accession countries, see Begg et al. (2003). Keller and Richardson (2003) discuss monetary policy frameworks and exchange rate regimes in the CIS.

the nontraded sector, output is given by constant-returns technology production functions,

(A1) $\begin{aligned} Y_T &= A_T F(K_T, L_T) \\ Y_{NT} &= A_{NT} G(K_{NT}, L_{NT}), \end{aligned}$

where $K_i$ denotes capital used in sector $i$, and $L_i$ denotes labor in sector $i$. The supply of labor is fixed at $L = L_T + L_{NT}$. Labor is immobile internationally but can move between the two domestic sectors. This ensures that workers will earn the same wage in both sectors. Capital is mobile internationally, and because of this, domestic capital's rate of return is equal to the world interest rate, $r$. We can define capital–labor ratios in the two sectors as $k_T \equiv K_T/L_T$ and $k_{NT} \equiv K_{NT}/L_{NT}$ and express output per worker as $y_T = A_T f(k_T) \equiv A_T F(k_T, 1)$ and $y_{NT} = A_{NT} g(k_{NT}) \equiv A_{NT} G(k_{NT}, 1)$. The relative price of nontradable goods in terms of tradables is $p$. With this notation, we can write four first-order conditions (two relating to traded sector and two to the nontraded sector) from representative companies' profit-maximization problems:

(A2) $\begin{aligned} A_T f'(k_T) &= r \\ A_T \left[ f(k_T) - f'(k_T)k_T \right] &= w \\ p A_{NT} g'(k_{NT}) &= r \\ p A_{NT} \left[ g(k_{NT}) - g'(k_{NT})k_{NT} \right] &= w. \end{aligned}$

As $r$ is given by the international capital markets, the four first-order conditions allow us to determine the four unknowns: $w$, $p$, $k_T$, and $k_N$.

To assess the dynamic implications of the aforementioned analysis, one can take logarithmic derivative of $p$:

(A3) $\hat{p} = \dfrac{\mu_{LNT}}{\mu_{LT}} \hat{A}_T - \hat{A}_{NT}$.

Here, variables marked with $^\wedge$ denote logarithmic derivatives (or very small percentage changes), and $\mu_{LT}$ and $\mu_{LNT}$ are labor's share of income generated in the tradable and nontradable sectors, respectively. As wages are equal across sectors, the ratio of $\mu_{LNT}$ to $\mu_{LT}$ can be written in the following form:

(A4) $\dfrac{\mu_{LNT}}{\mu_{LT}} = \dfrac{L_{NT} Y_Y}{p L_T Y_{NT}}$.

The Balassa-Samuelson effect assumes that purchasing power parity holds for traded goods, that is, their price is the same across countries (when expressed in the same currency). In the following, we use the price of tradables as the numeraire and set it to be 1. If one writes the price level both in the home country $(P)$ and rest of the world (or in the relevant trading partner, $P^*$) as a geometric average of the tradable and nontradable goods, with the weight of tradables being $\gamma$, the ratio of home to foreign price level is

$$(A5) \quad \frac{P^*}{P} = \left(\frac{p^*}{p}\right)^{1-\gamma}.$$

Here, $p$ is the price of nontradables in the home country and $p^*$ is the price of nontradables in the foreign country. By log differentiating (A.5) and using the expression for changes in the price of nontradables (A.3), we can assess the effect of relative productivity changes on real exchange rates (or the ratio of two countries' price levels):

$$(A6) \quad \hat{P}^* - \hat{P} = (1-\gamma)(\hat{p}^* - \hat{p}) = (1-\gamma)\left[(\hat{A}_{NT} - \hat{A}^*_{NT}) - \frac{\mu_{LNT}}{\mu_{LT}}(\hat{A}_T - \hat{A}^*_T)\right].$$

If the ratio of $\mu_{LNT}$ to $\mu_{LT}$ is larger than 1, the real exchange rate of a country will appreciate if productivity in its tradable sector, relative to the foreign country, rises faster than productivity in its nontradables, again relative to the foreign country. It is generally assumed that this is the case in poorer countries, which are in the process of catching up with more affluent economies.

## ACKNOWLEDGMENTS

The authors appreciate the research assistance of Lisa Lixin Xu, Elif Sisli, and Diana Kniazeva. Comments from the conference discussants, J. David Lopez-Salido and Werner Hermann, helped us sharpen the discussion and avoid errors. Finally, discussions with Oleh Havrylyshyn, Gerorges de Menil, and Jukka Pirttilä provided some important insights, which we are grateful to be able to use. Of course, all remaining errors are solely our own responsibility.

## REFERENCES

Arratibel, O., D. Rodriguez-Palenzuela, and C. Thimann. 2002. Inflation Dynamics and Dual Inflation in Accession Countries: A "New Keynesian" Perspective. Working Paper No. 132, European Central Bank.

Begg, D. 1997. Monetary Policy during Transition: Progress and Pitfalls in Central and Eastern Europe, 1990–6. *Oxford Review of Economic Policy* 13(2): 33–46.

Begg, D. 1998. Disinflation in Central Europe: The Experience to Date. In *Moderate Inflation: The Experience of the Transition Economies,* ed. C. Cottarelli and G. Szapary. Washington, DC: International Monetary Fund and National Bank of Hungary.

Begg, D., B. Eichengreen, L. Halpern, J. von Hagen, and C. Wyplosz. 2003. Sustainable Regimes of Capital Movements in Accession Countries. Policy Paper No. 10, Centre for Economic Policy Research.

Bonin, J., and P. Wachtel. 2003. Financial Sector Development in Transition Economies: Lessons from the First Decade. *Financial Markets, Institutions, and Instruments* 12(1): 1–66.

Brada, J. C., and A. M. Kutan. 2002. The End of Moderate Inflation in Three Transition Countries? Working Paper No. 433, William Davidson Institute.

Budina, N., and S. van Wijnbergen. 2001. Fiscal Deficits, Monetary Reform and Inflation Stabilization in Romania. *Journal of Comparative Economics* 29(2): 293–309.

Coorey, S., M. Mecagni, and E. Offerdal. 1998a. Achieving Low Inflation in Transition Economies: The Role of Relative Price Adjustment. *Finance and Development* 35(1): 30–33.

Coorey, S., M. Mecagni, and E. Offerdal. 1998b. Disinflation in Transition Economies: The Role of Relative Price Adjustment. In *Moderate Inflation: The Experience of the Transition Economies,* ed. C. Cottarelli and G. Szapary. Washington, DC: International Monetary Fund/National Bank of Hungary.

Coricelli, F., and B. Jazbec. 2001. Real Exchange Rate Dynamics in Transition Economies. Discussion Paper No. 2869, Centre for Economic Policy Research.

Cottarelli, C., and P. Doyle. 1999. *Disinflation in Transition.* Washington, DC: International Monetary Fund.

Cottarelli, C., and G. Szapary, eds. 1998. *Moderate Inflation: The Experience of the Transition Economies.* Washington, DC: International Monetary Fund/National Bank of Hungary.

Cukierman, A., G. P. Miller, and B. Neyapti. 2002. Central Bank Reform, Liberalization and Inflation in Transition Economies—An International Perspective. *Journal of Monetary Economics* 49(2): 237–64.

Dabrowski, M., ed. 1999. Disinflation, Monetary Policy and Fiscal Constraints: Experience of the Economies in Transition. CASE Report No. 16, Center for Social and Economic Research.

Dabrowski, M., ed. 2003. *Disinflation in Transition Economies,* Budapest, Hungary: Central European Press.

De Broeck, M., and T. Sløk. 2001. Interpreting Real Exchange Rate Movements in Transition Countries. Discussion paper, Bank of Finland Institute for Economies in Transition.

de Menil, G. 2003. History, Policy and Performance in Two Transition Economies: Poland and Romania. In *In Search of Prosperity,* ed. D. Rodrik. Princeton, NJ: Princeton University Press.

Domac, I., and C. Elbirt. 1998. The Main Determinants of Inflation in Albania. Policy Research Working Paper No. 1930, World Bank.

Égert, B. 2003. Nominal and Real Convergence in Estonia: The Balassa-Samuelson (Dis)connection. Working paper, Bank of Estonia.

Filer, R. K., and J. Hanousek. 2003. Inflationary Bias in Mid to Late Transition Czech Republic. http://econwpa.wustl.edu:8089/eps/dev/papers/0306/0306001.pdf.

Fischer, S., R. Sahay, and C. A. Vegh. 1998. From Transition to Market: Evidence and Growth Prospects. Working Paper No. WP/98/52, International Monetary Fund.

Groshen, E. L., and M. E. Schweitzer. 1997. Inflation Goals: Guidance from the Labor Market? *Current Issues in Economics and Finance* 3(15): 1–6.

Havrylyshyn, O. 1997. Economic Reform in Ukraine: Late Is Better than Never—But More Difficult. In *Macroeconomic Stabilization in Transition Economies*, ed. M. Blejer and M. Skreb. New York: Cambridge University Press.

International Monetary Fund (IMF). 2003. *Romania: 2002 Staff Report* (Country Report No. 03/11). Washington, DC: IMF.

Jones, J., and F. Mishkin. 2003. Inflation Targeting in Transition Countries: Experience and Prospects. Working Paper No. 9667, National Bureau of Economic Research.

Keller, P. M., and T. Richardson. 2003. Nominal Anchors in the CIS. Working Paper No. 03/179, International Monetary Fund.

Koen, V., and P. De Masi. 1997. Prices in Transition: Ten Stylized Facts. Working Paper No. 97/158, International Monetary Fund.

Mihaljek, D. 2002. The Balassa-Samuelson Effect in Central Europe: A Disaggregated Analysis. Paper presented at the 8th Dubrovnik Economic Conference, National Bank of Croatia, June.

Obstfeld, M., and K. Rogoff. 1996. *Foundations of International Macroeconomics.* Cambridge, MA: MIT Press.

Odling-Smee, J., and G. Pastor. 2001. The IMF and the Ruble Area, 1991–93. Working Paper No. 01/101, International Monetary Fund.

Organisation for Economic Co-operation and Development (OECD). 2002a. *Economic Surveys: Poland.* Paris: OECD.

Organisation for Economic Co-operation and Development. 2002b. *Romania: Economic Assessment.* Paris: OECD.

Randveer, M. 2000. The Income Convergence between EU and Accession Countries. Working Paper No. 6, Bank of Estonia.

Rother, P. C. 2000. Inflation in Albania. Working Paper No. 00/207, International Monetary Fund.

Roubini, N., and P. Wachtel. 1999. Current Account Sustainability in Transition Economies. In *Balance of Payments, Exchange Rates, and Competitiveness in Transition Economies,* ed. M. Blejer and M. Skreb. Dordrecht, Netherlands: Kluwer Academic.

Wozniak, P. 1998. Relative Prices and Inflation in Poland 1989–97: The Special Role of Administered Prices. Working paper, World Bank.

# Commentary

*Werner Hermann*

Wachtel and Korhonen's essay provides an overview of the disinflation process in central and eastern Europe and case studies of selected countries. Its main finding is that disinflation is the result of institution building and structural reforms, but it is independent of the exchange rate regime and the monetary policy approach. The authors do not rule out the possibility that global shocks are an important factor for disinflation in transition countries. I broadly share these conclusions. Wachtel and Korhonen also warn that European Union (EU) accession countries cannot achieve both price-level and exchange rate stability during a period of income convergence. I hope this warning will be heard in Europe.

Before I go into some of the issues discussed in the foregoing chapter, let me point out, by way of introduction, that the transition countries are a very diverse group. They differ so widely that their common history over the past few decades is probably the only reason for pooling them in a group. Transition countries share few characteristics that might distinguish them clearly from other countries. Their cultural traditions differ considerably. At one end of the spectrum covered by the transition countries, we find a number of famous harbor towns in the Hanseatic League and at the other end the greatest oases on the Silk Road. In the richest transition country, gross domestic product per capita at purchasing power parity started out 20 times higher than in the poorest, with the differential widening during transition. Some transition countries tolerated private enterprise even before the Berlin Wall came down, and made fast progress thereafter. Others are still command economies barely disguised as market economies. In a few of them, decision making might be even more centralized now than it was under the Soviet Union. It is not self-evident that something we observe in central Asia should be relevant for Slovenia, let's say, and vice versa. Two main groups of more homogeneous types of transition countries can be distinguished: central and eastern Europe (including the Baltics) and the other former republics of the Soviet Union. The chapter by Wachtel and Korhonen is mainly about the first group.

As I see it, Wachtel and Korhonen pose four main questions: (1) Why did transition economies succeed in reducing inflation quickly? (2) How did the transition countries disinflate? (3) Is inflation inevitable in transition? (4) Did inflation do its job? I would like to focus my commentary on these four questions.

254

## 1. WHY DID TRANSITION ECONOMIES SUCCEED IN REDUCING INFLATION QUICKLY?

Wachtel and Korhonen discuss several underlying causes of disinflation. I will comment on four of them and propose a fifth that they do not mention.

### 1.1 Institution Building

Inflation is a hidden tax on cash balances, and it transfers wealth from creditors to debtors. Inflation can be an indicator of a distribution conflict that is unresolved in the political debate. Strong institutions render political debate more efficient and reduce the attractiveness of the inflation tax, partly because they lower the costs of tax collection. Strong institutions are associated with solid government finances, with independent and accountable central banks that have a clear mandate, and with low inflation. Because institutions were weak or nonexistent at the beginning of the transition process, it is very plausible that institution building explains disinflation to a large extent.

### 1.2 European Integration

The prospect of EU accession can be a powerful motivation to engage in institution building and disinflation. Disinflation resulting from institution building should not, however, be attributed to integration, but explicitly to institution building. The question here is, does actual or expected EU integration have an effect that is independent of institution building? Such an effect could be attributed, for instance, to better growth prospects, increased confidence, and a lower level of risk. It is easy to imagine such an effect. In order to be certain whether the effect plays a role, one would have to isolate EU accession and compare transition countries with a similar improvement in institutions but different prospects with regard to EU accession. A disinflation advantage of EU accession countries would be an indication of a positive EU integration effect. Later in my remarks, I will touch on an aspect of EU integration that could have the opposite effect: a rise in inflation in the accession countries.

### 1.3 Global Disinflation

Disinflation is a worldwide phenomenon, and one would expect global disinflation to foster disinflation in the transition countries. Wachtel and Korhonen do not rule out important global factors. By concentrating on transition countries, all they can do is speculate that disinflation is not transition specific but largely the result of global factors. A larger sample, in which transition countries are compared with others, would be required to shed light on this question. Instead, Wachtel and Korhonen opt for an in-depth treatment in which they compare transition countries only.

## 1.4 Faulty Data

Faulty data cannot explain the fact that disinflation occurred, but it might explain why disinflation was reported. Wachtel and Korhonen ask whether we can trust the figures and present some very convincing arguments why inflation, particularly in early transition, was overstated. A decreasing trend in the bias creates the appearance of disinflation even if inflation is constant. On the other hand, there are cases in which the reliability of official figures was questioned by IFIs because they looked suspiciously low. Overall, it seems reasonable to work from the assumption that disinflation took place, but the data to some extent overstate disinflation.

## 1.5 Currency Substitution

One additional reason why inflationary policies became less attractive in transition countries, which Wachtel and Korhonen do not mention, might have to do with the increasing threat of currency substitution. In the Commonwealth of Independent States, financing government expenditures by expanding money supply was attractive during the first stage of transition because there were no inflation expectations, no established tax collection mechanism, no tradition of paying explicit taxes, and thus tax collection was extremely costly. An excess supply of money, of course, led to inflation. People adapted quickly and began to monitor the exchange rate of the domestic currency carefully. Soon the U.S. dollar became not only a stable store of value and tacit unit of account, but indeed the only commonly accepted means of payment for larger transactions, such as the sale of second-hand cars, even among residents. As more and more people tried to substitute dollars for domestic currency, inflationary policies became less attractive.

## 2. HOW DID THE TRANSITION COUNTRIES DISINFLATE?

One would expect that a credible nominal anchor would be quite important for disinflation. However, according to Wachtel and Korhonen, the monetary policy regime adopted during disinflation does not seem to matter. They contend that the method of disinflation is inconclusive, and the predominant monetary policy regime was a matter of discretion rather than a hard-and-fast rule. This finding might have to do with the fact that disinflation is a worldwide phenomenon. Anecdotal evidence suggests that the exchange rate was an important indicator for monetary policy, at the very least, and I would not be surprised if a thorough empirical analysis of the data revealed some regularity.

### 3. IS INFLATION INEVITABLE IN TRANSITION?

It may sound provocative to ask whether inflation is inevitable in transition, but I think inflation is, indeed, almost inevitable in transition—not because transition cannot theoretically take place without inflation, but because of the inevitable political tensions and turmoil, so that, in practice, inflationary episodes cannot be avoided. This is, however, not what Wachtel and Korhonen have in mind. What they mean is that the economics of transition, not the politics of it, lead to inflation.

They argue that inflation stems from an appreciating real exchange rate in transition economies because of income convergence and the Balassa-Samuelson effect. This might arise under fixed exchange rates, when real appreciation takes place through a price-level increase in the transition economies (or a price-level decrease in the rest of the world). However, it is not true in general because the adjustment can take place through the exchange rate mechanism. Transition economies can keep their price levels constant if they wish, experiencing a real appreciation through an appreciating nominal exchange rate. To the extent that EU accession countries try to stabilize their exchange rates in relation to the euro, income convergence could, however, have an inflationary effect.

Even with fixed exchange rates, I would question the existence of labor mobility between the tradable and the nontradable sectors in transition countries, a crucial assumption if the Balassa-Samuelson effect is to come into play. Transition economies, however, are characterized by heavily segmented labor markets, high unemployment, and large wage differentials, so a high level of labor mobility seems unlikely.

Another reason inflation appears inevitable in transition will be discussed in the next section.

### 4. DID INFLATION DO ITS JOB?

Wachtel and Korhonen suggest that inflation might have played a useful role in transition. Two assumptions are required to make their case: first, that relative prices are initially distorted, necessitating subsequent adjustment, and second, that sellers refuse to cut prices. Under these conditions, relative prices can only be adjusted through nominal price increases, and this results in an upward shift in the price level. How well do these assumptions conform to reality in the transition countries? I do not want to dispute the need for relative price changes during the process of transition, but I would like to note that the underestimation of quality improvements and the corresponding overestimation of inflation that Wachtel and Korhonen discuss might entail an overestimation of the requisite relative price adjustments.

How about the nominal price rigidity assumption? This has traditionally been used to justify moderate inflation at times when small adjustments in relative wages were required for labor markets to clear. The argument hinges on the advantage of allowing relative price adjustments to take place unnoticed. This is not the situation at the beginning of transition. Clearly, transition represents an extreme shock that shifts many markets far out of equilibrium and necessitates drastic price changes to clear markets. So even if we can accept the argument in the case of the labor market in the United States and in western Europe, it is not immediately clear that it also applies to markets in general, particularly in the case of transition countries.

For now, let us accept the proposition of downward nominal price rigidity in principle and hazard a guess at the order of magnitude in practice: How much change in the price level is needed? Let us look at the example of Poland, which is not an extreme case at all. According to Wachtel and Korhonen's table 1, the price level in Poland went up by a factor of about 7.5 between 1990 and 1997. If half of all goods, measured by their weight in the basket, had needed the same reduction in their relative price, they could have slashed their relative price by 90% to 95%. I leave it to the reader to judge whether such a big a shift in the price level might plausibly be attributed to the need to adjust relative prices or whether a smaller dose of inflation could have done the job.

# 8

# Inflation and Financial Market Performance:

# What Have We Learned in the Last Ten Years?

*John Boyd and Bruce Champ*

## 1. INTRODUCTION

This study investigates the relationship between inflation and financial market performance. Largely, our objective is to review the extensive literature that has grown up on this topic over the last ten years or so, through the end of 2003. We also provide a few new empirical findings, primarily on the association between inflation and interest rates and between inflation and bank profits. Our review of the theory is relatively brief, compared to what it could be. This is not because the theory literature is small or unimportant but because an excellent review piece was written by our friend and colleague Bruce D. Smith just before his untimely death in 2002.

Why the recent interest in inflation and financial markets? The empirical finding of a negative association between inflation and real economic growth (e.g., Barro 1995) generated enormous interest and much subsequent work. An obviously important issue was to determine whether this association really exists and, after that had been done, to try to explain why. Another important empirical finding at about the same time was that financial intermediaries (banks and markets) seem to play a key role in economic development (King and Levine 1993a, 1993b; Levine and Zervos 1998). This finding, too, generated a great deal of subsequent interest and follow-up research. The obvious link between the two findings is the possibility that inflation might be affecting real growth *through* the financial markets—specifically, by damaging financial markets or impeding their operation. Several of the theoretical models that we discuss in the following section allow for this possibility, and much of the empirical work reviewed or presented later looks for evidence of such effects.

We spend much more time investigating banks and banking markets than we do looking at stock and bond markets, for two reasons. The first is simply that there has been relatively more work on the former than on the latter. The second is that, in many respects, banks are a more "substantial" component of the financial sector. Relatively poor countries often have very primitive markets for equity, with no trading on organized exchanges. Bond markets are also uncommon. Only about 25% of the sample countries we look at have government bonds outstanding, and an even smaller fraction have significant private bond issues. But all countries, rich and poor, have banks.

If this study in some part achieves two objectives, we would view it as a resounding success. The first is to make empiricists better aware of recent advances in the theory of financial intermediation, money, and inflation. The second is to make monetary and macro theorists more aware of recent empirical findings. The body of relevant empirical literature on inflation and finance is growing exceptionally rapidly, and work is now being done by finance scholars as well as by economists. One unfortunate result of this recent outpouring is that there are surely excellent studies that we have neglected to mention here. To the aggrieved, we apologize.

The rest of this study proceeds as follows. Section 2 contains a brief review of the theory literature on inflation and financial markets. Sections 3 and 4 review empirical work on inflation and markets for traded financial securities, such as stocks and bonds. Section 5 looks at empirical work on inflation and commercial banking. Section 6 investigates inflation and asset return volatility. Finally, Section 7 summarizes our findings.

## 2. RECENT THEORETICAL STUDIES

### 2.1 Macro Models without a Role for Banking

Smith argues that macroeconomic models that ignore banking lead to "some fairly embarrassing results" (2002b, 2). These models either generate a Mundell-Tobin effect in which higher permanent inflation leads to higher real economic activity or to superneutrality, where higher inflation has no effect on real interest rates or real activity. These results contradict the empirical results that demonstrate that, above a certain level, inflation and real economic activity are negatively correlated.

Another result that emerges from macroeconomic models that ignore financial intermediation is optimality of the Friedman rule. This finding does not appear to be empirically interesting because periods of low nominal interest rates are often associated with suboptimal economic performance. The case of the Great Depression in the United States and Japan currently come to mind. Furthermore, as we will discuss later, models that include intermediation often exhibit suboptimality of the Friedman rule.

## 2.2 Models of Financial Intermediation and Economic Growth

Gurley and Shaw (1955, 1960, 1967) noted that at low levels of economic development, most capital investment is self-financed. Only with higher levels of per capita income do banks arise and play an important role in investment finance. With further increases in per capita income, sophisticated financial markets, such as equity markets, facilitate capital creation. A conclusion suggested by the Gurley–Shaw observations is that without the development of financial institutions and financial markets, the allocation of funds to productive investment is restrained. The resultant lower levels of capital investment inhibit economic growth. Furthermore, their observations imply that financial development and economic growth are jointly determined.

The theoretical literature of the last decade or so has attempted to incorporate the Gurley–Shaw observations in the form of models emphasizing the importance of bank provision of liquidity as a factor promoting economic growth. One such early model is that of Bencivenga and Smith (1991). This model demonstrates that liquidity provision by banks can affect the composition of savings in such a manner that promotes the accumulation of private capital.

It may also be that monetary policy plays a role in the low levels of financial development in developing countries. Developing countries tend to have relatively high levels of nominal interest rates. At first glance, high nominal interest rates would seem to encourage the development of banks. However, this ignores the fact that banks must insure against depositors' need for liquidity. Bencivenga and Smith (2003) present a model in which high nominal interest rates caused by high money growth rates imply that banks are unable to adequately insure against the liquidity needs of agents, and hence they are not utilized. Economic development suffers as a result. They point to historical episodes in which monetary reforms that caused substantial declines in money growth rates and nominal interest rates spurred the development of banks.

## 2.3 The Impact of Nominal Interest Rates and Inflation on Financial Development

Two important observations come out of the empirical literature. First, low nominal interest rates tend to be associated with low levels of real investment and low economic growth rates. This may call into question the optimality of the Friedman rule. Second, permanently higher levels of inflation, above a certain rate, adversely affect economic growth. This appears inconsistent with the Mundell-Tobin effect that arises in many standard macro models. How can we understand these observations? Many of the theoretical models discussed here have, to a great extent, attempted to explain these empirical observations.

The level of nominal interest rates affects bank portfolio decisions. Low nominal interest rates lower the opportunity cost of bank holdings of cash reserves, resulting in less investment in productive capital. In essence, with low interest rates, money becomes "too good" of an asset, and banks have little incentive to make productive investments. This, in turn, hinders economic growth. In such cases, a monetary policy that adheres to the Friedman rule may be suboptimal.

High levels of inflation can also adversely affect economic growth. If, as some empirical studies suggest, higher inflation does not tend to result in proportionately higher nominal interest rates, high inflation results in lower real rates of return (Barnes, Boyd, and Smith 1999). This increases the demand for loanable funds but reduces their supply. More importantly, sufficiently high inflation rates may exacerbate credit market frictions. Empirical evidence suggests that credit market frictions are stronger in developing countries than in developed countries (McKinnon 1973; Shaw 1973). In a world with credit market frictions, higher inflation can lead to heightened rationing of credit and lower overall investment. Smith (2002b) presents a model with costly state verification in which high rates of inflation cause credit rationing and lower investment. Azariadis and Smith (1996) also show that credit market frictions may bind with sufficiently high levels of inflation. This is consistent with the empirical observation that there is a critical inflation level above which higher inflation adversely affects economic growth.

Smith and van Egteren (2003) suggest another mechanism by which inflation can affect real output. In their model, inflation both lowers the real value of internal funds used by firms to make investment and distorts firms' incentives to accumulate internal funds. This causes firms to rely more heavily on external sources of funds, exacerbating informational frictions in financial markets. This adversely affects the level and efficiency of investment, resulting in lower real output. These effects arise not only with higher inflation but also with greater volatility in inflation.

The effect of inflation on real economic activity appears to be nonmonotonic. For example, Bullard and Keating (1995) show that for economies with an initially low level of inflation, a permanent increase in the rate of inflation can stimulate long-run economic activity. But, consistent with the aforementioned studies, in economies with relatively high initial inflation rates, further increases in inflation lead to reductions in economic activity.

Another potential linkage between high inflation and lower levels of financial development is through reserve requirements. High rates of inflation can serve as a significant tax on banks, especially in those developing countries with high levels of reserve requirements.

## 2.4 The Impact of Inflation on Crises and Economic Volatility

The empirical literature also notes an important relationship between high, sustained rates of inflation and financial crises (Demirguc-Kunt and Detragiache 1998). Friedman and Schwartz (1963), of course, noted the strong correlation between crises and recessions present in the U.S. economy. In some cases, but not all, crises have led to significant, long-lasting reductions in real output (Boyd et al. 2001). The recent theoretical literature suggests that financial market frictions may play an important role in banking crises.

The early theoretical literature on banking panics did not incorporate monetary economies (Bryant 1980; Diamond and Dybvig 1983). However, many of the empirical facts associated with banking crises involve observations about the behavior of monetary variables, such as currency–deposit and reserve–deposit ratios. This argues for incorporating money into models of banking in order to adequately explain the empirical observations. The Demirguc-Kunt and Detragiache (1998) observations about a possible inflation–crisis link further argue for integrating monetary considerations into models of banking.

Models featuring monetary considerations have often done so by incorporating financial market frictions. One common feature of such models is the propensity for the model economies to exhibit significant volatility. For example, Williamson (1987), Bernanke and Gertler (1989), and Carlstrom and Fuerst (1997, 1998) show that financial market frictions can amplify the magnitude of real exogenous shocks. Furthermore, financial market frictions can also lead to increased endogenous volatility (Azariadis and Smith 1996, 1998; Boyd and Smith 1998). Models incorporating credit market frictions often imply a critical value of the inflation rate, beyond which the model economies exhibit oscillatory dynamics outside the steady state (Boyd and Smith 1998; Schreft and Smith 1998).

Smith (2002b) presents a model in which banks facing stochastic withdrawals insure agents against relocation shocks. When the proportion ($\pi$) of relocating agents exceeds a critical level, bank panics occur in which bank reserves are exhausted. For even higher levels of $\pi$, banks liquidate storage investments and receive a low rate of return on those scrapped investments. Lower output results. In this model, higher rates of inflation are associated with a higher probability of a banking crisis. This model also shows that adherence to the Friedman rule causes banks to hold 100% reserves. This implies that the probability of a banking panic is zero. Nonetheless, setting the nominal interest rate to zero is not optimal in this model. Raising the nominal interest rate above zero induces banks to hold more of the productive storage asset and increases the steady-state welfare of agents.

Smith (2002b) also presents a costly state-verification model with credit market frictions. In this model, two steady states arise, one with a low capital stock and one with a high capital stock. Which steady state the economy approaches depends on the economy's initial capital stock. Equilibrium paths that approach the high-capital steady state can display indeterminacy with a multiplicity of equilibrium. Furthermore, the possibility of endogenous volatility arises in the neighborhood of the high-capital-stock steady state, but only if steady-state inflation is sufficiently high. This implies that high inflation may be associated with increased volatility of inflation, an observation made in the empirical literature.

In Choi, Boyd, and Smith (1996), financial intermediaries are faced with an adverse selection problem with the potential for credit rationing. For low rates of inflation, credit market rationing may not occur. In such a case, the model gives rise to a Mundell-Tobin effect. However, with higher rates of inflation, the model gives rise to endogenous rationing of credit. Higher rates of inflation reduce the real rates of return for savers, and when credit is rationed, informational frictions worsen. In such cases, economic activity suffers. High inflation can also result in development traps. When inflation is sufficiently high, economic volatility results and inflation becomes more variable, as do rates of return on savings. Boyd and Smith (1998), in a costly state-verification model, yield similar results.

**Summary.** This theoretical literature makes a number of empirical predictions. One is that inflation that is "too low" can hinder the financial intermediary sector and thus reduce real output. However, we review no empirical studies that investigate deflationary environments. Sustained deflation has been relatively rare in modern times and therefore not much studied. The cross-sectional data used in this study have few countries with periods of deflation lasting over a year or so. Past periods of deflation, such as the Great Depression or the late 1800s in the United States, suffer from a dearth of adequate data to thoroughly study the impact of inflation on the financial sector.

A second prediction of the theoretical models is that inflation that is "too high" can hinder the financial intermediary sector and thus reduce real output. There are several reasons. One is the possibility of the existence of inflation thresholds. Depending on the model, economic behavior is different on the high side of the threshold; for example, credit rationing may occur. As we shall see, there has been a good deal of work on the existence of such thresholds and some work on the possibility of endogenous credit rationing.

Finally, a third important prediction of several studies is that asset return volatility will be positively related to the rate of inflation, perhaps with a discrete jump at a threshold. There has been good deal of work on this topic, and we present a few new results in the present study.

## 3. THE STOCK MARKET

Most of the theoretical work we have reviewed deals with inflation, banks, and the economy. However, the effects of inflation on securities markets are potentially important, too (Levine and Zervos 1998), and therefore we begin our review of empirical work with studies of inflation and equity markets.

### 3.1 Inflation and Stock Market Size and Performance

Boyd, Levine, and Smith (2001) employ cross-country data to examine the relationship between inflation and four measures of stock market size or performance: total stock market capitalization as a percentage of gross domestic product (GDP), total value traded as a percentage of GDP, the ratio of stock value traded to stock market capitalization, and a measure of return volatility.[1] Their tests are country cross-sections employing data averaged over a 36-year period, 1970–95, for 48 countries. The idea of the long time averages is to look at steady-state relationships. They include as control variables initial (1970) real per capita GDP, initial (1970) secondary education, the number of coups and revolutions, the black-market currency premium, and a measure of the government's fiscal deficit.

They find that inflation is negatively and significantly associated with the first three stock market measures after controlling for the other variables mentioned. They also report strong evidence of "threshold effects" for these three relationships. Specifically, the inflation–stock market performance relationship flattens significantly for high values of inflation (above 15%) so that further increases in inflation are not associated with significant further deterioration in stock market capitalization, total value traded, or turnover.

Boyd, Levine, and Smith (2001) find that stock market volatility, on the other hand, is best represented by a simple, positive, linear relationship with inflation, which is highly statistically significant.[2] All these relationships are statistically significant and seemingly robust; however, the authors make no pretense of having established direction(s) of causality.

In figures 1 and 2, we reproduce some results similar to those of Boyd, Levine, and Smith using our own data. Figure 1 shows total equity market capitalization as a fraction of GDP (*mcap*) after sorting the data into inflation

---

[1] The first three stock market variables have been found to be significantly correlated with real economic development (King and Levine 1993a, 1993b). Stock market volatility is computed as a 12-month rolling standard deviation, cleansed of 12 months of autocorrelations following the procedure defined by Schwert (1989).

[2] We will return to the inflation-volatility issue in the new work presented in section 6 of this paper.

*John Boyd and Bruce Champ*

**Figure 1. Total Equity Market Capitalization/GDP by Inflation Quartile, 1980–95**

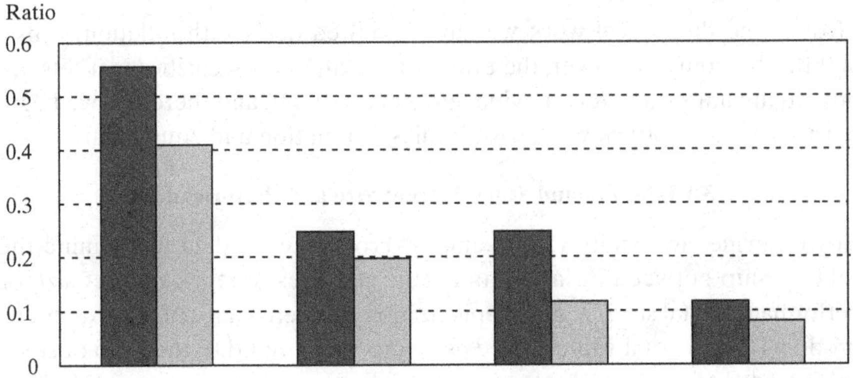

Ratio

| | First Quartile | | Second Quartile | | Third Quartile | | Fourth Quartile | |
|---|---|---|---|---|---|---|---|---|
| $N = 68$ | Mean | Median | Mean | Median | Mean | Median | Mean | Median |
| *mcap* | 0.5551 | 0.4092 | 0.2473 | 0.1977 | 0.2475 | 0.1169 | 0.1165 | 0.0811 |
| *cpirate* | 1.0363 | 1.0366 | 1.0664 | 1.0656 | 1.1161 | 1.1140 | 1.3249 | 1.2466 |

**Note:** Left bars are means; right bars are medians.

**Figure 2. Total Value of Equity Traded/GDP by Inflation Quartile, 1980–95**

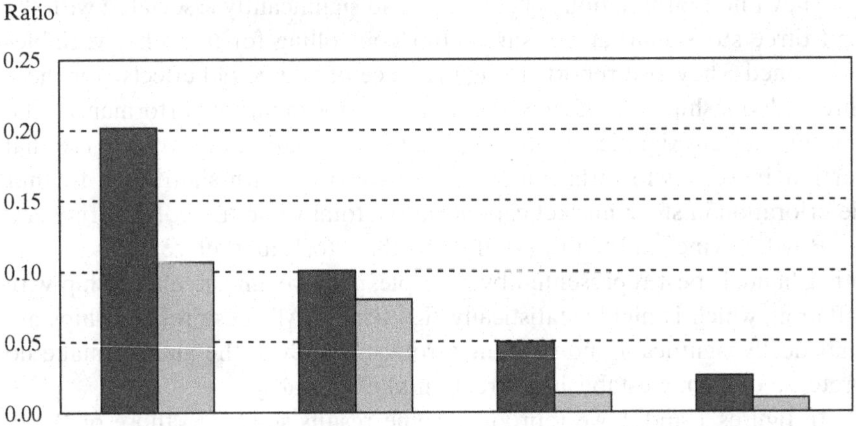

Ratio

| | First Quartile | | Second Quartile | | Third Quartile | | Fourth Quartile | |
|---|---|---|---|---|---|---|---|---|
| $N = 68$ | Mean | Median | Mean | Median | Mean | Median | Mean | Median |
| *tvt* | 0.2016 | 0.1067 | 0.1005 | 0.0801 | 0.0497 | 0.0134 | 0.0255 | 0.0098 |
| *cpirate* | 1.0363 | 1.0366 | 1.0678 | 1.0666 | 1.1194 | 1.1225 | 1.3249 | 1.2466 |

**Note:** Left bars are means; right bars are medians.

quartiles. These data are averaged over the period 1980–95, and there are 68 countries. The figure clearly shows the negative relationship between *mcap* and inflation, as reported by Boyd, Levine, and Smith. Figure 2 shows the total value of equity trading as a fraction of GDP (*tvt*) for the same countries and time period and exhibits the same negative relationship with inflation. In this case, we see clear evidence of flattening in the two higher-inflation quartiles. For quartile 3, the median value of *tvt* is 0.013 and for quartile 4, it is hardly different at 0.010.[3]

### 3.2 Inflation and Equity Returns

In this same study, Boyd, Levine, and Smith (2001) examine the relationship between inflation and nominal stock returns for 38 countries, employing the same set of control variables. In simple linear regressions, inflation enters with a positive and highly significant coefficient and an elasticity a bit greater than 1. However, there is also evidence of a threshold effect in the inflation–equity return relationship. For countries with average annual inflation less than 15%, there is no significant relationship between the long-run rate of inflation and the nominal return on equity. However, for economies with rates of inflation in excess of 15%, marginal increases in inflation are matched by even greater than one-for-one increases in nominal stock returns.[4]

To verify their results, we estimated equations (1) and (2) using a sample of equity returns for 31 countries, averaged over the 10-year period 1989–98. The dependent variable, *eqrate*, is the gross nominal rate of return on each country's major stock exchange, averaged geometrically over the 10 years. The inflation measure, *cpirate*, is the geometric average of gross changes in the consumer price index (CPI) over the same period.[5] To control for the level of economic development, which could be associated with the rate of inflation, we include a measure of initial wealth represented by real per capita GDP in the year 1980 (*initial*). In many economies, exchange rate risks (or distortions) could be associated with the level of asset returns. Therefore, we include the black-market currency premium (*bmp*) as an additional control variable. For obvious reasons, political risk could be associated with asset returns, and the number of coups and revolutions (*revc*) in also included as a control.[6] We split

---

[3] For a different perspective on inflation thresholds, see Rousseau and Wachtel (2002).
[4] This study did not attempt to search for the "best" threshold in these tests. However, this has been done in Barnes and Hughes 2002.
[5] A data appendix at the end of the paper describes the variables used in this study and provides their sources.
[6] We experimented with a variety of different control variables. Except as noted, the results were qualitatively little affected.

the sample into low-inflation and high-inflation halves, and equation (1) is estimated with the low-inflation countries. Standard errors are robust, and $t$ values are given in parentheses.

It is clear that there is no significant relationship between equity returns and inflation for the low inflation countries. Equation (2) is estimated with the high-inflation group, and here the inflation coefficient is almost exactly equal to 1 and highly statistically significant.[7] Both equations (1) and (2) have negative and significant coefficients on the black-market currency premium, $bmp$, suggesting that currency problems are not good for equity investments, all else being equal. Not surprisingly, $bmp$ is correlated with average inflation rates, but excluding this variable has little effect on the other coefficients and $t$ values in equations (1) and (2).

(1)   $eqrate = 1.932 - 0.855cpirate + 3.332initial - 0.504bmp + 0.038revc$

              (0.36)         (0.75)         (4.78)         (0.46)

   $n = 16, R^2 \text{ adj} = 0.52$

(2)   $eqrate = 0.005 + 1.026cpirate + 7.637initial - 0.003bmp - 0.144revc$

              (150.43)        (0.82)         (3.07)         (0.43)

   $n = 15, R^2 \text{ adj} = 0.99$

### 3.2.1 Inflation and Equity Returns: Time-Series Studies

Some previous studies of equity returns using time-series data have obtained results similar to those of Boyd, Levine, and Smith (2001) for low-inflation countries in the sense that, when inflation rates are relatively low, nominal equity returns are found to be essentially uncorrelated with inflation (Amihud 1996; Boudoukh and Richardson 1993; Choudry 2001). Kutan and Aksoy (2003) studied the relationship between inflation and equity returns in Turkey over the period December 1986–March 2001 using monthly data and an asymmetric GARCH (generalized autoregressive conditional

---

[7] In this case, the sample median inflation rate was just less than 5%. We could not split the sample at a 15% inflation rate, as did Boyd, Levine, and Smith (2001), because there are too few countries with average inflation exceeding that threshold. Our data come from a later, lower-inflation time period. If these regressions are rerun excluding very high-inflation countries (net inflation exceeding 100% per year), the results change little except that the inflation coefficient is much larger for the high-inflation group.

heteroskedastic) model. These authors found that average equity returns on a composite stock index and an index of industrial stocks were essentially unrelated to inflation, represented by changes in the CPI lagged by one, two, and three months.

Kutan and Aksoy (2003) also found that returns on financial-sector equities were positively and significantly correlated with inflation in all specifications. As they put it, "In these results, for the financials, anticipated inflation continues to have the most significant impact. All the estimated inflation coefficients are positive, and individually and jointly significant. The sum of the coefficients is 2.08: A 1% increase in the expected inflation rate raises the financial returns by 2.08%, all else constant" (236). This is an unexpected finding because results presented in section 5 of this paper suggest that banks are not particularly well hedged against inflation.

Barnes, Boyd, and Smith (1999) study a sample of 25 countries employing quarterly time-series regressions for periods as long as February 1957 through March 1996, depending on country. Their dependent variable is the nominal rate of return on equity, represented by changes in the country's major stock exchange index. Inflation is represented by the percentage change in the CPI, contemporaneous and lagged by one quarter. Sample inflation experience ranged from Switzerland, with a 0.86% average annual rate of inflation, to Peru, with a 54.0% average annual inflation rate. The simple cross-country correlation between the average rate of inflation and average equity returns was 0.84. However, in 15 out of 25 countries, the contemporaneous inflation coefficient was negative in the time-series regressions, and for only four countries was this coefficient positive and significantly different from zero. These were the *four highest-inflation countries in the sample:* Chile, Israel, Mexico, and Peru. On the other hand, the United States, Australia, and Japan, three of the lowest-inflation countries, had inflation coefficients that were *negative* and significantly different from zero at usual confidence levels.[8]

Obviously, the time-series findings are generally very consistent with the cross-country evidence. With the time-series tests, however, there are a number of cases with a *negative* relationship between inflation and nominal equity returns, always in low-inflation countries. This is an advantage over the time-series approach because such cases may be obscured by the time-averaging procedure in the country cross-sections. However, the time-series tests themselves suffer from the problem of using relatively high-frequency data to

---

[8] The one-quarter lagged inflation rate was only significant in eight of the 25 cases. In four of these cases, the coefficient was negative and of that four, three were low-inflation countries (Netherlands, Philippines, and Spain).

estimate what are believed to be steady-state relationships. In addition, in the time-series tests, there is the question of whether and to what extent inflation has been fully anticipated by market participants. For present purposes, these issues are irrelevant because both time-series and cross-sectional work lead to largely the same conclusions, which we will summarize next.

**Summary.** The response of nominal equity returns to inflation appears to depend on the level of inflation. In low-inflation environments, cross-country tests find that inflation and nominal equity returns are essentially uncorrelated. Time-series tests suggest that the two are significantly correlated in some countries and not in others. However, when this correlation is statistically significant, it is negative about as frequently as it is positive. In sum, in relatively low-inflation environments, inflation and real equity returns are negatively associated. In high-inflation environments, the findings are quite different. There, it appears that nominal equity returns increase at least enough to leave real returns unaffected. Time-series tests support this conclusion in the sense that stock returns seem to respond more positively to inflation changes in high-inflation environments.

## 4. DEBT MARKETS: INFLATION AND INTEREST RATES

In their study of Turkish financial markets over the period January 1987–December 2000, Kutan and Aksoy (2003) found no evidence of any relationship between inflation, lagged by one, two, and three months, and changes in interest rates. As they put it, "[T]he bond market does not act well as a hedge against anticipated inflation in Turkey" (232).

Barnes, Boyd, and Smith (1999) investigated the relationship between inflation and nominal interest rates for 25 countries using quarterly time-series over periods as long as February 1957–March 1996. They studied two interest rate series—a money market rate and a bank lending rate—and estimated both equations in first differences and ARMA (2,1) processes. When the money market rate is dependent, with either specification, less than half the countries exhibit inflation coefficients that are positive and statistically significant. Similar results are obtained when the bank lending rate is the dependent variable. In all cases and with both interest rates, the inflation coefficient is quite small, and when it is significantly different from zero, it is also significantly less than 1.

### 4.1 New Cross-Country Inflation and Interest Rate Tests

Our review of the literature found no previous research that looked at the relationship between inflation and interest rates employing country cross-sections with long time averaging. Therefore, we carried out some work of this nature for the present study. We estimated two kinds of regressions: those with nominal rates of interest as the dependent variable (table 1) and those with real rates of interest as the dependent variable (table 2). We include the same control variables—*initial, revc,* and *bmp*—discussed earlier.

**Table 1. Nominal Interest Rate Regressions, 1989–98**

| | Dependent Variables | | | | |
|---|---|---|---|---|---|
| | **1.** *mmrate* | **2.** *tbillrate* | **3.** *tdeprate* | **4.** *loanrate* | **5.** *govrate* |
| *cpirate8998* | 0.8721 (30.75)*** | 0.4825 (6.32)*** | 0.5895 (4.30)*** | 0.8548 (2.70)*** | 0.9376 (6.10)*** |
| *revc* | 0.0257 (0.36) | 0.0148 (1.07) | 0.0200 (1.13) | –0.0072 (0.35) | –0.0372 (2.67)** |
| *bmp* | –0.0005 (1.14) | 0.0001 (2.48)** | –0.0002 (0.80) | –0.0007 (0.97) | –0.0025 (2.41)** |
| *initial* | –0.3772 (0.45) | –2.3370 (1.88)* | –1.9550 (1.62) | –4.1382 (2.34)** | –2.1118 (3.12)*** |
| *constant* | 0.1792 (6.13)*** | 0.6016 (6.83)*** | 0.4737 (3.07)*** | 0.2717 (0.80) | 0.1390 (0.85) |
| *N* | 34 | 34 | 69 | 69 | 26 |
| Adjusted $R^2$ | 0.94 | 0.90 | 0.79 | 0.64 | 0.96 |
| Elasticity of *cpirate8998* | 0.8326 | 0.4666 | 0.5808 | 0.7973 | 0.8925 |
| Medians: Dep. Var. | 1.0939 | 1.0940 | 1.0977 | 1.1595 | 1.0839 |
| *cpirate8998* | 1.0444 | 1.0581 | 1.0815 | 1.0816 | 1.0317 |
| *revc* | 0.0000 | 0.0000 | 0.0000 | 0.0000 | 0.0000 |
| *bmp* | 0.1839 | 7.4965 | 7.5075 | 7.8157 | 0.0000 |
| *initial* | 0.0071 | 0.0041 | 0.0019 | 0.0019 | 0.0093 |

**Note:** Robust *t* statistics in parentheses. All regressions intentionally exclude countries with average inflation exceeding 200% per annum.
\* significant at 10%; \*\* significant at 5%; \*\*\* significant at 1%.

John Boyd and Bruce Champ

**Table 2. Real Interest Rate Regressions, 1989–98**

| | Dependent Variables | | | | | | |
|---|---|---|---|---|---|---|---|
| | **1.** *rmmrate* | **2.** *rtbillrate* | **3.** *rtdeprate* | **4.** *rloanrate* | **5.** *rgovrate* | **6.** *rtbillrate* | **7.** *rloanrate* |
| *cpirate8998* | −0.0920 (4.11)*** | −0.2979 (9.21)*** | −0.2534 (3.54)*** | −0.1214 (0.62) | 0.0128 (0.09) | 0.4105 (1.38) | 1.1203 (1.61) |
| *bmp* | −0.0005 (1.44) | 0.00004 (1.25) | −0.0001 (0.94) | −0.0004 (0.94) | −0.0023 (2.52)** | −0.00001 (0.21) | −0.0005 (1.02) |
| *revc* | 0.0244 (0.40) | 0.0160 (1.71)* | 0.0138 (1.01) | −0.0067 (0.40) | −0.0275 (1.95)* | 0.0172 (2.12)** | −0.0095 (0.55) |
| *initial* | −0.1123 (0.15) | −0.6342 (0.74) | −0.8344 (1.05) | −2.8014 (2.30)** | −1.2440 (2.01)* | 0.6118 (0.65) | −1.1138 (0.70) |
| *cpirate8998²* | | | | | | −0.2467 (2.48)** | −0.4580 (2.20)** |
| *constant* | 1.1375 (47.67)*** | 1.3522 (34.50)*** | 1.2960 (16.05)*** | 1.2273 (5.86)*** | 1.0491 (7.37)*** | 0.8682 (4.16)*** | 0.4127 (0.80) |
| *N* | 34 | 34 | 69 | 69 | 26 | 34 | 69 |
| Adjusted $R^2$ | 0.26 | 0.83 | 0.63 | 0.16 | 0.88 | 0.86 | 0.22 |
| Elasticity of *cpirate8998* | −0.0925 | −0.3059 | −0.2698 | −0.1230 | 0.0127 | −0.0851 | 0.2070 |
| Medians: Dep. Var. | 1.0390 | 1.0304 | 1.0159 | 1.0668 | 1.0456 | 1.0304 | 1.0668 |
| *cpirate8998* | 1.0444 | 1.0581 | 1.0815 | 1.0815 | 1.0317 | 1.0581 | 1.0815 |
| *bmp* | 0.1839 | 7.4965 | 7.5075 | 8.1157 | 0.0000 | 7.4965 | 7.8157 |
| *revc* | 0.0000 | 0.0000 | 0.0000 | 0.0000 | 0.0000 | 0.0000 | 0.0000 |
| *initial* | 0.0071 | 0.0041 | 0.0019 | 0.0019 | 0.0093 | 0.0041 | 0.0019 |

**Note:** Robust *t* statistics in parentheses. All regressions intentionally exclude countries with average (gross) inflation exceeding 200% per annum. If these data points are included, equation (2) is unaffected. In all other regressions, the inflation coefficient becomes insignificantly different from zero except in equation (1) where it is positive and marginally significant. * significant at 10%; ** significant at 5%; *** significant at 1%.

In table 1, the dependent variables are, in order, the nominal interest rate on money market securities, Treasury bills, time deposits, bank commercial loans, and medium- to long-term government bonds. Each interest rate is represented by its gross geometric average rate over the time period, 1989–98, employing annual data. Inflation is measured as the geometric average of gross changes in the CPI, averaged over the same period. In the tests with real interest rates reported in table 2, the dependent variables are these same five geometric average nominal interest rates divided by the same-period geometric average rate of CPI inflation.

In table 1, the coefficient of inflation is positive and highly significant for all interest rate measures. In all cases, the interest rate elasticity with respect to inflation (at the sample median values) is less than 1; in fact, it is significantly less than 1 in all cases except for the loan rate and government bond rate.

The real interest rate regressions in table 2 show generally the same picture. In regressions 1 through 5, the inflation coefficient is negative and highly significant in the equation for the real money market rate, the real Treasury bill rate, and the real time deposit rate. However, it is not statistically different from zero for the real loan rate and the real government rate.

Two of these relationships, the real Treasury rate and the real loan rate, appear to exhibit nonlinearity according to standard goodness-of-fit criteria, and we have included quadratic specifications for these two cases in regressions 6 and 7 of table 2. In both instances, the coefficient of the linear term is positive and the coefficient of the squared term negative, implying that real interest rates "worsen" as inflation increases. There is no positive rate of inflation for which the inflation elasticity of the real Treasury bill rate is positive. That is, $d(rtbillrate)/d(cpirate) < 0$ for any positive rate of inflation. The inflation elasticity of the real loan rate is positive for inflation rates up to about 22% and negative thereafter. Thus, according to this estimate, banks can increase loan rates to offset (or more than offset) inflation for low and intermediate rates of inflation but not for extremely high rates.

Figures 3–7 show means and medians for each of the five real interest rates, sorted into inflation quartiles. The (mean and median) real money market rate shows no obvious pattern, except that the highest quartile is relatively low. The (mean and median) real Treasury bill rate declines with each inflation quartile, as does the real time deposit rate. The mean real loan rate increases between the first and second quartiles and then declines in the third and fourth quartile. The median real loan rate is basically constant across the first two quartiles and decreases markedly in the third and fourth quartiles. Finally, the (mean and median) real government bond rate is essentially flat for the first three quartiles and then drops precipitously in the fourth quartile. Table 3 presents summary statistics for our measures of real interest rates and for the correlation coefficients between the real interest rates and inflation.

274      *John Boyd and Bruce Champ*

**Table 3. Real Interest Rates, 1989–98:**
**Means, Medians, and Correlations with Average Inflation**

|  | Mean | Median | Correlation with Average Inflation |
|---|---|---|---|
| *rmmrate* | 2.49% | 3.79% | −0.7077 |
| *rtbillrate* | 1.46% | 2.98% | −0.8809 |
| *rtdeprate* | −0.11% | 1.28% | −0.7969 |
| *rloanrate* | 6.26% | 6.64% | −0.4182 |
| *rgovrate* | 3.27% | 4.21% | −0.8465 |

**Figure 3. Real Money Market Rate by Inflation Quartile, 1989–98**

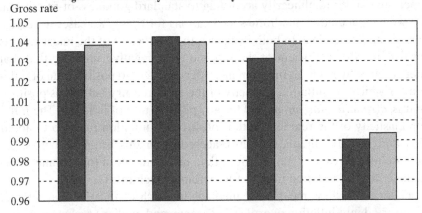

|  | First Quartile | | Second Quartile | | Third Quartile | | Fourth Quartile | |
|---|---|---|---|---|---|---|---|---|
| $N = 44$ | Mean | Median | Mean | Median | Mean | Median | Mean | Median |
| *rmmrate* | 1.0353 | 1.0385 | 1.0427 | 1.0399 | 1.0314 | 1.0391 | 0.9904 | 0.9937 |
| *cpirate* | 1.0218 | 1.0234 | 1.0329 | 1.0326 | 1.0628 | 1.0583 | 1.2676 | 1.1766 |

**Note:** Left bars are means; right bars are medians.

**Figure 4. Real Treasury Bill Rate by Inflation Quartile, 1989–98**

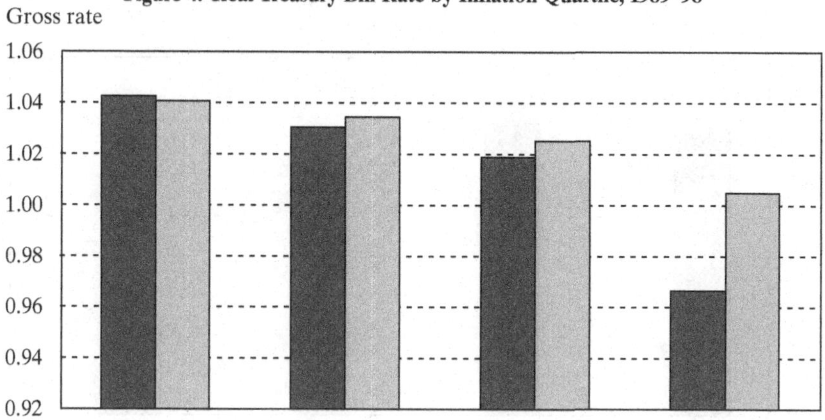

Gross rate

| | First Quartile | | Second Quartile | | Third Quartile | | Fourth Quartile | |
|---|---|---|---|---|---|---|---|---|
| $N = 52$ | Mean | Median | Mean | Median | Mean | Median | Mean | Median |
| *rtbillrate* | 1.0427 | 1.0408 | 1.0306 | 1.0347 | 1.0188 | 1.0252 | 0.9664 | 1.0049 |
| *cpirate* | 1.0234 | 1.0253 | 1.0360 | 1.0332 | 1.0892 | 1.0959 | 1.3181 | 1.2377 |

**Note:** Left bars are means; right bars are medians.

**Figure 5. Real Time Deposit Rate by Inflation Quartile, 1989–98**

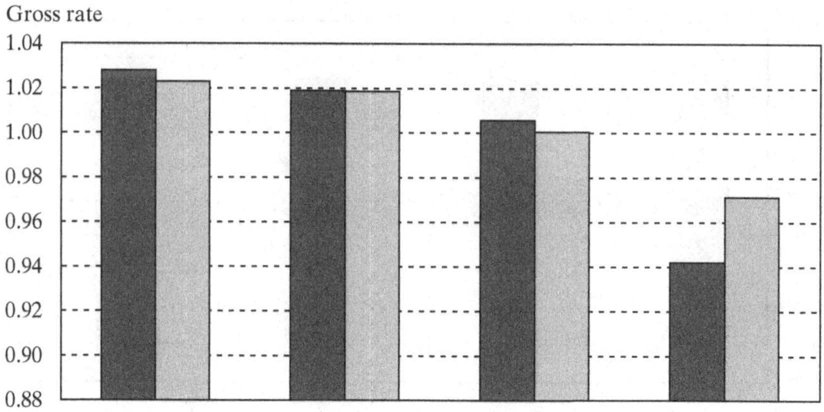

Gross rate

| | First Quartile | | Second Quartile | | Third Quartile | | Fourth Quartile | |
|---|---|---|---|---|---|---|---|---|
| $N = 102$ | Mean | Median | Mean | Median | Mean | Median | Mean | Median |
| *rtdeprate* | 1.0279 | 1.0230 | 1.0189 | 1.0187 | 1.0057 | 1.0004 | 0.9419 | 0.9714 |
| *cpirate* | 1.0241 | 1.0254 | 1.0461 | 1.0448 | 1.1043 | 1.1119 | 1.3451 | 1.2613 |

**Note:** Left bars are means; right bars are medians.

*John Boyd and Bruce Champ*

**Figure 6. Real Loan Rate by Inflation Quartile, 1989–98**

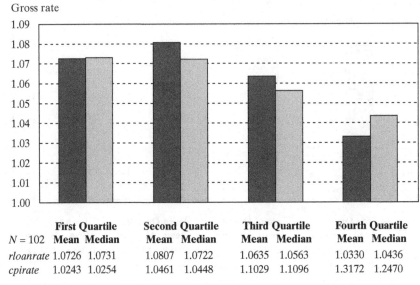

| | First Quartile | | Second Quartile | | Third Quartile | | Fourth Quartile | |
|---|---|---|---|---|---|---|---|---|
| $N = 102$ | **Mean** | **Median** | **Mean** | **Median** | **Mean** | **Median** | **Mean** | **Median** |
| *rloanrate* | 1.0726 | 1.0731 | 1.0807 | 1.0722 | 1.0635 | 1.0563 | 1.0330 | 1.0436 |
| *cpirate* | 1.0243 | 1.0254 | 1.0461 | 1.0448 | 1.1029 | 1.1096 | 1.3172 | 1.2470 |

**Note:** Left bars are means; right bars are medians.

**Figure 7. Real Government Bond Rate by Inflation Quartile, 1989–98**

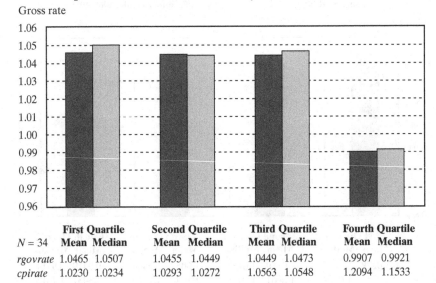

| | First Quartile | | Second Quartile | | Third Quartile | | Fourth Quartile | |
|---|---|---|---|---|---|---|---|---|
| $N = 34$ | **Mean** | **Median** | **Mean** | **Median** | **Mean** | **Median** | **Mean** | **Median** |
| *rgovrate* | 1.0465 | 1.0507 | 1.0455 | 1.0449 | 1.0449 | 1.0473 | 0.9907 | 0.9921 |
| *cpirate* | 1.0230 | 1.0234 | 1.0293 | 1.0272 | 1.0563 | 1.0548 | 1.2094 | 1.1533 |

**Note:** Left bars are means; right bars are medians.

**Summary.** The pattern in figures 3–7 is fairly clear and generally consistent with the regression results just presented. Time-averaged real interest rates tend to fall as inflation rises—if not at low to moderate inflation rates—and then when inflation enters the fourth quartile. A "representative" high-inflation economy, one that has inflation at the fourth-quartile sample medians, would have real money market rates and real Treasury bill rates of essentially zero. Its real time deposit rate would be –3% and its real government bond rate about –1%. Only its real loan rate would be meaningfully positive at about 4.4%.

## 5. INFLATION AND THE BANKING INDUSTRY

### 5.1 Inflation and Banking Development Indicators

Boyd, Levine, and Smith (2001) study the relationship between inflation and three banking development indicators that have been used widely in the literature: (1) the ratio of liquid liabilities of the financial sector to GDP; (2) the ratio of total assets of "deposit money banks" to GDP; and (3) the ratio of bank lending to the private sector to GDP. All three variables have been found to be strongly associated with the level and/or rate of change in real per capita GDP (King and Levine 1993a, 1993b). All variables were averaged over the period 1960–95, and cross-country regressions were estimated involving 94 countries. The development indicators were regressed against inflation and a set of control variables including initial (1960) real per capita GDP, initial (1960) secondary school enrollment, the number of coups and revolutions, the black-market premium, and the government deficient. In linear regressions, the inflation coefficient was negative and significant at the 1% confidence level in all cases.

However, there was also evidence of threshold effects. Essentially, inflation was negatively associated with all three financial development indicators in countries with inflation of less than 15%. But as inflation exceeded the 15% threshold, there was a discrete drop in the development indicator, and its relationship with inflation disappeared. This is very similar to the threshold results for stock market development measures from the same study that we reported earlier. To summarize in the authors' words,

> [T]here appears to be some evidence of a threshold in the empirical relationship between inflation and financial activity. At moderate inflation rates, there is a strong negative association between inflation and financial development. For countries whose inflation is above some critical level, the estimated intercept of the bank development relation is much lower than it is for countries below the threshold. Moreover, in economies with rates of inflation exceeding this threshold, the partial correlation between inflation and financial activity essentially disappears. (237)

**Figure 8. Commercial Banking Lending to Private Sector/GDP by Inflation Quartile, 1980–95**

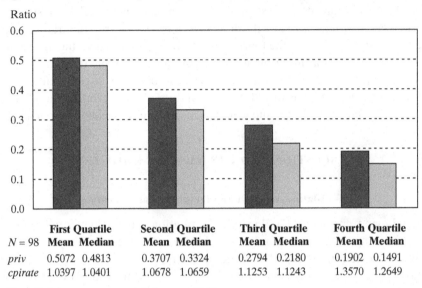

| $N = 98$ | First Quartile Mean Median | Second Quartile Mean Median | Third Quartile Mean Median | Fourth Quartile Mean Median |
|---|---|---|---|---|
| *priv* | 0.5072  0.4813 | 0.3707  0.3324 | 0.2794  0.2180 | 0.1902  0.1491 |
| *cpirate* | 1.0397  1.0401 | 1.0678  1.0659 | 1.1253  1.1243 | 1.3570  1.2649 |

**Note:** Left bars are means; right bars are medians.

Figure 8 is our own work, and it shows the relationship between bank lending to the private sector as a percentage of GDP (*priv*) and inflation after the data have been sorted into inflation quartiles. For this purpose, we have data for 98 countries, averaged over the 15-year period 1980–95.[9] Clearly, bank private lending is much greater, relative to the size of the economy, in low-inflation economies. In the lowest inflation quartile, this ratio averages more than 50% and in the highest, it averages about 19%. Boyd, Levine, and Smith (2001) also report statistical evidence that inflation exerts a causal effect on banking development as represented by *priv*.

**Summary.** These results, along with the results on stock markets, suggest that cross-sectionally, higher inflation goes hand-in-hand with a smaller financial intermediary sector. For banking (but not securities markets), there is evidence of causality running from inflation to financial markets.

### 5.2 Inflation and Credit Availability from Banks: Attitude and Opinion Data

Two recent studies have investigated external financing obstacles in different countries, employing a 1999 survey data set from the World Business Environment Survey. In the survey, almost 5,000 firms in 49 countries responded to questions about the obstacles they encountered in obtaining

---

[9] This is a much shorter time period and somewhat larger sample of countries than was employed by Boyd, Levine, and Smith (2001). However, the results are very similar.

external financing. There were three questions: (1) How problematic is financing for the operation and growth of your firm? (2) Is the need for special connections with banks an obstacle for the operation and growth of your business? (3) Is the corruption of bank officials an obstacle for the operation and growth of your business? Respondents employed a four-point scale from 1 (no obstacle) to 4 (major obstacle). It has been shown that survey responses significantly correlate to actual, measurable outcomes (Hellman et al. 2000) and are especially correlated with firm growth after controlling for many other factors (Beck, Demirguc-Kunt, and Maksimovic 2002).

Beck, Demirguc-Kunt, and Levine (2003b) use this data set to study the effects of banking supervision on the availability of external financing. Beck, Demirguc-Kunt, and Maksimovic (2003) use it to study the relationship between banking structure (competition) and availability of external finance. For our purposes, the two studies produce almost identical results, and therefore we confine our comments to the first, which provides somewhat more detail. In Beck, Demirguc-Kunt, and Levine (2003b) the dependent variables are the survey responses, and inflation is included as a control variable along with the ratio of private bank lending to GDP, the growth rate of real GDP per capita, and a variety of legal and institutional variables. When "general financing obstacles" (question 1) was the dependent variable, the coefficient of inflation was positive and statistically significant at usual confidence levels in almost all specifications. The clear implication is that, all else being equal, more inflation is associated with greater difficulty in obtaining external financing.[10] Essentially, the same results are obtained when the dependent variable is "bank corruption" (question 3).[11]

**Summary.** The findings of this body of research suggest that higher inflation is associated with greater impediments to credit access. It would surely be useful to employ this unique data set for a full investigation of the influence of inflation on credit availability. These "soft" attitude and opinion data may be expected to capture nonprice credit rationing of the sort modeled by Boyd and Smith (1998), Choi, Boyd, and Smith (1996), and others.

---

[10] The only exception is when a variable representing the liberality of deposit insurance coverage is also included. In that case, the inflation coefficient drops to insignificance. However, adding this variable also results in a very large decline in effective sample size, which could also explain the change.

[11] Surprisingly, when the dependent variable is "need for a special connection" (question 2), the inflation coefficient becomes negative and statistically significant at the 95% confidence level in most specifications. The study does not discuss this sign difference, which is inconsequential to its research objectives. It is worth noting that responses to the three questions seem to be capturing attitudes about different phenomena, as the simple correlations between the three responses are never larger than 0.42.

### 5.3 Banking Crises

Several studies have examined which economic forces are associated with or "cause" banking crises. In at least three cases, inflation, although not the variable of primary interest, was included as a control variable. For example, Demirguc-Kunt and Detragiache (1998) examine the role of moral hazard due to deposit insurance in causing banking system instability. In their study, the dependent variable was a (0,1) dummy variable that took on the value 1 if a country experienced a banking crisis, zero otherwise. Banking crisis dates were taken from a data set constructed and updated by the World Bank (Caprio and Klingebiel 1999). The study employed a multivariate logit model with a panel of 61 countries experiencing 40 banking crises over the period 1980–97. Inflation was included as a control variable, along with the growth rate of real GDP, the terms of trade, the ratio of M2 to foreign exchange reserves, and the beginning-of-sample real GDP per capita.

Under a variety of different specifications, the inflation variable had a positive coefficient that was statistically significant (at high confidence levels) as an explanator of banking crisis probabilities. However, in later revisions of this same study, the real interest rate was added as an additional control variable and the sample was expanded. With these changes, the inflation coefficient dropped to insignificance. We believe that adding the real interest rate as an explanatory variable could easily obscure the true effect of inflation on banking crisis probabilities. Although inflation is arguably exogenous, the real interest rate is clearly endogenous and (by construction) a function of inflation. In this study, the simple correlation between the rate of inflation and the real interest rate is extremely high at –0.98.[12] However, the authors inform us that most of the change in the partial correlation with inflation results from the change in sample composition. Interestingly, even with the larger sample, the simple correlation between inflation and banking crisis probability (reported by Beck, Demirguc-Kunt, and Levine 2003a) is positive and significant at the 1% confidence level.[13]

---

[12] Another recent study by Beck, Demirguc-Kunt, and Levine (2003a) examines the relationship between banking concentration and the probability of banking crises. It employs essentially the same data set as Demirguc-Kunt and Detragiache (1998) and produces, from our perspective, identical results. That is, inflation never enters as a significant explanation of banking crisis probability, but inflation is always entered alongside the real interest rate. All our comments on the previous study apply equally to this one.

[13] It is important to note that for the purposes of the Demirguc-Kunt and Detragiache studies (1998) that such multicollinearity is not at all an issue. They are not interested in separating the effects of inflation and real interest rates, only to control for them.

Another recent study by De Nicolo, Bartholomew, Zaman, and Zephirin (2004) took a different approach to empirically representing the occurrence of banking crises. Instead of trying to date crisis beginnings and endings, they construct a continuous crisis-probability measure for the five largest banks in a country. This "$z$ score" measure is the probability that the five largest banks will experience combined losses great enough to eradicate their consolidated equity capital. The $z$ score depends on mean profits, the variability of profits, and the equity capital of the five banks. All of these are represented as a percentage of total assets and measured with annual accounting data over the period 1993–2000. Depending on specification, up to 97 countries are included.

In the reported results, inflation enters as a control variable, along with a set of regional dummy variables, real GDP growth, and a government intervention variable that is intended to capture the effect of government bailouts on banks' profit distributions. In none of the various specifications did inflation enter with a coefficient significantly different from zero. However, the six regional dummy variables, in conjunction with the real growth variable, could be serving as a reasonably good proxy for inflation. So, we asked the authors whether they would provide us with a $z$ score regression with inflation and the government intervention variable as the only explanatory variables. They were gracious enough to do so, and the results are shown in equation (3). The dependent variable is the $z$ score, *cpirate* is the sample average rate of inflation, and *crisis* is the government intervention variable discussed previously. Estimation is by ordinary least squares with robust standard errors, and $t$ values are given in parentheses.

(3)    $z$ score = $3.262 - 2.048 crisis - 3.028 cpirate$         $R^2$ adj = .152

             (5.87)         (3.029)                                    $n = 112$

Inflation enters with a negative coefficient, significant at the 5% confidence level. Because lower $z$ scores are associated with banking instability, inflation reduces banking stability, all else being equal. The coefficient of the government intervention variable, *crisis*, is also negative and significantly different from zero at a high confidence level, reflecting the effect of banking crises. [14]

---

[14] We have reproduced results very similar to equation (3), employing our own data set. Specifically, we find that a $z$ score measure is negatively and significantly related to *cpirate*, controlling for *bmp*, *revc*, and *initial*. We do not reproduce those results here because they depend on the standard deviation of bank borrowing and lending spreads, not of bank profits, and therefore are not strictly comparable to equation (3). Time-series data for bank profits were not available to us.

Boyd et al. (2001) investigate the characteristics of countries that experienced multiple banking crises. A common feature, especially in Latin America, is that such countries often have high rates of inflation during a banking crisis that is going to be followed by another banking crisis. There are not a sufficient number of multiple-crisis countries for formal statistical analysis, but this feature of the data is quite striking.

**Summary.** On the basis of existing work, it is probably premature to conclude that inflation is (not) a major factor associated with banking crises. This is difficult to ascertain empirically, especially given the problems in dating and defining banking crises. In the next two sections of this paper, we will present some new evidence on this topic that is also suggestive; specifically, higher inflation is, all else being equal, associated with declining real profits margins of banks and increasing return volatility.[15]

### 5.4 Bank Profits, Borrowing and Lending Spreads, Net Interest Margins, and Value Added: How Are These Associated with Inflation?

A number of studies have looked at the relationship between inflation and bank profits or between inflation and bank net interest margins, represented by *(interest income – interest expense)/total assets.* In several of these studies, inflation was included as a control variable but was not itself the main variable under investigation. One example is Demirguc-Kunt, Laeven, and Levine (2003), which investigates the relationship between bank concentration and net interest margins. These authors employ a large cross-country panel with data for about 1,400 banks and 72 countries over the period 1995–99. Domestic inflation enters as a control variable, along with a number of other controls. These authors report a positive and significant relationship between inflation and bank net interest margins, robust to a variety of specifications. In their regressions, the coefficient of inflation is consistently about 0.04, sample mean inflation is 4.37, and the mean net interest margin 3.61. This implies an inflation rate elasticity of bank net interest margins of only about 0.05, which is (undoubtedly) significantly less than 1.

A related study by Levine (2004) uses another cross-country panel data set to investigate the effect of entry restrictions on bank net interest margins. This study includes observations on 1,165 banks in 47 countries over the same period, 1995–99, and many of the same control variables are included. The inflation coefficient is again positive and highly significant, with a value of about 0.11 depending on the specifications. The mean net interest margin is 3.46, but sample mean inflation is not reported. However, mean inflation

---

[15] It is also difficult to separate the effects of banking and currency crises (Kaminsky and Reinhart 1999).

should be close to the 4.37% value reported in Demirguc-Kunt, Laeven, and Levine (2003).[16] Assuming mean inflation of 4.37%, the elasticity of bank profit margins with respect to inflation is about 0.14 in this study. That is, again, almost certainly significantly less than 1.

An interesting recent study of inflation and bank profitability is by Honohan (2003), who examines country cross-sections for approximately 72 countries. His data are for the years 1988–99, split into the subperiods 1988–95 and 1995–99. For the 1988–95 subsample, Honohan only studies the relationship between inflation and bank profits. For the 1995–99 subsample, he investigates the relationships between inflation and bank profits, inflation and bank value added (as a fraction of bank assets),[17] and inflation and bank net interest margins.

In many specifications, Honohan includes banking balance-sheet ratios and/or the real interest rate as additional variables. For our purposes, their inclusion is problematic because these right-side variables are arguably endogenous and themselves functions of inflation.[18] Thus, we prefer Honohan's simplest specification, in which inflation is the only right-side variable. With this specification, he finds that bank profits are positively related to inflation in both subperiods and at very high confidence levels. The same is true when net interest margins and bank value added are the dependent variables. The author indicates that the inflation elasticity of bank profits (1988–95) is about 0.51, evaluated at the sample median values of both variables. He also reports an inflation elasticity of net interest margins of about 0.29. Again, these results suggest that real bank profitability is negatively associated with the level of inflation.

### 5.4.1 Legal Reserves and the Inflation Tax on Banks

Perhaps the most interesting results reported by Honohan are those on inflation, bank reserves, and their joint effect on bank profits. It is a hoary notion in monetary economics that governments can effectively tax banks by forcing them to hold non-interest-bearing reserves and inflating. Such a tax, like the inflation tax on nonbank currency holdings, may be an important revenue source in developing or transitional economies in which collecting other taxes is problematic. However, Honohan finds no evidence of such a reserve tax on banks. Indeed, he reports, that "inflation strongly interacts with reserves—not to reduce profits, but instead to increase them! Rather than the

---

[16]  The two studies cover the same period and use approximately the same data set.
[17]  The value added of banks is essentially bank profits before taxes plus wages, salaries, and some other operating expenses.
[18]  For example, the simple correlation between inflation and the real interest rate is –0.98, making it almost impossible to separate the two effects.

reserve holdings being involuntary, in countries with high reserve holdings and high inflation the banks are likely finding ample remuneration, at least on their marginal reserve holdings. A look at some of the high profit countries in the scatter shows Russia and Romania to be prominent" (392–93).[19]

### 5.4.2 The Inflation Tax on Bank Reserves: Some New Results

Honohan's results are sufficiently interesting that we decided to reexamine the relationship between inflation, reserves, and bank profits, employing data for up to 84 banks averaged over the period 1991–95. Two measures of bank reserve holdings are employed—*rrat* (*legal reserves/total deposits*) and *rrat1* (*legal reserves/M2*)—and both produce very similar results.[20] In table 4.1, equation (1), the dependent variable is *rrat* the explanatory variables are the net *cpirate* (*infl1*) and the same controls we have employed previously. The coefficient of *infl1* is positive and significant, suggesting that as inflation increases, official reserve holdings increase also. In equation (2), the alternative definition of the reserve ratio is used and produces very similar results. These findings suggest that governments *might* be using a reserve tax on banks. But they are only suggestive because we cannot be sure that reserves are involuntarily held or are paying below-market rates of interest.

Equations (3) and (4) examine the relationship between the two reserve ratio measures and net interest margins. In both cases, the reserve ratio coefficients are positive, with the coefficient on *rrat* statistically significant, which is consistent with what Honohan (2003) reports. However, in equation (5), we regress net interest margin on *rrat* and our usual control variables and, with this change, the coefficient of *rrat* becomes statistically insignificant. Next, in equation (6) of table 4.2, we include the variable *inter* = *rrat* × *cpirate* to represent the interaction between reserve holdings and inflation. In this case, the coefficient of *rrat* is positive and highly significant, whereas the coefficient of the interaction term is negative and highly significant also. This suggests that reserve holdings could have a positive association with bank profits, as reported by Honohan (2003), but only when inflation is below some threshold. Once inflation exceeds that threshold, higher reserve holdings may be associated with lower bank returns. According to these estimates, that threshold

---

[19] This result is obtained with the first subperiod, 1988–95. In the second subperiod, a positive interaction between inflation and reserve holdings is also reported, except that here, the dependent variable is net interest margin (table 13.4, equation [5]).

[20] We only have data on bank reserve holdings, not reserve requirements, and thus cannot distinguish reserves that are voluntarily held from those that are not. Honohan's empirical investigation is confronted with exactly the same problem. Also, these tests would be greatly improved if we had the data to control for other bank regulatory policies—for example, entry restrictions.

**Table 4.1. Reserve Holding, Inflation and Bank Net Interest Margins, 1991–95**

| | Dependent Variables | | | | |
|---|---|---|---|---|---|
| | **1.** *rrat* | **2.** *rrat1* | **3.** *net* | **4.** *net* | **5.** *net* |
| *infl1* | 0.1892 (3.53)** | 0.6236 (2.33)* | | | |
| *initial* | –8.9773 (4.76)** | –7.2112 (0.98) | | | –0.9221 (2.02)* |
| *bmp* | –0.00006 (0.60) | –0.0009 (2.89)** | | | 0.00002 (0.97) |
| *revc* | 0.0611 (1.39) | 0.1289 (1.17) | | | –0.0059 (0.88) |
| *rrat* | | | 0.0810 (3.08)** | | –0.0106 (0.52) |
| *cpirate9195* | | | | | 0.0786 (7.01)** |
| *rrat1* | | | | 0.0123 (1.77) | |
| *constant* | 0.1552 (6.47)** | 0.3090 (4.85)** | 1.0303 (283.27)** | 1.0397 (264.22)** | 0.9579 (68.12)** |
| *N* | 84 | 74 | 77 | 67 | 73 |
| Adjusted $R^2$ | 0.35 | 0.15 | 0.16 | 0.03 | 0.55 |
| Elasticities: *infl1* *cpirate9195* | 0.1363 | 0.2463 | | | 0.0835 |
| Medians: Dep. Var. *infl1* *initial* *bmp* *revc* *rrat* *cpirate9195* *rrat1* | 0.1437 0.1035 0.0014 9.0407 0.0500 | 0.2842 0.1123 0.0012 12.3059 0.1000 | 1.0374 0.1237 | 1.0409 0.2823 | 1.0388 0.0017 9.5628 0.0000 0.1332 1.1046 |

**Note:** Robust *t* statistics in parentheses. All regressions intentionally exclude countries with average (gross) inflation exceeding 200% per annum. When the high inflation data points are included, the inflation coefficient becomes negative in equations (1) and (2) and is statistically significant in equation (1).

\* significant at 10%; ** significant at 5%; *** significant at 1%.

**Table 4.2. Reserve Holding, Inflation, and Bank Net Interest Margins, 1991–95**

| | Dependent Variables | | | |
| | 6. net | 7. rnet | 8. rnet | 9. rnet |
|---|---|---|---|---|
| rrat | 0.5040 (3.06)** | -0.4846 (4.21)** | -0.0555 (1.99) | -0.1308 (0.47) |
| initial | -0.2750 (0.55) | | 0.8927 (1.99) | 0.7981 (1.37) |
| revc | -0.0047 (0.84) | | -0.0094 (1.17) | -0.0096 (1.18) |
| bmp | 0.00000005 (0.00) | | -0.00003 (1.77) | -0.00003 (1.51) |
| cpirate9195 | 0.1911 (5.49)** | | -0.4990 (16.75)** | -0.5154 (6.18)** |
| inter | -0.4536 (3.18)** | | | 0.0663 (0.26) |
| constant | 0.8314 (20.89)** | 0.9871 (84.37)** | 1.5013 (46.91)** | 1.5198 (16.59)** |
| N | 73 | 77 | 73 | 73 |
| Adjusted $R^2$ | 0.61 | 0.30 | 0.97 | 0.97 |
| Elasticity of cpirate9195 | 0.2033 | | -0.5839 | -0.6032 |
| Medians: Dep. Var. | 1.0388 | 0.9530 | 0.9439 | 0.9439 |
| rrat | 0.1332 | 0.1237 | 0.1332 | 0.1332 |
| initial | 0.0017 | | 0.0017 | 0.0017 |
| revc | 0.0000 | | 0.0000 | 0.0000 |
| bmp | 9.5628 | | 9.5628 | 9.5628 |
| cpirate9195 | 1.1046 | | 1.1046 | 1.1046 |
| inter | 0.1490 | | | 0.1490 |

**Note:** Robust $t$ statistics in parentheses. All regressions intentionally exclude countries with average (gross) inflation exceeding 200% per annum. If the high inflation observations are included, the coefficient of inflation becomes insignificant in equation (6). In equation (9), the coefficient of inflation changes sign and remains significant at a high confidence level.
* significant at 10%; ** significant at 5%; *** significant at 1%.

occurs at an inflation rate of about 13%, which is close to the sample mean inflation rate, or the 60th sample inflation percentile. Thus, with this specification, there are plenty of sample data points both above and below the threshold.

In equations (7), (8), and (9), we deflate bank net interest margins by the rate of inflation, creating a real net interest margin measure, *rnet* = *net* /*cpirate*. In equation (7), with no control variables, the coefficient of *rrat* is negative and highly significant. However, when the control variables are added in equation (8), the coefficient of *rrat* drops to only marginal significance. Finally, in equation (9), there is no evidence of a significant interaction effect between the reserve ratio and inflation.

**Summary.** We conclude from Honohan's work and our own that if there is an inflation tax operating through bank reserves, it is either not large and/or was not commonly employed during the sample period. The empirical evidence seems somewhat mixed and dependent on specification. Moreover, as Honohan (2003) notes, the results could be importantly affected by special reserve subsidies in a few sample countries.

None of this is to suggest, however, that real bank profits are unaffected by inflation. We will see momentarily that is surely incorrect.

### 5.5 Some New Results on Inflation and Bank Profitability

Given the importance of banking in most economies and given the finding that inflation tends to shrink the relative size of the banking sector according to previous empirical work, we decided to carry out some additional tests of our own. Specifically, we investigate the effect of inflation on bank profitability. Table 5 shows the results of regressions in which the dependent variables are bank lending minus borrowing spreads, net interest margins, profits before taxes, and value added to GDP. All these dependent variables are regressed against inflation and the usual set of control variables. The dependent variable in the first regression is *spread*, defined as the difference between commercial loan rates and time deposit rates (*spread* = 1 + *loanrate* − *tdeprate* ).[21] In this specification, the inflation coefficient is positive but not significant at usual confidence levels. The elasticity of *spread* with respect to the inflation rate at the sample medians is only about 0.34.[22]

---

[21] These are averages of annual commercial loan and time deposit interest rates reported in the IFS data set. Definitions and averaging methods may vary from country to country.

[22] Because of the large standard error, the coefficient of 0.33 is not significantly less than 1.0 at usual confidence levels.

Table 5. Inflation's Association with Bank Interest Spreads,
Net Interest Margins, Profits, and Value Added

| | Dependent Variables | | | | | | |
|---|---|---|---|---|---|---|---|
| | 1. *spread* | 2. *rspread* | 3. *rroa* | 4. *rnim* | 5. *rvalad* | 6. *rnet* | 7. *rval* |
| *cpirate8998* | 0.3309 (1.45) | −0.4163 (2.84)** | | | | | |
| *initial* | −1.2479 (1.04) | 0.3694 (0.37) | 0.2424 (0.90) | −0.1214 (0.28) | 0.4472 (1.15) | 1.2224 (2.89)** | 1.2083 (2.15)* |
| *bmp* | −0.0003 (0.59) | −0.0002 (0.47) | 0.0001 (7.23)** | 0.00004 (1.14) | 0.0001 (3.39)** | −0.00003 (1.47) | −0.000008 (0.32) |
| *revc* | −0.0186 (1.18) | −0.0207 (1.50) | −0.0044 (1.23) | −0.0012 (0.19) | 0.0023 (0.41) | −0.0134 (1.41) | −0.0052 (0.41) |
| *cpirate9599* | | | −0.7880 (31.14)** | −0.6190 (10.14)** | −0.6609 (13.59)** | | |
| *cpirate9195* | | | | | | −0.5119 (17.86)** | −0.4728 (17.23)** |
| *constant* | 0.7185 (2.98)** | 1.4372 (9.24)** | 1.7882 (63.17)** | 1.6416 (25.10)** | 1.6816 (32.05)** | 1.5073 (45.32)** | 1.4959 (46.06)** |
| $N$ | 64 | 64 | 51 | 51 | 51 | 76 | 76 |
| Adjusted $R^2$ | 0.31 | 0.64 | 0.98 | 0.90 | 0.92 | 0.97 | 0.93 |
| Elasticities: *cpirate8998* *cpirate9599* *cpirate9195* | 0.3359 | −0.4557 | −0.8588 | −0.6490 | −0.6925 | −0.5920 | 0.0000 −0.5291 |
| Medians: Dep. Var. *cpirate8998* *initial* *bmp* *revc* *cpirate9599* *cpirate9195* | 1.0571 1.0731 0.0019 7.4965 0.0000 | 0.9805 1.0731 0.0019 7.4965 0.0000 | 0.9581 0.0026 4.4806 0.0000 1.0442 | 0.9960 0.0026 4.4806 0.0000 1.0442 | 0.9966 0.0026 4.4806 0.0000 1.0442 | 0.9540 0.0018 9.0407 0.0000 | 0.9860 0.0018 9.0407 0.0000 1.1033 |

**Note:** Robust $t$ statistics in parentheses. All regressions intentionally exclude countries with gross inflation greater than 200% per year.
\* significant at 10%; \*\* significant at 5%; \*\*\* significant at 1%.

In equation (2), *rspread* is the *spread* variable deflated by the average rate of inflation (*rspread* = *spread* /*cpirate*). In this specification, the inflation coefficient is negative and significant at the 1% confidence level. In essence, this result suggests that, although bank lending rate–borrowing rate spreads increase with the rate of inflation, they don't increase fast enough to remain unaffected in real terms.

In equations (3) and (4), the dependent variables are bank profits before taxes and net interest margins, both deflated by the average rate of inflation. These are related and correlated measures, and they produce very similar results. The coefficient of inflation is negative and highly significant in both cases, with the implication that inflation hurts real bank returns according to either measure.

The dependent variable in equation (5) is the value added of the banking industry, again deflated by inflation.[23] Note that this is quite different from a return or profitability measure because it is the sum of operating profits *and* operating expenses. Rather, it roughly represents the output of the banking industry divided by bank assets. This variable, too, is negatively and very significantly related to average inflation during the sample period. Equations (6) and (7) are identical to equations (4) and (5), except that they employ data over the period 1991–95 instead of 1995–99. They produce very similar results, suggesting robustness.

**Summary.** The main conclusion to take away from the results in table 5 is that banks appear to be harmed by inflation. Their net interest margins, net profits, rates of return on equity, and value added all appear to decline in real terms as inflation rises. All this seems quite consistent with the finding, reported earlier, that the relative size of the banking industry also declines relative to the overall economy.

## 6. INFLATION AND ASSET RETURN VOLATILITY

Several of the theoretical models discussed earlier (e.g., Boyd and Smith 1998; Choi, Boyd, and Smith 1996) predict a positive relationship between steady-state inflation and asset return volatility, at least when the rate of inflation is above some threshold. It is clear that the volatility of inflation itself is very closely associated with average inflation. For example, in the cross-sectional tests of Boyd, Levine, and Smith (2001), the simple correlation between mean inflation and inflation volatility is 0.98, based on a sample of 48 countries and 36 years of data. Barnes, Boyd, and Smith (1999) estimated the correlation

---

[23] Our measure of value added is bank profits before taxes plus overhead costs, primarily in the form of wages and salaries.

between mean inflation and the standard deviation of inflation to be 0.99, based on data for 25 countries and about 20 years of data. As both studies note, these correlations are so high that it would be almost impossible to empirically separate the effects of mean inflation and inflation volatility.

Both studies also report high correlations between the average rate of inflation and the volatility of equity returns. In Barnes, Boyd, and Smith (1999), the simple correlation between the mean rate of inflation and the standard deviation of equity returns is 0.74. Boyd, Levine, and Smith (2001) use a more complicated measure of equity return volatility and find that this measure exhibits a simple correlation of 0.84 with average inflation. They also examine the partial correlation of equity return volatility and inflation, after controlling for a number of other factors. This partial correlation is positive and significant at the 1% level.

Table 6.1. Inflation and Asset Return Volatility, 1989–98

| | Dependent Variables | | | | | |
|---|---|---|---|---|---|---|
| | 1. stbill | 2. stbill | 3. smm | 4. smm | 5. stdep | 6. stdep |
| cpirate8998 | 0.3171 (3.99)** | 0.4401 (21.27)** | 0.2584 (3.48)** | 0.3316 (12.40)** | 0.3801 (2.46)* | 0.2269 (4.05)** |
| initial | | 1.5227 (2.51)* | | 0.1625 (0.12) | | 0.8853 (1.90) |
| bmp | | −0.0001 (1.45) | | 0.0003 (1.47) | | − 0.0000009 (0.02) |
| revc | | −0.0089 (0.70) | | −0.0537 (0.98) | | −0.0036 (0.37) |
| constant | −0.3093 (3.63)** | −0.4468 (19.11)** | −0.2354 (3.02)** | −0.3104 (9.16)** | −0.3709 (2.41)* | −0.2229 (3.64)** |
| N | 52 | 34 | 44 | 34 | 103 | 69 |
| Adjusted $R^2$ | 0.72 | 0.92 | 0.56 | 0.76 | 0.07 | 0.63 |
| Elasticity of cpirate8998 | 13.0616 | 16.1249 | 9.4986 | 11.6766 | 19.5107 | 10.2050 |
| Medians: Dep. Var. cpirate8998 initial bmp revc | 0.0254 1.0461 | 0.0289 1.0581 0.0041 7.4965 0.0000 | 0.0284 1.0443 | 0.0297 1.0444 0.0071 0.1839 0.0000 | 0.0208 1.0694 | 0.0240 1.0694 0.0019 7.5075 0.0000 |

Note: Robust $t$ statistics in parentheses. All regressions intentionally exclude countries with average (gross) inflation greater than 200% per year. If these data points are included, the coefficient of inflation in equations (3) and (4) becomes an order of magnitude larger, but statistically insignificant. In equations (5) and (6), the inflation coefficient becomes an order of magnitude larger but remains positive and significant at high confidence levels.
* significant at 10%; ** significant at 5%; *** significant at 1%.

Table 6.2. Inflation and Asset Return Volatility, 1989–98

| | Dependent Variables | | | | | |
|---|---|---|---|---|---|---|
| | **7.** *sloan* | **8.** *sloan* | **9.** *sgov* | **10.** *sgov* | **11.** *sspread* | **12.** *sspread* |
| *cpirate8998* | 0.8408 (2.34)* | 0.3858 (4.28)*** | 0.2667 (5.14)*** | 0.2368 (6.30)*** | 0.5121 (1.51) | 0.1174 (3.01)** |
| *initial* | | 1.4808 (3.22)** | | −0.9289 (1.23) | | −0.4406 (1.17) |
| *bmp* | | −0.0003 (1.19) | | | | −0.00007 (0.74) |
| *revc* | | −0.0046 (0.69) | | −0.0566 (1.76) | | −0.0047 (0.77) |
| *constant* | −0.8662 (2.28)* | −0.3906 (4.10)** | −0.2595 (4.88)** | −0.2130 (6.05)** | −0.5342 (1.45) | −0.1040 (2.43)* |
| *N* | 103 | 69 | 34 | 28 | 98 | 64 |
| Adjusted $R^2$ | 0.16 | 0.75 | 0.63 | 0.71 | 0.25 | 0.50 |
| Elasticity of *cpirate8998* | 35.8435 | 15.4524 | 16.9427 | 13.8939 | 37.4289 | 8.3843 |
| Medians: Dep. Var. *cpirate8998* *initial* *bmp* *revc* | 0.0251 1.0694 | 0.0270 1.0815 0.0019 7.8157 0.0000 | 0.0164 1.0408 | 0.0176 1.0317 0.0101 0.0000 | 0.0145 1.0631 | 0.0150 1.0731 0.0019 7.4965 0.0000 |

**Note:** Robust *t* statistics in parentheses. All regressions intentionally exclude countries with average (gross) inflation greater than 200% per year. If these high inflation data points are included, the coefficient of inflation becomes much larger in all regressions except (9) and (10). All coefficients remain positive. Statistical significance increases in (8), (11), and (12) but is unchanged or decreases in (7), (9), and (10).
* significant at 10%; ** significant at 5%; *** significant at 1%.

From this work, there is evidence that across countries, inflation volatility and equity return volatility are strongly and positively associated with mean inflation. What has not been done before, to our knowledge, is to examine the relationship between average inflation and interest rate volatility in country cross-sections. Therefore, some tests of this kind are presented in tables 6.1 and 6.2.

We find that inflation and interest rate volatility are positively associated. In regressions 1 through 10, the dependent variable is the sample standard deviation of a nominal interest rate calculated over the period 1989–98. The explanatory variables are either average inflation by itself or average inflation and our usual set of control variables. The interest rates examined are the Treasury bill rate, money market rate, time deposit rate, bank loan rate. and a government bond rate. In all 10 regressions, the inflation coefficient is positive. In eight cases, it is significant at the 1% level and in two cases significant at the 5% level. The largest effect is on the bank loan rate, and the smallest on the government bond rate.

In equations (11) and (12), the dependent variable is the standard deviation of the spread between bank loan rates and bank deposit rates. We employ this interest rate spread as a proxy variable for bank profitability because the available data do not allow us to compute the volatility of bank profits. In any case, this return volatility measure is positively associated with average inflation. The coefficient is not quite statistically significant at usual confidence levels in the simple regression, but when the control variables are added, it is significant at the 1% confidence level. This finding may suggest that as inflation increases, all else being equal, bank profitability becomes more variable. It is even more certain that as inflation rises, the rates at which banks lend and borrow become more variable.

## 7. SUMMARY AND CONCLUSIONS

**1. All else being equal, higher inflation is associated with smaller equity markets and smaller banking industries.** Both stock market capitalization and trading volume have been found to be smaller relative to the size of the overall economy in higher-inflation economies. Existing studies have not investigated the direction of causality. Similarly, the size of the banking industry relative to the size of the overall economy has been found to be smaller in high inflation environments. In this instance, formal tests suggest causality running from inflation to banking-sector size. The present study has presented results suggesting that the real value added of the banking industry is negatively and significantly associated with average inflation across countries.

2. **For both stock market and banking industry size, there is evidence of threshold effects in the relationship with inflation.** For sufficiently high rates of inflation, the negative associate between inflation and intermediary sector size essentially disappears after a discrete drop. Nominal rates of return on equity also exhibit a threshold that is almost the exact reflection of intermediary sector size. That is, equity returns are essentially uncorrelated (or negatively correlated) with inflation up to a threshold and then, after a discrete drop, move roughly one for one with inflation.

3. **Asset returns do not generally seem to conform to the predictions of "monetary neutrality."** In both cross-sectional and time-series work, asset returns do not seem to adjust fully for inflation, even after (in the cross-sections) extended periods of time. The only exception to this statement is equity returns in relatively high-inflation environments. In time-series tests, equity returns are often unrelated to inflation changes, and they are not infrequently *negatively* related to inflation changes in low-inflation environments. New cross-country tests in this study found that of five different interest rates studied, most were not fully indexed to inflation, even when data were averaged over 10-year periods.

4. **These results on inflation and asset returns are consistent with the theoretical possibility that high inflation results in real rates of interest that are "too low."** As in a number of theoretical studies reviewed, this could restrain real investment, exacerbate credit market frictions, lead to credit rationing, and so on. Indeed, cross-sectional tests with attitude and opinion data suggest that, all else being equal, high inflation is associated with problems of credit availability.

5. **Based on work we have done, it appears that, on average, banks are not able to hedge their profits against inflation well, especially when inflation is high.** Across countries, nominal bank profits increase with inflation but not at fast enough rates so as to leave real profits unaffected. Bank profits, net interest margins, and lending–borrowing rate spreads all were found to decline, in real terms, as inflation rose across countries. However, there is little evidence in the data of the most obvious and talked-about mechanism whereby inflation harms banks—that is, a combination of binding reserve requirements and non-interest-bearing reserves. Indeed, there is even evidence of a "bank reserve subsidy" in some countries, at least during the limited sample periods that have been studied.

What remains less clear, however, is why inflation, especially high inflation, seems so harmful to banks. Banks are financial institutions, and in principle, they can set loan and deposit rates as appropriate for given market conditions. One would think they are relatively sophisticated and not subject to money illusion. One possible explanation is that our time averaging is not long enough in the cross-country tests, and as a result, the data reflect transitional effects of inflation (capital losses) that would disappear in the long run. Frankly, we are skeptical of this explanation. As a general rule, banks borrow shorter term and lend longer term so that they are temporarily hurt by *rising* interest rates. We doubt that this is a pervasive phenomenon that could drive our results simply because, on average, interest rates have been declining over the period examined. But it is still a possibility.

A second possibility is that interest rate regulation hinders banks' abilities to adjust their interest rates upward in response to inflation. This could be to the result of ceilings on loan rates or on deposit rates that result in dis-intermediation out of banking. What is clear from our results is that loan rates are much more responsive to inflation than deposit rates. In table 1, the inflation elasticity of time deposit rates is 0.58, and the inflation elasticity of commercial loan rates is 0.80. In table 2, the inflation elasticity of real time deposit rates is –0.27, and the inflation elasticity of real commercial loan rates is –0.12. This suggests that, relatively speaking, if regulation is affecting rate setting, it is having greater effect in deposit than in loan markets. This is not necessarily good for banks if deposit rate regulation results in disintermediation.

**6. For a variety of financial assets, rate of return volatility is positively associated with inflation across countries.** Based on our own work and that of others, there is evidence that higher inflation is associated with more volatile equity returns, nominal interest rates, and bank returns. All of this suggests that inflation may be associated with higher probability of banking crises, all else being equal, and there is at least some empirical work suggesting that is so. These findings are consistent with the predictions of a number of theoretical studies discussed earlier.

They are also potentially relevant to the observed negative relationship between inflation and real bank profitability measures. That is, banks solve a portfolio problem in which they trade off risk versus expected profitability. As conditions in bank asset and liability markets become more volatile (as we have found they do in high-inflation environments), the risk–return frontier confronting banks has shifted inward (e.g., worsened). Under quite general conditions, banks would be expected to respond by reducing both their risk exposure and their expected profits.

## DATA APPENDIX

This appendix contains a description of the variables used in this study. The source of the data is listed with each variable name. Those variables referenced as "IFS" come from the *International Financial Statistics* CD-ROM (May 2003) published by the International Monetary Fund. The IFS variables include the corresponding IFS line item.

| Variable | Description | Source |
|---|---|---|
| *bmp* | Black-market currency premium, average over 1980–92 | *World's Currency Yearbook*; Wood (1988) |
| *cpirate* | Gross geometric average of annual CPI inflation, 1989–98 (some derived series use a shorter time average) | IFS: 64 |
| *eqrate* | Gross annual rate of return on country's principal stock exchange. Does not include divident returns, 1989–98 | IFS: 62 |
| *govrate* | Gross annual rate of interest on medium- to long-term government bonds, 1989–98 | IFS: 61 |
| *initial* | Per capital real GDP in 1980 (in millions) | Loayza, López, Schmidt-Hebbel, and Sérven (1998) |
| *inter* | Derived from *inter = rrat\* cpirate*, 1989–98 | |
| *loanrate* | Gross annual rate of interest on bank commercial loans, 1989–98 | IFS: 60P |
| *mcap* | Stock market capitalization as share of GDP, 1980–95 | Beck, Demirguc-Kunt, and Levine (1999) |
| *mmrate* | Gross annual rate of interest on money market securities, 1989–98 | IFS: 60B |
| *net* | Derived from net = 1 + (interest income – interest expense)/total assets, 1991–95 | Beck, Demirguc-Kunt, and Levine (1999) |
| *revc* | Revolutions and coups over the 1980s | Banks (1994) |
| *rgovrate* | Derived from *rgovrate = govrate/cpirate*, 1989–98 | |
| *rloanrate* | Derived from *rloanrate = loanrate/cpirate*, 1989–98 | |

| | | |
|---|---|---|
| *rmmrate* | Derived from *rmmrate* = *mmrate/cpirate*, 1989–98 | |
| *rnet* | Derived from *rnet* = *net/cpirate*, 1989–98 | |
| *rnim* | Derived from *rnim* = (1 + net interest margin)/ *cpirate*, 1995–99 | Net interest margin from Demirguc-Kunt, Laeven, and Levine (2003) |
| *rrat* | Derived from *rrat* = official reserves/(time deposits + demand deposits), 1991–95 | IFS: Official reserves 20, Time deposits 25, Demand deposits 24 |
| *rrat1* | Derived from *rrat1* = official reserves/M2, 1991–95 | IFS: Official reserves 20, M2 33 |
| *rroa* | Derived from *rroa* = [1 + (profits before taxes/total assets)]/*cpirate*, 1995–99 | Profits before taxes/total assets from Demirguc-Kunt, Laeven, and Levine (2003) |
| *rroe* | Derived from *rroe* = [1 + (profits before taxes/ owners' equity)]/*cpirate*, 1995–99 | Profits before taxes and owners' equity from Demirguc-Kunt, Laeven, and Levine (2003) |
| *rspread* | Derived from *rspread* = *spread/cpirate*, 1989–98 | |
| *rtdeprate* | Derived from *tdeprate/cpirate*, 1989–98 | |
| *rval* | Derived from (net + overhead costs)/*cpirate*, 1991–95 | Overhead costs from Beck, Demirguc-Kunt, and Levine (1999) |

| | | |
|---|---|---|
| *rvalad* | Derived from *rvalad* = [1 + profits before taxes + operating expenses)/total assets]/*cpirate*, 1995–99 | Profits before taxes, operating expenses, and total assets from Demirguc-Kunt, Laeven, and Levine (2003) |
| *sgov* | Derived from *sgov* = standard deviation of *govrate*, 1989–98 | |
| *spread* | Derived from spread = 1 + *loanrate* – *tdeprate*, 1989–98 | |
| *sloan* | Derived from sloan = standard deviation of *loanrate*, 1989–98 | |
| *smm* | Derived from smm = standard deviation of *mmrate* 1989–98 | |
| *stbill* | Derived from stbill = standard deviation of *tbillrate*, 1989–98 | |
| *stdep* | Derived from stdep = standard deviation of *tdeprate*, 1989–98 | |
| *sspread* | Derived from sspread = standard deviation of *spread*, 1989–98 | |
| *tdeprate* | Gross annual rate of interest on bank time deposits, 1989–98 | IFS: 60L |
| *tbillrate* | Gross annual rate of interest on Treasury bills, 1989–98 | IFS: 60C |
| *tvt* | Total value traded on the stock market as share of GDP, 1980–95 | Beck, Demirguc-Kunt, and Levine (1999) |

REFERENCES

Amihud, Y. 1996. Unexpected Inflation and Stock Returns Revisited: Evidence from Israel. *Journal of Money, Credit, and Banking* 28: 22–33.

Azariadis, C., and B. D. Smith. 1996. Private Information, Money, and Growth: Indeterminacy, Fluctuations, and the Mundell-Tobin Effect. *Journal of Economic Growth* 1: 309–32.

Azariadis, C., and B. D. Smith. 1998. Financial Intermediation and Regime Switching in Business Cycles. *American Economic Review* 88: 516–36.

Banks, A. S. 1994. Cross-National Time Series Data Archive. Center for Social Analysis, State University of New York–Binghamton.

Barnes, M., and A. W. Hughes. 2002. A Quantile Regression Analysis of the Cross Section of Stock Market Returns. Working Paper No. 02-2, Federal Reserve Bank of Boston.

Barnes, M., J. H. Boyd, B. D. Smith. 1999. Inflation and Asset Returns. *European Economic Review* 43: 737–54.

Barro, R. J. 1995. Inflation and Economic Growth. *Bank of England Quarterly Bulletin*, May, 166–176.

Beck, T., A. Demirguc-Kunt, and R. Levine. 1999. A New Database on Financial Development and Structure. Policy Research Working Paper No. 2146, World Bank.

Beck, T, Demirguc-Kunt, A., and R. Levine. 2003a. Bank Concentration and Crises. Working Paper No. 9921, National Bureau for Economic Research.

Beck, T., Demirguc-Kunt, A., and R. Levine. 2003b. Bank Supervision and Corporate Finance. Unpublished manuscript, World Bank.

Beck, T., Demirguc-Kunt, A., and V. Maksimovic. 2002. Financial and Legal Constraints to Firm Growth: Does Size Matter? Unpublished manuscript, World Bank.

Beck, T., Demirguc-Kunt, A., and V. Maksimovic. 2003. Bank Competition and Access to Finance. Unpublished manuscript, World Bank.

Beck, T., R. Levine, and N. Loyaza. 2000. Financial Intermediation and Growth: Causes and Causality. *Journal of Monetary Economics* 46: 31–77.

Bencivenga, V. R., and B. D. Smith. 1991. Financial Intermediation and Economic Growth. *Review of Economic Studies* 58: 195–209.

Bencivenga, V. R., and B. D. Smith. 2003. Monetary Policy and Financial Market Evolution. *Federal Reserve Bank of St. Louis Review* 85: 7–25.

Bernanke, B. S., and M. Gertler. 1989. Agency Costs, Net Worth, and Business Fluctuations. *American Economic Review* 79: 14–31.

Boudoukh, J., and M. Richardson. 1993. Stock Returns and Inflation: A Long Term Perspective. American Economic Review 83: 1346–55.

Boyd, J. H., and B. D. Smith. 1997. Capital Market Imperfections, International Credit Markets, and Nonconvergence. *Journal of Economic Theory* 73: 335–64.

Boyd, J. H., and B. D. Smith. 1998. Capital Market Imperfections in a Monetary Growth Model. *Economic Theory* 11: 241–73.

Boyd, J. H., R. Levine, and B. D. Smith. 2001. The Impact of Inflation on Financial Market Performance. *Journal of Monetary Economics* 47: 221–48.

Boyd, J. H., P. Gomis-Porqueras, S. Kwak, and B. D. Smith. 2001. A User's Guide to Banking Crises. Unpublished manuscript, University of Minnesota.

Bryant, J. 1980. A Model of Reserves, Bank Runs, and Deposit Insurance. *Journal of Banking and Finance* 4: 335–44.

Bullard, J., and J. Keating. 1995. The Long-Run Relationship between Inflation and Output in Postwar Economies. *Journal of Monetary Economics* 36: 477–96.

Caprio, G., and D. Klingebiel. 1999. Episodes of Systematic and Borderline Financial Distress. Unpublished manuscript, World Bank.

Carlstrom, C., and T. Fuerst. 1997. Agency Costs, Net Worth, and Business Cycle Fluctuations: A Computable General Equilibrium Approach. *American Economic Review* 87: 893–910.

Carlstrom, C., and T. Fuerst. 1998. Agency Costs and Business Cycles. *Economic Theory* 12: 583–99.

Champ, B., B. D. Smith, and S. D. Williamson. 1996. Currency Elasticity and Banking Panics: Theory and Evidence. *Canadian Journal of Economics* 29: 828–64.

Chari, V. V., L. J. Christiano, and P. J. Kehoe. 1996. Optimality of the Friedman Rule in Economies with Distorting Taxes. *Journal of Monetary Economics* 37: 203–23.

Choi, S., J. H. Boyd, and B. D. Smith. 1996. Inflation, Financial Markets and Capital Formation. *Federal Reserve Bank of St. Louis Review* 78: 9–35.

Choudry, T. 2001. Inflation and Rates of Return on Stocks: Evidence from High Inflation Countries. *Journal of International Financial Markets, Institutions and Money* 11: 75–96.

Demirguc-Kunt, A., and E. Detragiache. 1998. The Determinants of Banking Crises in Developed and Developing Economies. *IMF Staff Papers* 45: 81–109.

Demirguc-Kunt, A., and E. Detragiache. 1999. Does Deposit Insurance Increase Banking System Stability? An Empirical Investigation. Policy Research Working Paper No. 2247, World Bank.

Demirguc-Kunt, A., and R. Levine. 2001. *Financial Structure and Economic Growth: A Cross-Country Comparison of Banks, Markets, and Development*, Cambridge, MA: MIT Press.

Demirguc-Kunt, A., L. Laeven, and R. Levine. 2003. Regulations, Market Structure, Institutions, and the Cost of Financial Intermediation. *Journal of Money, Credit, and Banking* 36: S593–623.

De Nicolo, G., P. Bartholomew, J. Zaman, and M. Zephirin. 2004. Bank Consolidation, Internationalization, and Conglomeration: Trends and Implications for Financial Risk. *Financial Markets, Institutions and Instruments* 13(4): 173–217.

Diamond, D. W., and P. H. Dybvig. 1983. Bank Runs, Deposit Insurance, and Liquidity. *Journal of Political Economy* 91: 401–19.

Friedman, M., and A. J. Schwartz. 1963. *A Monetary History of the United States, 1867–1960*. Princeton, NJ: Princeton University Press.

Goldsmith, R. W. 1969. *Financial Structure and Development*. New Haven, CT: Yale University Press.

Gurley, J. G., and E. S. Shaw. 1955. Financial Aspects of Economic Development. *American Economic Review* 45: 515–38.

Gurley, J. G., and E. S. Shaw. 1960. *Money in a Theory of Finance*. Washington, DC: Brookings Institution Press.

Gurley, J. G., and E. S. Shaw. 1967. Financial Structure and Economic Development. *Economic Development and Cultural Change* 15(3): 257–68.

Hellman, J. S., G. Jones, D. Kaufmann, and M. Schankerman. 2000. Measuring Governance and State Capture: The Role of Bureaucrats and Firms in Shaping the Business Environment. Working Paper No. 51, European Bank for Reconstruction and Development.

Honohan, P. 2003a. The Accidental Tax: Inflation and the Financial Sector. Unpublished manuscript, World Bank.

Honohan, P. 2003b. Avoiding the Pitfalls in Taxing Financial Intermediation. Policy Research Working Paper No. 3056, World Bank.

Huybens, E., and B. D. Smith. 1999. Inflation, Financial Markets, and Long-Run Real Activity. *Journal of Monetary Economics* 43: 283–315.

Kaminsky, G., and C. M. Reinhart. 1999. The Twin Crises: The Causes of Banking and Balance of Payments Problems. *American Economic Review* 89: 437–500.

King, R. G., and R. Levine. 1993a. Finance and Growth: Schumpeter Might Be Right. *Quarterly Journal of Economics* 108: 717–37.

King, R. G., and R. Levine. 1993b. Finance, Entrepreneurship and Growth: Theory and Evidence. *Journal of Monetary Economics* 32: 513–42.

Kutan, A. M., and T. Aksoy. 2003. Public Information Arrival and the Fisher Effect in Emerging Markets: Evidence in Stock and Bond Markets in Turkey. *Journal of Financial Services Research* 23: 225–39.

Levine, R. 2004. Denying Foreign Bank Entry: Implications for Bank Interest Margins. In *Bank Market Structure and Monetary Policy,* edited by Luis Antonio Ahumada and J. Rodrigo Fuentes, 271–292. Santiago, Chile: Banco Central de Chile.

Levine, R., and D. Renelt. 1992. A Sensitivity Analysis of Cross-Country Growth Regressions. *American Economic Review* 82: 942–63.

Levine, R., and S. J. Zervos. 1998. Stock Markets, Banks, and Economic Growth. *American Economic Review* 88: 537–58.

Levine, R., N. Loayza, and T. Beck. 2000. Financial Intermediation and Growth: Causality and Causes. *Journal of Monetary Economics* 46: 31–77.

Loayza, N., H. López, K. Schmidt-Hebbel, and L. Servén. 1998. The World Saving Database. Mimeo, World Bank.

McKinnon, R. 1973. *Money and Capital in Economic Development.* Washington, DC: Brookings Institution Press.

Rousseau, P., and P. Wachtel. 2002. Inflation Thresholds and the Finance-Growth Nexus. *Journal of International Money and Finance* 21: 777–93.

Schreft, S. L., and B. D. Smith. 1997. Money, Banking and Capital Formation. *Journal of Economic Theory* 73: 157–82.

Schreft, S. L., and B. D. Smith. 1998. The Effects of Open Market Operations in a Model of Intermediation and Growth. *Review of Economic Studies* 65: 519–50.

Schwert, W. 1989. Why Does Stock Market Volatility Change over Time? *Journal of Finance* 44: 1115–53.

Shaw, E. 1973. *Financial Deepening in Economic Development.* New York: Oxford University Press.

Smith, B. D. 2002a. Monetary Policy, Banking Crises, and the Friedman Rule. *American Economic Association Papers and Proceedings* 92: 128–34.

Smith, B. D. 2002b. Taking Intermediation Seriously. Unpublished manuscript.

Smith, R. T., and H. van Egteren. 2003. Inflation, Investment, and Economic Performance: The Role of Internal Financing. Unpublished manuscript.

Williamson, S. D. 1986. Costly Monitoring, Financial Intermediation, and Equilibrium Credit Rationing. *Journal of Monetary Economics* 18: 159–79.

Smith, B. D. 1987. Financial Intermediation, Business Failures, and Real Business Cycles. *Journal of Money, Credit, and Banking* 31: 469–91.

Smith, B. D. 1993. Finance, Entrepreneurship, and Growth: Theory and Evidence. *Journal of Monetary Economics* 32: 513–42.

Wood, A. 1988. Global Trends in Real Exchange Rates: 1960–84, Discussion Paper No. 35, World Bank.

# Commentary

*Nicola Cetorelli*

John Boyd and Bruce Champ have put together a very useful survey of the literature on inflation and the real economy and have produced some empirical updates and refinements. The basic lesson, which is sensible, is that inflation is bad. Theory offers good intuition as to why that should be the case. Mainly, inflation can have a direct impact on the optimization strategies of economic agents. For instance, banks may alter their incentives to lend as the opportunity cost of money changes with inflation. Similarly, firms may modify their choice between using internally generated funds or external sources to finance new capital investments. That, in turn, may have an additional impact on banks' decision making because banks perceive a modification in the quality distribution of prospective entrepreneurs.

I offer a main point of discussion. This should not be read as a criticism of Boyd and Champ but as an observation on possible directions to improve the current literature. Boyd and Champ state that their main objective is to increase mutual awareness between theorists and applied economists. The underlying text of their comment is that perhaps theory and empirical analysis of inflation have proceeded in an independent fashion, and this may have limited the scope of the results attained so far. I agree fully with this characterization, and I dare to add that perhaps theorists have been ahead of the game in this particular line of research.

Reading through Boyd and Champ's survey of the literature, we learn that all of the empirical evidence on inflation and its links with other economic variables has been obtained from studies based on aggregate, cross-country data sets. The endemic problem with this approach is that it lends itself—too easily—to objections related to omitted variable biases, common factor determination, endogeneity, and reverse causality. This is indeed a common refrain in the results of what can now be defined as "traditional" studies on the link between financial development and economic growth: The seminal empirical work of King and Levine (1993a, 1993b), for example, was instrumental in confirming the original Schumpeterian intuition of the existing causal link between financial market development and growth. This intuition is well grounded and hard to dispute, and by now, there is widespread consensus that the link does indeed exist. And yet, such a consensus was not really reached until more recent times, as scholars started to depart from the traditional approach and, thanks to richer data sets becoming available, began directly testing specific theoretical predictions related to the finance–growth nexus, making use of more and more disaggregated information on industries and firms (e.g., Rajan and Zingales 1998; Demirguc-Kunt and Maksimovic 1998). The empirical analysis of the impact of inflation on the real economy suffers from the same type of criticism. However, the problem is even more serious: In establishing the causal link between finance and growth, scholars became relatively comfortable in performing the thought experiment of comparing two otherwise identical economies differing in, say, the number of banks in operation or the size of the stock market. Which one is likely to display more growth? More generally, we are fairly at ease in applying the "natural experiments" methodology while testing the impact of structural variables that can be related to the functioning and depth of the financial sector.

I am, however, a little uncomfortable extending this methodological approach to the analysis of inflation—or more precisely, to empirical studies based on comparisons of economies in a persistent state of low or high inflation. Taken at face value, the results of the cross-sectional studies surveyed by Boyd and Champ imply that in going from a high-inflation to a low-inflation environment, growth will improve and banks and capital markets will thrive. I have no doubt that it is better to be in a low-inflation environment, but I do not know how to interpret such findings. States of persistently high or low inflation are, in fact, achieved as a result of fundamentally different conditions. Undisciplined, excessive money growth—which is often needed to satisfy unsustainable fiscal spending—in an environment with poor institutions and regulations typically leads to persistent high inflation. Inflation thus changes as an economy goes through a deep, pervasive transformation of its fundamentals. Indeed, inflation will change as a result of such transformations.

Take the example of most Latin American countries during the last 25 years. Average inflation in the region was about 180 percent per year in 1980 and peaked at 235 percent during the first half of the 1990s. Inflation is currently at one-digit levels in Chile, Brazil, Colombia, Peru, and Mexico (Bernanke 2005). The remarkable success of these countries in shifting to a low-inflation environment was achieved, as Bernanke points out, through aggressive fiscal discipline, the development of better institutions, the modernization of the banking system, and a commitment to improve the independence of central banking institutions. Consequently, in a very fundamental way, these nations are not the same today as they were 20 years ago. Hence, my main point is that being in a high- or low-inflation environment is the end result of major structural differences that make the ceteris paribus principle behind the natural experiment approach very difficult to apply in this case.

This comment is not limited to Latin American countries. Table 1 reports mean values and the statistical significance of the mean difference for a number of variables describing institutional and regulatory characteristics across

*Nicola Cetorelli*

Table 1. **Institutional and Regulatory Environment:**
**Low-Inflation versus High-Inflation Countries**

| Variable | Mean, Low-Inflation Countries | Mean, High-Inflation Countries | Mean Difference Statistical Significance |
|---|---|---|---|
| Rule of law | 5.25 | 2.66 | *** |
| Contract enforceability | 3.05 | 1.95 | *** |
| Corruption | 4.32 | 2.87 | *** |
| Bureaucracy | 4.52 | 2.67 | *** |
| Property rights | 4.37 | 3.07 | *** |
| Entry regulation | 3.48 | 2.67 | *** |
| Bank entry denied | 0.09 | 0.20 | *** |
| Domestic bank entry denied | 0.12 | 0.10 | |
| Foreign bank entry denied | 0.03 | 0.19 | *** |
| Bank activity restrictions | 8.37 | 11.00 | ** |
| Bank overhead costs | 0.02 | 0.07 | *** |
| Nonperforming loans | 0.06 | 0.07 | *** |
| Net interest margin | 0.02 | 0.07 | *** |
| Bank government ownership | 0.11 | 0.26 | *** |
| Private monitoring | 6.68 | 5.79 | ** |

**Note:** Rule of law is an indicator measuring the law and order tradition of a country; it ranges from 10 (strong law and order tradition) to 1 (weak law and order tradition). Contract enforceability measures the relative degree to which contractual agreements are honored and complications presented by language and mentality differences; it is scored 0–4, with higher scores for superior quality. Corruption is an indicator that measures the level of corruption on a scale ranging from 0 (high level of corruption) to 10 (low level of corruption). Bureaucracy is an indicator scored 0–6; high scores indicate autonomy from political pressure and the strength and expertise to govern without drastic changes in policy or interruptions in government services, as well as the existence of an established mechanism for recruiting and training. Property rights is an indicator scored 1–5; greater protection of private property receives a higher score. Entry regulation rates regulation policies related to opening and keeping open a business; it is scored 0–5, with higher scores meaning that regulations are straightforward and applied uniformly to all businesses and that regulations are less of a burden to business. Bank entry denied is the fraction of bank entry applications denied. Domestic bank entry denied is the fraction of entry applications from domestic banks denied. Foreign bank entry denied is the fraction of entry applications from foreign banks denied. Bank overhead costs and nonperforming loans are the indicator's respective shares of total bank assets. Net interest margin is net interest revenue divided by total bank assets. Bank government ownership is the share of publicly owned bank assets as a share of total bank assets. Private monitoring is an aggregator of indexes indicating the degree of private oversight of banking firms; a higher score implies a higher degree of private oversight.

**Source:** Demirguc-Kunt and Levine (2001); Barth, Caprio and Levine (2004).

*** significant at the 1% level; ** significant at the 5% level.

109 countries. I focus specifically on variables measuring characteristics of the banking industry because Boyd and Champ devote special attention to the impact of inflation on banks' pricing strategies and overall profitability. The data sources are Demirguc-Kunt and Levine (2001) and Barth, Caprio, and Levine (2004). High-inflation countries are defined as those in the top quartile of the distribution, and low-inflation are those in the bottom quartile.

As the numbers indicate, high-inflation countries score systematically worse along all dimensions. An overall weaker institutional environment is marked by an inferior legal structure, more pervasive corruption, heavier bureaucratic burden, poorer contract enforceability, and less protection of property rights.

High-inflation countries are also characterized by much larger obstacles to opening a business. Higher overall regulatory costs of entry are reflected in worse entry conditions in banking, as indicated by higher rejection rates of entry applications. But the constraints on the banking industry are not only prevalent at entry. Incumbent banks operate in significantly more restricted environments and in conditions of worse overall efficiency. Complementing this fact is the much higher fraction of banks that are government owned. Finally, banks in high-inflation environments operate in conditions of poorer market discipline.

Hence, the data in the table are indicative of fundamental differences between high- and low-inflation countries. This argument, however, does not just underscore the problem of omitted variables. Simply controlling for institutional and regulatory differences and for firm- or industry-specific characteristics would not solve the fundamental problem that inflation is not just another structural variable to be added in a reduced form equation but is itself a result of a number of economic factors. For example, focusing on banks, Boyd and Champ review empirical work and add some of their own, showing that banks' pricing and overall performance is significantly affected by moving from a low- to a high-inflation environment. But the casual evidence in table 1 indicates that the conditions of entry in the industry are different, as are important determinants of a bank's cost function and the ownership or managerial characteristics of incumbents, indicated by the significantly different proportion of government-owned banks. These are all first-order determinants of the equilibrium dynamics within the industry, and hence the prevailing pricing and performance measures. I am very comfortable with the predictions of the theoretical models on the impact of inflation, but I am not sure that this is what we are picking up with the current empirical methodology.

A more convincing approach, in my opinion, would be to focus on low-inflation economies and look at the impact of recognizable, exogenous inflationary shocks, such as a shift in the aggregate supply. In such a better-controlled environment, it would be possible to analyze, say, individual banks' propensity to lend, banks' lending standards, or firms' demand for external finance in response to increasing (or decreasing) prices—in sum, more direct testing of the theoretical implications of the models that Boyd and Champ review and in a more controlled environment.

In conclusion, Boyd and Champ should be praised for providing such a systematic compilation and analysis of the theory behind inflation and the real economy. In that respect, they have achieved their main objective—to raise mutual awareness between theorists and applied scholars. I suspect the latter group is bound to benefit the most from this exchange.

### REFERENCES

Barth, J. R., G. Caprio, Jr., and R. Levine. 2004. Bank Regulation and Supervision: What Works Best? *Journal of Financial Intermediation* 13: 205–48.

Bernanke, B. 2005. Inflation in Latin America—A New Era? *BIS Review* 8: 1–7.

Demirguc-Kunt, A., and V. Maksimovic. 1998. Law, Finance, and Firm Growth. *Journal of Finance* 56: 2107–37.

Demirguc-Kunt, A., and R. Levine, eds. 2001. *Financial Structure and Economic Growth.* Cambridge, MA: MIT Press.

King, R., and R. Levine. 1993a. Finance and Growth: Schumpeter Might Be Right. *Quarterly Journal of Economics* 108: 717–37.

King, R., and R. Levine. 1993b. Finance, Entrepreneurship and Growth. *Journal of Monetary Economics* 32: 513–42.

Rajan, R. G., and L. Zingales. 1998. Financial Dependence and Growth. *American Economic Review* 88: 559–86.

# Commentary

*Peter L. Rousseau*

## 1. INTRODUCTION

Identifying the channels through which inflation affects real economic activity is an undertaking that has never strayed far from the top of the macro-economic research agenda. Indeed, a large literature has long articulated its presumed costs, ranging from those associated with the very acts of changing prices and economizing on money holdings to the inhibition of long-term contracting (see Driffill, Mizon, and Ulph 1990 and the sources cited therein). It is also well known that these effects are quite difficult to quantify. But progress has been made over the past several years, with one strand of the inflation literature building on the cross-country framework introduced by Barro (1991) and first applied to the study of the finance–growth relationship by King and Levine (1993). The latter piece, like many others that have followed, emphasized the role of financial factors in economic growth, and inflation entered the empirical specifications on the right-hand side as a control variable, if at all.

However, a number of recent studies, of which Boyd, Levine, and Smith (2001) is the most notable, have turned more serious attention to inflation and its potential to reduce the efficiency of financial institutions and markets in directing resources to their best uses. It is this newer literature that John Boyd and Bruce Champ survey and extend in their present contribution. In this commentary, I offer my own views on what has been accomplished to date on this particular front and then look beyond the effects of inflation on financial development to examine its effects on economic growth through the financial sector.

## 2. INFLATION AND FINANCIAL DEVELOPMENT

Boyd and Champ begin their survey with a useful review of the relevant the-ory on inflation, growth, and financial market frictions but quickly direct attention to empirics, which is where most of the contributions of the recent literature have been made. They first consider studies that measure the impact of inflation on broad proxies for the extent of financial activity, namely, the ratios of aggregates such as money, stock market capitalization, and value of traded stocks to GDP. Though one may question whether such measures actually reflect the efficiency with which financial services are delivered or even the intensity of financial intermediation, the limited number of data items that are usually available for cross-country analyses requires such assumptions to be made, and the measures have become widely accepted. When inserted as the dependent variable in a cross-country regression with inflation accompanying the standard explanatory variables from a growth regression on the right-hand side, Boyd, Levine, and Smith (2001) find that inflation is negatively correlated with measures of banking and stock market development when the inflation rate lies beneath a threshold of about 15%, but that the link appears to be severed in higher-inflation environments.

Though this finding is not problematic in and of itself, the interpretation that it usually receives is suspect. Boyd and Champ, for example, assert that the inflation–stock market performance relationship flattens significantly for high values of inflation (above 15%) so that further increases in inflation are not associated with further deterioration in stock market capitalization, total value traded, or turnover. The potential problem lies in giving a time-series interpretation to a cross-sectional finding—in this case, one implying that financial sectors can tolerate ever-higher inflation rates once a given threshold is reached. This all but ignores the observation that countries with high inflation (i.e., above the threshold) have low levels of financial development generally and that there is little relationship between finance and inflation in the higher-inflation subset. In other words, once inflation is so high that financial-sector activity is already seriously dampened, even higher inflation rates are unlikely to cause much further damage.

At the same time, the authors do an admirable job of surveying the progress that has been made to date with this type of specification and extending our understanding by looking at alternative measures of financial market performance on the left-hand side. In particular, the finding that inflation is unrelated to nominal equity returns in low-inflation environments yet positively related in high-inflation ones suggests a lack of response on the part of investors to unanticipated price-level shocks that is reminiscent of the Lucas (1972) "confusion" model. They also find that inflation is negatively related to bank profits, loan–deposit rate spreads, net interest margins, and the amount of value added by banks, all of which represent new evidence that inflation is not only associated with financial repression but also impedes bank performance.

I must point out, however, that the cross-country specification used by the authors and many others whom they cite is rather ad hoc. One could easily argue, for example, that it resembles a long-run money-demand equation more than a model of the supply side of the credit-creation process. After all, agents faced with consistently high-inflation environments economize on money holdings, and if the banking system is unable to offer an adequate and reliable real return to depositors, they will substitute consumption goods and durables for financial securities, thus lowering even the broadest monetary aggregates. The point here is that the financial development regression, with standard conditioning variables from the typical cross-country growth regression on the right-hand side, does not conform to any particular model of how finance emerges and deepens. On the other hand, the standard cross-country growth regression seems more firmly rooted in the Solow model and thus is better equipped to address questions about how inflation affects the smooth operation of the financial sector under the premise that higher conditional economic growth rates are the ultimate outcome measure.

### 3. INFLATION, FINANCE, AND ECONOMIC GROWTH

An analysis of how inflation affects growth both directly and through the financial sector is beyond the scope of the Boyd and Champ survey, yet it seems important given the problems of interpretation just described. This section considers aspects of this neglected theme, calling on some of my own work with Paul Wachtel (Rousseau and Wachtel 2001, 2002).

When it comes to inflation and growth, there are two facts that seem well established: First, inflation is bad for growth, with negative and statistically significant coefficients usually appearing on inflation variables when added to the right-hand side of a Barro-type growth regression (Barro 1996). Second, this result is largely the result of the inclusion of high-inflation observations in the sample. Bruno and Easterly (1998), for example, show that the negative relation between inflation and growth vanishes in the baseline growth regression when countries with average inflation rates over 40% are excluded from the analysis. But perhaps the effects of inflation on growth reach beyond the direct ones captured by such regressions.

Table 1 presents the results of four instrumental variables regressions in which the dependent variable is the average growth rate of real GDP per capita averaged over five-year periods from 1960 to 1995 for as many as 84 countries. The explanatory variables are the levels of real income per capita and the secondary school enrollment rate at the start of each five-year period, as well as the inflation rate and ratio of broad money (M3) to GDP averaged across each five-year period. Inflation and the M3/GDP ratio are instrumented by their own initial values and by the initial ratios of international trade (imports plus exports) and government expenditure to GDP.

Table 1. Cross-Country IV Growth Regressions, 1960–95

| | Dependent variable: Per capita real GDP growth (percent) | | | |
|---|---|---|---|---|
| | (1) | (2) | (3) | i < 500% |
| Log initial real per capita GDP | −0.133 (−1.1) | −0.219 (−1.7) | −0.259 (−2.0) | −0.244 (−1.9) |
| Log initial secondary school enrollment rate | 1.026 (5.1) | 0.832 (3.9) | 0.907 (4.0) | 0.848 (3.9) |
| Inflation rate | −0.004 (−2.4) | | −0.003 (−2.5) | 0.004 (0.7) |
| M3 (percent of GDP) | | 0.025 (4.6) | 0.023 (4.2) | 0.025 (4.6) |
| Adjusted $R^2$ (Number of observations) | .169 (517) | .231 (479) | .221 (479) | .219 (479) |

Note: $T$ statistics appear in parentheses beneath the coefficient estimates. Instruments include initial values of the ratios of M3, international trade, and government expenditures to GDP, with initial values taken as the first observation in each five-year period. Dummy variables for five-year periods are included in all regressions but are not reported.

Table 2. Cross-Country IV Growth Regressions by Inflation Rate, 1960–95

| | Dependent variable: Per capita real GDP growth (percent) | |
|---|---|---|
| | i < 8.3% | i > 8.3% |
| Log initial real per capita GDP | −0.389 (−2.3) | −0.114 (−0.6) |
| Log initial secondary school enrollment rate | 1.023 (3.7) | 0.796 (2.3) |
| M3 (percent of GDP) | 0.033 (5.3) | 0.005 (0.5) |
| Adjusted $R^2$ (Number of observations) | .305 (240) | .160 (239) |

Note: $T$ statistics appear in parentheses beneath the coefficient estimates. Instruments include initial values of the ratios of M3, international trade, and government expenditures to GDP, with initial values taken as the first observation in each five-year period. Dummy variables for five-year periods are included in all regressions but are not reported.

An important commonality in all four regressions is the positive and significant correlation between financial depth (i.e., M3/GDP) and conditional growth rates, regardless of whether inflation enters the specification. The coefficients on inflation reflect the usual finding that any negative relationship with growth is driven by high inflation observations. In this case, the fourth column of the table indicates that it even vanishes when only hyperinflationary events (average five-year annual inflation of more than 500%) are excluded. All of this seems to suggest that inflation does not hamper the operation of the finance–growth nexus at all and that even moderate to high inflation rates do not inhibit growth!

But, as Boyd and Champ suggest with their financial development regressions, this cannot be the end of the story. Table 2 presents the same regressions as table 1, this time excluding inflation as an explicit explanatory variable and splitting the sample at the median five-year average inflation rate of about 8.3%. Now financial development is a statistically significant growth determinant for the low-inflation subset and not for the higher-inflation one, once again suggesting that the relationship between finance and growth is severed in higher inflation environments.

Just how high must inflation be for this severance to occur? Figure 1 shows the evolution of the coefficients on the M3/GDP ratio for the same specification reported in table 2, but now starting with the 50 highest inflation observations in the sample only and then rolling in additional observations one at a time. In other words, the final point on the solid line represents the coefficient on M3/GDP from a growth regression with all of the observations included. The dotted lines are two-standard-error bands around the coefficient estimates. Note that the solid line crosses the horizontal zero line as the observation with an inflation rate of 13.4% is added to the sample and that the lower two-standard-error band crosses the same horizontal line at 6.5%. This implies that the threshold at which inflation matters for growth by disrupting the smooth operation of finance is likely to lie somewhere between 6.5% and 13.4%, which is consistent with but a bit lower than the threshold found by Boyd, Levine, and Smith for the inflation–finance link.

*Peter L. Rousseau*

**Figure 1. Observations Ordered by Decreasing Inflation**

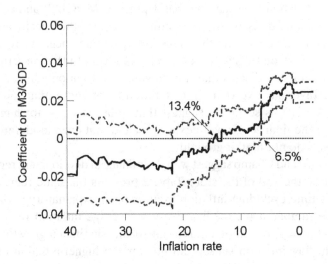

**Note:** Evolution of coefficients on the M3/GDP ratio in growth regressions as the sample increases, 1960–95.

At this point, a few summary comments are appropriate. First, it seems that the negative effects of inflation on growth in cross-country samples are driven by a few extreme observations. But more importantly, the ability of a given level of financial development to affect growth seems linked to the inflation rate when inflation rates are not too high. This suggests that finance cannot operate smoothly in promoting growth even in moderately high-inflation environments and that the negative effects of inflation on the finance–growth nexus rise quickly even at low inflation rates. On the other hand, the effects of inflation on growth, if confined to their traditional roles in the inflation literature, are probably quite small, at least under nonhyperinflationary circumstances. This suggests that Boyd and Champ continue to be on the right track in seeking to determine the conditions under which inflation affects finance at low inflation rates; this seems to be where relatively small fluctuations in inflation can have relatively large effects on financial development. We have accomplished much in the past 10 years on this front, as the survey suggests, but the results all point to there being much left to be learned. I look forward to the authors' next contribution to our common cause.

REFERENCES

Barro, R. J. 1991. Economic Growth in a Cross-Section of Countries. *Quarterly Journal of Economics* 106: 407–43.

Barro, R. J. 1996. Inflation and Growth. *Federal Reserve Bank of St. Louis Review* 78: 153–69.

Boyd, J. H., R. Levine, and B. D. Smith. 2001. The Impact of Inflation on Financial Sector Performance. *Journal of Monetary Economics* 47: 221–48.

Bruno, M., and W. Easterly. 1998. Inflation Crises and Long-Run Growth. *Journal of Monetary Economics* 41: 3–26.

Driffill, J., G. E. Mizon, and A. Ulph. 1990. Costs of Inflation. In *Handbook of Monetary Economics*, vol. II, ed. B. M. Friedman and F. H. Hahn, 1013–66. New York: Elsevier North-Holland.

King, R. G., and R. Levine. 1993. Finance and Growth: Schumpeter Might Be Right. *Quarterly Journal of Economics* 108: 717–37.

Lucas, R. E. 1972. Expectations and the Neutrality of Money. *Journal of Economic Theory* 4: 103–24.

Rousseau, P. L., and P. Wachtel. 2001. Inflation, Financial Development and Growth. In *Economic Theory, Dynamics and Markets: Essays in Honor of Ryuzo Sato*, ed. T. Negishi, R. Ramachandran, and K. Mino, 309–24. Boston: Kluwer Academic.

Rousseau, P. L., and P. Wachtel. 2002. Inflation Thresholds and the Finance-Growth Nexus. *Journal of International Money and Finance* 21: 777–93.

# Index

Printed in the United States
by Baker & Taylor Publisher Services